NEW LIGHT ON FORMULAS IN ORAL POETRY AND PROSE

UTRECHT STUDIES IN MEDIEVAL LITERACY

57

UTRECHT STUDIES IN MEDIEVAL LITERACY

General Editor

Marco Mostert (Universiteit Utrecht)

Editorial Board

Gerd Althoff (Westfälische-Wilhelms-Universität Münster)
Pierre Chastang (Université Versalles St-Quentin-en-Yvelines
Erik Kwakkel (University of British Columbia)
Mayke de Jong (Universiteit Utrecht)
Rosamond McKitterick (University of Cambridge)
Arpád Orbán (Universiteit Utrecht)
Francesco Stella (Università degli Studi di Siena)
Richard H. Rouse (UCLA)

NEW LIGHT ON FORMULAS IN ORAL POETRY AND PROSE

edited by

Daniel Sävborg and Bernt Ø. Thorvaldsen

BREPOLS

British Library Cataloguing in Publication Data

A catalogue record for this book is available from the British Library

© 2023 – Brepols Publishers n.v., Turnhout, Belgium

All rights reserved. No part of this publication may be reproduced, stored in a retrieval system, or transmitted, in any form or by any means, electronic, mechanical, photocopying, recording, or otherwise, without the prior permission of the publisher.

D/2023/0095/76

ISBN 978-2-503-60428-2

e-ISBN 978-2-503-60429-9

DOI: 10.1484/M.USML-EB.5.132161

ISSN 2034-9416

e-ISSN 2294-8317

Printed in the EU on acid-free paper

Table of Contents

List of Illustrations   vii

Formulas and Formula Research: An Introduction
    DANIEL SÄVBORG and BERNT Ø. THORVALDSEN   1
Fee, Fi, Fo, Formula: Getting to Grips with the Concept and Deciding on a Definition
    FROG   17
Formulas, Collocations, and Cultural Memory
    STEPHEN A. MITCHELL   59
A Formula Is a Habit Colliding with Life
    SLAVICA RANKOVIĆ and MILOŠ RANKOVIĆ   81
Chunks, Collocations and Constructions: The Homeric Formula in Cognitive and Linguistic Perspective
    CHIARA BOZZONE   113
A Further History of Orality and Eddic Poetry
    PAUL ACKER   141
Formulas in Scottish Traditional Narrative: Finding Poetry in the Prosaic
    WILLIAM LAMB   163
Towards a Typology of Runic Formulas, with a Focus on the One-Word Formula in the Older Runic Inscriptions
    MICHAEL SCHULTE   191
Revisiting Formula and Mythic Patterns and the Interplay between the *Poetic Edda* and *Vǫlsunga Saga*
    SCOTT A. MELLOR   227
Same Meanings, Different Words: Retelling as a Mode of Transmission in Old Norse-Icelandic *Konungasögur* Tradition
    DARIA GLEBOVA   259

Depicting Violence in *Íslendingasögur*: A Formula on the Verge
   of Legal Tradition
        EUGENIA KRISTINA VOROBEVA   287
Formulaic Word-Play in the Poems of the *Anglo-Saxon Chronicle*
        INNA MATYUSHINA   303
Freeman's Formulas: Openings, Transitions and Closes
        JONATHAN ROPER   327
The Aesthetics of Russian Folktale Formulas: A View
   from Translation Studies
        TATIANA BOGRDANOVA   353

List of Illustrations

[Slavica RANKOVIĆ and Miloš RANKOVIĆ:]

Fig. 1	The 'formula joke'. Cartoon by Miloš RANKOVIĆ.	82
Fig. 2	Grettir's Temper Management. Image by Miloš RANKOVIĆ.	99
Fig. 3	An instant note. Image by Slavica RANKOVIĆ, produced in Evernote.	100
Fig. 4	A note on the formulaic expression. Image by Slavica RANKOVIĆ, produced in Evernote.	102
Fig. 5	The 'yes or no' dimension. Image by Slavica RANKOVIĆ, produced in Evernote.	103
Fig. 6	The multi-value dimension. Image by Slavica RANKOVIĆ, produced in Evernote.	104
Fig. 7	The logistical dimension. Image by Slavica RANKOVIĆ, produced in Evernote.	105
Fig. 8	Offence type vs. restrained exercised. Image by Miloš RANKOVIĆ.	106
Fig. 9	Action type vs. number of previous offences. Image by Miloš RANKOVIĆ.	107
Fig. 10	PCA analysis: The space of Grettir's temper management. Image by Miloš RANKOVIĆ.	108
Fig. 11	PCA, X and Y axes. Image by Miloš RANKOVIĆ.	109

[Chiara BOZZONE:]

Fig. 1	Type and Token Counts of 2-, 3-, 4-, and 5-word collocations in the LOB corpus of written English.	119
Fig. 2	Type and Token Counts of 2-, 3-, 4-, and 5-word collocations in Herodotus.	119
Fig. 3	Type and Token Counts of 2-, 3-, 4-, and 5-word collocations in Homer.	120
Table 1	Select definitions of the Homeric formula.	128
Table 2	Some unique and repeated expressions reflecting the collocation ἀλη- 'pain' + παθ- 'suffer' in Homer.	136

Table 3	Some unique and repeated expressions reflecting the collocations πηματ- 'misery' + παθ- 'suffer', κακ 'bad, ill' + παθ- 'suffer', and αἰν- 'terrible' + παθ- 'suffer' in Homer.	137
Table 4	From themes to formulas.	138

[Paul ACKER]

Fig. 1	MS U, p. 8, bottom margin.	147
Fig. 2	MS AM 147 8vo, f. 12v.	152
Fig. 3	Rök stone.	157

[William LAMB]

Table 1	Parallelisms in metrical and measured poetry.	165
Table 2	Coda types per position (raw counts).	184
Fig. 1	Coda phoneme type per position.	185
Fig. 2	Onset density per order.	186
Table 3	Coda obstruence per binomial position.	186
Fig. 3	Binomial element syllable counts per position.	187
Table 4	Stressed vowel length in Element 2, where $SYL_1 > SYL_2$.	188

[Michael SCHULTE]

Fig. 1	Års 2 bracteate with the one-word formula **laukaR** (Picture credit: IK 8).	198
Fig. 2	Sjælland II bracteate with the inscription **hariuha haitika : farauisa : gibu auja** (Picture credit: IK 98).	199
Fig. 3	Sjælland II bracteate with the inscription **hariuha haitika : farauisa : gibu auja** (Picture credit: IK 98).	201
Table 1	Distribution of the formulaic words **alu**, **laþu**, and **laukaR** on gold bracteates.	205
Fig. 4	The runestone from Elgesem featuring the one-word formula **alu**. Photo: Julius Magnus Petersen, National Museum of Denmark.	207
Fig. 5	Lellinge bracteate with the reduplication formula **salu-salu** and a swastika (picture credit: IK 105).	208
Fig. 6	Skodborg B-bractate with the inscription **auja alawin auja alawin auja alawin j (= ú) alawid** (picture credit: IK 161).	209
Fig. 7	Vadstena bracteate with the reduplication formula **tuwa-tuwa** followed by the complete rune-row of the older fuþark (picture credit: IK 377,1).	211
Table 2	Diffusion of the *ǫrð / upphiminn* formula in Old Germanic.	214
Fig. 8	Skåne I bractate with the twin formula **laþulaukaR** and the charm word **alu** (picture credit: IK 149,1).	216

Fig. 9	Darum I bracteate featuring the inscription **frohila laþu** (picture credit: IK 42).	220
Fig. 10	Danmark 1 bracteate displaying the shortened word formula **lkaR** for laukaR (Picture credit: IK 229).	222

[Daria GLEBOVA]

Table 1	265
Table 2	267
Table 3	268
Table 4	270
Table 5	273
Table 6	274
Table 7	279
Table 8	282
Table 9	283

Formulas and Formula Research: An Introduction

DANIEL SÄVBORG and BERNT Ø. THORVALDSEN

The concept of the formula has during the last ninety years revolutionised the entire view on oral poetry and narrative art, and therefore the entire view of orality in general. The so-called 'Oral-Formulaic Theory', which forms the basis of a major part of the analysis of oral poetry, uses the notion already in its name. The formula has to a high extent been regarded as the core of the distinctive character of oral poetry. It is a concept which has influenced scholars of cultures and poetic traditions all over the world.

But formula research has developed considerably during these ninety years. Although several basic views from the 1930s are still relevant in the scholarly discussion, an abundance of new ideas, interpretations, concepts, and theories have emerged since then. New fields of research have also emerged, such as formulas in oral prose and in oral-derived written literature, and more disciplines have also been involved in formula research. In addition to the literary studies in which this research started (in the study of Homeric poetry), linguists and folklorists have become important contributors in interdisciplinary formula research. The distinction between verbal formulas in the original definition and other recurring, meaning-bearing units has been problematised, which has also led to new research topics and questions.

New Light on Formulas in Oral Poetry and Prose, ed. Daniel SÄVBORG and Bernt Ø. THORVALDSEN, *Utrecht Studies in Medieval Literacy*, 57 (Turnhout: Brepols, 2023), pp. 1-15.

The present volume is an offshoot of a symposium organised in Tartu in December 2019 under the title 'The Formula in Oral Poetry and Prose: New Approaches, Models and Interpretations'. Most of the articles in the volume are based on papers presented there. The volume aims to reflect the boiling research activity within the field that surfaced at the symposium, which included material from a variety of geographical and literary contexts. We hope that the volume will inspire the further development of formula research and increase the knowledge of the new ideas and research questions, and a collaboration between scholars of different disciplines and cultures.

Already before the twentieth century, scholars from different fields had long observed more or less fixed expressions, or formulas, in literary texts, and collections of formulas have been published since the nineteenth century according to varying criteria and with different opinions on the functions and aesthetic qualities of such phrasing. In the Germanic area, the formula collections of Richard Meyer (1889) and Otto Hoffman (1885) serve as examples of early focus on formulaic expression.[1] Although these scholars made very useful catalogues of such expressions in poetry, they offered limited and diverging theoretical understanding and delimitation of the phenomenon.[2]

The Oral-Formulaic Theory from the 1930s spurred more activity in this field, and a higher level of theoretical consciousness. Milman Parry and Albert Lord based this theory on studies of the Homeric poetry, where the use of formulas played a key role. Parry's famous definition of formula was "a group of words which is regularly employed under the same metrical conditions to express a given essential idea".[3] The function of the formulas was to serve as the fixed elements in a basically improvised oral performance, as a tool for the rapid performance in verse.[4] Parry's theory on the Homeric poetry was soon considered relevant for oral narrative in general. The scholar mainly responsible for that was Albert Lord, whose main focus was the still living oral poetry

---

[1] R. MEYER, *Die altgermanische Poesie nach ihren formelhaften Elementen beschrieben* (Hildesheim, Zürich and New York, 1985; originally published in1889) ; O. HOFFMAN, *Reimformeln im Westgermanischen* (Darmstadt, 1885).

[2] Paul Acker presents some of the early research in P. ACKER, *Revising Oral Theory: Formulaic Composition in Old English and Old Icelandic Verse* (New York, 1998).

[3] M. PARRY, "Studies in the epic technique of oral verse-making: I: Homer and Homeric style", *Harvard Studies in Classical Philology* 41 (1930), pp. 73-148, at p. 80; cf. already M. PARRY, *L'Epithète traditionnelle dans Homère: Essai sur un problème de style homérique* (Paris, 1928), p. 16.

[4] A. LORD, *The Singer of Tales*, 2nd edn., ed. S. MITCHELL and G. NAGY (Cambridge, MA, 2000), p. 4 (first edn. 1960).

in what was Yugoslavia at the time,[5] but the Oral-Formulaic Theory was fashionable in the research on, e.g. Old Norse, Old English, Middle High German, and Homeric poetry from the 1960s to the 1990s. In Old Norse research this trend was influential in the study of Eddic poetry.[6] Although supplying important insights in those fields, the limits of the Oral-Formulaic theory has been increasingly clear, especially when the objects of study are prose texts, or memorised texts, or when formulaic expression occur in texts that are remote from oral tradition and performance.

Parry's original definition of *formula* as "a group of words which is regularly employed under the same metrical conditions to express a given essential idea" is possible to apply only to metric poetry, and it presupposes the formula as a verbally fixed unit.[7] This has caused trouble for analysing formulas in

---

[5] LORD, *The Singer of Tales*.

[6] See the useful surveys in ACKER, *Revising Oral Theory*, pp. 85-110; FROG, "*Alvíssmál* and orality I: Formula, alliteration and categories of mythic being", *Arkiv för nordisk filologi* 126 (2011), pp. 19-28; B.Ø. THORVALDSEN, "The generic aspect of the Eddic style", in: *Old Norse Religion in Long-Term Perspectives: Origins, Changes, and Interactions: An International Conference in Lund, Universitetet i Lund (3.-7. juni 2004)*, ed. A. ANDRÉN, K. JENNBERT, and and C. RAUDVERE (Lund, 2006), pp. 19-34; J. HARRIS, "Eddic poetry", in: *Old Norse-Icelandic Literature: A Critical Guide*, ed. C. CLOVER and J. LINDOW (Ithaca, 1985), pp. 68-156, at 112. In Old English scholarship, Parry's theory and view of formulas were introduced already in 1953 by F.P. Magoun, "Oral-formulaic character of Anglo-Saxon narrative poetry", *Speculum* 28 (1953), pp. 446-467 (although Magoun had actually discussed formulas in *Beowulf* and Eddic poetry already in 1929, in ID., "Recurring first elements in different nominal compounds in *Beowulf* and the *Elder Edda*", in: *Studies in English Philology, a Miscellany in Honor of Frederick Klaeber*, ed. K. MALONE and M. RUUD (Minneapolis, 1929), pp. 73-78, at pp. 73-74). Later, D.K. Fry developed the Oral-Formulaic Theory considerably in D.K. FRY, "Old English formulaic themes and type-scenes", *Neophilologus* 52 (1968), pp. 48-54. For an overview of the Anglo-Saxonist formula research, see S.C.E. HOPKINS, "Of scopas and scribes: Reshaping oral-formulaic theory in Old English literary studies", in: *Weathered Words: Formulaic Language and Verbal Art*, ed. FROG and W. LAMB (Cambridge, MA, 2022). For examples of the trend of applying the oral-formulaic theory to Eddic poetry (with or without reservations), see L. LÖNNROTH, "Hjálmar's death-song and the delivery of Eddic poetry", *Speculum: A Journal of Medieval Studies* 46 (1971), pp. 1-20; ID., "*Iǫrð fannz æva né uphiminn*: A formula analysis", in: *Speculum Norrœnum: Norse Studies in Memory of Gabriel Turville*-Petre, ed. Ursula Dronke (Odense, 1981), pp. 310-27; R. KELLOGG, *A Concordance to Eddic Poetry* (East Lansing, MI, 1988), p. VII; G. SIGURÐSSON, "On the classification of Eddic heroic poetry in view of the oral theory", in: *Poetry in the Scandinavian Middle Ages, Spoleto, 4-10 September 1988: The Seventh International Saga Conference*, ed. T. PÀROLI (1990), pp. 245-255, at p. 245; S.A. MELLOR, *Analyzing Ten Poems from The Poetic Edda: Oral Formula and Mythic Patterns* (New York, 2008), pp. 114-124. For other types of formula analyses of Eddic poetry, see MELLOR, *Analyzing Ten Poems*, pp. 62-63, 69-112, and 169-287; FROG, "*Alvíssmál* and orality", pp. 28-63; and ACKER, *Revising Oral Theory*, pp. 63-83.

[7] PARRY, "Studies in the epic technique of oral verse-making", p. 80.

prose as well as in poetic traditions with less fixed verbal constructions which nonetheless seem to be the same devices as the ones called 'formulas' by Parry and Lord.

To consider the formula as a broader linguistic phenomenon has turned out to be a fruitful development of the research during the last decades.[8] A leading scholar within this field of 'formulaic language' is Alison Wray, who was quoted by several of the scholars attending the Tartu symposium. She uses the terms 'formulaic sequence', which seems to cover the unit otherwise called 'formula'. Her definition of 'formulaic sequence' is:

> a sequence, continuous or discontinuous, of words or other elements, which is, or appears to be, prefabricated: that is sorted and retrieved whole from memory at the time of use, rather than being subject to generation or analysis by the language grammar.[9]

For Wray, formulaic sequences constitute a central feature of language in general, and many of her examples come from everyday language ('nice to see you' etc.).[10] Wray's definition is very wide and inclusive and may need to be sharpened when, for example, analysing formulas as devices in oral or oral-derived literature. One might, for example, add that the sequence in question is a 'sequence in a certain discourse' or in specific genres to avoid inclusion of idioms from ordinary discourse, and one could also follow William Lamb in excluding phrases that seem to be idiolectic.[11] Furthermore, the 'other elements' in Wray's definition are open to a variety of 'units' that may leave the formulaic sequence to be a very heterogeneous unit. Yet, a broader definition than

---

[8] This type of research does indeed have a long history. It has since long been a trend not least among Russian scholars; see, e.g. V.V. VINOGRADOV, *Sovremennyi russkiy literaturnyi yazyk* (Moscow 1938), p. 121; N.Yu. SHVEDOVA, *Ocherki po sintaksisu russkoi razgovornoi rechi* (Moscow, 1960); and O.A. LAPTEVA, "Normativnost nekodifitsirovannoi literaturnoi rechi", in: *Sintaksis i norma*, ed. G.A. ZALOTOVA (Moscow, 1974), pp. 5-42. For a relatively early discussion of the relevance of this research in relation to the formula research in literary studies of traditional poetry, see G.I. MALTSEV, *Traditsionnye formuly russkoy narodnoy neobryadovoy liriki* (Leningrad, 1989).

[9] A. WRAY, *Formulaic Language and the Lexicon* (New York, 2002), p. 9.

[10] A. WRAY, "Identifying formulaic language: Persistent challenges and new opportunities", in: *Formulaic Language*, 1, *Distribution and Historical Change*, ed. R. CORRIGAN et al. (Philadelphia, 2009), pp. 27-51, at p. 38.

[11] W. LAMB, "Verbal formulas in Gaelic traditional narrative: Some aspects of their form and function", in: *Registers of Communication*, ed. A. AGHA and FROG (Helsinki, 2015), pp. 193-220, at p. 226-227.

Formulas and Formula Research: An Introduction 5

that given by Lord is clearly needed if the scope of formula studies extends beyond oral narrative poetry.

It may be challenging to reach a definition which is acceptable to scholars from different fields and with diverging aims. There is, for example, a difference between studying formulas as literary devices and studying them as part of human language in general.[12] What appears to be a formula from the latter perspective may have little or no significance from the perspective of literary composition. If a student of a given literary genre aims to delimit formulas specific to a single genre and its specific mode of composition, it goes without saying that Wray's definition would not be precise enough. The scholar would need to work with the delimitation of formulas restricted to the genre in question while excluding those formulas belonging to human language in general. On the other hand, Lord's definition is too narrow to be useful when studying other texts than oral verse. Still, the relationship between formulas and verse which is emphasised by Lord, and the reason for the inclusion of 'metrical conditions' in Lord's definition, is clearly a very important background to the use of formulas in some cases, while in other cases (such as in prose) it is irrelevant. Wray's definition calls for more fine-grained groupings of formulas according to the scope of each study and the specifics of each field. Yet, Wray's work may have much to offer as an overarching definition and may enable discussions across disciplines and across diverging perspectives on formulas.

At several points, more recent research has revised Parry's and Lord's views and developed alternative explanations and broadened the field of interest. Partly due to its origins in oral performance, formula research has been much concerned with poetry. Much less has been written about formulas in prose. William Lamb, however, in a recent work has examined the form and categories of formulas in Gaelic traditional narrative.[13] His investigation might so far be the most thorough attempt to analyse formulas in narrative prose.

The Icelandic saga literature can be seen as an oral-derived genre.[14] Nonetheless, the research on formulas in saga prose is very limited. Formulas are

---

[12] Such differences have since long been underscored in Russian formula research, for instance the effective discussion in MALTSEV, *Traditsionnye formuly*, p. 7.

[13] LAMB, "Verbal formulas in Gaelic traditional narrative". For an overview of previous studies of formulas in traditional prose, see FROG and W. LAMB, "A Picasso of perspectives on formulaic language", in: *Weathered Words: Formulaic Language and Verbal Art*, ed. FROG and W. LAMB (Cambridge, MA, 2022), pp. 1-21, at p. 4.

[14] For the concept of oral-derived texts, see J.M. FOLEY, *Traditional Oral Epic: The Odyssey, Beowulf, and the Serbo-Croatian Return Song* (Berkeley, 1990), p. 5.

indeed frequently mentioned in connection with saga style,[15] but in spite of that, there is remarkably little analysis on the formulas in the saga prose. The scholars who have paid attention to the formulas in the sagas have hardly ever put the term into a larger context of formula use or into any kind of theoretical model. Lars Lönnroth has devoted some research on the types and function of the saga formulas, and, in 2018, Daniel Sävborg sketched some of the general ideas for such studies.[16] Scholarly analysis and description of the formula as a phenomenon in saga literature is still very limited, but, due to newer views on the relationship between orality and literacy, the subject is clearly well worth pursuing. In the study of formulas in prose, the definitions and approaches from linguistic formula research have turned out to be fruitful in the analysis.

Another important development in formula studies is the mediation of the previously overemphasised difference between oral and written communication. Parry's and Lord's theory of formulas paved the way for seeing the formula as an oral device only, and the density of formulas in a text was even seen as a criterion of its orality. For a period of time, formulas were often seen as expressions of orality as opposed to literacy, but this opposition is now played down by most scholars.[17] In the case of the Old Norse corpus, as in that of other older corpora of written texts, the idea of a fundamental divide between oral and written culture is cumbersome, since all textual sources are in written states and thus firmly located in literary culture. The interplay between the oral and written forms is more complex than any dichotomy justifies, and in contempo-

---

[15] E.g. V. ÓLASON *Dialogues with the Viking Age: Narration and Representation in the Sagas of the Icelanders*, trans. A. WAWN (Reykjavík, 1998), p. 112; M. CLUNIES ROSS, *The Cambridge Introduction to the Old Norse-Icelandic Saga* (Cambridge, 2010), pp. 16, 26; L. LÖNNROTH, *Njáls saga: A Critical Introduction* (Berkeley, 1976), pp. 44-45; D. SÄVBORG, "Style", in: *The Routledge Research Companion to the Medieval Icelandic Sagas*, ed. Á. JAKOBSSON and S. JAKOBSSON (London and New York, 2017), pp. 111-126, at pp. 115-118; and ID., *Sagan om kärleken: Erotik, känslor och berättarkonst i norrön litteratur* (Uppsala, 2007), p. 55; S. RANKOVIĆ, "The performative non-canonicity of the canonical: Íslendingasögur and their traditional referentiality", in: *The Performance of Christian and Pagan Storyworlds: The Non-Canonical Chapters of the History of Nordic Medieval Literature*, ed. L.B. MORTENSEN et al. (Turnhout, 2013), pp. 247-272, at p. 259, and EAD., "Immanent seas, scribal havens: Distributed reading of formulaic networks in the sagas of icelanders", *European Review* 22 (2014), pp. 45-65, at pp. 46, 49; cf. also K. LIESTØL, *Upphavet til den islendske ættesaga* (Oslo, 1929), p. 30.

[16] LÖNNROTH, *Njáls saga*, pp. 44-45; D. SÄVBORG, "The formula in Icelandic saga prose", *Saga-Book* 42 (2018), pp. 51-86.

[17] Parry's method of assessing the orality of a text on the basis of the statistics of its formula density was followed, e.g. by MAGOUN, "oral-formulaic character of Anglo-Saxon narrative poetry", pp. 446-467, but has been shown to be problematic, e.g. by J.A. RUSSO, "Is 'oral' or 'aural' composition the cause of Homer's formulaic style?" in: *Oral Literature and the Formula*, ed. B.A. STOLZ and R.S. SHANNON (Ann Arbor, 1976), pp. 31-54.

Formulas and Formula Research: An Introduction

rary scholarship this opens up a range of new approaches to the older material. For example, formulaic language may well be studied in genres that are, at least from one perspective, heavily dependent on the written medium. The concept 'oral-derived text' of the folklorist John Miles Foley refers to written literature with clear oral roots, and might serve as a fruitful theoretical starting point.[18]

The actual function of the formulas has to a remarkably small degree been the focus of the leading scholars. For Parry and Lord, the function of formulas was to serve as a tool for the rapid 'composition in performance', the 'semi-improvised' performance of a non-memorised text in verse.[19] For Lord, the formulas "were useful not, as some have supposed, merely to the audience if at all, but also and even more to the singer in the rapid composition of his tale".[20] Such a view is of course less relevant for both prose and fixed poetry, and this is a point where it has been necessary to search for alternative interpretations. Some scholars have seen them as purely decorative clichés. Walter Baetke described them as "*Floskeln*", and Lars Lönnroth described most of the formulas of the Icelandic saga literature as "commonplaces for presenting recurrent but fairly trivial motifs".[21]

At this point, formula research has changed considerably over the last decades. "Less prevalent is the view of the formula as exclusively or even primarily a compositional unit; instead, it is now more often understood as an integer of traditional meaning", according to John Miles Foley and Peter Ramey, describing this development.[22] They consider this as a general change of the Oral Theory: "Oral Theory has grown less concerned with questions of composition *per se* and more interested in issues of meaning and aesthetics".[23] This break with Parry's and Lord's view of the essential issue of the function of the formulas in oral tradition is indeed a general tendency in international scholarship

---

[18] He defines the concept 'oral-derived texts' as "the manuscript or tablet works of finally uncertain provenance that nonetheless show oral traditional characteristics" (FOLEY, *Traditional Oral Epic*, p. 5).

[19] E.g. LORD, *The Singer of Tales*, p. 4. It should be mentioned that the entire idea of oral poetry as non-memorised, a cornerstone on Parry's and Lord's view of oral poetry and its use of formulas, has been challenged by modern scholars on the basis of research on poetry from other cultures (see, e.g. K. REICHL, "Formulas in oral epics: The dynamics of meter, memory, and meaning", in: *Weathered Words*, pp. 27-47, at p. 36, on Turkic oral poetry).

[20] LORD, *The Singer of Tales*, p. 30.

[21] W. BAETKE, *Über die Entstehung der Isländersagas* (Berlin, 1956), p. 29; LÖNNROTH, *Njáls saga: A Critical Introduction*, p. 45.

[22] J.M. FOLEY and P. RAMEY, "Oral theory and medieval literature", in: *Medieval Oral Literature*, ed. K. REICHL (Berlin, 2012), pp. 71-102, at p. 80.

[23] FOLEY and RAMEY, "Oral theory and medieval literature", p. 79.

since the 1970s. This is true for the field where modern formula research originated, Homeric studies, where the 'meaning' of the formulas and other traditional elements now constitutes a central focus area.[24] It is similarly true for the current research of formulas of other cultures.[25]

To understand the function of the formula it seems more fruitful to connect with folkloristic research on oral tradition. Paul Zumthor describes the formulaic style as a discursive and intertextual strategy, where the various fragments – such as formulas – send the listener back to a familiar semantic universe by making the fragments functional within their exposition.[26] This view is developed by John Miles Foley in his theory of 'traditional referentiality', where traditional elements, such as formulas,

> reach out of the immediate instance in which they appear to the fecund totality of the entire tradition, defined synchronically and diachronically, and they bear meanings as wide and deep as the tradition they encode".[27]

The consequence of this view can be demonstrated by examples from Old Norse literature. In Eddic poetry, formulas do contribute to the structuring of texts, but they also appear to function as references to tradition. Eddic poetry contains the *jǫrð / upphiminn*-formula ('earth' / 'up-heaven'), and the latter noun is only present in poetry, and only in this specific formula. It has, so to speak, its meaning within the confines of tradition. Other devices in Old Norse poetry serve the same function, such as the numerous *heiti*, or poetic synonyms, that are chosen instead of the more common words typically used in prose. The view of formulas as parts of an intertextual strategy, which relate them to pre-existing messages of the same genre or tradition, seems to be fruitful, as well as

---

[24] In M.N. NAGLER, *Spontaneity and Tradition: A Study in the Oral Art of Homer* (Berkeley, 1974), one of the main chapters bears the title "Meaning and Significance" (pp. 27-63). A similar view of formulas is found among many recent Homer scholars, such as G. NAGY, *The Best of the Achaeans: Concepts of the Hero in Archaic Greek Poetry* (Baltimore, 1999), p. 4; R. SACKS, *The Traditional Phrase in Homer: Two Studies in Form, Meaning and Interpretation* (Leiden, 1987); and D.F. ELMER, *The Poetics of Consent: Collective Decision Making and the Iliad* (Baltimore, 2013), pp. 15, 25.

[25] See, e.g. FROG and LAMB, "A Picasso of perspectives", p. 5; in Russian scholarship of traditional poetry and prose, a similar development from viewing formulas as 'clichés' of the kind appearing in everyday language to a focus on the artistic, aesthetic, character of the formulas can be observed (e.g. MALTSEV, *Traditsionnye formuly*, pp. 6-7; cf. pp. 2-5).

[26] P. ZUMTHOR, *Oral Poetry: An Introduction*, trans. K. MURPHY-JUDY (Minneapolis, 1990), pp. 89-90.

[27] J.M. FOLEY, *Immanent Art: From Structure to Meaning in Traditional Oral Epic* (Bloomington, 1991), p. 7.

Formulas and Formula Research: An Introduction 9

to see them as meaning-bearing units, whose meaning in the particular cases must be decoded in the light of the entire tradition or genre. In this view, an introductory formula such as *X hét maðr* in the Icelandic saga literature, is anything but trivial: it signals narrative discourse, the genre of *Íslendingasögur*, and places this particular *Íslendingasaga* in the tradition of all other *Íslendingasögur*. It awakes our expectations to the succeeding story and creates a framework for understanding it. When this formula is used, the listener or reader is invited to compare this event with all other similar cases in the same tradition, something that strongly influences our expectations, and we hear or read the whole episode in the light of all the others we know. The formulas in this view are, in contrast to Lord's view, relevant for the audience or readers, providing them with tools for their interpretation and understanding of the text.[28]

This view means that the formulas are signals from the performer / author to the audience / reader. This makes it necessary to ask: *What* do they signal? Lars Lönnroth's study of the Eddic *jǫrð-upphiminn* formula reveals that it brings about associations to the wide cosmological order and is especially related to creation and apocalypse. Daniel Sävborg has analysed several formulas in the saga literature, pointing to the fact that they are often charged with meaning and their correct interpretation is necessary for understanding the behaviour and reactions of characters and plot development,[29] and that a reading based only on the literal surface results in an incorrect interpretation of sagas and saga episodes.[30]

A main challenge to Parry's and Lord's formula theory concerns the form, and thus the definition, of the concept. Their definition, and the rules they singled out, were based on the comparison between Homeric and Serbian poetry, and it has eventually become obvious that neither their definition nor the rules can be considered universal. As John Miles Foley and Peter Ramey have stressed, the majority of the oral traditions of the world do not follow these rules and there is a general agreement among scholars today "that any definition of the formula must be tailored to its respective tradition".[31]

---

[28] The view that formulas might guide our 'interpretation' of a traditional work is found also in recent research; e.g. in ELMER, *The poetics of Consent*, p. 15, regarding the *Iliad*.

[29] SÄVBORG, "The formula in Icelandic saga prose", pp. 60-67.

[30] For an example of such a misinterpretation, see M.I. STEBLIN-KAMENSKIJ, *The Saga Mind*, trans. K.H. OBER (Odense, 1973), pp. 87, 90-94, and the discussion in SÄVBORG, *Sagan om kärleken*, pp. 340-362.

[31] FOLEY and RAMEY, "Oral theory and medieval literature", p. 81 (the quotation), and 78-79. The fact that Parry's definition of *formula* was too narrow even for Homeric poetry has also been underscored by several recent scholars; e.g. J.B. HAINSWORTH, *The Flexibility of the Homeric Formula* (Oxford, 1968); G. MACHACEK, "The occasional contextual appropriateness

Some oral poetic traditions are so different from the material analysed by previous scholars in the Parry-Lord tradition that it has been seen as impossible to talk about formulas here. Those difficulties have led some scholars to avoid the strict term 'formula', replacing it with substitutes such as 'traditional phrase', 'formulaic phraseology', 'multiform' concepts indeed including formulas in Parry's original sense, but broader and open to far more flexibility in form.[32] However, recent scholarship has also developed alternative approaches and definitions which might make it possible to talk about 'formulas' here too.

One such case is the Old Norse skaldic poetry. Since it is an oral genre, we could expect that formulas were present in it, according to the standard view. The allegedly memorised (non-improvised) character of the genre, and its avoiding of lexical repetition, have resulted in a view that skaldic poetry is an exception in international oral poetry, completely lacking formulas.[33] However, scholars have searched for possibilities of using the notion of 'formula' here too. With a new definition and concept of formula, free from the limits of the Parry-Lord model, it may be possible to analyse formulas also in skaldic poetry. Attempts have been made by Frog.[34] Bjarne Fidjestøl's analysis of the frequent stereotype 'feed the corpse-eating animals' (with the meaning 'to kill enemies') is another attempt. Fidjestøl demonstrated the stereotype form of these expressions, although they could have "*synonymutskiftning i alle led*" ("synonym replacement in all parts"),[35] cf. e.g. "*brǫ́ð fekk hrafn*" ("the raven

---

of formulaic diction in the Homeric poems", *The American Journal of Philology* 115 (1994), pp. 321-335; ELMER, *The Poetics of Consent*, p. 15; cf. also FROG and LAMB, "A Picasso of perspectives", p. 3.

[32] 'Traditional phrase' is used by NAGLER, *Spontaneity and Tradition*, pp. 1-63; 'traditional phraseology' by, e.g. FOLEY, *Traditional Oral Epic*, p. 167, note 22; 'formulaic phraseology' by, e.g. FOLEY and RAMEY, "Oral theory and medieval literature", p. 81, and W. LAMB, "From motif to multiword expression: The development of formulaic language in Gaelic traditional narrative", in: *Weathered Words*, pp. 193-220, at p.195; the 'multiform' concept was established by L. HONKO and A. HONKO, "Multiforms in epic composition", in: *The Epic: Oral and Written*, ed. L. HONKO, J. HANDOO, and J.M. FOLEY (Mysore, 1998), pp. 31-79, and was recently developed by FROG, "Multiform Theory", in: *Weathered Words*, pp. 115-146.

[33] So, e.g. B. BIRGISSON, *Inn i skaldens sinn: Kognitive, estetiske og historiske skatter i den norrøne skaldediktingen*, PhD thesis University of Bergen (Bergen, 2008), p. 15.

[34] FROG, "Mythological names and *dróttkvætt* formulae II: Base-word determinant indexing", *Studia Metrica et Poetica*, 1.2 (2014), pp. 39-70, and ID., "Metrical entanglement and *dróttkvætt* composition – A pilot study on battle kennings", in: *Approaches to Nordic and Germanic Poetry*, ed. K. ÁRNASON et al. (Reykjavík, 2016), pp. 149-229.

[35] B. FIDJESTØL, *Det norrøne fyrstediktet* (Bergen, 1980), p. 320.

got prey")[36] and "*ímr gat krǫ́s*" ("the wolf had a delicious meal"),[37] something which Fidjestøl called a "*formelprega variasjonsteknikk*" ("formula-based technique of variation").[38] Daniel Sävborg has in two works discussed such 'formulaic' variations in another stereotype in skaldic poetry, 'the woman causes the man grief' (with the meaning 'the man loves the woman') and indeed used the notion 'formula' there.[39]

Sometimes, the variation in verbal expression is so extensive that the term 'formula', or even 'formulaic phrase', might be problematic to use. This underscores the importance to discuss the distinction and relationship between verbal formulas proper and other meaning-bearing units of a formulaic kind (e.g. recurring motifs, scenes, story patterns and stereotype descriptions; cf. Parry's and Lord's notions of system, themes, type-scenes etc.).[40] These phenomena often interact intersectionally with verbal formulas proper and have recently been examined by Slavica Ranković and Daniel Sävborg.[41]

The present volume aims at shedding new light on formulas in oral tradition and in oral-derived texts. The authors have been invited to contribute both with theoretical discussion on the topic and with analysis of concrete cases. In some articles, the former task dominates, in others the latter. The volume has a particular focus on Old Norse literature, reflecting the background of the editors, but there are also several studies on Greek, Russian, English and American

---

[36] *Skaldic poetry of the Scandinavian Middle Ages: Poetry from the Kings' Sagas* 2.1, ed. K.E. GADE (Turnhout, 2009), p. 74.

[37] *Skaldic poetry of the Scandinavian Middle Ages*, p. 117.

[38] B. FIDJESTØL, *Det norrøne fyrstediktet*, p. 321.

[39] D. SÄVBORG, "The woman causes me grief: An Old Norse formula and concept of passion", in: *Germanisches Altertum und europäisches Mittelalter*, ed. W. HEIZMANN and J. VAN NAHL (Berlin, 2023), pp. 371-338; cf. also ID., *Sagan om kärleken*, pp. 310-312.

[40] Frog has noted that the relation between *formulas* and *themes* is "unclear" (FROG, "Multiform theory", p. 119) something indicated also by ZUMTHOR, *Oral Poetry*, p. 92. In Anglo-Saxonist scholarship, D.K. Fry used a 'formula' concept based on Parry's, and distinguished it from motifs, type-scenes, and themes, which were also described as "formulaic" (FRY, "Old English formulaic themes and type-Scenes", p. 49). William Lamb has discussed the possible distinction extensively and suggested the new concept 'formulaic motif' for "a motif conventionally expressed in part or whole through formulaic phraseology in a particular genre or across genres" (LAMB, "From motif to multiword expressions", p. 195). Daniel Sävborg coined the name 'formulaic motif' already in 2017 for a similar phenomenon in Icelandic saga prose (SÄVBORG, "The formula in Icelandic saga prose", p. 79).

[41] E.g. S. RANKOVIĆ, "The performative non-canonicity of the canonical", p. 259; EAD., "The temporality of the (immanent) saga: tinkering with formulas", in: *Dating the Sagas: Reviews and Revisions*, ed. E. MUNDAL (Copenhagen, 2013), pp. 147-190; EAD., "Immanent seas, scribal havens", pp. 46, 49; SÄVBORG, "The formula in Icelandic saga prose", pp. 78-81; ID., *Sagan om kärleken*, pp. 45-64.

cases, both ancient and modern. Altogether, this makes the volume relevant for scholars of formulas in many cultures, while at the same time the various topics are far from scattered, and the different articles supplement each other in a fruitful way.

***

Stephen A. Mitchell's article "Formulas, collocations, and cultural memory" opens with a discussion on the notion of 'collocation', "particular words which native speakers routinely place in the juxtaposition", and its relation to 'idioms' and 'formulas'. The first part of the article consists of a thorough discussion of the definition of these notions as well as of their distinguishing features, a discussion contributing to the theoretical discussion in the field. The second part demonstrates the practical usefulness of the notion 'collocation' by an examination of a particular case of oral tradition, Nordic charms.

In "Fee, fi, fo, formula: Getting to grips with the concept and deciding on a definition", Frog starts with the basic question: "what is a formula?" He then provides a thorough analysis of various definitions of the notion and of how the discussion of it has evolved since the early twentieth century. He notes the strong differences between the definitions and examines the consequences of these differences for scholarship. A main part of the article consists of a discussion of the different needs and purposes behind the choice of a certain 'formula definition'. This moves the focus from the traditional theoretical problem of 'definition of formula' to the problem of deciding how to define it.

The article by Jonathan Roper, "Freeman's formulas: Openings, transitions and closes", takes as its starting point the audio-recordings from the 1960s and 1970s in Newfoundland, when the tradition of telling wonder-tales was still alive. Roper uses one wonder-tale told by a certain storyteller on three occasions as a case study. His analysis focuses on the opening and closing of the tale in all three versions, especially examining the formulas used. The investigation concludes with a discussion of the differences between the oral, actually performed, folktales and edited versions in the printed editions. The use of formulas constitutes one of these differences: genuine oral folktale performances are far less formulaic than the book-folktale we are used to.

Tatian Bogrdanova's "The aesthetics of Russian folktale formulas: A view from translation studies" discusses the aesthetics of the Russian folktale from the perspective of translation studies. Bogrdanova examines a group of English translations of Russian folktales. Her main focus is the way they render the formulas of this particular genre, and she notes how the differences in the translators' approaches depend on the level of their awareness of this particular folklore tradition.

In an article by Eugenia Vorobeva, "Depicting violence in *Íslendingasögur*: A formula on the verge of legal tradition", the use of formulas in Old Norse prose is the focus. She investigates violence-related language in Old Norse prose literature, both in the sagas and in the law codes. The article demonstrates that depiction of violence and wounds in Old Norse prose is full of certain formulas, which the author identifies and analyses for the first time ever. She coins the new notion 'legalistic formulas' for formulas in the saga prose which are not strictly legal but reflect legalistic discourse and thereby charge the narrative with broader meaning.

Scott A. Mellor attempts in "Revisiting formula and mythic patterns and the interplay between *The Poetic Edda* and *Vǫlsunga saga*" to develop the view and definition of 'formula' found in Parry's and Lord's works to work better for Eddic poetry and its distinctive features. In particular, he enters into a dialogue with Paul Acker's similar attempts. In the latter part of the article, Mellor moves on to 'mythic patterns', a concept established by Albert Lord. Mellor examines two such patterns, e.g. the so-called 'absence – devastation – return' pattern in the Eddic *Vǫlsungr* cycle and *Vǫlsunga saga*. The result confirms Lord's claim that such patterns go beyond culture, time, and mode.

In "Same meaning, different words: Retelling as a mode of transmission in Old Norse-Icelandic *Konungasögur* tradition", Daria Glebova examines variation between different versions of the same stories in three specific Old Norse cases: the stories about Bjǫrn Hítdœlakappi, Hákon jarl's death, and Snæfríðr and King Haraldr. In her thorough analysis, she discusses micro-variation on the lexical level as well as 'retelling' with the clear goal to improve the text.

Paul Acker's article "A further history of orality and Eddic poetry" addresses the interface between the oral and the written by studying a kind of abbreviation which in the Old Norse context is typical in the written representation of Eddic poetry. In several cases, the manuscripts abbreviate sections that are similar to a previous section written in full, and in some cases even without the abbreviated text being written out at all. Acker relates this kind of abbreviation to oral tradition and shows how this method continues into the writing of ballads. Acker also connects this phenomenon to recent trends in research on Old Norse orality.

In "Toward a typology of runic formulas", Michael Schulte discusses formulas present in the runic material, and he suggests a fine-grained typology of these formulas. He presents six useful categories of runic formulas based on linguistic and metrical criteria. What is termed the 'formulaicity' of an expression is carefully considered on the basis of several factors, among them frequency, function, semantics, and etymology. As Schulte points out, runic formulas are by their very nature hybrid when it comes to the distinction between orality and literacy. Yet parts of this material have a considerable age, and it is thus of great interest to students of formulas, even in a Germanic perspective.

Chiara Bozzone approaches the Homeric material and investigates the concept of the formula from a linguistic perspective in "Chunks, collocations, and constructions: The Homeric formula in cognitive and linguistic perspective". Through numerous examples, Bozzone illustrates how formulas may be seen as expressions of what some linguists have termed 'chunking', which is related to the limits of human memory. Bozzone also characterises formulas as constructions, templates that allow for the production of formulaic expressions, and she presents a fivefold categorisation of formulas with different degrees of fixity and semantic characteristics.

In "Formulaic word-play in the poems of the *Anglo-Saxon Chronicle*", Inna Matyushina studies formulaic language in the *Anglo-Saxon Chronicle* and discusses the presence of formulaic wordplay in a text that may primarily be seen a product of literary production rather than oral performance and tradition. Matyushina finds that formulaic language is used to establish associations with traditional and Christian poetry, and thus functions primarily as an aesthetic device. This is an important function of formulaic language which was understated in the works of Parry and Lord but has later been claimed also in the case of more traditional oral-formulaic use, and in a variety of cultural contexts.

Slavica and Miloš Ranković present a work in two parts in their "A formula is a habit colliding with life". In the first part they discuss the theoretical basis of the formula and reach a definition covering both prose and poetry. In the second part of the paper, they present a case study from the saga of Grettir Ásmundarson in the light of a method termed 'distributed reading'. They focus on formulas and networks of formulas involved in situations where Grettir's considerable temper is challenged. The method enables a refined understanding of formulas and how they contribute to the narrative.

In "Formulas in Scottish traditional narrative: Finding poetry in the prosaic", William Lamb discusses the distinction between poetry and prose, an argues for a broader view of poetry when considering the qualities and formulaicity of traditional narrative, such as in the Scots and Gaelic narratives investigated in the first part of the paper. Lamb also presents an analysis of binominals and addresses the question which of them are common to language in general and which are specific to traditional genres. Lamb argues that both types should be considered when investigating the formulaicity of traditional narrative.

Fee, Fi, Fo, Formula: Getting to Grips with the Concept and Deciding on a Definition

FROG

In memoriam of John Miles Foley

What is a formula? The answer to this question often seems self-evident, whether we feel confident in our explanation or stupid because we are not sure what to say. The intuition of self-evidence is rooted in encountering the term all over the place, with a tendency to take its meaning for granted. The handling of the word conceals the diversity of definitions attached to it, some of which are incompatible, while many scholars who use it in passing would be hard pressed to define it if anyone suddenly asked. The problem of definitions can be particularly acute for researchers in Old Norse or Old English studies, owing to their quite different relations to so-called Oral-Formulaic Theory (OFT), also called Oral Theory. In both cases, tethering to OFT has impacted research, not least because OFT built on and propagated a definition of formula stemming from one of Milman Parry's dissertations, written nearly a century ago (1928).[1] Parry's definition makes formulaic language a phenomenon exclusive to poetry, handicapping the concept's extension to prose. More generally, these fields and others where OFT ascended remain generally unaware of the diversity of approaches to formulaic language, which have developed across a variety of disciplines. The present chapter offers a general perspective on the issue of choosing, adapting, or creating a formula definition.

This chapter is structured around the FAQs of choosing or developing a formula definition for your research.[2] It starts off with an overview of why there are many definitions for 'formula' and the associated concept, briefly introducing the three branches in which formula research has developed and their recent convergence. Attention then turns to a longstanding stumbling block to the development of open dialogue across branches of research, which is also of central interest in the present volume: the deep-rooted idea that poetry and prose are fundamentally different. This idea is aired out and, rather than imagining poetry and prose as a pair of mutually exclusive categories, an alternative approach is outlined. This approach views all forms of linguistic discourse as organised on a hierarchy of principles that may vary between one type of discourse and another. From this perspective, any type of discourse can have features like alliteration, rhyme, or parallelism, but some make these primary principles organising language into units (e.g. lines), and, within that form of discourse, formulaic language is shaped through these organising principles. This leads to considering definitions of 'formula' as falling into different types according with whether they are descriptive or stipulative (i.e. based on *a priori* stipulations of what a formula is) and how a definition is calibrated, which can range from proposing a definition as universal to something intended for use only within a single study. Once the range of potential ways of defining a formula have been surveyed, factors to consider when choosing a definition are reviewed. The chapter closes with a response to the key question: *How can I tell what sort of definition will work best for me?*

The discussion offered here is oriented to readers who are working with forms of verbal art, from traditions of medieval law and literature to improvisational rap battles. The prominence of Old Norse and Old English in the present

---

[1] M. PARRY, *L'épithète traditionnelle dans Homère* (Paris, 1928) and ID., *Les formules de la métrique d'Homère* (Paris, 1928); for translations into English, see ID., *The Making of Homeric Verse: The Collected Papers of Milman Perry*, ed. A. PARRY (Oxford, 1971).

[2] This structure was used by John Miles Foley in J.M. FOLEY, "*Guslar* and *Aoidos*: Traditional register in South Slavic and Homeric epic", *Transactions of the American Philological Association* 126 (1996), pp. 11-41, of which this chapter is a humble echo.

Fee, Fi, Fo, Formula

volume leads traditions in these languages and scholarship surrounding them to be a central frame of reference and source for examples. In fields where OFT has held a prominent or dominant position, it remains common for scholars to think about formulaic language as specific to poetry, but the more general view today is that formulae are ubiquitous in language.[3] From that perspective, the question of *whether* the concept of formula is relevant to your research is analogous to asking whether you need the concept of 'verb'. Anyone working with formulaic language in oral poetry should be aware that formulaic language is recognised as a phenomenon of language generally. Anyone interested in formulaic language outside of metred poetry will likely stumble over Parry's definition and should be aware of the rich and varied discussions of formulaic language in other forms of discourse. Whereas other contributions to this book illustrate the potential of different types of formula analysis, the current chapter introduces the variety of definitions with perspectives on how to navigate these in relation to your own interests and research aims.

Question 1: Why Isn't There Just One Definition That Everybody Uses?

Formulaic language did not start off as a category that everybody intuitively understood, and it is indeed only relatively recently that the word 'formula' has become fairly standard for such units of language. Today, formula research can be viewed as having three main branches, which I describe as 'lexicon-centred', 'discourse-centred', and 'oral-poetic'. Lexicon-centred and discourse-centred research, elaborated below, tend to be more or less in dialogue. These can best be seen as extremes on a spectrum with a variety of work between their poles. The fissure is deep, however, between these and the oral-poetic branch, owing in large part to the mainstream view that 'poetry' is fundamentally different from other types of language usage. Rather than each branch being founded on a single, defining framework, they have taken shape as different approaches have become linked or superseded one another; historical changes have unified some discussions while earlier approaches simultaneously remained in play. Thus, within each branch, there are multiple, historically stratified discussions, some of which are centred in particular disciplines or fields. The complexity of

---

[3] Rephrasing W. LAMB, "From motif to multiword expression: The development of formulaic language in Gaelic traditional narrative", in: *Weathered Words: Formulaic Language and Verbal Art*. ed. FROG and W. LAMB (Cambridge, MA, 2022: *Milman Parry Collection of Oral Literature*), pp. 193-220, at p. 214.

the situation is in large part owing to interest in formulaic language coming from so many angles independently, but without being concerned with theorising the general concept so much as exploring a phenomenon of language observed in particular material. The discussions have thus tended to evolve within networks of scholars whose interests are aligned, with dialogue between some of these networks or clusters of such networks and not between others. Although the diversity might be considered to reflect the fragmented nature of formula research, it is more accurate to say that formulaic language is addressed in several multidisciplinary discussions that have remained largely separate where their concerns have been historically separate.

Because the term 'formula' has gradually become pervasive across research, it easily gives the impression that the concept is generally established and uncontroversial. Individual scholars are often only aware of discussions in particular networks, so many researchers pick up a definition or approach for a particular study without being aware of alternatives, especially when the topic is new for them or only forms part of a broader research interest. Taking up a definition in this way is unsurprising, because there has been a lack of centralised entry points to formula research. In lexicon-centred and discourse-centred branches, volumes devoted to formulaic language readily recognised through 'formula' in the title are concentrated in the present century, among which Alison Wray's *Formulaic Language: Pushing the Boundaries* (2008) and Koenraad Kuiper's *Formulaic Genres* (2009) now offer key points of entry.[4] The situation in the oral-poetic branch was different: the publication of Albert Lord's *Singer of Tales*[5] produced the initial boom of OFT in the 1960s and 1970s,[6] which stimulated and propagated the respective formula research. Although Lord's *magnum opus* is now quite dated, it has never been superseded

---

[4] E.g. *Formulaic Language*, ed. R. CORRIGAN *et al.*, 2 vols. (Amsterdam, 2009: *Typological Studies in Language* 82-83); K. KUIPER, *Formulaic Genres* (Basingstoke, 2009); *Formulaic Sequences: Acquisition, Processing and Use*, ed. N. SCHMITT (Amsterdam, 2004); A. WRAY, *Formulaic Language: Pushing the Boundaries* (Oxford, 2008); EAD., *Formulaic Language and the Lexicon* (Cambridge, 2002); see also *Formula: Units of Speech – 'Words' of Verbal Art: Working Papers of the Seminar-Workshop, 17th-19th May 2017, Helsinki, Finland* ed. FROG (Helsinki, 2017: *Folkloristiikan Toimite* 21).

[5] A.B. LORD, *The Singer of Tales* (Cambridge, MA, 1960: *Harvard Studies in Comparative Literature* 24).

[6] For an accessible overview of these decades of OFT, see J.M. FOLEY, *The Theory of Oral Composition: History and Methodology* (Bloomington, 1988).

as a central point of entry into this branch of research, although now *Weathered Words* (2022)[7] will help to fill this gap, along with the present book.

Among the three branches, the lexicon-centred branch arguably has the deepest roots, and formulaic language in oral poetry began receiving attention during the nineteenth century. Lexicon-centred research sprang from attention to idioms, both in lexicography and interest in so-called 'folk speech', with research concentrated on European and North American national languages. It focused on expressions that diverged in lexicon (*beyond the pale*), syntax (*believe you me*), or meaning (*monkey business*) from the lexicon and grammar of everyday speech, often with an etymological interest. From that perspective, formulaic language was a marginal and insignificant part of language. The oral-poetic branch began to emerge in research on languages other than the researcher's own, whether foreign or historical. Poetry in those languages was seen as separate from more general language use, sometimes addressed in terms of the 'style' of traditional narrative or song.[8] Spoken or written idioms that were *also* found in poetry could make poetic texts relevant as sources. Oral poetry held a valued position in lexicography because of the vocabulary that could be found there.[9] There was no explicit theoretical principle on which poetry and other types of discourse were separated, but idioms tended to be examined as belonging in either one or the other.

A number of transformative changes occurred in discussions of formulaic language across the middle of the twentieth century. Attention shifted from language as an abstract system to how it relates to people and situations. Basic ideas that had long been part of discussion became reframed in terms of cognitive processes. Ferdinand de Saussure, for example, had considered the process whereby people internalise language in both simple and complex (i.e. formulaic) units, anticipating cognitive approaches to language acquisition by almost half a century.[10] Similarly, Parry's theory of formulaic language was an early

---

[7] *Weathered Words: Formulaic Language and Verbal Art*, ed. FROG and W. LAMB (Cambridge, MA, 2022: *Milman Parry Collection of Oral Literature* 6).

[8] E.g. A. NUTT, in collaboration with D. MACINNES, "Notes", in: *Folk and Hero Tales*, ed. and trans. D. MACINNES (London, 1890), pp. 395-491.

[9] *Dictionaries as Sources of Folklore Data*, ed. J. ROPER (Helsinki, 2020: *FF Communications* 321).

[10] Ferdinand de Saussure's observation that "*la langue ne se présente pas comme un ensemble de signes délimités d'avance [...] c'est une masse indistincte où l'attention et l'habitude peuvent seules nous faire trouver des éléments particuliers*" (F. DE SAUSSURE, *Cours de linguistique générale* (Paris, 1967; first published in 1916), p.146) ("language does not present itself as a set of signs delimited in advance [...] it is an indistinct mass, in which only habit and attention allow us to distinguish particular elements") anticipates Alison Wray's theory of 'needs-only

formulation of the idea that pre-fabricated chunks of language lighten the cognitive load for producing utterances at the rate of speech,[11] now recognised as part of commonplace conversation and especially of situations of regular interaction, like when making a purchase at your local shop.[12] The terminology and research concepts available to these scholars were very different, yet they were considering aspects of formulaic language that are today commonly viewed through a lens of cognitive processing in some branches of formula research. Of course, the cognitive dimension of their ideas did not receive widespread interest until much later, in the cascade of shifts in interest and attention in research that followed the so-called postmodern turn. These shifts led to fundamental changes in the lexicon-centred branch of approaches, produced the distinct discourse-centred branch, and also eventually transformed the oral-poetic branch.

Especially across the past several decades, lexicon-centred approaches have shaken formulaic language free from being somehow aberrant. It is now widely distinguished only by being more complex than an individual word and functioning as a discreet unit. Formulaic language has thus been reconceived to include everything from *thank you* to complex verbs like *shake free*. From there, it may also be understood to include one or more words in a construction with preferred choices for completing accompanying variable slots and any constraints on how the slots are completed.[13] For example, *a pain in ARTICLE / PRONOUN X* is completed with *neck* or *ass* but never *foot* or *back* (unless in semantic play). Such slots may also be governed by what is called 'semantic prosody' – i.e. an evaluative stance is regular for the formula – like *bordering on X* in its primary, non-physical usage, meaning 'approaching an undesirable state (of mind)', in which the negative evaluation is key to its meaning.[14] The developments during this period are connected with the recognition that how

---

analysis' (WRAY, *Formulaic Language and the Lexicon*, pp. 130-132), according to which "the process of analysis which the child engages in would not be that of breaking down as much linguistic material as possible into its smallest components. Rather, nothing would be broken down unless there were a specific reason, and although rules were derived and words stored in the lexicon as the result of the analysis that did occur, few, if any, implicit generalizations would be made from one piece of linguistic data to another" (*ibid.*, p. 130).

[11] PARRY, *L'épithète traditionnelle* and ID., *Les formules*.

[12] E.g. KUIPER, *Formulaic Genres*, and WRAY, *Formulaic Language: Pushing the Boundaries*.

[13] E.g. *Formulaic Language*, ed. CORRIGAN et al.; *Formulaic Sequences*, ed. SCHMITT; and WRAY, *Formulaic Language and the Lexicon*.

[14] N. SCHMITT and R. CARTER, "Formulaic sequences in action: An introduction", in: *Formulaic Sequences*, ed. SCHMITT, pp. 1-22, at p. 8.

things are actually expressed in a language are far more limited than what the lexicon and grammar make hypothetically possible.[15] From this perspective, formulae are pervasive in language use. Alison Wray's definition of a formulaic sequence has been widely accepted and is increasingly treated as a potential standard definition:[16]

> a sequence, continuous or discontinuous, of words or other elements, which is, or appears to be, prefabricated: that is, stored and retrieved whole from memory at the time of use, rather than being subject to generation or analysis by the language grammar.[17]

Discourse-centred approaches emerged especially across the past half century as attention shifted from language as an abstract system to language in situated practices. This shift included attention to how language is used in relation to structures and scripts or interactive scenarios. Scholars looked beyond the scope of a clause's or sentence's syntax and also began to consider embodied behaviour. Research faced the question of a formula's minimum complexity, and whether a single word could constitute a formula. From the perspective of the lexicon, *thank you* is a formula while *thanks* is not, because, although they are generally interchangeable in other respects, the former is considered two words while the latter is only one. Discourse-centred research could operate under the same principle, but the consideration of extra-linguistic features and structures of interaction resulted in a change in the features qualifying complexity. This allowed a formula to be one word combined with something else, such as intonation, gesture, and so on, rather than a formula being constituted exclusively of lexical material.[18] In English, for example, *No!* and *No way!* both have formulaic usage expressing the elicitation of surprise at something heard or seen, but in oral discourse this meaning as opposed to another is dependent on intonation and is customarily accompanied by at least some degree of bodily performance of surprise. Wray's definition of a 'formulaic sequence' rather than of a 'formula' more generally should be viewed in this light. Allowing

---

[15] A. PAWLEY and F. HODGETTS SYDER, "Two puzzles for linguistic theory: Nativelike selection and nativelike fluency", in: *Language and Communication*, ed. J.C. RICHARDS and R.W. SCHMIDT (London, 1983), pp. 191-227.

[16] Cf. works collected in *Formulaic Language*, ed. CORRIGAN et al., and also in *Weathered Words*, ed. FROG and LAMB.

[17] WRAY, *Formulaic Language and the Lexicon*, p. 9.

[18] A. PAWLEY, "Grammarians' languages versus Humanists' languages and the place of speech act formulas in models of linguistic competence", in: *Formulaic Language*, ed. CORRIGAN et al., 1, pp. 3-26.

one-word formulae led discourse markers like *Hi* or *thanks* to get discussed as formulae sometimes without clarifying why, leading the distinction between word and formula to blur. The difference in principles for considering complexity have enabled the address of one-word formulae, but the principles are often implicit rather than explicit and theorised (and thus open to variant interpretations). The rationale can be viewed as the binding of the particular word with a script of interaction, which structures its usage, rather than simply using words of the lexicon in combination with the rules of the grammar. The central point here, however, is that the criteria qualifying a formula in the discourse-centred branch of research expand considerably from that in the lexicon-centred branch, allowing for formulae of only one word.

This brings us to the oral-poetic branch of research, which warrants a more developed introduction in the present context. In fields where OFT and its definitions of 'formula' became dominant, the invisibility of work in other branches has concentrated formulaic language research in poetry, even when discussions developed on very different trajectories, as in Old Norse and Old English research. Prior to the boom of OFT, formulaic language tended to be seen as a fact of oral style rather than as a phenomenon of interest in its own right. The language of poetry was recognised as distinct already from an early stage[19] and its phraseology was of interest already in the nineteenth century. This led Eduard Sievers to append a remarkably detailed *Formelverzeichnis* ('formula index') to his edition of the Old Saxon epic *Heliand*[20] and Richard Meyer to produce a massive study of *formelhafte Elemente* ('formulaic elements') in Old Germanic poetry.[21] The recurrent linguistic units were approached on the same principles as in lexicon-centred approaches, although the category remained fuzzy. Much as English 'formula' today has a number of usages beyond formulaic language, German 'Formel' ('formula') had a broader range of use, for instance as the term coined for what today is commonly called a tale-type in comparative folk narrative research.[22] The terminology was by no means uniform. Recurrent phraseology was often referred to with terms like 'cliché' or '*locus communis*' ('commonplace'), aligning with an ideology of the *Volk* as

---

[19] Old English poetry, e.g. was characterised as composed in a distinct dialect of language already at the beginning of the eighteenth century (G. Hickesius, *Linguarum vett: Septentrionalium thesaurus grammatico-criticus et archæologicus* 2 (Oxford, 1705), pp. 101-134).

[20] *Heliand*, ed. E. SIEVERS (Halle, 1878), pp. 389-496.

[21] R.M. MEYER, *Die altgermanische Poesie nach ihren formelhaften Elementen beschrieben* (Berlin, 1889).

[22] *Griechische und albanesische Märchen*, ed. and trans. J.G. VON HAHN (Leipzig, 1864).

uncreative and mechanical reproducers of inherited traditions. Milman Parry's research that formed the foundation of OFT developed within this ideology.[23]

Parry focused on formulaic language in Homeric epics as evidence of their oral background, an argument made within a long debate concerning whether the epics were of oral or literary origin. Oral epic traditions were documented and researched throughout the nineteenth century. Parry's argument was based on the idea that long oral epics are neither memorised nor is it possible for singers to compose each metrical line at the pace of performance; instead, recurrent phrases common in oral epics were considered prefabricated phrases fitted to metrical lines and parts of lines on which singers relied in order to compose at the rate of performance. His formula definition later circulated globally with OFT:

> a group of words which is regularly employed under the same metrical conditions to express a given essential idea.[24]

The cognitive implications of the definition are implicit, but note that it formally corresponds to Wray's definition of a formulaic sequence above, except that it includes an additional criterion that the words should occur in particular metrical positions.

Parry's work on formulaic language initially received little attention in Homeric scholarship. His model shifted focus from tradition as text to tradition as practice in order to explain the Homeric epics. However, interest in how texts relate to people and vary across different situations only became of widespread interest with the cross-disciplinary shifts described as postmodernism. In 1949, Parry's student and fieldwork collaborator Albert Lord completed his doctoral dissertation comparing South Slavic, Homeric, and Germanic poetries in terms of oral composition.[25] Lord then regularly gave a seminar at Harvard on 'Medieval Epic and Romance' that concentrated on formulae and the corre-

---

[23] PARRY, *L'épithète traditionnelle*; ID., *Les formules*; ID., *The Making of Homeric Verse*; on the research leading up to Parry's dissertations, see FOLEY, *The Theory of Oral Composition*, pp. 1-18.

[24] M. PARRY, "Studies in the epic technique of oral verse-making 1: Homer and Homeric style", *Harvard Studies in Classical Philology* 40 (1930), pp. 73-147, at p. 80; Parry first published his definition in French as *"une expression qui est régulièrement employée, dans les mêmes conditions métriques, pour exprimer une certaine idée essentielle"* (PARRY, *Les formules*, p. 16).

[25] A.B. LORD, *The Singer of Tales: A Study in the Processes of Composition of Yugoslav, Greek, and Germanic Oral Narrative Poetry* (unpublished doctoral dissertation, Harvard University, 1949).

sponding traditional units of narration called 'themes'.[26] In this seminar, Lord and his students wrestled with the applicability of "Parry's [formula] definition to the specific metrical and rhythmic conventions of the several cultures involved".[27] OFT percolated in Harvard circles during the 1950s. It created a stir in Old English studies through an invited series of lectures by Francis Peabody Magoun, Jr., at the University of London in 1952 and the associated publication of his paper "The oral-formulaic character of Anglo-Saxon narrative poetry" in the following year. Magoun reproduced Parry's definition,[28] but defining a formula as a repeated phrasal unit did not accommodate Old English poetry's verbal variation: the metrical requirement of alliteration drove the poetry to develop systems of vocabulary and phraseology to 'say the same thing' with words beginning with different sounds to meet the alliteration of particular lines.[29] This situation gradually accrued a focused discussion that made Old English studies a hotbed for working with the definition of formula and its applicability.[30] The publication of Lord's revised dissertation as *The Singer of Tales* followed in 1960.[31] This work formalised OFT, establishing what can today be described as Classic OFT, and gradually became viewed internationally as a basic entry point for approaching formulaic language in verbal art. Its reproduction of Parry's formula definition[32] made this the standard for fields where discussions of formulaic language developed centrally from Lord's *Singer of Tales*, as in Old Norse studies.[33] The remarkable reception of Lord's book

[26] A.B. LORD, "Perspectives on recent work on the oral traditional formula", *Oral Tradition* 1.3 (1986), pp. 467-503, at p. 479; on the units called themes, see also PARRY, *The Making of Homeric Verse*, pp. XLI-XLII; LORD, *The Singer of Tales*, pp. 68-98; J.M. FOLEY, *Traditional Oral Epic: The Odyssey, Beowulf, and the Serbo-Croatian Return Song* (Los Angeles, 1990), esp. pp. 240-245, 279-284, 329-335.

[27] LORD, "Perspectives on recent work", p. 479.

[28] F.P. MAGOUN, "The oral-formulaic character of Anglo-Saxon narrative poetry", *Speculum* 28.3 (1953), pp. 446-467, at p. 449.

[29] See also J. ROPER, "Synonymy and rank in alliterative poetry", *Sign Systems Studies* 40.1-2 (2012), pp. 82-93.

[30] See also S.C.E. HOPKINS, "Of *scopas* and scribes: Reshaping oral-formulaic theory in Old English literary studies", in: *Weathered Words*, ed. FROG and LAMB, pp. 49-79.

[31] LORD, *The Singer of Tales*.

[32] LORD, *The Singer of Tales*, p. 4.

[33] E.g. J. HARRIS, "Eddic poetry as oral poetry: The evidence of parallel passages in the Helgi poems for questions of composition and performance", in: *Edda: A Collection of Essays*, ed. R.J. GLENDINNING and H. BESSASON (Manitoba, 1983), pp. 210-242; P. ACKER, *Revising Oral Theory: Formulaic Composition in Old English and Old Icelandic Verse* (New York, 1998), ch. 4; S. MELLOR, *Analyzing Ten Poems from* The Poetic Edda*: Oral Formula and Mythic Patterns* (Lewiston, 2008); see also B.Ø. THORVALDSEN, Svá er sagt í fornum vísindum*: Tekstualiseringen av de mytologiske eddadikt* (unpublished doctoral thesis, University of Bergen, 2006);

reflects its resonance with changing interests that would gradually precipitate the so-called performance-oriented turn.[34]

Classic OFT spread as a methodological package and superseded alternative approaches to relevant traditions, uniting a wide range of research. Parry's definition became the default point of reference in those discussions, but the definition remained tangled up with the methodological framework. The 'theory' of Classic OFT concerned formulaic language as a product of a performer's needs while composing metred lines *in situ*. However, Parry developed it with the aim to demonstrate that the Homeric epics originated in an oral tradition on the basis of the density of formulaic language in the written texts. Lord extended this argument to Old Germanic poetries, illustrating the principles through the fieldwork on South Slavic epic. There were adaptations of Classic OFT to prose traditions,[35] but Parry's definitional criterion of "under the same metrical conditions" formally excluded language in unmetred discourse. Moreover, although Parry's definition corresponds formally to Wray's with a single additional criterion, it was embedded in a broader 'theory' that viewed formulae as produced by the needs of the composition in performance of metred poetry. The argument asserted a polarised contrast between oral poetry and written composition, in which formulaic language was specifically linked to the needs of oral poetry, and more specifically to oral poetry that was composed in the process of performance. Although poetry had long held an implicit status as 'different' from language use in other contexts, the spread of OFT reified that divide through both its explicit definition and the ideas carried with it.[36]

In the boom of the 1960s and 1970s, several developments went on simultaneously. Vocabulary was impacted so that, wherever OFT got a foothold, 'formula' superseded terms like 'cliché', 'commonplace', 'idiom', '*locus commu-*

FROG, '*Alvíssmál* and Orality I: Formula, alliteration and categories of mythic being", *Arkiv för Nordisk Filologi* 126 (2011), pp. 17-71. OFT was already being tested against Old Norse poetry in the Harvard circle, leading to Robert Kellogg's doctoral dissertation, R. KELLOGG *A Concordance of Eddic Poetry* (PhD dissertation, Harvard University, 1958), although this had little early impact because it remained unpublished until 1988 (R. KELLOGG, *A Concordance to Eddic Poetry* (East Lansing, 1988: Medieval Texts and Studies 2)).

[34] E.g. R. BAUMAN, *Verbal Art as Performance* (Prospect Heights, 1984; first published in 1975); *Folklore: Performance and Communication*, ed. D. BEN-AMOS and K. GOLDSTEIN (The Hague, 1975).

[35] E.g. A. BRUFORD, "Gaelic folk-tales and mediaeval romances: A study of the early modern Irish 'Romantic tales' and their oral derivatives", *Béaloideas* 34.1-5 (1969), pp. 1-165, 167-285; R. SCHOLES and R. KELLOGG, *The Nature of Narrative* (Oxford, 1966).

[36] See also FROG and W. LAMB, "A Picasso of perspectives on formulaic language", in: *Weathered Words*, ed. FROG and LAMB, pp. 1-21.

nis', and so forth. Inspired by the new drive to identify formulae in historical texts, philological scholars began designating almost any recurrent phenomenon discovered inside poetic lines as a 'formula'. This produced a plethora of terms like 'structural formula',[37] 'metrical formula',[38] 'syntactic formula',[39] and so on, which have largely fallen out of use, but that inadvertently reinforced the view that formulaic language in oral poetry is separate from formulaic language in other contexts. At the same time, controversy erupted on two fronts in particular. The 'theory' that the density of formulae in a historical text like the *Iliad* indicate an origin from oral poetry was hotly debated, which included raising methodological issues concerning how to calculate formulaic density in written texts.[40] As OFT was being tested on an ever-increasing variety of traditions, Classic OFT was getting viewed as *the* model for how oral poetries work, yet it described a particular type of variable long epic poetry, and the model was not viable for many oral traditions.[41] Indeed, the composition-in-performance model was not even uniformly applicable to all oral long epic traditions, some of which maintained extended passages that were quite regularly reproduced from memory.[42] The spread of OFT was rapid and pervasive where the respective poetry aligned with its model; where an oral poetry tradition did not exhibit full composition-in-performance variation, OFT was only engaged on a limited basis, but it could nevertheless have subtle impacts on how researchers conceived of formulaic language and how it was discussed.

---

[37] Referring to a distribution of words within a line or part of a line according to their syllabic or moraic patterns, irrespective of their syntactic relations (J. RUSSO, "A closer look at Homeric formulas", *Transactions and Proceedings of the American Philological Association* 94 (1963), pp. 235-247, on Homeric epic).

[38] Referring to the preferred rhythmic-metrical form of a line among possible alternatives (FOLEY, "Formula and theme in Old English poetry", in: *Oral Literature and the Formula*, ed. B.A. STOLZ and R.S. SHANNON III (Ann Arbor, 1976), pp. 207-232, on Old English poetry).

[39] Referring to a preferred organisation of syntax within a line (S.B. GREENFIELD, "The canons of Old English criticism", *English Literary History* 34.2 (1967), pp. 141-155, on Old English poetry).

[40] E.g. J.A. RUSSO, "Is 'oral' or 'aural' composition the cause of Homer's formulaic style", in: *Oral Literature and the Formula*, ed. B.A. STOLZ and R.S. SHANNON III (Ann Arbor, 1976), pp. 31-54.

[41] E.g. R. FINNEGAN, *Oral Poetry: Its Nature, Significance and Social Context* (Cambridge, 1977).

[42] K. REICHL, "Formulas in oral epics: The dynamics of metre, memory and meaning", in: *Weathered Words*, ed. FROG and LAMB, pp. 23-47; ID. "Oral tradition and performance of the Uzbek and Karakalpak singers", in: *Fragen der mongolischen Heldendichtung*, 3, ed. W. HEISSIG (Wiesbaden, 1985), pp. 613-643.

Viewing formulae narrowly as general resources of a composition-in-performance type significantly impacted discussions. Parry's definition was approached within that framework, which polarised the contrast between composition in performance and 'memorisation' or 'remembering' lines that had been composed. Aligning formulae with one side of that contrast excluded it from the other,[43] which meant that Classic OFT denied formulaic language as being linked to mnemonics rather than composition only. Consequently, it was not enough to be "a group of words which is regularly employed under the same metrical conditions to express a given essential idea".[44] The group of words had to be found in different sequences of text, because if they were found in different examples of the same text sequence, such as two versions of an Old Norse poem, the passage might simply have been memorised.[45] If there were only two examples of the potential formula, these had to be separated sufficiently, that the second was not reproduced from short-term memory of the first.[46] The critical mass of discussion about formulaic language in Old English with its active rethinking of formula definitions was not paralleled in research on Old Norse eddic poetry, for which the composition-in-performance model was not a good fit because it exhibits a much heavier reliance on memory. Engagements with OFT were generally limited and testing it on cases in the corpus only supported the view that it was not composition-in-performance poetry.[47] Nevertheless, Classic OFT's definition made scholars cautious of considering a phrase as a formula if it was only attested in one poem,[48] while sequences of lines with similar phraseology commonly remained interpreted through text-loan models.[49]

During the 1970s and 1980s, some attempts were made to link OFT research with formula studies in other fields. Paul Kiparski's pioneering attempt was

---

[43] On this phenomenon, see S. GAL and J. IRVINE, *Signs of Difference: Language and Ideology in Social Life* (Cambridge, 2019).

[44] PARRY, "Studies in the epic technique", p. 80.

[45] This principle is visible, for example, in L., LÖNNROTH, "Hjalmar's death-song and the delivery of eddic poetry", *Speculum* 46.1 (1971), pp. 1-20.

[46] LORD, "Perspectives on recent work", p. 480. Assessing whether the potential example was an accidentally independent generation of the same phrase from the lexicon and grammar rather than being a formula proper (e.g. RUSSO, "Is 'oral' or 'aural' composition the cause") is a methodological concern that remains valid in current approaches today (cf. WRAY, *Formulaic Language: Pushing the Boundaries*).

[47] E.g. LÖNNROTH, "Hjalmar's death-song"; HARRIS "Eddic poetry as oral poetry".

[48] This continues into recent research – e.g. MELLOR, *Analyzing Ten Poems*, p. 96.

[49] For discussion, see B.Ø. THORVALDSEN, "Om Þrymskviða, tekstlån og tradisjon", *Maal og Minne* (2008), pp. 142-166; for an early dynamic approach, see HARRIS, "Eddic poetry as oral poetry".

made already in the 1970s; it also sought to connect OFT to Finno-Karelian kalevalaic poetry, which was viewed at the time as 'memorised'.[50] Another noteworthy attempt was made by Koenraad Kuiper and D.C. Haggo, working with the calls of livestock auctioneers rather than epic.[51] The most significant for Old Norse and Old English research was in Paul Acker's dissertation in 1983,[52] although this remained largely unknown until its publication in 1998.[53] Acker made a major innovation of introducing, from formula research in contemporary linguistics, the concept of formulae as potentially having variable slots that are completed in use. His work is also representative of a more general turn from focusing on formulae only in composition-in-performance practices to treating the concept as equally relevant for oral poetry that relies more heavily on memory. However, none of these or similar attempts had much impact in bridging the divide between branches of formula research.

Around 1990, OFT research underwent a turn from formal analysis and the inventorying of formulae and themes to exploring their meanings and functions.[54] These interests could be found in earlier scholarship,[55] but they became integrated with a concern for performance and practice, and they connected with an interdisciplinary trend to look beyond one's own discipline. This turn produced a secondary boom in OFT research by creating new relevance to traditions like Old Norse eddic poetry, where meaning in oral or oral-derived variation was interesting and pertinent even if Classic OFT's model of composition in performance did not apply. The shifts in interest opened OFT to numerous theoretical advances, and it integrated a broader range of approaches to oral traditions. This process brought it into alignment with some frameworks that remain distinct, such as ethnopoetics, while others have been absorbed.[56]

---

[50] P. KIPARSKY, "Oral poetry: Some linguistic and typological considerations", in: *Oral Literature and the Formula*, ed. STOLZ and SHANNON III, pp. 73-106.

[51] K. KUIPER and D.C. HAGGO, "Livestock auctions, oral poetry and ordinary language", *Language in Society* 13 (1984), pp. 205-234.

[52] P. ACKER, *Levels of Formulaic Composition in Old English and Old Icelandic Verse* (unpublished doctoral dissertation, Brown University, 1983).

[53] ACKER, *Revising Oral Theory*.

[54] J.M. FOLEY and P. RAMEY, "Oral theory and medieval studies", in: *Medieval Oral Literature*, ed. K. REICHL (Berlin, 2012), pp. 71-102.

[55] E.g. L. LÖNNROTH, "*Iǫrð fannz æva né upphiminn*: A formula analysis", in: *Speculum Norroenum: Studies in Memory of Gabriel Turville-Petre*, ed. U. DRONKE et al. (Odense, 1981), pp. 310-327; P. BEEKMAN TAYLOR, "The structure of *Vǫlundarkviða*", *Neophilologus* 47 (1963), pp. 228-236.

[56] Cf. J.M. FOLEY, *The Singer of Tales in Performance* (Bloomington, 1995).

The problems of using formulaic density as a test for oral origin became widely recognised by the end of the 1980s,[57] but the process of leaving those problems behind was long, and its shadow was even longer. The turn to meanings was also gradual, along with the shift of interest to relationships of traditions to individuals in social contexts. The differences in OFT before and after these processes led some scholars to distinguish Classic OFT from current research by designating the latter as 'Oral Theory'. The distinction is not very widely made but penetrated into Old Norse and Old English research to some degree.[58] However, this terminological distancing has proven more confusing than effective, since the epithet 'oral-formulaic' was never used by Lord and actually spread through the title of Magoun's seminal article from 1953.[59] Lord consistently referred to OFT as 'Oral Theory', often specifying that it is Parry's oral theory.[60] The term 'Oral Theory' was thus the label propagated through *The Singer of Tales*, used internationally as a synonym for OFT from 1960 onwards, and, ironically, its use referred specifically to Parry's ideas from which later scholarship wanted to distance itself. The turn in research built on the more formally-centred studies of Classic OFT and the infrastructures it developed, while retaining its central concepts and terms of formula and theme. The differences that were in such sharp focus in the 1990s appear today as integrated with continuities. Although the term 'Oral Theory' has been seen as more open, the research has never sought to theorise the vast spectrum of orality and has been characterised instead by its focus on prefabricated resources in traditions of verbal art. Thus the preference here for the more specific epithet 'Oral-Formulaic' and the distinction as between 'Classic' and 'Current' OFT rather than as the distinction between OFT and something else.

Following the turn of the 1990s, ways of thinking about formulae in OFT research have gradually changed. Questions of formulaic density as an indicator of orality were centrally a concern for traditions preserved only in manuscripts. The move away from these questions obviated the implicit criterion that a formula should be a common social resource for the *in situ* composition of new lines. At the end of his career, Lord himself turned attention to forms of oral poetry that were not of the composition-in-performance type. He was on the path to developing a new theory of these types of poetry and how they vary in

---

[57] See also FOLEY, *The Theory of Oral Composition*.

[58] This terminological distancing gained a foothold in Old Norse scholarship through the work of Paul Acker (ACKER, *Revising Oral Theory*, pp. xiv-xv).

[59] MAGOUN, "The oral-formulaic character"; the title of his 1952 lecture series was the same except in its use of 'formulaic' rather than 'oral-formulaic'.

[60] E.g. LORD, *Singer of Tales*, p. 5; ID., *The Singer Resumes the Tale* (Ithaca, 1995), p. 167.

terms of what he had earlier described as 'runs' and later as 'blocks of lines'.[61] His earlier view of runs was based on South Slavic and Homeric epics, where he proposed that they were linked to an individual singer's memory and would not be sustained in the long term, let alone in social transmission.[62] In his later work, he brought into focus these more complex verbal sequences as units in which many traditions were composed. His interest was shaped by a concern to show that such poetry was not 'memorised', which he conceived as unique to literate culture, and he explored variation in these larger units, both in their internal phraseology and their organisation into larger texts.[63] By that time, general interest had already moved away from formal units, so this work did not have significant impact on OFT research, yet his findings are relevant here:

> It can truly be said that even with short lyric songs [i.e. verbally conservative oral poems], which are erroneously thought to have a fixed text kept verbatim in the memory, the concept of a fixed text needs to be modified. The larger the sample with which one works, the less adequate is the concept of word-for-word memorization as a means of song transmission.[64]

The bigger the data on such poetry, the clearer it becomes that what were previously viewed as memorised lines operate as formulae that simply have a highly specialised meaning or usage. They can vary verbally and be adapted to uses in other contexts to produce different sorts of meanings.[65] The latter types of usage were simply not often documented in medieval records or in early folklore collection because they were in personal or situational expressions rather than circulating as social tradition with potential as heritage for modern societies and nations.

During the present century, the approaches to formulaic language in different branches of research have been coming into alignment. In the 1990s, John

---

[61] Lord's term *run* for such units (LORD, *Singer of Tales*, pp. 58-60) was coined by Alfred Nutt (NUTT, 'Notes', pp. 448-449), who considered them in prose narration; in A.B. LORD, *Epic Singers and Oral Tradition* (Ithaca, 1991), Lord's use of 'run' is found in some chapters (pp. 22-23, 90, 152, 161, 183) while 'block of lines' is used in others, but remains without definition and Lord varies regarding whether a block may be a couplet (pp. 77, 82, 88); the latter term is preferred in the posthumous collection, LORD, *The Singer Resumes the Tale*.

[62] A.B. LORD, "Memory, fixity, and genre in oral traditional poetry", in: *Oral Traditional Literature: A Festschrift for Albert Bates Lord*, ed. J.M. FOLEY (Columbus, 1981), pp. 451-461.

[63] Esp. LORD, *The Singer Resumes the Tale*; see also FROG, "Multiform theory", in: *Weathered Worlds*, ed. FROG and LAMB, pp. 115-146.

[64] LORD, *The Singer Resumes the Tale*, p. 62.

[65] E.g. L. TARKKA, "'Word upon a word': Parallelism, meaning, and emergent structure in Kalevala-meter poetry", *Oral Tradition* 31.2 (2017), pp. 259-292.

Fee, Fi, Fo, Formula

Miles Foley sought to sidestep the problem of formula definitions by proposing instead a turn to the vernacular concept of a 'word',[66] which he later describes with Peter Ramey "as an integer of traditional meaning".[67] This definition corresponds directly to Alison Wray's influential reconception of a formula as a "morpheme-equivalent unit" – i.e. as a unitary sign in the mental lexicon of users. When Parry's metrical criterion, returned to below, is omitted, his definition becomes a "group of words which is regularly employed ... to express a given essential idea".[68] Now that this definition has gradually been shaken free of implicit ideas from Classic OFT, it directly corresponds to Wray's description of a formulaic sequence as "a sequence, continuous or discontinuous, of words or other elements, which is, or appears to be, prefabricated".[69] The uses of 'formula' remain diverse, yet they generally tend to agree that a formula is a thing made of language more complex than a single word and that expresses a coherent unit of meaning or discourse function. There is variation on where to draw the line between a word and a formula, which is not always clear, and approaches vary concerning what types of features are included when considering complexity – only lexical items, non-linguistic features, structures or metrical templates, etc. – but the principles are otherwise generally stable while the 'formula'-terms for structural patterns in oral poetry coined in the boom of Classic OFT have generally fallen out of use. Atop of the convergence of approaches especially over the past few decades, there has been a rising trend especially in oral poetry research to look across branches of formula studies and to work toward a more synthetic model of the formula. This trend may be moving toward a critical mass of change through workshops, conferences, and publications, such as the present book.[70]

Question 2: But Aren't Poetry and Prose Fundamentally Different?

The idea that poetry is somehow free of the rules of customary language use stems from modern literary poetry, where unique expression and innovative, unexpected formulations are valorised, and where poets draw more or less

---

[66] J.M. FOLEY, *How to Read an Oral Poem* (Urbana, 2002); ID., *The Singer of Tales in Performance*; ID., "Word-power, performance and tradition", *The Journal of American Folklore* 105 (1992), pp. 275-301.
[67] FOLEY and RAMEY, "Oral theory and medieval studies", p. 80.
[68] PARRY, "Studies in the epic technique", p. 80.
[69] WRAY, *Formulaic Language and the Lexicon*, p. 9.
[70] See also *Formula*, ed. FROG; and *Weathered Words*, ed. FROG and LAMB.

freely on any and all linguistic resources available to accomplish the desired effects.[71] In contrast, oral traditions are characterised by conventional ways of speaking called 'registers'. Oral-poetic registers may diverge considerably from conversational language but remain regular and predictable on their own terms no less than how lawyers and judges speak in a courtroom setting.[72] Performers might do exceptional things for various effects, as may any language user, but variation must remain within limits or performers will either lose their audience or not be considered to perform within the tradition.

The contrast between 'poetry' and 'prose' is itself a construct based on thinking through written rather than oral texts. In the context of written materials, 'prose' refers to text organised in an ongoing series of sentences and that lacks a periodic metre.[73] The division of these categories is fundamental and intuitive in modern societies, reflected pervasively in editorial practices of presenting poetic texts (prose poems aside) according to metrical lines or corresponding visual arrangements, whereas 'prose' is organised as continuous text with breaks according to structuring by paragraphs and often also by turns of reported speech. Old English and Old Norse poetry are thus commonly described as written out as prose in the earliest manuscripts because these present poems without beginning each new metrical line as a new line of text. In contrast, contemporary scribes laid out Latin poetry as verse, which reflects a different ideology of texts today considered poetry in each language.[74] This is not to suggest that medieval writers conceived of these texts as 'prose' in the modern sense, only that they also had such categories that yield the striking contrast with our own of systematically writing out verse as 'prose'.[75] Today, concern-

---

[71] E.g. R. HASAN, *Linguistics, Language, and Verbal Art* (Oxford, 1989).

[72] E.g. FOLEY, '*Guslar* and *Aoidos*'; FROG, "Registers of oral poetry", in: *Registers of Communication*, ed. A. AGHA and FROG (Helsinki, 2015: *Studia Fennica Linguistica* 18), pp. 77-104; on registers generally, see M.A.K. HALLIDAY, *Language as Social Semiotic: The Social Interpretation of Language and Meaning* (London, 1978); A. AGHA, "Registers of language", in: *A Companion to Linguistic Anthropology*, ed. A. DURANTI (Malden, 2001), pp. 23-45; ID., *Language and Social Relations* (Cambridge, 2007).

[73] Conversation tends not to be linked as such to the category 'prose' unless it is embedded as reported speech in a longer stretch of oral or written text. However, the relevant individual utterances in a conversation are naturally classed as prose and the intuitive obstacle to describing conversation as 'prose' is that it is constituted of an accumulation of discontinuous texts, and it is viewed as interaction rather than as a text itself.

[74] K. O'BRIEN O'KEEFFE, *Visible Song: Transitional Literacy in Old English Verse* (Cambridge, 1990); FROG, "Text ideology and formulaic language", *Saga-Book* 48 (2024) (forthcoming).

[75] This may have been because Latin poetry is organised by *metrum* (i.e. 'metre' in the Classical sense of counting syllables and their quantities), while accentual verse is organised by

ing oral discourse, prose becomes a negatively defined category as 'not poetry', so it can also include utterances in rudimentary conversation. As a result, 'prose' encompasses a wide range of registers of discourse. Nevertheless, the distinction being made is formal, and it reveals what differentiates 'poetry' and 'prose'.

In an oral context, researchers' etic categories of poetry and 'not poetry' or prose are, as Nigel Fabb has so astutely described it, distinguished through the hierarchy of organising principles of discourse that govern the text or utterance.[76] In 'not poetry', syntax and prosody are the primary principles organising language into units. Parallelism, alliteration, metre, and perhaps extra-linguistic rhythms may be added features that structure stretches of text for rhetorical or aesthetic effect without characterising the text as a whole. These features often structure idioms used within non-poetic discourse, such as *right as rain*, or even produce nonsense elements as in rhyme reduplications like *okey-dokey*. Such structuring principles are not only common in idioms but also operate as a mnemonic device that ultimately makes idioms structured in this way more stable in historical transmission than those which are not. Nevertheless, the poetic principles of these phrases remain limited to the scope of the idiom rather than extending to the surrounding text. In contrast, poetry is characterised by other principles receiving precedence over syntax and prosody in organising a text into units – i.e. lines and perhaps groups of lines – also with the potential for other poetic features to be added. Ethnopoetics, which gained traction in the 1980s,[77] has revealed the fluidity between these categories. Conventions of non-poetic discourse may also be regularly structured into lines and stanzas or strophes at a higher level of prosody, without being systematically marked by metre, parallelism, alliteration, or rhyme. Rather than being restricted to prose

---

rhythmus (i.e. other recurrent patterning, hence giving both the modern words *rhythm* and *rhyme*), and that Classical rhetoric distinguished 'poetry' as composed with *metrum*, a view that was dominant until the influential work of Robert Lowth (R. LOWTH, *De sacra poesi Hebræorum: Prælectiones academicæ* (Oxford, 1753); see also FROG, "An eighteenth-century origin of modern metrical studies? – Or – Robert Lowth as a pioneer of ethnopoetics", *NordMetrik News* 1 (2018), pp. 5-14). Conversely, vernacular verse may have simply been classed as a category of speech, much as English speakers today conventionally class the scripts of songs as 'lyrics' and not as 'poetry'.

[76] N. FABB, *What is Poetry? Language and Memory in the Poems of the World* (Cambridge, 2015).

[77] See, e.g. D. HYMES, *'In Vain I Tried to Tell You': Essays in Native American Ethnopoetics* (Philadelphia. 1981); J. SHERZER, *Kuna Ways of Speaking: An Ethnographic Perspective* (Austin, 1983); D. TEDLOCK, *The Spoken Word and the Work of Interpretation* (Philadelphia, 1983).

in the conventional sense, poetic structuring principles have been shown to operate even in co-produced conversation, where they are often introduced to create cohesion and rhetorical effects between utterances in individual turns.[78]

The hierarchy of principles shapes language use and its organisation, of which formulaic language is only one part among a variety of phenomena. When one or more poetic principles are elevated as primary, these subordinate syntax and prosody.[79] In an oral tradition, this subordination is regularised and conventional, from which point syntax and prosody evolve in a symbiotic relationship with metre. The initial boom of OFT research was anticipated by a rising awareness that the organisation of language in actual lines of oral poetry is far more limited and repetitive than what would be hypothetically possible according to the lexicon and grammar of the language. Parry's dissertations are built on this observation for phraseology.[80] Rather than being unique to formulae, the type of linkage Parry saw between metre and formulaic sequences was also found for individual words, merely as an outcome of convention, a phenomenon described as 'localisation' – i.e. a word or phrase that regularly occurs in certain metrical positions, whether or not it may also occur in other metrical positions.[81] Once recognised, lexical localisation in combination with poetic syntax can be viewed as supporting formulaic phraseology and its variation, as well as producing types of one-word formulae with an open slot, such as with a verb localised in certain positions in a line and its variable subject or object in other particular positions. If the relationship of a lexeme to a line's metrical

---

[78] E.g. J.W. Du Bois, "Towards a dialogic syntax", *Cognitive Linguistics* 25.3 (2014), pp. 359-410; G. Jefferson, "On the poetics of everyday talk", *Text and Performance Quarterly* 16.1 (1996), pp. 1-61; D. Tannen, "Repetition in conversation: Towards a poetics of talk", *Language* 63.3 (1987), pp. 574-605.

[79] When poetic principles are applied as periodic, syntax and prosody must either be subordinated to them as the primary organising principles of discourse or be arbitrary to the poetic principles, otherwise they will interfere with those principles and produce irregularities. An oral-poetic meter will not be based on features not present in a language and perceivable by its speakers, and a metre may be affected by changes in phonology and grammatical inflection. The latter is linked to recognising linguistic signs as 'the same' across different forms of discourse, even through variations such as archaic or dialectal forms. Syntax and prosody, on the other hand, may be perceived as registral features governing the arrangement and articulation of linguistic signs in ways that might systematically deviate from other forms of speech. For instance, in certain line types of Old Norse *ljóðaháttr* metre, monosyllabic prepositions are regularly used postpositionally, which deviated from conventional word order already at the time when the metre formed (i.e. post-syncope).

[80] Parry, *L'Épithète traditionnelle*, and id., *Les formules*.

[81] E.G. O'Neill Jr., "The localization of metrical word-types in the Greek hexameter: Homer, Hesiod, and the Alexandrians", *Yale Classical Studies* 8 (1942), pp. 105-178, on Homeric epic.

template or a larger discourse structure is accepted as a form of complexity, then Old English line-initial *Hwæt!*, opening a sequence of narration, can be viewed as a formula. Linkages between ways words are used and metrical templates were also brought into focus in the boom of OFT, producing the plethora of now devalued terms calling these types of formula, such as syllabic – or moraic – structures,[82] syntactic patterns,[83] or rhythmic-metrical forms,[84] as well as the more open-ended patterning of sound and form in which variations may change words or syntax.[85] In Old English alliterative poetry, it was observed that certain words are more commonly used to carry alliteration than others, irrespective of their position in a line, which was calculated as the words' 'alliterative rank'.[86] Alliterative rank only received concentrated interest following the boom of OFT research,[87] and alliterative 'collocations' came into focus as an extension of formula research – i.e. words or word stems customarily paired to carry alliteration.[88] Corresponding phenomena can also be observed for rhyme, although these did not receive the sort of focused attention as Old and Middle English alliteration.[89] The dazzling variety of phenomena affecting word choice, position, and organisation within a line becomes comprehensible when considered against the different traditions' hierarchies of organising principles.[90]

In non-poetic language, formulae take shape in relation to the dominant principles of syntax and prosody for the expression of units of meaning or discourse functions. Semantic links can also produce collocations more generally – i.e. a statistical tendency for words to be used together although not necessarily forming a coherent unit of meaning. For example, *green grass* might be

---

[82] A so-called 'structural formula' (RUSSO, "A closer look", on Homeric epic).

[83] A so-called 'syntactic formula' (GREENFIELD, "The canons of Old English criticism", on Old English poetry).

[84] A so-called 'metrical formula' (FOLEY, "Formula and theme", on Old English poetry).

[85] A so-called *Gestalt* (M.N. NAGLER, *Spontaneity and Tradition: A Study in the Oral Art of Homer* (Berkeley, 1974), on Homeric poetry).

[86] A. BRINK, *Stab und Wort im Gawain: Eine stilistische Untersuchung* (Halle a.S., 1920), already in 1920.

[87] M. BORROFF, *Sir Gawain and the Green Knight: A Stylistic and Metrical Study* (New Haven, 1962), on Middle English poetry; see also ROPER, "Synonymy and rank".

[88] R. QUIRK, "Poetic language and Old English metre", in: *Essays on the English Language Medieval and Modern*, ed. A. BROWN and P. FOOTE (London, 1968; first published in 1963), pp. 1-19, on Old English poetry.

[89] Cf. D. BUCHAN, *The Ballad and the Folk* (London, 1972), p. 154.

[90] See further FROG, "Metrical entanglement: The interface of language and meter", in: *Versification: Metrics in Practice*. ed. FROG, S. GRÜNTHAL, K. KALLIO, and J. NIEMI (Helsinki, 2021: *Studia Fennica Litteraria* 12), pp. 249-294.

considered a formulaic sequence, but *green* is more generally a collocate of *grass*, as in *How does the grass look to you? – Not very green*. *Green* is more common to use when talking about *grass* than *healthy*, *lush*, or any number of alternative expressions, a tendency that is bound up with the expression *green grass*, but which functions far more flexibly.[91] When other organising principles receive precedence, they place constraints on lexical choices and their organisation, reducing the number of possible ways to 'say the same thing'. The more restrictive those constraints, the more challenging it can be to generate new expressions freely in the flow of performance. Since genres of oral poetry tend to be used for certain things rather than for others, the register becomes equipped for talking about those things. In poetic registers, formulaic language also takes shape in relation to meaning or discourse function, but this is structured by the poetic form. Parry's definition of formula is relevant to verbal art with a periodic metre that only governs syllables or 'morae'.[92] Where the poetic form is organised through systematic semantic parallelism, words regularly paired across lines can express a single unit of meaning as a formula, whether the two words are connected by synonymy, such as Rotenese *inak//fetok* ('woman'//'girl'), metonymy, such as K'iche' Mayan *aqan//q'ab'* ('foot'//'hand' = PERSON), metaphor, such as K'iche' Mayan *tz'aaq//k'axtuun* ('wall'//'fortress' = HOME), or some other principle.[93] In Old English alliterative poetry, the register evolved ways to 'say the same thing' with alternative words that began with different sounds, and some formulaic sequences were equipped to accommodate this sort of lexical alternation according to the alliteration in the line, like the *X bealdor* formula, in which the open slot is completed by a noun in the genitive that carries alliteration and forms an expression meaning 'lord'. However, collocations also evolved to accommodate the metrical need of alliteration. These are often semantically compatible or associated, like *grass* and *green*, but Old English verse commonly has a break between independent clauses in the middle of an alliterating line, separating the alliterative collocation, such as the *wuldor* : *weorod* ('glory: troop') collocation in the long line "*weoroda wealdend. / Is ðæs wuldres ful*".[94] Thus, an alliterative collocation

---

[91] J.R. FIRTH, *Papers in Linguistics 1939-1951* (Oxford, 1957); T. LEHECKA, "Collocation and colligation", in: *Handbook of Pragmatics* (Amsterdam, 2015), pp. 1-20.

[92] A 'mora' is a unit of syllabic quantity: one short syllable constitutes one mora while a long syllable constitutes two morae, and thus two short syllables are interchangeable with one long syllable in mora-counting metres.

[93] FROG, "Metrical entanglement", p. 274; see also J.J. FOX, *Explorations in Semantic Parallellism* (Canberra, 2014).

[94] FROG, 'Metrical entanglement', p. 269-270, citing *Elene* 751.

may fulfil its metrical role while the words are used in separate sentences. Although such collocations have been addressed as 'formulae', this potential for distribution across independent clauses affects their relationship to formula definitions, as discussed below.

These basic phenomena are the same as in non-poetic usage; they are simply shaped or driven by additional factors of the poetic form, resulting in many formulae that are structured by formal principles in addition to meaning or function, and also collocations that are formally driven rather than only semantic. Linkages that form between certain words and their use in alliteration or metrical position might seem unique to poetry, but conventions of word placement are also common where phraseology is governed only by syntax and prosody, such as *too* but not *also* being conventionally usable in clause-final position, and conventions linked to words like *but, however, yet*, and so on in initial position in different clause types. Many languages have conventions concerning whether such words should be clause-initial, clause-second, clause-final, or have variable placement.[95] The difference in a poetic register is not *that* there are conventions of placement, but that those conventions may be linked to the respective poetic organising principles of discourse. The process of forming formulaic sequences, collocations, linkage to formal structures, and so on occurs in relation to those principles and their hierarchy.

Question 3: Does This Mean That All Formula Definitions Are More or Less the Same?

Formula definitions come in all shapes and sizes. Wray highlights that, on the one hand, definitions may either be 'stipulative' or 'descriptive', and, on the other hand, they may vary considerably in their scope of relevance or intended

---

[95] Although this might be viewed as fundamentally different from placement of language in a metrical template, it concerns binding with the primary principle of organising discourse into units. It gets taken for granted in syntax, where it is viewed abstractly at the level of a clause. Ethnopoetic analysis is built on the oft-implicit observation that utterances manifest metered frames in relation to which subsequent units of utterance become perceived and assessed (e.g. Hymes, Dell, *'In Vain I Tried to Tell You'*; see also Du Bois, 'Towards a Dialogic Syntax'; on the history of the term *metered frame*, see FROG, "Parallelism and orders of signification (Parallelism dynamics I)", *Oral Tradition* 31.2 (2017), pp. 425-484, at pp. 427-28). Words' conventions of initial, second, penultimate, and final placement allow them to function as markers in organising discourse into lines and line groups or stanzas (e.g. *Oh, ... / but ... / but ... / but ..., too.*; see also J. BLOMMAERT, "Applied ethnopoetics", *Narrative Inquiry* 16.1 (2006), pp. 181-190).

applicability.[96] Both factors are important to be aware of when choosing or developing a definition. In addition to being complementary to, and determinants on, the criteria of a particular definition, the factors contributing to a definition's formation are not always the same as those surrounding its use.

A stipulative definition is one that is determined by a researcher and provides a frame of reference for the analysis of particular data. A descriptive definition is, ideally, arrived at inductively through empirical data in order to model the particular phenomenon. In practice, these categories can be rather fluid. Concerning many definitions, it is immediately clear that they are intended to be stipulative. Wray's definition of a formulaic sequence above is a case in point: it is postulated as a universal definition that can be used as a frame of reference for considering any phenomenon, whether the aim is to identify things as formulae or to look at a variety of phenomena and consider ways that they may align with or diverge from the definition. Descriptive definitions tend to take as their point of departure certain criteria, like assuming that a formula is (*a*) a linguistic unit that (*b*) expresses a unit of meaning. The respective criteria become a lens for identifying, in the data under consideration, material on the basis of which is formed a descriptive model of formulae. The premises are stipulative, but the resulting definition may be – at least ideally – inductively arrived at through the examination of empirical data. Of course, the history of research illustrates that implicit stipulations may shape what researchers consider when identifying examples for comparison and how they handle a definition. In this respect, the case of Parry's definition is instructive. It was treated as stipulative within OFT research. The definition explicitly included criteria (*a*) and (*b*) along with (*c*) metrical conditions under which a formula occurs, yet it also imported Classic OFT's implicit criterion of (*d*) belonging to a collective tradition of units used in *in situ* composition and variation. The implicit criterion reflects an ideological dimension of discussion, which is further reflected in the debates that surrounded Classic OFT.

Most researchers rely on definitions that others have proposed, such as Parry's. His definition was then adapted by researchers to make it applicable to other traditions. The adaptations may ultimately rest on inductive knowledge of the operation of language in a tradition, while the formulation becomes stipulative. For example, the applicability problem of Parry's criterion of 'under the same metrical conditions' might be exchanged for an alternative, as in James J.

---

[96] A. WRAY, "Identifying formulaic language: Persistent challenges and new opportunities", in: *Formulaic Language*, ed. CORRIGAN *et al.*, 1, pp. 27-51; EAD. *Formulaic Language: Pushing the Boundaries*.

Fox's adaptation for formulaic language in traditions of canonical parallelism as "a group of words which is regularly employed *under the conditions of strict parallelism* to express a given essential idea".[97] Once formulated, Fox's definition then operates as stipulative. The history of discussion of formulaic language in Old English verse, on the other hand, can be viewed as an evolution of stipulative definitions, beginning from Parry's being refined and adapted in relation to the corpus.[98] Although Wray's definition can be considered transparently stipulative, it is also an outcome of synthesis and testing against a variety of material rather than a wholly artificial construct. The difference between a stipulative and descriptive definition might thus be considered to have less to do with inherent qualities of the definition itself than with how one handles it.

Definitions vary most based on their intended relevance or applicability. Whereas Wray's definition is intended to work universally, irrespective of language, culture, or medium, other definitions are specific to a type of tradition, like Fox's for traditions of canonical parallelism, while some are designed specifically for a particular study, without intending for it to be usable as a definition outside of the investigation or research material.[99] I normally work with a definition that is not bound to a particular language or medium. This is a preference motivated by two factors. The first is my general interest in linking formula research across disciplines. The second is a more pragmatic preference to use a consistent definition irrespective of the research focus or type of discourse under consideration, from Austronesian ritual poetry to Donald Trump's impacts on American racial discourse. Commensurate definitions or at least a common frame of reference is necessary in order to make insights and theoretical perspectives applicable from one study to another. Descriptively-oriented definitions or otherwise tradition-specific models can take into account distinctive features related to the poetic form or conventions of usage.

The more closely the model reflects the tradition and its variation, the more nuanced the perspectives it may enable in analyses of specific cases and variation. For example, Fox's definition above is not well suited to research on Old Norse or Old English poetry, but it provides a sound basis for studies on how the lexical makeup of such formulae in Rotenese ritual poetry vary by dialect and the networks formed by words that are used in multiple formulaic pairs.[100] Highly specified definitions may also move into formula typology. Rather than

---

[97] J.J. FOX, *Master Poets, Ritual Masters: The Art of Oral Composition among the Rotenese of Eastern Indonesia* (Canberra, 2016), p. XI, original emphasis.
[98] I.e. in MAGOUN, "Oral-formulaic character".
[99] See also WRAY, *Formulaic Language: Pushing the Boundaries*.
[100] FOX, *Explorations*; ID., *Master Poets*.

accounting for all Old Norse formulae, a kenning formula in Old Norse *dróttkvætt* poetry might be defined as

> a kenning with a particular referent of which the base word and determinant each regularly occur in the same metrical positions of a *dróttkvætt* line or lines although the words used for them vary in relation to alliteration and rhyme.

This definition would not account for other formulae used in the metre, but it could be used to analyse variations, such as when the determinant of the formula is replaced by the base word of another kenning. It can also be used to analyse examples of semantic play or allusion, such as the kenning *Kraka drífa* ('sleet of Kraki (a sea king)') in the line "*ósvífr Kraka drífu*", where it corresponds formally to a common battle-kenning formula (determinant in positions 3-4, base word in positions 5-6) of the 'weather of an agent of battle' type. However, it is used instead to refer to gold in the complex kenning *Kraka drífu Hlǫkk* ('Hlǫkk (valkyrie) of gold' = woman).[101] The kenning is used in a description of women weeping in the wake of war, and the use of this kenning formula with a flex of its semantics appears intended to allude to the context. Such definitions or models need not be considered exclusive of more abstract and generally applicable definitions, and especially definitions that distinguish formula types may be developed within a more abstract formula definition.

In practice, descriptive definitions arrived at inductively begin from an explicit or implicit idea of what a formula is – i.e. you begin with an *a priori* assumption of what a formula is and then explore the form or forms taken by that phenomenon in particular material. Broad comparative approaches are alo often not simply concerned with the basic principles of a more abstract definition; comparison is an instrument for bringing tradition-specific features into focus, developing or supporting the development of better accounts of the respective traditions. The idea of developing a study-specific definition might sound odd and perhaps even pointless, but it can also be a tool for narrowing the focus of research. Study-specific definitions narrow the field of vision, cutting out peripheral and ambiguous data, and they may potentially avoid the often messy problem of theoretical definitions of formula. For instance, the kenning formula above might be further specified as

---

[101] Grani *skáld, Poem about Haraldr harðráði 1*, ed. K.E. GADE, in: *Poetry from the Kings' Sagas*, 2, *From c. 1035 to c. 1300* (Turnhout, 2009: *Skaldic Poetry of the Scandinavian Middle Ages* 2), pp. 296-297, l. 2.

occurring in a single line with a one-word determinant preceding and adjacent to the base word.

Such a definition might be to test a hypothesis of syntax in what should be a short article. The rationale would be that it provides a practical means to restrict examples to what are syntactically the most basic kennings, leaving aside all others as variations, which might cloud the pattern with associated variations in the surrounding syntax or simply require more discussion than space allows. Alternately, the same definition might be used in a study testing whether kennings with different referents are used with the same or different relative frequency in particular metrical positions. The rationale then might simply be that the definition provides a practical means to limit the corpus to only a few metric-structural formula types. The same might be accomplished with a broader definition and an explicit delimitation of your data. This type of definition is best suited to quantitative studies based on a hard-sciences model, in which a hypothesis is proposed and the definition itself becomes one of the tools for analytically testing the hypothesis. Study-specific definitions are not exclusive of broad theoretical or descriptive approaches, which might be considered too inclusive to be practical for some studies. Generally speaking, formula studies on oral poetry tend not to be concerned with *any* formulae and focus on particular formulae or particular types that are distinctive of the respective genre or of a dedicated register. There is nothing inherently 'wrong' with defining 'formula' in this way (even if some people may be critical of it), but it is crucial when introducing such a definition that it is qualified as 'in this paper' or something similar, making it immediately clear that the definition is not intended to be more broadly applicable, and providing and explanation as to why.

Recognising the differences between types of definitions is not only relevant to choosing a definition best suited to your research; it can also be important for recognising issues that can result from how a particular definition is used. When shopping for a definition, and especially when adopting one used by others, it is important to consider its background and the baggage that it may carry with it. For example, the prominence of OFT in cultural research has, as mentioned above, made it a primary point of entry into formula research for many researchers. Many of these researchers then stumble over the applicability of the concept 'formula' to their material if it is not metred poetry. The problem is that Parry's definition gets viewed as universal, when it was originally study-specific. The observation of recurrent phrases being linked to metrical positions led Parry to systematically look for words that recur in the same metrical positions in the Homeric epics, and to collate and compare these. His definition is descriptive of what is found with his method,[102] describing each specific phrase as a formula; cases where one word was in a regular position while a second had been exchanged for a metrically equivalent word were interpreted as a distinct formula or phrase generated on analogy.[103] Parry was not attempting to theorise formulaic language generally and presented his definition as specifically linked to Homeric poetry.[104] It was also bound up with his ideas of the role of formulaic language in the flow of live performance, which structured his entire investigation, so that it really only describes Homeric formulae of a particular type.[105] The tension surrounding Parry's definition stems from its origin as an investigation-specific stipulation that became propagated as a universal model. The ability of the definition to spread reflects both its, and Classic OFT's, analogical applicability for considering how language works in many forms of oral poetry. Nevertheless, it is a definition designed for a certain type of research method as a tool connected to a theory of the role of formulae in the performance of highly variable oral poetry. As stressed above, Parry's definition is formally consistent with other approaches common today, except that it has an added criterion of metrical positions, but its applications have been shaped by Classic OFT's ideological baggage. It has been around for almost a century, which is plenty of time to recognise and understand what happened to it as it was reused and to shake it loose from implicit assumptions. Many definitions developed more recently in other fields are similarly bound up with theoretical models, and their biases and baggage may be more challenging to bring into focus.

Question 4: Is It Better to Work with a Definition Like Parry's, Known in My Own Field, Start from a More Theoretical One Like Wray's, or Just Make up My Own?

When choosing a definition, several factors should be considered, in particular:

- The source material being studied;
- The aims of the investigation;

---

[102] FROG and LAMB, 'A Picasso of Perspectives'.
[103] PARRY, *L'épithète traditionnelle* and *Les formules*.
[104] This generally unacknowledged detail has recently been drawn attention to by Karl Reichl (REICHL, "Formulas in oral epics").
[105] J.B. HAINSWORTH, *The Flexibility of the Homeric Formula* (Oxford, 1968).

- The field with which the material or type of analysis is identified;
- The intended audience.

The first two factors concern the practical side of analysis, while the latter two concern making your study accessible and relevant to other scholars. Relying on a definition familiar to the field with which both your audience and data are related has an advantage of working within a familiar frame of reference. It requires less explanation or justification if your study does not need to look beyond it. In Old Norse eddic scholarship, for example, breaking from Parry's definition and using Wray's would easily create confusion or at least difficulty in seeing how to relate this to familiar ways of looking at formulae in the field. Whether generating a new definition or adopting one from discussions outside a field, it is important to situate the definition in relation to approaches currently under discussion so that it becomes clear how your study relates to others'. If your study engages material associated with another field, it may also be important to be aware of how formulaic language is currently discussed for such material. For example, Parry's definition might be unsurprising for Old Norse researchers but it could appear quite narrow and dated in the context of Old English research, where the concept is often much more flexible and has long been a nexus of discussion.[106] Most important is to choose something that is well-suited to your study and its aims, and to consider this in relation to your broader interests. For instance, if you plan on working with formulaic language in further studies, you might like the definition you use to remain consistent. Issues of relating to scholarship can be accommodated by introducing your approach and positioning it in relation to other approaches more familiar in the field or fields.

When considering whether to work with a dominant approach within a field or to look outside of it, a key factor is whether your study is aligned with that approach. If the aim is to study meanings or the usage and variation of formulae as commonly recognised, the conventional approach will probably be fine for you. If the aim is to explore types or dimensions of formulaic language not usually assessed, alternative approaches can offer different points of view that may enable critical perspectives on conventional approaches or bring into focus types or uses of formulaic language that have remained outside of researchers' fields of vision. In Old Norse studies, for instance, in addition to limitations on what have been considered formulae in eddic poetry, skaldic poetry was consid-

---

[106] See, e.g. A. HENNESSEY OLSEN, 'Oral-formulaic research in Old English studies: 1", *Tradition* 1.3 (1986), pp. 548-606; FOLEY, *Traditional Oral Epic*, chs. 6 and 9.

ered 'memorised', so the presence of formulaic language there was simply never discussed. Although the changes since the 1990s have led to considering the mnemonic potential of formulae, their potential role in the composition and reproduction of skaldic poems has received little attention.[107] Also, the view that the poetry is 'memorised' still tends to imagine this in terms of literary texts with an objectively existing exemplar as though every word is fixed, without consideration of variation in oral transmission and performance, which link to formulaic phraseology. These issues are rooted in the ideologies of Classic OFT, which became the dominant approach in the field. Whether working from that approach or drawing on one from another branch of research, it remains important to recognise and address these issues in order to get past them.

Question 5: How Can I Tell What Sort of Definition Will Work Best for Me?

A formula definition is a tool, and the best tool to use depends on the job. Definitions are constituted of criteria, and they can be selected or formulated according to the criteria relevant for the investigation.[108] Basic criteria for defining a linguistic formula are:

- A linguistic unit;
- More complex than a single 'word' (however complexity is being defined);
- With unitary meaning or function at the level of words.

Parry's explicit criterion linking formula to metre makes it a poor choice when working with unmetred discourse. Classic OFT's implicit criterion of being commonly used to generate new, composition-in-performance-type expressions will be relevant if those are the dynamics of formula use in focus. Alternately, it may be an undesirable obstacle if focus is on meanings and variation in phraseology in lines that are only known from a single passage in a single poem. There are three versions of many passages of the Old Norse poem *Vǫluspá*[109] that seem to have been documented independently from the oral tradition,

---

[107] See, however, FROG, "Metrical entanglement and *dróttkvætt* composition : A pilot study on battle-kennings", in: *Approaches to Nordic and Germanic Poetry*, ed. K. ÁRNASON et al. (Reykjavík, 2016), pp. 149-229.

[108] See also WRAY, *Formulaic Language and the Lexicon*.

[109] All eddic poems are cited according to the fourth edition of Neckel and Kuhn (*Edda: Die*

but comparative analysis of variation in the presence, absence, organisation, and phraseology of lines in relation to formulaic language requires shaking free of Classic OFT's baggage. In line with Lord's observation quoted above,[110] in a corpus of a hundred thousand or more examples of poetry, it becomes clear that even a line customary to a single passage of a single song can both vary and be adapted to other contexts: it operates as a formula although it will presumably always carry associations of its conventional usage. The 'baggage' of Classic OFT's methodology excluded treating such lines and passages as formulae. Consideration of formulaic language in texts' variation between manuscripts was thereby considerably limited in Old Norse studies. Outside of Joseph Harris's seminal article written in 1975 (appearing only in 1983),[111] there has been almost no discussion in Old Norse research of what is called 'scribal performance'. Scribal performance describes how manuscript copyists or transcribers vary oral-derived text based on their knowledge of the respective tradition,[112] which has become a lively topic of discussion in Old English research.[113] For example, copies of Snorri Sturluson's *Edda* exchange the formulae in one (but not the second) quotation from the eddic poem *Alvíssmál* to correspond to the text of the preserved poem, which seems likely to reflect knowledge of the copyist.[114] Similarly, the Upsaliensis *Edda* seems to exhibit an addition of the long line found as *Vǫluspá* 45.11-12 to the quotation of that passage among other features that point to a scribe competent in eddic poetry.[115] It then becomes relevant to consider whether this long line should be considered a formula, and the same for examples of variation that may reflect alternative forms of a common line, whether in independently documented versions of a particu-

---

Lieder des Codex Regius nebst verwandten Denkmälern, ed. G. NECKEL and H. KUHN, 1, *Text*, 4th edn. (Heidelberg, 1963).

[110] LORD, *The Singer Resumes the Tale*, p. 62.

[111] HARRIS, "Eddic poetry as oral poetry".

[112] For a recent literature review, see J.L. READY, *Orality, Textuality, and the Homeric Epics: An Interdisciplinary Study of Oral Texts, Dictated Texts, and Wild Texts* (Oxford, 2019).

[113] E.g. A.N. DOANE, "The ethnography of scribal writing and Anglo-Saxon poetry: Scribe as performer", *Oral Tradition* 9.2 (1994), pp. 420-439; see also M. AMODIO, *Writing the Oral Tradition: Oral Poetics and Literate Culture in Medieval England* (South Bend, IN, 2004); O'BRIEN O'KEEFFE, *Visible Song*.

[114] FROG, "Text ideology and formulaic language".

[115] A more recent or perhaps the most recent scribe of this manuscript clearly had difficulty with the poetry, but, e.g. the addition of an eddic quotation to a story about Þórr and use of extended abbreviations familiar to manuscript copies of full poems (see Snorri Sturluson, *The Uppsala Edda: DG 11 4to*, ed. H. PÁLSSON (London, 2013)) point to an earlier scribe with knowledge of the poetry.

lar poem or passage or introduced through scribal performance.[116] Examples of this type are numerous, although largely unexplored, but approaching such lines in terms of formulae requires shaking free of Classic OFT's baggage.

Because almost anything recurrent at the level of poetic lines got called a formula during the boom of Classic OFT, it is relevant to critically consider whether 'formula' is the concept you need at all. Owing to the current trajectory of formula research, I strongly advocate sticking with a formula definition that is compatible with the three points above. Qualifying a formula in this way excludes several types of phenomena closely related to formulae, such as collocations or more complex verbal systems,[117] and also the various structural patterns that may exhibit regular recurrence in a corpus without expressing a verbal unit of meaning.[118]

Research on collocations in Old and Middle English, and more recently in Old Norse, has been centrally interested in their potential to carry connotative meanings and associations.[119] However, these semantics operate at a different level than that of their constituent words. In the Old English example above, words of a collocation carried alliteration, linking independent clauses across the line's caesura. Treating these as formulae creates the issue that they do not have unitary meaning in the same way as a formulaic sequence like *swift-footed Achilles*. The connotative meaning of the collocation operates independently of

---

[116] For example, there are several slight variations between copies of eddic poems preserved in the Codex Regius (GKS 2365) and AM 748 I a 4to, many of which are owing to a sloppy copyist of the latter, but some of which appear to reflect competence in the poetry (presumably already in the exemplar). An interesting example is in *Hymiskviða*, where the Codex Regius reads *Hreingálkn hlumðo / en hǫlkn þuto* ("the sea-beast dashed / and the stony field howled") and AM 748 1 a 4to has *hruto* ("was flung") for *hlumðo* (*Hymiskviða* 24.1-2). The rhyme may seem anomalous for eddic verse, but light disyllables are the most common structure for end-rhymed lines in this meter (FROG, "Rhyme in alliterative oral poetry: A look at Old English, Old Norse, and Finno-Karelian traditions", in: *Rhyme and Rhyming in Verbal Art and Song*, ed. N. FABB and V. SYKÄRI (Helsinki, 2022: *Studia Fennica Folkloristica* 25), pp. 74-98). Other examples in the Codex Regius make it seem unlikely that it was emended as an anomaly (*Vǫluspá* 52.5-6; *Hávamál* 85.1-2; *Brot af Sigurðarkviða* 4.1-2), which opens the possibility that it was introduced in manuscript transmission in a type of scribal performance, which could then reflect variant forms of the same formula.

[117] On more complex verbal systems, see FROG, "Multiform theory".

[118] For discussions of several of these, see FROG, "Metrical entanglement".

[119] For Old English, see M. REINHARD, *On the Semantic Relevance of the Alliterative Collocations in* Beowulf (Berne, 1976: *Schweizer anglistische Arbeiten* 92); E.M. TYLER, *Old English Poetics: The Aesthetics of the Familiar in Anglo-Saxon England* (York, 2006); for Old Norse, see M.E. RUGERRINI, "Alliterative lexical collocations in eddic poetry", in: *A Handbook of Eddic Poetry: Myths and Legends of Early Scandinavia*, ed. C. LARRINGTON, J. QUINN, and B. SCHORN (Cambridge, 2016), pp. 310-330.

the meanings produced through words' syntagmatic relations, where each constituent of the collocation operates as an independent linguistic sign, as opposed to *swift-footed Achilles*, which operates as a unitary sign. Of course, there are alliterative collocations that are also formulae, such as the paired use in Old Norse of *æsir* ('gods') and *álfar* ('elves') to refer to the whole divine community. This is used as a syndetic a-line formula *æsir ok álfar* ('gods and elves') and also in parallel clauses, as in "*Hvat er með ásom? / Hvat er með álfom?*" ("What is with the gods? / What is with the elves?"),[120] where the lexical pair *æsir//álfar* is used to express a single unit of meaning across parallel lines in the type of formula discussed by Fox.[121] However, the unitary meaning of the pair that qualifies it as a formula concerns denotative rather than connotative semantics.

The same issue is created for extended stretches of text of "up to a dozen or so [lines] in number"[122] that are conventional in the tradition. Earlier scholarship could also describe such a text sequence as a formula. These units can express unitary meaning in the sense of regularly presenting the same image or motif in narration. However, that meaning operates at the level of what is linguistically mediated rather than at the level of the syntagmatic relations of linguistic signs, and variation at the level of constituent lines may produce different propositional meanings.[123] The recognisability of the complex unit allows it to be apprehended as meaning-bearing, yet, like the different versions of passages of *Vǫluspá*, the meanings of individual lines through which it is articulated, and their relations to one another, may not be regular. In Classic OFT, such extended sequences were described by Lord as 'runs' or 'blocks of lines', but the upper limit of a formula's complexity was not a topic of concern: formula research concentrated on the level of the line. Lexicon- and discourse-centred approaches have also had no interest in the question of upper complexity, where the focus on unitary meaning in usually highly variable forms of discourse leads syntax to provide a natural threshold at the level of a clause or sentence, which a formula will not usually exceed.[124] Although larger units may operate like formulae, they can be distinguished as 'macro-formulae'.[125] In cases such as these, a formula definition is still relevant, not because it is used

---

[120] *Vǫluspá*, st. 48.1-2.
[121] Fox, *Master Poets*.
[122] C.M. Bowra, *Heroic Poetry* (London, 1952), p. 222.
[123] Frog, "Multiform theory".
[124] Systematic parallelism produces a syntactic condition where formulaicity may operate at the level of paired clauses that express the same unit of meaning.
[125] Frog, "Multiform theory".

to identify the phenomenon, but as a point of reference for considering sameness and difference. Because I have found the upper threshold of complexity significant, I would normally define a linguistic formula as:

> a linguistic sign, or equivalent signifier, more complex than a single word but not normally exceeding a clause or sentence, while having unitary meaning or functional value so that it operates as a distinct unit of the lexicon.

This definition corresponds to Wray's, or to Parry's without the metrical criterion, bringing into focus lower and upper complexity criteria. It is stipulative, works across branches of research and can be applied to any language or form of discourse. It accounts for complex units of the lexicon, which, through their operation as distinct linguistic signs, can operate with particular conventions, meanings, and / or functions. Today, the ideology inherited from Classic OFT remains commonplace especially in research on medieval poetry, leading the concept of formula to remain strongly linked to expressions in particular metrical positions and associated with a functional role in composition and / or, in more recent decades, as a mnemonic. The above definition is not incompatible with such views, but does not define a formula in terms of such roles. This type of broad definition can be taken as a base, adding criteria such as placement in certain metrical positions or a criteria of some function, which should not be conflated as the same thing.[126] It is also worth keeping in mind that Parry's definition was criticised already in the boom of the 1960s as too limited even for Homeric verse.[127]

---

[126] Parry's theory was that formulae enable composition at the rate of performance, much as formulae of spoken language enable fluent speech, but it does not follow that all formulae are accounted for as enabling such composition. Wray's theory of 'needs-only analysis' (WRAY, *Formulaic Language and the Lexicon*, pp. 130-132) is useful to consider here. It accounts for formulae as complex units of language that simply do not get broken down and analysed according to their parts in relation to the grammar, which allows for archaisms, the greater fixity of less frequently used idioms, and so on. The role of formulae as a compositional resource in an oral-poetic register is undeniable, but usage of such resources may be more semantically than functionally driven, and formal structuring may be as much a constraint on an expression's usage as it is a resource.

[127] HAINSWORTH, *The Flexibility of the Homeric Formula*. In Old Norse eddic poetry, for example, such an approach should consider the formal and functional differences between a traditional unit like the *ljóðaháttr* b-line formula PREPOSITION *ása sonum* ('PREPOSITION sons of the gods'), which is of the classic Parryan type, the *æsir//álfar* ('the whole divine community') collocation, which is an alliterative collocation of unitary meaning that may be distributed across lines, and the *fornyrðislag* expression ... *æsir* ... *á þingi* ('... gods ... at assembly'), found both as a b-line formula (*Vǫluspá* 48.3-4) and with *æsir* at the end of the a-line and carrying alliteration

The emphasis on identifying formulae with formal compositional resources linked to metrical lines is what produced a variety of 'formula' terms disconnected from particular phraseology in the boom of Classic OFT that have fallen out of use. Preferred patterns of syntax, arrangements of words in a line, and so on can be framed in different terms. Here, those formal aspects are treated as complementary to formulaic language or built into some but not all formulae. Every oral-poetic register has syntax that is organic to it, irrespective of how much it might diverge from that of conversational speech.[128] Syntax can be considered to become 'entangled' with the poetic form,[129] which both structures it and with which it evolves. This process of entanglement can produce preferred structures that also remain flexible, for instance allowing an inversion of word order so that a different word carries alliteration. The inclination to describe such patterns as formulae stems from a desire to connect them to OFT via one of its central terms, but such use of 'formula' has become inconsistent with the term's current usage and is thus more likely to cause confusion today. The same is true of the organisation of words in a line so that word breaks, stresses, and / or syllabic rhythms align with metrical positions in a certain way or produce a particular metrical line type (in Old Germanic poetries). These can equally be viewed in terms of the entanglement of word rhythms rather than as formulae proper.

A terminological distinction does not devalue the respective phenomenon, which may instead be brought into focus in better ways. For example, many verse narrative traditions exhibit formally regular rhythms of formulae for naming characters.[130] This structural pattern can be associated with making the names compatible with other formulae related to action or speaking, which they can accompany within a line.[131] Rather than the respective structural paradigm being a formula proper, it can be approached as a 'prosodic morpheme', a pattern of rhythm and sound that is corollary to a unit of sense, like forming nicknames in English by reducing the name to a monosyllable followed by -*y* (*Catherine* > *Kathy*, *John* > *Johnny*).[132] The prosodic morpheme can then be

with the following word (*Baldrs draumar* 1.1-2; *Þrymskviða* 14.1-2), which would not conform to a definition like Parry's.

[128] FOLEY, '*Guslar* and *Aoidos*', p. 25.

[129] On the concept of metrical entanglement, see FROG, "Metrical entanglement".

[130] E.g. PARRY, *L'épithète traditionnelle*; J. SAARINEN, "Formula and structure: Ways of expressing names in the northern Runosong tradition", in: *Weathered Words*, ed. FROG and LAMB, pp. 243-258.

[131] FROG, "Multiform theory".

[132] T. RIAD, "Meter as improvement" (unpublished keynote lecture presented at the conference "Versification: Metrics in Practice", Helsinki, Finland, 25th-27th May 2016).

viewed as metrically localised[133] or entangled with certain metrical positions as opposed to others.[134] The concept of prosodic morpheme is then complementary to that of 'formula', and may be used to approach formula families that are formally, semantically, and / or functionally linked. For example, Tim William Machan finds that Old Norse appositional phrases for a named person and constituted of a kinship term like *faðir* ('father'), *sonr* ('son'), *bróðir* ('brother'), *systir* ('sister'), and so on, combined with a name or noun in the genitive, like *Buðla dóttir* ('Buðli's daughter') accompanying the name *Brynhildr*, appear systematically in the second half of a long line and the kinship term never carries the alliteration.[135] While *Buðla dóttir* may be viewed as a b-line formula, which is in turn a specification of the open-slot *X-GEN dóttir* formula, the open slot formula itself belongs to a family of formulae linked to kinship terms that are regularly structured. Viewing these in terms of a prosodic morpheme then opens the question of whether *Loki / Laufeyiar sonr*[136] should be viewed as a variation of the pattern, although the majority of examples have a trochaic rhythm, while *Þrymr / þursa dróttinn*[137] might be considered to reflect the same prosodic morpheme although *dróttinn* ('lord') is not a kinship term. It is not necessary to use the concept of prosodic morpheme any more than it is necessary to use one rather than another definition of formula, but the concept presents a complementary tool that may offer perspectives on the material.

As broader patterns of language use are brought into focus, having a suitable formula definition is certainly relevant. However, caution is needed to avoid two traps into which it is easy to fall. The first is of defining the primary material through the concept rather than using a stipulative definition as a point of reference when examining that material. The second is of becoming invested in the term 'formula', so that you either cannot see outside of it or try to stretch it to account for all of the variation in the data and inadvertently obscure the respective phenomenon. The latter problem in Old English led Donald K. Fry to redefine 'formula' to account for the dynamic variation in the poetry by focusing on 'formula systems' as groups of phrases that seem to be generated on analogy to one another and to define a formula as any product of such a

---

[133] O'NEILL, "The localization of metrical word-types".
[134] FROG, "Metrical entanglement".
[135] T.W. MACHAN, [review of] "Robert Kellogg: 'A Concordance to eddic Poetry'", *Scandinavian Studies* 63.1 (1991), pp. 126-127, at p. 127.
[136] *Þrymskviða*, st. 18.1-2, etc.
[137] *Þrymskviða*, st. 6.1-2, etc.

system.[138] This approach is an extension of Parry's use of 'system',[139] reproduced by Lord,[140] before the concept of 'variable slots' had been introduced. Each specific phrase was then described as a formula, some of which might be generated uniquely on analogy to one known from the tradition. The concept is thus consistent with principles of Classic OFT, but adapted to the highly variable phraseology of Old Germanic alliterative poetries. Fry's approach leads Old Norse *Buðla dóttir* ('Buðli's daughter') and *þursa dróttinn* ('giants' lord') to be considered formulae produced by the same system. Just for fun, I swept through the Old English corpus and created a preliminary database of about one thousand kennings and genitive kenning-like constructions meaning 'lord'. According to Fry's model, all of these would be equally considered formulae produced by the 'system'. This model meets Classic OFT's concerns for assessing formulaic density by identifying phrases that may appear unique as formulae, but the approach does not distinguish between expressions that circulated as highly crystallised phrases and those found only once that may have been generatively produced. It also obviates consideration of formal differences: most form a complete half-line, but the syllabic structure of the constituent words are not regular, so some require additional words in a line. Although Fry's approach was effective for the interests of his time, it obscures the dynamics of how language is working in the poetry. The words used to generate these expressions exhibit differences in the frequency with which they carry alliteration and they may also exhibit preferred placement in a line; in many cases, they exhibit preferred pairing with certain words or types of word (e.g. ethnonyms, place names) as opposed to others.[141] Where such tendencies especially with word combinations are apparent, these can be approached as discreet formulae with preferred ways of completing the formula's open slot, but addressing them as formulae in isolation obscures the fact that both words being combined can exhibit such tendencies, and that the tendencies linked to each

---

[138] D.K. FRY, "Old English formulas and systems", *English Studies* 48.1-6 (1967), pp. 193-204.

[139] PARRY, *L'épithète traditionnelle* and *Les formules*.

[140] LORD, *Singer of Tales*.

[141] The relative frequency in carrying alliteration, called alliterative rank (BORROFF, *Sir Gawain and the Green Knight*) or alliteration rate (D. CRONAN, "Alliterative rank in Old English poetry, *Studia Neophilologica* 58.2 (1986), pp. 145-158), tends to be assessed only for usage in the corpus as a whole (see also ROPER, "Synonymy and rank"), while preferred placement by metrical position has only been assessed for all uses of a word in a single poem (O.A. SMIRNITSKAYA, *The Verse and Language of Old Germanic Poetry*, ed. and trans. I.V. SVERDLOV (Tempe, in press, ch. 5). These observations concern usage in a certain type of rhetorical figure within the whole corpus.

word may align or contrast as they are combined. The operation of language in generating these expressions is extremely dynamic, and developing an accurately representative model for it seems to require looking beyond the concept of formula.

Many issues of definition are related to trying to contain a complex phenomenon in a single term. In addition to the countless things that move outside of the central criteria of formula above, a general definition like Wray's, Foley's, or Parry's without the metrical criterion can contain a huge variety of phenomena – indeed, so many that it would be difficult or perhaps impossible to review them exhaustively.[142] The more criteria that are added, the more probable that the definition specifies formulae of a particular type. Classic OFT's concern with identifying and inventorying formulae and how they vary was built around formulae of a very basic type as a regularly-positioned phrasal unit like *swift-footed Achilles*. The definition excluded formulae that could vary in their metrical positions,[143] 'telescoping formulae', that in some traditions may expand or contract,[144] parallel terms that form a coherent unit of meaning like *æsir//álfar* above,[145] and so on. The definition excluded distinctions by formal type and, in spite of the great interest in identifying every formulaic phrase in a text, it also generally excluded interest in the principles of their combination, which were taken for granted under the aegis of the 'grammar' of the poetry.[146] Acker's work stands out in this respect, both for making distinctions between formula types, such as the syndetic formula of two words linked by a conjunction, like *æsir ok álfar* ('gods and elves'), and also for observing systemic relations in variation between selected formulae driven by alliteration in a line.[147]

---

[142] See also the discussion in L. HARVILAHTI, *Kertovan runon keinot: Inkeriläisen runoepiikan tuottamisesta* (Helsinki, 1992).

[143] HAINSWORTH, *The Flexibility of the Homeric Formula*; cf. the Old Norse *fornyrðislag* formula ... *æsir* ... *á þingi* ('... gods ... at assembly') in note 127 above.

[144] E.g. in the syllable-counting Kalevala-meter, using curly brackets to indicate the hierarchy of omissible elements: *{{vaka} vanha} Väinämöinen* ('{{sturdy} old} Väinämöinen') (FROG, "Metrical entanglement", p. 257); in Karelian laments, organised in 'strings' of variable length organised according to a single pattern of alliteration: *{{kumbane olet kallehilla ilmoilla piäl'ä {kaheksien kuuhuzien} kandelija} kalliz} kandaja{ze}ni* ('{{one who is into the dear.PL world. PL {for eight.PL months.DIM.PL} bringer} dear} carrier{.DIM}.POSS' = MOTHER) (adapted from E. STEPANOVA, "The register of Karelian lamenters", in: *Registers of Communication*, ed. AGHA and FROG, pp. 258-274, at p. 265; layout from FROG, "Metrical entanglement", p. 271).

[145] Also FOX, *Master Poets*.

[146] LORD, *Singer of Tales*.

[147] ACKER, *Levels of Formulaic Composition*; ID., *Revising Oral Theory*; on syndetic formulae, see also E.A. GUREVIČ, "The formulaic pair in eddic poetry", in: *Structure and Meaning in*

If your definition distinguishes formulae of a particular type, it may be relevant to keep alternative types and distinctions between them in sight. The distinction might be in the usage within the tradition, like formulae used across poems in a poetic system as opposed to those specific to a particular poem, the narrative event, or another unit expressed. It might also be formal, like a syndetic formula or parallel terms used for unitary meaning like *æsir//álfar*. The additional point of reference has the potential to lead to new observations on their usage or relations.

For example, the *æsir//álfar* collocation can be considered an 'ordered pair' – i.e. *æsir* always precedes *álfar*, with the exception of a single long line ... *álfa / né ása sona* (' ... elves' / 'nor gods' sons'), with its repetition in a dialogic exchange.[148] The expression includes a formula of the *X's synir* ('sons of X') type formed with a term for a category of being to reciprocally refer to the same category – i.e. 'sons of gods' = 'gods'. This formula type is widely attested, although it is specific to the metre called *ljóðaháttr*, where it is regularly used in either a b-line or in the line type called a *Vollzeile*. The *X's synir* formula is used exclusively for gods, humans, and giants, with the exception of a manuscript variation of the formula above, in which *álfa né ása sona* is written *ása eða álfa sona*, producing a unique expression 'sons of elves'. Two types of formulae are in interaction in this line, requiring that either the *æsir//álfar* collocation is inverted to produce a conventional *ása synir* formula or that the collocation retains its conventional order and produces an anomalous *álfa synir* formula. It is not relevant here which phrasing is most likely for the common exemplar of the two manuscripts. What is relevant is that the interaction of the formulae creates a tension that resulted in a copyist's scribal performance, 'correcting' one phrasing with the other. In order to approach and explicate this type of phenomenon, it is necessary not only to have a definition of formula but also to distinguish between formulae of different types.

When choosing a definition of formula, the challenges are manifold and often they are not immediately recognisable. Consequently, there may be some trial and error. The most important things to be aware of are:

- What sorts of definitions are out there and to be able to recognise them as constituted of different criteria;

Old Norse Literature: New Approaches to Textual Analysis and Literary Criticism, ed. J. LINDOW, L. LÖNNROTH, and G.W. WEBER (Odense, 1986), pp. 32-55.

[148] *Skírnismál*, st. 17.1-2, 18.1-2.

- That not all criteria are universally applicable and some definitions may not work for you;
- That you should not be afraid of trying out different definitions and testing what they can and cannot do with your material;
- That a definition of formula is something to hold up to your material and compare it to, but does not define cases in that material;
- That you might end up using multiple definitions;
- That not everything is a formula and that a definition of formula may not be significant for every study.

Although it is most common to take up someone else's definition, you should not be afraid of modifying it or proposing your own, for instance as a study-specific or tradition-specific definition. All three possibilities have advantages. If you have not yet worked a lot with the problem of definitions, the safest course is to take up someone else's definition. Established definitions not only provide a recognisable frame of reference, they also locate responsibility for it with someone else: you become responsible for the *choice* of definition, not for any issues that might be raised with the definition itself. This strategy has the advantage that you can comment critically on that definition and its background or applicability to your material without committing to any particular definition as how a formula *should be* defined. The flipside is that the definition you choose may not be well-suited to your material or investigation and can carry all sorts of baggage with it, baggage that could interfere with how your work is received or leave invisible aspects of what you are trying to study. Rather than trying to formulate a definition proper, you can also simply make a list of criteria, consider which criteria are relevant to your material, and which are not, and figure out which ones are or are not relevant and in what ways. In this case, a whole study could be built up with different criteria in focus, only turning to the question of whether or not the things in question are formulae and how 'formula' should be defined when writing it all up. Whatever the case, just remember that research is a process of which the trial and error of finding something that works is an organic part for all of us, so there is no reason to be intimidated by it, even if it can be frustrating.

In more general terms, if the point is to interpret or otherwise analyse certain formulae that have already been identified, it is practical to remain with the definition that you started out with. Whenever the point is to interpret things already identified as formulae, most important is simply to make the definition clear so that people working with different approaches can situate your work in relation to their own. If the point is to analyse formulae of a conventionally identified type and their variation in a particular tradition, the same principle can be followed. Such a study might also benefit considerably from developing a descriptive definition or model rather than working from a stipulative definition. The scope of the model might be general for the tradition, limited to formulae distinctive of that tradition as opposed to others, or specific to the particular formula type. When research spans different traditions, a tradition-dependent definition may be methodologically problematic unless it is uniformly applicable to both or all traditions in question. The greater the variety of traditions compared, the more probable that a broader stipulative definition is needed. If a study is exploratory, it may be relevant to work with multiple definitions in mind, in order to remain open to the widest possible range of forms that formulaic language can take. The same is true if the aim is to critically assess current formula research on the tradition in question or otherwise 'think outside the box'. In other words, for some jobs, the most basic and familiar tool works just fine, while other jobs might require a variety of tools and a great deal more tinkering before you're done. But the best way to start is just to pick up a definition and see what you can do with it. And if it doesn't go perfectly the first time around, at least juggling definitions is safer than juggling knives, so there's nothing to be worried about when you pick them back up and try again.

Formulas, Collocations, and Cultural Memory

STEPHEN A. MITCHELL

Introduction

An issue of great interest in the study of charm magic concerns how such materials maintained themselves over time, especially in cases where there has been only irregular recourse to written documents. I am here echoing the goal set by the authors of a very important study of Serbian charms, Barbara Kerewsky Halpern and John Foley, "[w]e want to discover why as well as how orality works as a vital means of preservation and transmission".[1] But I am not only interested in the oral dimension of this problem, but rather in how language – written, oral, and / or moving back and forth between these communication channels – acts in a variety of ways to preserve and transmit meaning. I readily accept that whatever boundary existed between oral and inscribed transmission of magic in the northern world, the membrane was porous and becoming more so over time, as seems clear in the case of the Nordic 'black book' tradition.[2] At the same time, even given the possibility of multiple com-

---

[1] B. KEREWSKY HALPERN and J.M. FOLEY, "The power of the word: Healing charms as an oral genre", *The Journal of American Folklore* 91 (1978), pp. 903-924 at p. 903.

[2] Often referred to as 'black books' (*svartaböcker, sortebøger,* or in its fuller form, *svartkonstböcker* and so on), these often mixed collections of magical lore, medical knowledge,

---

New Light on Formulas in Oral Poetry and Prose, ed. Daniel SÄVBORG and Bernt Ø. THORVALDSEN, *Utrecht Studies in Medieval Literacy*, 57 (Turnhout: Brepols, 2023), pp. 59-79.

munication channels, it must be said that there exist a number of Nordic charm texts from post-medieval folklore sources whose nature and very existence have beguiled researchers for a very long time,[3] at least in some instances within a primarily or even strictly oral context. What factors contribute to the relative stability of such verbal charms over time? Adding to our understanding of this question and its possible answers is the nub of what I want to address.

In addition to the role played by grimoires in the later periods, observations of living traditions of charm magic often note the role of learning magic person-to-person, usually from older generations. Thus, in the Balkans, for example as Kerewsky Halpern and Foley note,

> Charms are regarded as an inheritance, items of great usefulness to be preserved and passed on. Young girls are taught these *basme* [healing charms] by their mothers or grandmothers, and they may also be present while a grandmother is actually performing. An in-marrying bride can learn from her mother-in-law or grandmother-in-law.[4]

Although we lack for our materials the sort of detail these modern observations from southeastern Europe provide, we do have significant evidence suggesting

---

and veterinary medicine were extremely popular from the late medieval period to relatively modern times, and it is their contents that form much of the bases for the various national collections of magical formulae. For orientation and basic older bibliography, see F. HØDNEBØ, "Trolldomsbøker", in: *Kulturhistorisk leksikon for nordisk middelalder fra vikingetid til reformasjonstid*, ed. J. BRØNDSTED et al. (Copenhagen, 1982 [1956-1978]), 18, cols. 670-674. In recent decades these remarkable texts have attracted a great deal of attention: see, e.g. K. STOKKER, *Remedies and Rituals: Folk Medicine in Norway and the New Land* (St. Paul MN, 2007); O. DAVIES, *Grimoires: A History of Magic Books* (Oxford, 2009), pp. 126-128 and *passim*; A. OHRVIK, *Medicine, Magic and Art in Early Modern Norway: Conceptualizing Knowledge* (London, 2018: *Palgrave Historical Studies in Witchcraft and Magic*); and T.K. JOHNSON, *Svartkonstböcker: A Compendium of the Swedish Black Art Book Tradition* (Seattle WA, 2019). Of related interest, see S.A. MITCHELL, "Leechbooks, manuals, and grimoires: On the early history of magical texts in Scandinavia", *ARV: Nordic Yearbook of Folklore* 70 (2014), pp. 57-74.

[3] E.g. the different perspectives one can infer by comparing the opening section of *Norske Hexeformularer og magiske Opskrifter*, ed. A.C. BANG (Christiania, 1901-1902: *Videnskabsselskabet i Christiania Skrifter II: Historisk-filosofisk klasse* 1), pp. 1-17, "*Odin og Folebenet*", with the conclusion in R.T. CHRISTIANSEN, *Die finnischen und nordischen Varianten des zweiten Merseburgerspruches: Eine vergleichende Studie* (Hamina, 1914: *Folklore Fellows Communications* 18). Cf. the similar comment in J. ROPER, *English Verbal Charms* (Helsinki, 2005: *FF Communications* 288), p. 99, on the extreme conservatism of some English charms of the second Merseburg type. On the substantial work that has been conducted on this problem, a very useful point of departure is A. HOPTMAN, "The second Merseburg charm: A bibliographic survey", *Interdisciplinary Journal for Germanic Linguistics and Semiotic Analysis* 4.1 (1999), pp. 83-154.

[4] KEREWSKY HALPERN and FOLEY, "The power of the word", p. 906.

a tradition of individuals learning magic in the medieval Nordic world, both as represented in literary sources and in trials of various sorts (e.g. *Eyrbyggia saga*, the early fourteenth-century case of Ragnhildr Tregagaas).[5] And, of course, we have every reason to believe that inter-generational oral transmission of charm texts, as well as dissemination by way of writing (including runes), took place in Nordic tradition.[6]

In addition to the transmission of magical recipes, important extra-narrative aspects help explain how charms may have been used in ways that led to their being carefully recalled (and also being recalled, but much mutated), such as the possibility that incantations connected with particular saints may have been regularly invoked on their saint's day.[7] Lea Olsan, building on theories of memory, has suggested the importance of what she terms "semantic motifs", the "link between the symptom (or need) a charm serves and the specific incantational words or signs (...) that serve as the cure",[8] an idea close to what Timothy Tangherlini in a much broader sense has suggested we may want to term "tradition memory".[9]

In other cases, exploration of directly linguistic and poetic features, such as prosody, alliteration, and poetic metre, have been viewed as key considerations. In his important examination of Estonian charms, for example, Jonathan Roper points to the following factors in accounting for *variation* in the performance of charm traditions: sound patterns, syntactic templates, organising numbers, metrical form, and interference,[10] but several of these same features (sound

---

[5] These and a number of other instances are detailed in S.A. MITCHELL, "Magic as acquired art and the ethnographic value of the sagas", in: *Old Norse Myths, Literature and Society*, ed. M. CLUNIES-ROSS (Viborg, 2003: *The Viking Collection* 14), pp. 132-152, and ID., *Witchcraft and Magic in the Nordic Middle Ages* (Philadelphia, 2011).

[6] A particularly useful case study of this same problem within a different tradition is found in T.M. SMALLWOOD, "The transmission of charms in English, medieval and modern", in: *Charms and Charming in Europe*, ed. J. ROPER (New York, 2004), pp. 11-31.

[7] In addition to KEREWSKY HALPERN and FOLEY, "The power of the word", see, e.g. J.M. FOLEY, "*Læcdom* and *Bajanje*: A comparative study of Old English and Serbo-Croatian charms", *Centerpoint: A Journal of Interdisciplinary Studies* 4 (1981), pp. 33-40; L.T. OLSAN, "Latin charms of medieval England", *Oral Tradition* 7(1992), pp. 116-142; K.L. JOLLY, *Popular Religion in late Saxon England: Elf Charms in Context* (Chapel Hill NC, 1996); L.T. OLSAN, "Charms in medieval memory", in: *Charms and Charming in Europe*, ed. ROPER, pp. 59-88; and P.M. JONES and L.T. OLSAN, "Performative rituals for conception and childbirth in England, 900-1500", *Bulletin of the History of Medicine* 89.3 (2015), pp. 406-433.

[8] OLSAN, "Charms in medieval memory", p. 63.

[9] See T.R. TANGHERLINI, "'Where was I?': Personal experience narrative, crystallization and some thoughts on tradition memory", *Cultural Analysis* 7 (2008), pp. 41-76.

[10] J. ROPER, "Charms, change and memory: Some principles underlying variation", *Folk-*

patterns and syntactic templates in particular) might also serve to account for longevity as much as variation.

In this essay, I examine a further vector that may play an important yet largely overlooked role in the transmission of the Nordic magical charms, collocations, what one might describe as particular words which native speakers routinely place in juxtaposition (described more narrowly below). These semi-fixed phrases have, I suspect, an important function in the preservation of charm texts, especially as regards the status and semantic register of the lexemes in popular tradition, yet they are rarely considered in most charm studies.[11] Collocations, by definition, indicate the habituation of certain words and phrases, especially in such marked contexts as ritual observance (or parallel frameworks, such as liturgy, prayer, and song), processes through which they become normalised within a speech community, and contribute to what has been called "word-power".[12] Although the relationship of the collocates appears to be based more in semantics than grammatical structures or formal phonological features, that is not to suggest that other factors do not also help account for their persistence and use over time.

The essay begins with some very broad definitions, and then refines the notion of collocations in relation to idioms and formulas, illustrated with examples highlighting how the principle may have contributed to the relative stability of charms of different types throughout the medieval and early modern periods. I use examples that often but do not always touch on magic, as well as those that are directly connected to magic and other forms of religious life – in the end, I am principally concerned with the applicability of this issue to what might be broadly termed 'spiritual' culture over many centuries.[13]

---

lore: Electronic Journal of Folklore 9 (1998) = <http://www.folklore.ee/folklore/vol9/roper.htm>.

[11] And exception to this tendency, albeit with reference to epics, is J.M. FOLEY, *Traditional Oral Epic: The* Odyssey, Beowulf, *and the Serbo-Croatian Return Song* (Berkeley CA, 1990), pp. 212-217, 228, 238.

[12] J.M. FOLEY, "Word-Power, performance, and tradition", *The Journal of American Folklore* 105 (1992), pp. 275-301.

[13] Without wanting to sound coy, I use 'spiritual' here in a broad, neutral sense, so as to capture what are in some instances highly institutionalised and carefully curated religious beliefs (i.e. in medieval Catholicism), while, at other times, the term is intended to include extra-institutional spiritual beliefs reflected in charm magic, which can also, but need not, be grounded in Christian belief. This question of materials being maintained over time (as well as its opposite, innovation within the charm tradition) is an issue I have addressed previously on several occasions: S.A. MITCHELL, "Continuity: Folklore's problem child?", in: *Folklore in Old Norse – Old Norse in Folklore*, ed. D. SÄVBORG and K. BEK-PEDERSEN (Tartu, 2014: *Nordistica Tartuensis* 20), pp. 34-51; ID., "Faith and knowledge in nordic charm magic", in: *Faith and*

Collocations, Idioms, and Prose Formulas

A collocation is a kind of phrasal association, that is, "The habitual juxtaposition or association, in the sentences of a language, of a particular word with other particular words" or "a group of words so associated".[14] Collocations form part of what are often referred to as "conventionalized expressions",[15] a somewhat inexact umbrella term which has understandably been seen as contributing to "the ungoverned country between lay metalanguage and the theoretical terminology of linguistics".[16] Still, there is value in the phrase, even if 'conventionalised expressions' may be slightly ambiguous and encompasses a very wide range of conventional speech forms, including idioms, proverbial expressions, and other patterned utterances.

Contrasting collocations with idioms and formulas, with which they share a number of features, highlights what is meant by the association of a particular

---

Knowledge in Late Medieval & Early Modern Scandinavia, ed. K. KJESRUD and M. MALES (Turnhout, 2020: *Knowledge, Scholarship, and Science in the Middle Ages* 1), pp. 193-211; and ID., "Notes on *historiolas*, referentiality and time in Nordic magical traditions", in: *Folklore and Old Norse Mythology*, ed. FROG (Helsinki, 2021), pp. 245-266.

[14] The definitions are those of the *Oxford English Dictionary* (online edition), referring to J.R. FIRTH, "Modes of meaning", *Essays and Studies*, n.s. 4 (1952), 118-149, specifically pp. 123 ff. I should be clear that I am only seeking a practical phrase to use in discussing such phenomena, and realise that these definitions have been important topics in linguistic research. A serviceable example for collocation might be, "Collocation is the co-occurrence of two items in a text within a specified environment" (J.M. SINCLAIR, S. JONES, and R. DALEY, *English Collocation Studies: The Osti Report* (London, 2004 [1970]), p. 10), but that definition is perhaps a bit too loose, as discussed further below. Cf. S-G. MALMGREN, *Begå eller ta självmord? Om svenska kollokationer och deras förändringsbenägenhet 1800-2000* (Göteborg, 2002) <http://hdl.handle.net/2077/18763>.

[15] E.g. J. BYBEE, "From usage to grammar: The mind's response to repetition", *Language,* 82 (2006), 711-733, speaks of "conventionalized word sequences, which include sequences that we might call formulaic language and idioms, but also conventionalized collocations" (p. 713). P. KIPARSKY, "Oral poetry: Some linguistic and typological considerations", in: *Oral Literature and the Formula*, ed. by B. A. STOLZ and R. S. SHANNON (Ann Arbor, 1976), pp. 73-106, for example, uses the term 'bound phraseology', which is perhaps more transparent than 'conventionalised expression', although the latter phrase importantly underscores the social dimension, i.e. use and habituation.

[16] G. NUNBERG, I.A. SAG, and T. WASOW, "Idioms", *Language,* 70 (1994), 491-538. The authors are specifically discussing the place of idioms. The full context of their expostulation is well worth noting, "In actual linguistic discourse and lexicographical practice, 'idiom' is applied to a fuzzy category defined on the one hand by ostension of prototypical examples like English *kick the bucket, take care of* NP, or *keep tabs on* NP, and on the other by implicit opposition to related categories like formulae, fixed phrases, collocations, clichés, sayings, proverbs, and allusions – terms which, like 'idiom' itself, inhabit the ungoverned country between lay metalanguage and the theoretical terminology of linguistics" (p. 492).

word with other particular words, although it must be said that the border between the groups is not always clear. I begin with idioms, a category defined as conventionalised word sequences that typically use standard word choices and syntax, but generally have figurative rather than literal meanings, with the result that they do not have predictable outcomes. Examples might include such English idioms as *kick the bucket, light a fire under someone*, and *tend to one's own rat-killing*, expressions that have literal (but little-used) meanings as well as figurative meanings.

The first two of these expressions are very commonly used figuratively to mean, respectively, 'to die' and 'to motivate'. Used in a variety of media, these idioms have become well-known and are often listed in dictionaries. That third idiom, on the other hand, meaning 'mind your own business', is, I suspect, one that relatively few native English speakers will recognise or understand.[17] The point is, of course, that 'conventionalised expressions' can be part of a standard language, or narrowly restricted to specific speech communities, defined by region, occupation, religion, or other factors, in other words, used only among those who belong to specific subcultural communities. Phrases of this sort resist recognition and interpretation from the outside, and can even be (and likely are) used as markers for the purposes of both social inclusion and social exclusion.

Collocations are also word sequences that are conventionalised, but unlike idioms, their meanings are predictable – these phrases do not typically run the risk of being incomprehensible to outsiders, only that they will be judged unacceptable by native speakers. One can, for example *make, brew, prepare*, or even (increasingly rarely) '*perk*' (< percolate) *coffee* in English, but one does not generally *cook coffee – of course, no one would actually misunderstand the meaning of such usage, but most English speakers would assume the author of such a phrase was not a native speaker. Similarly, but now focussing on the use of a more archaic word form, one *wends one's way* in English, but, so far as I know, native speakers would find unacceptable (or odd in any event) saying that an individual *wends her path, rather than *wends her way* – but there is no logical or grammatical reason why one should not be able to do so.[18]

---

[17] 'Tend to your own rat-killing' was in my childhood a completely normal way of saying 'mind your own business'. I later came to understand that this idiom was part of my mother's rural West Texas dialect (with antebellum family roots to Missouri and Kentucky) and part of a regional usage common among Dust Bowl immigrants to California's Central Valley – but when used elsewhere, especially (but not only) in urban areas, the expression inevitably leads to noticeably shocked (sometimes even angry) reactions from other native speakers.

[18] Because collocations are phrases that are preferred by native speakers over semantically and grammatically equivalent expressions, they present an interesting window onto issues of both

Key to collocations then is that they are word sequences of relatively loose association used in prose or poetry, and habituated through repeated use, especially in particular contexts. Learning through repetition is hardly unique to this category of speech, but in this case, we have reason to suspect that non-national speech communities are of particular significance, communities which may be regional and dialectal or sub-cultural, such as religious or other special types of communities. But slang these collocations are not, since part of their character is that they are not fleeting phenomena but used, and in evidence, over many generations.[19]

It is also useful to compare collocations with 'formulas' or 'prose formula' – of course, collocations need not be prose (although they often are). And our evolved nomenclature itself represents a further complicating factor, in that 'formula' has acquired a great many specialised meanings and associations that do not apply to collocations and thus might serve to complicate the matter.[20] That said, however, there are important and notable functional similarities: due to their usefulness to speakers, in a manner resembling the value of the formula to a singer composing in performance, such multi-word composites as collocations are sometime referred to in the scholarly literature as 'prefabs' (< prefabricated (*sc.* expressions)), that is, ready-made sequences that ease the production of speech.[21]

Citing Milman Parry's work on recurrence in Homeric epic,[22] Paul Kiparsky notes the possibility of "patterns which might be termed *echoes*, involving

---

style and multilingualism. See, e.g. SINCLAIR, JONES, and DALEY, *English Collocation Studies*, and BYBEE, "From usage to grammar".

[19] Cf. BYBEE, "From usage to grammar".

[20] This issue has been referred to as "a nagging and seemingly insoluble dilemma" in J.M. FOLEY, "Tradition and the collective talent: Oral epic, textual meaning, and receptionalist theory", *Cultural Anthropology* 1.2 (1986), pp. 203-222, at p. 203, in which he mentions "the academic jousting over analytical terms such as the phraseological 'formula'". Of course, the important developments in this saga have to do with the use of 'formula' in the context of Homeric poetry, especially by the work of Milman Parry, Albert Lord, and others. Cf. M. PARRY, *L'epithète traditionnelle dans Homère: Essai sur un problème de style Homérique* (Paris, 1928), translated as "The traditional epithet in Homer" in: *The Making of Homeric Verse: The Collected Papers of Milman Parry*, ed. A. PARRY (Oxford, 1971), pp. 1-190; ID., *Les formules et la métrique d'Htmère* (Paris, 1928), translated as "Homeric Formulae and Homeric Metre" in: *The Making of Homeric Verse*, ed. A. PARRY, pp. 191-239, as well as A.B. LORD, *The Singer of Tales*, 2nd edn, ed. S.A. MITCHELL and G. NAGY (Cambridge MA, 2000: *Harvard Studies in Comparative Literature* 24) (first edition 1960).

[21] So in, e.g. B. ERMAN and B. WARREN, "The idiom principle and the open choice principle", *Text* 20 (2000), pp. 29-62.

[22] PARRY, *The Making of Homeric Verse*, pp. 73, 328.

purely phonological repetition, without any necessary lexical or syntactic relationship".[23] Thus, in addition to formulas at deep and surface levels, speaking specifically of oral poetry (although with wider implications it seems), Kiparsky suggests a third type,

> that of phonological representations. Some of the stereotyped patterns of oral poetry are apparently coded in the singer's memory simply in terms of phoneme sequences, which can be matched in composition with syntactically and lexically divergent sequences. Exactly what these phonological patterns look like formally, and what are the dimensions and limits of their variability, is hard to tell for now.[24]

Patterns of these sorts, Kiparsky suggests, track neatly onto the findings of memory specialists, who find three types of verbal memory – auditory ('echoic') memory; sentences in surface structure form; and deep or semantic form – all of which contribute to long-term memory.[25]

Along similar lines, it would seem, in his study of this topic, David Rubin focusses on the repetition of sound (with a particular interest in rhyme) as a strong aid to memory, and reports on a striking research result: citing tests of recall in which two cues, one semantic and one phonological, are used, the results show that "each succeeded in producing a target 6% of the time when used individually, *but 86 % of the time when used together*" (emphasis added).[26] It is not difficult to imagine that in some instances this finding has implications for collocations. For example, alliteration seems to be common but

---

[23] KIPARSKY, "Oral poetry", p. 90; cf. the remarks in response to Kiparsky's paper in C. WATKINS, "Response to Kiparsky", in: *Oral Literature and the Formula*, ed. STOLZ and SHANNON, pp. 107-111. The phenomenon called 'echo-words' and 'echoic repetition' noted for Old English poetry may have relevance here as well, insofar as it represents a kind of wordplay that connects sound and sense through these repetitions. See J.O. BEATY, "The echo-word in *Beowulf* with a note on the *Finnsburh* fragment", *Publications of the Modern Language Association* 49 (1934), pp. 365-373, and E.R. KINTGEN, "Echoic repetition in Old English Poetry, especially *The Dream of the Rood*", *Neuphilologische Mitteilungen* 75 (1974), pp. 202-223.

[24] KIPARSKY, "Oral poetry", p. 91.

[25] "The existence of three levels of formulaic patterning would agree well with the results of psychological experiments on the way sentences are remembered", KIPARSKY, "Oral poetry", p. 91.

[26] D.C. RUBIN, *Memory in Oral Traditions: The Cognitive Psychology of Epic, Ballads, and Counting-Out Rhymes* (New York, 1995), p. 94. See also ID., "Oral traditions as collective memories: Implications for a general theory of individual and collective memory", in: *Memory in Mind and Culture*, ed. P. BOYER and J.V. WERTSCH (Cambridge, 2009), pp. 273-287; and D.C. RUBIN and D.L. GREENBERG, "The role of narrative in recollection: A view from cognitive and neuropsychology", in: *Narrative and Consciousness: Literature, Psychology, and the Brain*, ed. G. FIREMAN, T. MCVAY, and O. FLANAGAN (Oxford, 2003), pp. 53-85.

by no means necessary feature (e.g. *wend my way*); similarly, rhyme is also (but need not be) found in collocations (e.g. *nearest and dearest*). Overwhelmingly, however, it seems that repetition, habituation, and conventionalisation are far and away the key factors accounting for the vigour and longevity of such word sequences.

Are there lessons for us as regards the Nordic materials? I believe there are. Following the brief examination of a single Swedish collocation (*fröjd och glädje*, ('joy and delight') over some seven centuries in various genres, I present three cases of collocations related to Nordic charm traditions, where such features as rhyme and alliteration do sometimes appear to play roles: *til árs ok friðar* ('for prosperity and peace'); *þistill – mistill – kistill* ('thistle – mistletoe – and "little chest"'); and *iǫrð – upphiminn* ('earth – (high) heaven').

Nordic Collocations and Nordic Charms

Cal Watkins, in responding to the Kiparsky paper cited above, argues that in the case of the Vedic texts, "[t]here can be no doubt (...) that the presence of a traditional priestly class is a decisive factor in the preservation of fixed compositions", an argument I suggest is appropriate in many ways to medieval Christianity as well.[27] Interestingly, this comment comes as part of a discussion of mediality's role in the habituation process, where Kiparsky maintains that "it is not the *technique* (writing versus speech) that determines the fixity of a text, but rather the *function* which that text has in the society".[28]

The role of institutional authorities, of a 'traditional priestly class' and other elites, with considerable control over education and media, in conventionalising expressions should not to be underestimated. Naturally, we cannot know with certainty whether our surviving documents reflect existing language use or are shaping it, but a sense of a collocation in use over time can be seen in *fröjd och glädje*, roughly 'joy and delight', a collocation with a lengthy historical record and one still much in use.[29]

---

[27] WATKINS, "Response to Kiparsky", p. 107.
[28] KIPARSKY, "Oral poetry", p. 101,
[29] That is, the two lexemes are broadly equivalent expressions of good cheer – *fröjd*, 'joy, rejoicing, delight', etc., and *glädje,* 'delight, happiness, gladness, mirth'. Spot checking the other Nordic languages suggests that similar (but not identical) histories are applicable to them as well, but for the sake of this essay, I deemed a small set of examples within a single national language sufficient. Naturally, I can make no pretence of having scoured the textual inventory evenly, but I hope the examples in this instance represent a judicious 'grab sample' of the possibilities.

Already by the earliest decades of the fourteenth century, the *fröjd och glädje* collocation occurs in the translated literature of the Swedish court, appearing a number of times in *Herr Ivan*, for example (e.g. *medh glædhi ok frygdh*).[30] *Fröjd och glädje* (and its variants, for this collocation is quite loose in form) is very prominent in the religious literature of the late medieval and early modern eras, appearing in such diverse places as the Old Swedish legendary, *Fornsvenska legendariet* (e.g. *frygh ok glæþi*);[31] in the Swedish translation of Bonaventura's *Meditationes vitæ Christi* (*Bonaventuras betraktelser öfver Christi lefverne*) (e.g. *mz frygdh och glädhi*);[32] and frequently in prayers, especially, it would seem, in the private prayer books of Birgittine nuns (e.g. *äwärdeligha frögdh oc glädhi, mädh aldra största frögdh oc glädhi, all glädi oc ffrögdh, blifwe altidh i thinne frygdh oc glädhi*, and so on).[33] This same association of these two collocates can be readily seen in the treatment of biblical passages, as the language of the Vulgate is turned into the Swedish of various periods (e.g. *Esther* 8:15-17; *Psalms* 43:4; *Jeremiah* 48:33).[34] And perhaps especially through such use in biblical passages and other ecclesiastical contexts, such as prayers and other devotional literature, the collocation has maintained wide-spread use from the Middle Ages into nineteenth-century Swedish folktale collections,[35] and continues to be common in Swedish (e.g. the expression *mitt hjärtas fröjd och glädje* ('my heart's joy and delight').

[30] *Herr Ivan: Kritisk upplaga,* ed. E. NOREEN (Uppsala, 1931: *Svenska Fornskrift-Sällskapets Samlingar* 50), p. 19, l. 250. The frequency of the rhyme pair *frygdh-dygdh* ('joy-virtue') in this piece of chivalric romance is especially noteworthy.

[31] "Om vår Herre" in: *Fornsvenska Legendariet*, ed. V. JANSSON (Stockholm, 1838: *Svenska Fornskrift-Sällskapets Samlingar* 55), pp. 62-73, at p. 62.

[32] *Bonaventuras betraktelser öfver Christi lefverne: Legenden om Gregorius af Armenien*, ed. G.E. KLEMMING (Stockholm, 1859: Svenska Fornskrift-Sällskapets Samlingar 15), chaps. 44, 81, 94 (pp. 127, 234-235, 247). In this text, one even see forerunners of the modern *Mitt hjärtas fröjd och glädje*, e.g. '... *af store hiärtans* frygdh *oc* glädhi ...' (ch. 11, p. 7).

[33] *Svenska böner från medeltiden*, ed. R. GEETE (Stockholm, 1907-09: *Svenska Fornskrift-Sällskapets Samlingar* 38), pp. 50, 67, 184, 193, 253, 254, 316, 355, 379, 381, 399, 407, 442, 458, 503, 521.

[34] Cf. *Biblia sacra, iuxta Vulgatam versionem*, ed. B. FISCHER and R. WEBER. 4th rev. edn. (Stuttgart, 1994); the translations of Jöns Budde (*c.* 1437-1491) and others in *Svenska medeltidens bibel-arbeten*, ed. G.E. KLEMMING (Stockholm, 1853: *Svenska Fornskrift-Sällskapets Samlingar* 9.2). For the Gustav Wasa bible (1541) and Karl XII's bible (1703) translations, see the online editions at: <https://litteraturbanken.se/>. For Gustaf V's bible (1917), *Svenska Folkbibeln* 2015, and *Nya levande bibeln*, see <https://www.biblegateway.com>.

[35] E.g. *Svenska folk-sagor och äfventyr efter muntlig öfverlemning,* ed. G.O. HYLTÉN-CAVALLIUS and G. STEPHENS (Stockholm, 1844-1849), pp. 69, 106, 135, 224. Despite the reassuring subtitle that the tales are based on oral presentations, the collector-editors have no doubt massaged the texts, but I assume that such likely editorial intrusions notwithstanding, these collocations would have been part of the text as told.

There are other ways in which collocations seem paradoxically both to evolve and be maintained over time. Whereas I suspect that, in the case of the *fröjd och glädje* collocation, continuity may especially derive from habituation as the result of repeated prayers and other religious observances, there may also be instances where conventionalisation comes about through more formal rituals. A case in point is likely to be found in an expression often but not exclusively connected with ceremonial toasts. The custom of so-called commemorative or *minni* ('memory') toasts is highlighted in a number of medieval texts, and has been much discussed in recent decades, especially whether it should be understood as the reflex of pre-conversion native practice, as it is often presented, or an imported idea, based on Christian practices.[36]

Vivid reports of such a pagan tradition come mainly from Icelandic literary texts: for example, in Snorri Sturluson's mythological *ars poetica*, his so-called *edda*, he writes, "*Freyr er inn ágætasti af ásum ... ok á hann er gott at heita til árs ok friðar*" ("Freyr is the greatest of the Æsir ... and it is good to call on him for prosperity and peace").[37] Other texts, also believed to have been written by Snorri Sturluson, show very similar patterns as regards the *til árs ok friðar* collocation: *Hákonar saga Aðalsteinsfóstra*, for example, maintains, "*... skyldi fyrst Óðins full – skyldi þat drekka til sigrs ok ríkis konungi sínum – en síðan Njarðar full ok Freys full til árs ok friðar*" ("First Óðinn's toast should be drunk for victory and for power to the king, and then toasts to Njǫrðr and Freyr, for prosperity and for peace"), and later in the same saga, the farmers say that they want the king to make sacrifice (*blóta*) in order for them to have prosperity and peace, as his father had done ("*Bœndr segja, at þeir vilja, at konungr blóti til*

---

[36] Mentioned in the sagas (e.g. *Saga Hákonar góða,* ch. 14), ceremonial toasts, that is, the tradition of '*mæla fyrir minnum*', were long assumed to be a pre-Christian practice, a view challenged in K. DÜWEL, *Das Opferfest von Lade: quellenkritische Untersuchungen zur germanischen Religionsgeschichte* (Vienna, 1985: *Wiener Arbeiten zur germanischen Altertumskunde und Philologie* 27), who argues that the custom derived from a Christian tradition honouring Christ and the saints and came to Scandinavia with the conversion. For a recent review of the evidence on ceremonial drinking and commemorative 'memory' toasts, see L. LÖNNROTH, "Memorial toasts", in: *Handbook of Pre-Modern Nordic Memory Studies: Interdisciplinary Approaches*, ed. J. GLAUSER, P. HERMANN, and S.A. MITCHELL (Berlin, 2018), 1, pp. 695-698. For a survey on the phrase *til árs ok friðar*, see F. STRÖM, "År och fred", in: *Kulturhistorisk leksikon for nordisk middelalder fra vikingetid til reformasjonstid*, ed. J. BRØNDSTED *et al.* (Copenhagen, 1982 [1956-78]), 20, cols. 450-452.

[37] *Gylfaginning* in *Snorri Sturluson, Edda: Prologue and Gylfaginning,* ed. A. FAULKES. 2nd edn. (London, 2005), pp. 7-55, at p. 24. For ease of presentation, I am here using the English simplex 'prosperity', but *ár* (lit. 'plenty, abundance, fruitfulness', as well as 'year') might be better glossed as 'good harvest'.

árs þeim ok friðar, svá sem faðir hans gerði").[38] Similarly, *Óláfs saga Tryggvasonar* reports that when the king offers to make human sacrifice with the leading men among the pagans, the king says that he will sacrifice them for (that is, in order to have) peace and prosperity, " ... *hann vill þessum blóta til árs ok friðar* ...".[39]

The same phrase and the same practice – albeit with a different referent – are mentioned in several of the older Nordic law codes. But in these cases, the references are to the Christian world, so, for example: *"En þat ǫl ſkal igna til kriſt þacca. ok ancta Mariu. til árs. oc til friðar"* (*The Older Laws of Gulaþing*) ("The ale shall be blessed with thanks to Christ and Saint Mary for peace and prosperity").[40] This same collocation also appears in *The Older Law of Frostathing,* where the text, in discussing the preparations for various saints' days (Saint Mary and All Saints), directs that anyone twelve years and older should only eat bread and salt, *"til árs oc friþar oc til heill u allum mǫnnum"* ("for [that is, in order to have] peace and prosperity and the health of all men").[41] Elsewhere, the very opening line of *The Older Laws of Gulaþing* states that we should bow to the east and pray for *árs ok friðar*.[42] And it is surely no accident that the Old Swedish provincial law for Södermanland concludes its section on bodily harm (*"Manhælgis balker"*) with the same collocation, *"Guþ han giwi os friþ oc ar. oc lif for vtan ændæ"* ("May God grant us peace and prosperity and life without end").[43]

An even longer history of a collocation in use in the Nordic languages is attested by a curious set of words, whose origins and meaning have long been debated. In fact, it appears to be a particularly persistent collocation in the Scandinavian world, where the terms for 'thistle', 'mistletoe', and 'little chest' ('coffin'?) play key roles, i.e. the *þistill – mistill – kistill* word sequence. Variants of this phrase are in evidence in the Nordic region for well over a millen

---

[38] *Hákonar saga Aðalsteinsfóstra* in *Snorri Sturluson. Heimskringla I*, ed. BJARNI ADALBJARNARSON (Reykjavík, 1962 [1941]: Íslenzk fornrit 26), pp. 150-197 at pp. 168, 170 (chaps. 14, 16).

[39] *Óláfs saga Tryggvasonar*, in: *Snorri Sturluson, Heimskringla I*, pp. 225-372 at p. 316 (ch. 67).

[40] "Ældre Gulathings-Lov" in: *Norges gamle Love indtil 1387*, ed. R. KEYSER and P.A. MUNCH (Christiania, 1846-1895), 1, pp. 1-111 at pp. 6, 7.

[41] "Ældre Frostathings-Lov" in: *Norges gamle Love indtil 1387*, 1, pp. 121-258 at p. 141.

[42] "Ældre Gulathings-Lov", 1, p. 3.

[43] *Södermanna-Lagen*, ed. D.C.J. SCHLYTER (Lund, 1838: *Corpus iuris Sueo-Gotorum antiqui: Samlingar af Sweriges Gamla Lagar* 4), p. 161.

nium, possibly from the sixth-century By (Norway) runestone[44] right up to recent decades as part of a children's rhyme in southern Norway in the 1960s.[45] Runic variants of this sequence, often shortened in inscriptions to the initial graphemes, þmk, appear in some 15 inscriptions from throughout the non-insular Nordic world (and with one example from Poland),[46] and carry over into Icelandic saga writing, most famously in the so-called *Syrpuvers* "Syrpa Verses" of the *Buslubœn* "Busla's Prayer" in *Bósa saga ok Herrauðs*, an Icelandic saga preserved in three fifteenth-century manuscripts, and seems to be referred to obliquely in *Fǫr Scírnis*, one of the Eddic poems.[47]

Moreover, there appear to be analogues to parts of this collocation in other Germanic traditions (i.e. the Old English charm against the theft of cattle) which, if correctly identified,[48] may suggest even broader geographic distribu-

---

[44] N Kj71, By, Sigdal sogn, Norway. *NIærR* 6 (= *Norges indskrifter med de ældre runer*, ed. S. BUGGE, vol. 1 (Christiania, 1891-1903), pp. 89-116).

[45] According to M. SCHULTE, "*Tistel-mistel*-formelen i vikingtid og nordisk middelalder – Form, funksjon og symbolverdi", *Maal og Minne*, 112 (2020), 97-126, at p. 97, "*Tistel-mistel-formelen, slik jeg kaller den her, hadde mest sannsynlig direkte forløpere i senurnordisk tid på 500/600-tallet, og den har etterlevninger i moderne tid*". On the testimony to the use of the collocation in the 1960s, see SCHULTE, "*Tistel-mistel*-formelen", p. 98.

[46] See SCHULTE, "*Tistel-mistel*-formelen", pp. 103-105, especially with its new evidence for additional inscriptions, although not every possible variant is included (see p. 103, n. 9). On the runic evidence, see also M. MACLEOD and B. MEES, *Runic Amulets and Magic Objects* (Woodbridge, 2006), pp. 145-147, and *Runes, Magic and Religion: A Sourcebook*, ed. J. MCKINNELL, R. SIMEK and K. DÜWEL (Vienna, 2004: *Studia Medievalia Septentrionalia* 10), pp. 134-140. On cultural memory and its relevance to the study of runic inscriptions, see M. SCHULTE, "Memory culture in the Viking ages: The runic evidence of formulaic patterns", *Scripta Islandica* 58 (2007), pp. 57-74, and M. MALM, "Runology", in: *Handbook of Pre-Modern Nordic Memory Studies: Interdisciplinary Approaches*, ed. GLAUSER, HERMANN and MITCHELL, pp. 217-227.

[47] This engaging collocation has been the subject of much debate over the decades, including its possible connection to *Fǫr Scírnis*, e.g. M. OLSEN, "Fra gammelnorsk myte og kultus", *Maal og Minne* 1 (1909), pp. 17-36, at p. 23; ID., "De norröne runeinnskrifter", in: *Runorna*, ed. O. VON FRIESEN (Oslo, Stockholm, and Copenhagen, 1933: *Nordisk kultur* 6), pp. 83-113, at p. 108; A. LIESTØL, "Runer frå Bergen", *Viking* 27 (1964), pp. 5-53, at pp. 18-19; J. HARRIS, "Cursing with the thistle: 'Skírnismál' 31.6-8, and OE Metrical Charm 9.16-17", *Neuphilologische Mitteilungen* 76 (1975), pp. 26-33; W. HEINZMANN, "Der Fluch mit der Distel: Zu *Fǫr Scírnis* 31.6-8", *Amsterdamer Beiträge zur älteren Germanistik* 46 (1996), pp. 91-104; S.A. MITCHELL, "Anaphrodisiac charms in the Nordic Middle Ages: Impotence, infertility, and magic", *Norveg* 38 (1998), pp. 19-42; and B.Ø. THORVALDSEN, "The poetic curse and its relatives", in: *Along the Oral-Written Continuum: Types of Texts, Relations and their Implications*, ed. S. RANKOVIĆ, L. MELVE, and E. MUNDAL (Turnhout, 2010: *Utrecht Studies in Medieval Literacy* 20), pp. 253–267. This wide-ranging discussion has been significantly updated by the excellent analysis in the recent SCHULTE, "*Tistel-mistel*-formelen", which includes a substantial review of the secondary literature.

[48] See the cautious comments in *Runes, Magic and Religion*, ed. MCKINNELL, p. 140.

tion of whatever semantic aspect of these words it was that kept them alive in cultural memory.[49] In the most recent assessment of this charm collocation, Michael Schulte concludes that the "thistle – mistletoe formula", as he calls it, had roots in Roman, Celtic, and Germanic mythology, and had both fertility functions as well as apotropaic power against evil forces, elements central to both pre-Christian and Christian use of the complex.[50]

But how is it that a word sequence along these lines has been part of the North Germanic language community (and that is a very widely distributed and defined speech community) over so many centuries? Part of the reason in this instance must surely be the rhyming character of the phrase, in proof of which, it is notable that when the three lexeme sequence *pistill, mistill, kistill* is extended, as it is in the case of the Tønsberg rune stick, the added words fit the same rhyming pattern: *ristill* (? 'ringworm') and *histill* (?).[51]

Thus far, none of the examples have been what might be thought of as formulas in a classic sense (that is, roughly, as lexical conventions that function within poetic constraints), but one example where this manifestly *is* the case and which has been much discussed over the past three decades in particular is the earth and high heaven formula (*iǫrð fannz œva né upphiminn*), a phrase closely identified with Lars Lönnroth's article of the same name.[52] Lönnroth examines evidence of this formula from across the Germanic world, with an important postscript noting two charm texts, one in Old English, the other in Old Danish, which Gerd Weber had subsequently brought to his attention.

The evidence – arranged here as North Germanic, Anglo-Saxon, and Conti-

---

[49] Cf. HARRIS, "Cursing with the thistle"; HEINZMANN, "Der Fluch mit der Distel".

[50] "Fruktbarhetsmotivet og vernefunksjonen mot onde makter, som har røtter i den romerske, keltiske og germanske mytologien, står sentralt ved Bede den hedenske og den kristne bruken av *tistel-mistel*-formelen. Symbolverdien til tistelen og mistelen støtter opp om denne tolkningen" (SCHULTE, "*Tistel-mistel*-formelen", p. 117).

[51] Following in these cases the transcription and glosses in *Runes, Magic and Religion*, ed. MCKINNELL, pp. 137-138.

[52] L. LÖNNROTH, "*Iǫrð fannz œva né upphiminn*: A formula analysis", in: *Speculum Norroenum: Norse Studies in Memory of Gabriel Turville-Petre*, ed. U. DRONKE (Odense, 1981), pp. 310-327. As C.B. HIEATT, "Cædmon in context: Transforming the formula", *The Journal of English and Germanic Philology* 84 (1985), pp. 485-497, at p. 486, notes in her response to Lönnroth (citing A. Liberman), there had already been some earlier consideration of the same materials by *i.a.* Einar Ól. Sveinsson in 1965.

nental German (Old High German, Old Saxon) – thus offers the following picture (here largely after Schulte, with my modifications):[53]

iǫrð fannz æva | né *upphiminn* (*Vǫlospá* 3:5-6)
hvaðan *iǫrð* um kom | eða *upphiminn* fyrst, inn fróði iotunn (*Vafþrúðnismál* 20:4-6)
er eigi veit | *iarðar* hvergi | né *upphimins*: áss er stolinn hamri (*Þrymskviða* 2:5-7)
iǫrð dúsaði | oc *upphiminn* (*Oddrúnargrátr* 17:5-6)
iǫrð bið ec varða | oc *upphimin* (Ribe rune stick)
iǫrð s[c]al rifna oc *upphiminn* (Skarpåker rune stone)

eorðan ic bidde | and *upheofon* (*For Unfruitful Land* 4)
eorðan eallgrenel | ond *upheofon* (*Andreas* 798)
eorþan mid hire beorgum | ond *upheofon* torhtne mid his tunglum (*Christ* 967-968)
Ðu geworhtest *eorþan* frætwe | and *upheofon* (*Psalms* 101:22)

ero ni uuas | noh *ufhimil* (*Wessobrunn Prayer*)
thit uueroldriki, *ertha* | endi *upphimil* (*Heliand* 2885-2886)

Lönnroth makes several key arguments regarding this evidence: first, extending his thoughts from earlier publications, he sketches out how we should understand the medieval northern materials in the context of performance and mediality,[54] and he then tackles in a very substantive way some of the prevailing views about the Nordic materials. He suggests, for example, that as opposed to the ossified manuscript form in which we are accustomed to interpret the Eddic materials, these poems ought, in fact, to be viewed against their historical backgrounds,[55] that is, what we would today understand as their performance

---

[53] M. SCHULTE, "Memory culture in the viking age: The runic evidence of formulaic patterns", *Scripta Islandica* 58 (2007), pp. 57-74, at p. 61. The full range of materials have been recently reviewed in both SCHULTE, "Memory culture in the Viking ages", and in the broad context of the orality-literacy controversy in P. HERMANN, "Methodological challenges to the study of Old Norse myths: The orality and literacy debate reframed", in: *Old Norse Mythology – Comparative Perspectives*, ed. P. HERMANN, S.A. MITCHELL, and J.P. SCHJØDT (Cambridge MA, 2017: *Publications of the Milman Parry Collection of Oral Literature* 3), pp. 29-51. Cf. L. MELVE, "Literacy – eit omgrep til bry eller et brysamt omgrep?", *Scripta Islandica* 56 (2005), pp. 127-137.

[54] Lönnroth specifically mentions L. LÖNNROTH, "Hjálmar's death-song and the delivery of Eddic poetry", *Speculum* 46 (1971), pp. 1-20, but one naturally also thinks in this arena of ID., *Den dubbla scenen: Muntlig diktning fran Eddan till ABBA* (Stockholm, 1978), and ID., "The double scene of Arrow-Odd's drinking contest", in: *Medieval Narrative: A Symposium,* ed. H. BEKKER-NIELSEN *et al.* (Odense, 1979), pp. 94-119.

[55] "From a formal point of view, Eddic poetry must once have been closer to Anglo-Saxon verse than they appear in *Codex Regius*, and this means that they must also have been more

contexts.[56] And in line with this perspective, Lönnroth sees such formulaic language as *iǫrð – upphiminn* as parallel to the linguists' idea of collocations operating as 'pre-fabs',[57] writing,

> a Germanic scop or skald composing a text on the theme of Creation (Christian *or* pagan) might have used the *iǫrð - upphiminn* formula more or less automatically because it was part of the particular 'poetic grammar' in which he had learned to express his thoughts.[58]

In addition to these important reflections on the technical aspects of these examples, Lönnroth also explores the formula's key recurrent themes of Creation and Destruction.[59] Having been alerted to the Old English and Old Danish magical texts, Lönnroth treats them separately, in a postscript, suggesting that they demonstrate a norm for magical usage which runs as follows:

> 1. The speaker should invoke the holy cosmic powers, including 'heaven and earth', the sun (God and Saint Mary?), to give him the strength necessary to perform an act of magic. 2. The magic is thought of as an act of exorcism, whereby nature is cleansed from evil spirits and restored to health, fecundity and usefulness.[60]

As suggested above, Lönnroth's analysis is not particularly interested in, much less dependent on, source issues, but he does address the question of possible biblical inspiration and concludes rather emphatically that "Although most of the texts treat this theme [of Creation] in a Christian spirit, the use of

---

loosely structured and more formulaic in style; easier to improvise, more difficult to memorize", LÖNNROTH, "*Iǫrð fannz æva né upphiminn*', p. 312.

[56] For excellent surveys of this field, see T. GUNNELL, "Performance studies", in: *Handbook of Pre-Modern Nordic Memory Studies*, ed. GLAUSER, HERMANN, and MITCHELL, 1, pp. 107-119, and ID., "Old Norse poetry in performance: Introduction", in: *Old Norse Poetry in Performance*, ed. B. MCMAHON and A. FERREIRA (London, 2022), pp. 4-17.

[57] E.g. ERMAN and WARREN, "The Iidiom principle".

[58] LÖNNROTH, "*Iǫrð fannz æva né upphiminn*", p. 314. Cf. Lord's discussion in LORD, *The Singer of Tales*, p. 42, of the young singer's learning process and "the syntactic patterns which the boy now begins to store in his experience and to use as a basis for new phrases".

[59] As SCHULTE, "Memory culture in the Viking age", pp. 61-62, notes, Lönnroth "has shown that at least three different thought patterns or themes are invoked by this formula: the 'Creation Myth', the 'Destruction Myth', or *Ragnarǫk*, and a 'Healing Charm' against diseases and outer enemies. Thus, the formula is subordinate to a larger metaphysical theme of chaos versus cosmic and social order as depicted in the eddic poem of *Vǫlospá*".

[60] LÖNNROTH, "*Iǫrð fannz æva né upphiminn*", p. 325.

Formulas, Collocations, and Cultural Memory 75

the formula cannot be derived from the Bible".[61] Constance Hieatt accepts that judgment,[62] and also concludes that it would be "reasonable to accept Lönnroth's 'Creation theme' as a common Old English type-scene".[63] Of course, the creation of the universe and the heavenly bodies, and their destruction at the end of the world, are the stuff of mythologies on a broad world-wide basis,[64] whether Christian, pre-Christian, or non-Christian. To me, the existence of parallel structures indicates circumstances of what might just as well have been complementarity, rather than competition, for the lay people of the medieval North.[65] Thus, the many strikingly similar elements of the creation myths reflected in *Vǫlospá* and *Genesis*, similar both to each other and to other mythologies, would perhaps have represented conflict and concern to a Christian clergyman, but such parallel buttressing might to others have suggested an empowering world view.

Beyond the specific alliterative *iǫrð – upphiminn* formula, a looser habituated collocation reflecting the same ideas such as (again using Old Swedish as the example), *iordh – himil* ('earth – heaven'), appears not only in the expected places in Old Swedish Bible translations (e.g. *Aff ophowe kapadhe gudh aff ālȝāngo himil oc iordh*),[66] but also in a variety of ecclesiastical contexts, such as commentaries and paraphrases of the Genesis creation story.[67] And, of course, these specific collocations constitute part of a larger set of cosmological

---

[61] LÖNNROTH, "*Iǫrð fannz æva né upphiminn*", p. 315.

[62] "But there is no good reason to suppose that the Bible is the immediate or primary source (...) whatever the relationship to the Bible here, it appears likely that the poet was also drawing on various features of a familiar type-scene", HIEATT, "Cædmon in Context', p. 495.

[63] HIEATT, "Cædmon in Context', p. 494, and thereby usefully allowing her to add several more Old English texts to the tally.

[64] See, for example, motifs A600-A899 and A1000-A1099 in *Motif-Index of Folk-Literature*, ed. S. THOMPSON, rev. edn., 2nd printing (Bloomington, 1966), as supplemented by such later works as *In Their Own Words: Introduction, Concordance of New Motifs, and Bibliography*, ed. J. WILDBRET and K. SIMONEAU (Cambridge MA, 1992: *Folk literature of South American Indians*).

[65] In other words, I accept the usefulness of such agreements and parallels for Christian missionary and proselytising efforts, but simultaneously want to avoid falling prey to the sense that something that is not provably *echt germanisch* should lack interest for us. It must surely be the case that a story line which might have been traditional is only enhanced if the more recent prevailing cultural norm has similar views, as I believe would have been the case with such creation themes in medieval Scandinavia.

[66] *Svenska medeltidens bibel-arbeten*, ed. KLEMMING, pp. 155, 157, and 158. Cf. the Gustav Wasa bibel (1541), "*I begynnel en kapadhe Gudh himmel och iord. Och iorden war ödhe och toom / och mörker war på diwpet / och Guds ande weffde offuer watnet*".

[67] See, e.g. *Svenska medeltidens bibel-arbeten*, ed. KLEMMING, pp. 31, 35, 37, 38, 40, 48, 60, 119, 462.

references to the various heavenly bodies, such as "*Oc giordhe gudh to'r to liws ool oc maana (...) oc th<u>e</u>r til giordhe han manga tia'rnor / oc satte th<u>e</u>m i himilin at liw a ow*er *iordhina*".[68] Although average parishioners would have understood little in a text in Latin (but certainly all ecclesiastics did), the Latin equivalents of these terms also make up part of church rituals, as in the *Benedictio herbarum,* when God is addressed as the creator of man "*et condidisti terram, solem et lunam et stellas et omnia celestia et terrestria*" ("and who established the earth, the sun, and the moon, and the stars, and all things, heavenly and earthly").[69]

Building on Lönnroth's observation that the Old Danish and Old English charms "invoke the holy cosmic powers, including 'heaven and earth', the sun (God and Saint Mary?)",[70] it is notable that most of the instances of the *iǫrð – upphiminn* formula, not just the charm texts, follow a pattern where the 'earth and heaven' phrase is associated with deities or heroes, very often followed by tertiary references to various celestial bodies. In other words, cases where 'earth and heaven' is only used adjectivally as a descriptor, as appears to be the case in, e.g. *Christ* 967-968 and *Þrymskviða* 2, are the exceptions. Thus, the majority of the cases of the *iǫrð – upphiminn* formula appear in the context of what appear to be acts related to calling or summoning higher powers.[71]

This feature is prominent in the Ribe rune stick, *c.* 1300,[72] which begins, "*Iorþ biþ ak uarþæ ok uphimæn, sol ok santæ *Maria ok sialfæn *Guþ drottin ...*" ("I pray Earth to guard and High Heaven, the sun and Saint Mary and Lord God himself ...").[73] A few centuries later, this same sort of invocation involving religious figures, heaven, earth, and sun, expanded to include the moon and all the planets, can be seen in the so-called *Vinjeboka*, a remarkable late fifteenth / early sixteenth-century Norwegian collection of charms, medical remedies, and Marian devotional materials:

---

[68] *Svenska medeltidens bibel-arbeten*, ed. KLEMMING, pp. 156.

[69] From 1493 (Brev. Linc. 1493, f. 13 v) in: *Signelser ock besvärjelser från medeltid ock nytid,* ed. E. LINDERHOLM (Stockholm, 1917-1940: *Svenska landsmål och svenskt folkliv* B, 41), pp. 39-40. There are, of course, variations on these combinations, e.g. the heaven-earth-sea-sun-moon group (*caelum-terra-mare-sol-luna*) in a Latin charm again theft (*Contra furtum*) in *Signelser ock besvärjelser*, ed. LINDERHOLM, p. 55.

[70] LÖNNROTH, "*Iǫrð fannz æva né upphiminn*", p. 325.

[71] Cf. E. BOZÓKY, *Charmes et prières apotropaïques* (Turnhout, 2003: *Typologie des sources du Moyen Age occidental* 86), p. 38, on the "designation of adjuvant powers" ("*nomination des puissances adjuvantes*").

[72] DR EM85; 493 M in *Samnordisk Runtextdatabas*. Ed. L. ELMEVIK, L. PETERSON, H. WILLIAMS *et al.*, available at: <http://www.nordiska.uu.se/forskn/samnord.htm> (Uppsala, 1993-).

[73] The translation follows *Samnordisk Runtextdatabas*.

In nomine Patris et Filii er Spiritus Sancti. Jeeg maner dich, Icht, om the hellige .v. vundh'r. Ieg maner teg om the hellige .iij. naglele, som i giennemginge Gudz hendh'r och fødh'r. Ieg maner teg, Icht, vith thz hellige sūare kors, som Wor Herre Iesus Christus toldhe sin sinnide døth opaa. Ieg maner thig, Icht, om sol och mane och allæ planet'r. Ieg maner theg, Icht, vith Gudz domstoll + (...)

In the name of the Father, the Son, and the Holy Spirit. I exhort you, Gout, by the five holy wounds. I exhort you by the three holy nails that pierced God's hands and feet. I exhort you, Gout, by the rugged holy cross on which Our Lord, Jesus Christ, suffered His blessed death. I exhort you, Gout, by the sun and the moon and all the planets. I exhort you, Gout, by God's judgement seat + (...)[74]

Language not very dissimilar to these charms, with a similar 'designation of adjuvant powers' – that is, heaven and earth, plus celestial object(s), plus a deity or more (in any order) – is also reflected in such invocations as the following, a charm against various demonic forces, collected in Skåne in the 1870s, *"vid himmel och Iord, vid sol och måne och vid alla sju stjernorna, vid alla heliga menniskors och vid vår herre Jesu Kristi ärofulla födelse och uppståndelse ifrån det döda"* ("by heaven and earth, by sun and moon and by all seven stars, by all the saints and by our Lord, Jesus Christ's glorious birth and resurrection from the dead").[75] Likewise when a charm from Småland in the 1840s conjures against rats and mice, it does so *"vid den heliga graf, som vår Herre låg uti, vid himmel och Iord, vid sol och myne, vid stena och planet'r, vid Gatten och land"* ("by the holy grave in which our Lord lay, by heaven and earth, by sun and moon, by stones and plants, by water and land").[76]

Of course, references to the various celestial bodies of the solar system are hardly unique images to Nordic charms,[77] but these loose collocations involving heaven and earth, often in combination with the other heavenly bodies, had strength on the one hand from their histories and habituation within the tradi-

---

[74] *Vinjeboka: Den eldste svartebok fra norsk middelalder*, ed. O. GARSTEIN (Oslo, 1993), pp. 60-61, 68-70, 70-72 (nos. 6, 11, 13 [the last a Latin charm]). Garstein dates the earliest texts in the book to *c.* 1480.

[75] *Signelser ock besvärjelser*, ed. LINDERHOLM, p. 202 (No. 408). As Linderholm has conveniently brought all the Swedish charm materials together, I refer to his edition, but note that he has this charm from Eva Wigström, who collected the charm in Östra Göinge in the 1870s.

[76] *Signelser ock besvärjelser*, ed. LINDERHOLM, p. 220 (No. 431).

[77] A strikingly similar celestial list is invoked in, e.g. W.W. SKEAT, *Malay Magic, being an Introduction to the Folklore and Popular Religion of the Malay Peninsula* (London, 1900), p. 574.

tion, and simultaneously were reinforced by ecclesiastical ritual, and not surprisingly tend to permeate the various national charm traditions.[78]

Final Thoughts

As Jasper Frøkjær Sørensen has urged us to consider on numerous occasions, magic represents a "conceptual blending",[79] one where the role of language in all its many subtleties (e.g. often archaic and fossilised in form, emotional and expressive in mood, iterative and redundant in the context of ritual) can hardly be overstated.[80] It is perhaps tempting, because of the closeness of the function of collocations to that of formulas in a system based on 'composition-in-performance', to interpret them solely from the perspective of their potential usefulness to ritual performers, and to undervalue the evocative function of collocations to audiences / hearers. Although I by no means dismiss the 'pre-fab' function of collocations, my concern here is with their value as carriers of emotions and associations, as reflexes of traditional belief, and as associative conduits for hearers to such concepts as authority, power, and efficaciousness.

In considering the sort of emotional and intellectual resonance a collocation can have, we might remind ourselves of the important function so-called *historiolas* have in charms, where even very brief references can call to mind entire narratives.[81] Collocations, both as discreet habituated linguistic units and as part of larger patterned expressions of rituals and narratives, bring with them

---

[78] See, for example, the large number of such collocations among the charm materials in *Norske Hexeformularer og Magiske Opskrifter*, ed. A.C. BANG (Christiania, 1901-1902: heaven and earth: pp. 6, 32, 36, 38, 39, 42, 67, 86, 112, 122, 166, 379, 380, 416, 535, 547, 548, 583, 587, 650, 652, 657, 661, 664, 667, 670, 671, 705, 707, and 713; heaven and earth with other celestial bodies: pp. 40, 43-44, 46, 50, 146, 378, 591, 594, 602, 603, 653, 669, 708, 709, and 714.

[79] E.g. J. SØRENSEN, *A Cognitive Theory of Magic* (Lanham MD, 2007); ID., "Acts that work: A cognitive approach to ritual agency", *Method & Theory in the Study of Religion* 19.3-4 (2007), pp. 281-300.

[80] See SØRENSEN, *A Cognitive Theory of Magic*, pp. 88-93.

[81] The literature on this topic is enormous, of course; for theoretical orientation, see D. FRANKFURTER, "Narrating power: The theory and practice of the magical historiola in ritual spells", in *Ancient Magic and Ritual Power*, ed. M. MEYER and P. MIRECKI (Leiden, 1995: *Religions in the Graeco-Roman World* 129), pp. 455-476; D. FRANKFURTER, "Narratives that do things", in: *Religion: Narrating Religion*, ed. S.I. JOHNSTON (Farmington Hills MI, 2017), pp. 95-106. On the Nordic situation in contemporary light, see FROG, "Mythology in cultural practice: a methodological framework for historical analysis", *REM: The Retrospective Methods Network Newsletter* 10 (2015), pp. 33-57; and MITCHELL, "Notes on *historiolas*".

a different sort of quality, namely, their own previously established systems of emotional referents, what I believe Wolfgang Iser means when he speaks of the "virtual dimension", the meeting ground of text and imagination in the world of written literature, but an idea readily understood as the space between the spoken charm text and its audience.[82]

As Kerewsky Halpern and Foley found in their analyses of Serbian charms, "... the source of [the charm's] phenomenological power lies in the ritual act of making the collective inheritance of the past the living inheritance of the present",[83] a perspective very close, of course, to Tangherlini's idea of "tradition memory".[84] I would argue that collocations can in a small way be contributing factors in creating such sensations – minor, of course, when set against more significant elements like *historiolas*, remedies, ritual actions, and other foregrounded features. Still, collocations, redolent as they can be of spiritual traditions, are also capable of evoking strong emotional responses, and have their roles to play as well in the enduring power of charm magic over time.

---

[82] Cf. W. ISER, *The Implied Reader* (Baltimore, 1974), p. 290, "The literary text activates our own faculties, enabling us to recreate the world it presents. The product of this creative activity is what we might call the virtual dimension of the text, which endows it with its reality. This virtual dimension is not the text itself, nor is it the imagination of the reader: it is the coming together of the text and imagination".

[83] KEREWSKY HALPERN and FOLEY, "The power of the word", p. 924; later, this view has been later developed by Foley into his well-known formulation concerning "how performance serves as the enabling event, and tradition as the enabling referent, for the enactment and reception of verbal art" (FOLEY, "Word-power, performance, and tradition", p. 275).

[84] TANGHERLINI, "'Where was I?'".

A Formula Is a Habit Colliding with Life

SLAVICA RANKOVIĆ and MILOŠ RANKOVIĆ

In a recent article, Daniel Sävborg argued for a more formal, more theoretical and up-to-date approach to the formula in general and in the Icelandic saga prose in particular.[1] The same motivation provides the impetus for the present volume as a collective, cross-disciplinary attempt to address the issue from various angles, and so the first part of this article constitutes our contribution to the general debate. It also provides theoretical underpinnings for the 'Distributed Reading' project (featured in the second part) – a reading practice that traces networks of formulas in traditional literature, with those pertaining to the sagas of Icelanders and Grettir the Strong's temper being used as a case study here.

1. What Is the Formula?

Recognising the Formula

We will begin this section with a joke – a rhetorical decision which in itself

---

[1] D. SÄVBORG, "The formula in Icelandic saga prose", *Saga-Book* 42 (2018), pp. 51-86.

New Light on Formulas in Oral Poetry and Prose, ed. Daniel SÄVBORG and Bernt Ø. THORVALDSEN, Utrecht Studies in Medieval Literacy, 57 (Turnhout: Brepols, 2023), pp. 81-111.

might be recognisable as a formula – an opening formula, to be precise, the so-called 'icebreaker'. Here it comes:

Fig. 1 'The formula joke'. Cartoon by Miloš RANKOVIĆ.

In its light-hearted way, the cartoon in Fig. 1 attempts to address the question we are grappling with in this volume – that is, what is a formula – and is also indicative of the pervasive attitude towards it. Namely, not knowing *precisely* what the formula is has not prevented most scholars from studying its effects in a given text and, in some cases (very much including our own),[2] studying them in some detail. The main point seems to be that there is this recurring pattern and that it is recognised as such: 'here it comes again'. At first, this might seem like a topsy-turvy approach, as it stands to reason that one should first know what one's object of study is in order to study it, but more often than not, the other way around is the norm rather than the exception, as we tend to name phenomena – 'evolution', 'memory', 'dark matter' ... 'formula' – and study

---

[2] See, for example: S. RANKOVIĆ, "The temporality of the (immanent) saga: Tinkering with formulas", in: *Dating the Sagas: Reviews and Revisions*, ed. E. MUNDAL (Copenhagen, 2013), pp. 199-233; EAD., "The performative non-canonicity of the canonical: *Íslendingasǫgur* and their traditional referentiality", in: *The Performance of Christian and Pagan Storyworlds: Non-Canonical Chapters of the History of Nordic Medieval Literature*, ed. L.B. MORTENSEN *et al.* (Turnhout, 2013), pp. 247-272; EAD., "Immanent seas, scribal havens: Distributed reading of formulaic networks in the sagas of Icelanders", *European Review* 22.1 (2014), pp. 45-54; EAD., "In the refracted light of the mirror phrases *sem fyrr var sagt* and *sem fyrr var ritat*: Sagas of Icelanders and the orality-literacy interfaces, *Journal of English and Germanic Philology* 115.3 (2016), pp. 299-332; EAD., "The exquisite tempers of Grettir the Strong", *Scandinavian Studies* 89.3 (2017), pp. 375-412. EAD., "Traversing the space of the oral-written continuum: Medially connotative back-referring formula in *Landnámabók*", in: *Moving Words: Literacies, Texts and Verbal Communities of the Nordic Middle Ages*, ed. A.C. MULLIGAN and E. MUNDAL (Turnhout, 2019), pp. 255-278.

their manifestations and effects in nature and culture long before we can fully understand or define them. Of course, as Sävborg quite rightly warns us, the danger here is that the formula "might be regarded as an uncomplicated phenomenon, whose character, function and meaning are obvious".[3] And yet, just the same, this deceptively simple 'here-it-comes-again' principle might be adopted as a tentative point of departure for diametrically opposite reasons – out of sheer respect for the complexity of the phenomenon. For, while the formula seems easy enough to recognise, it is notoriously difficult to theorise.

Nowadays, artificial networks excel at recognising formulas too. We have in mind here GPT-2, the 2019 machine learning language model created at the OpenAI research laboratory in San Francisco, which has, among other impressive achievements, managed to produce a rather plausible newspaper article, following a short (and distinctly *im*plausible) human prompt about a herd of English-speaking unicorns supposedly being discovered somewhere deep in the Andes mountains.[4] Rising to the challenge, GPT-2 has not only successfully employed the relevant generic conventions regarding news reporting (e.g. supplying a credible name, area of expertise and academic affiliation of the South American researcher lucky enough to have made this "shocking discovery"), but has, in an attempt to address the very implausibility of the "bizarre creatures" it was tasked with writing about, also offered some 'scientific' hypotheses as to their origins and how they might have ended up speaking "perfect English". What is most difficult to fathom here is that GPT-2 came up with this text even though no explicit rules (e.g. pertaining to grammar and language in general or to article writing in particular) were ever programmed into it, nor was this language model in any way primed in advance to identify task-specific concepts such as, in this case, 'unicorn', 'scientist', or 'shocking'. And yet, much like a child learning a language, quite 'on its own' and purely on the basis of the trial-and-error principle (in this case, simply by trying to predict the next likely word, given all the previous ones), GPT-2 was able to pick up on all the relevant rules and conventions – the article writing formulas – just by virtue

---

[3] SÄVBORG, "The formula in saga prose", p. 51.
[4] See A. RADFORD et al., "Better language models and their implications", *OpenAI*, 14 February 2019 (available online at <https://openai.com/blog/better-language-models/>). Slavica discusses GPT-2 in S. RANKOVIĆ, "Spectres of agency: The case of *Fóstbrǿðra saga* and its distributed author", in: *In Search for the Culprit: Aspects of Medieval Authorship*, ed. S. GROPPER and L. RÖSLI (Berlin, 2021), pp. 175-192. We address the explosive developments in AI since 2021 in S. RANKOVIĆ and M. RANKOVIĆ, "Timing/taming Grettir's temper: A distributed reading", in: *Time, Space and Narrative in Medieval Icelandic Literature*, ed. B. ALLPORT and A. FINLEY (forthcoming).

of being exposed to *c*. eight million pages of the Reddit dataset[5] on which it was trained.[6] In a way, the experiments with GPT-2 seem to confirm Derrida's view of writing / text as a self-replicating machine: the "kind of machine that is in turn productive".[7] They also echo the view of the nineteenth century Serbian folklorist, Vuk Karadžić who, based on his vast experience of oral poetry in the Balkans, estimated that, for a person who knows around fifty different songs, it should be easy enough to compose a new one.[8]

Theorising the Formula

So much for recognising the formula. Theorising, as already noted, is quite another matter. Already, if we were to take our opening joke seriously for a moment and unpack it a little, this becomes instantly apparent. For example, what, exactly, has 'come again' in the above cartoon (Fig. 1)? Comparing closely the pattern in the first square with its re-enactment in the second – the circle-ellipse ratios of the 'head' bits of the individual pattern segments, the size of the angles formed by those with 'open mouths', the frequency and amplitudes of the looped bottom bits, the whirls of the end flourishes, the spaces between the segments, etc. – reveal variation and diversity at the very heart of repetition. And that is just the pure graphics and physics of the hand-written (as opposed to mechanically reproduced) mark that we are talking about. What about the variations along other important dimensions of the joke – linguistic, medial, performative, contextual, i.e. who is relating it, to whom, for what purpose, in what circumstances?

---

[5] Reddit <https://www.reddit.com/> is a social media platform, an online forum comprising user-generated content, news, conversations, images, videos, etc.

[6] Vastly more capable large language models have since been trained, such as GPT-3.5 and 4 used by ChatGPT (see <https://chat.openai.com>). Their 'emerging abilities' appear to correspond to their ever greater size more than to the intervening advances in machine learning algorithms (see <https://en.wikipedia.org/wiki/Large_language_model#Emergent_abilities>). We understand these abilities as formulas that did not emerge out of machine learning algorithms in the past few years, but from the evolution of language over millennia.

[7] Cf. J. DERRIDA, *Margins of Philosophy*, trans. A. BASS (Chicago, 1982), p. 316.

[8] In the preface to his 1823 Leipzig edition of Serbian folk poetry, Karadžić writes: "*Koji čovek zna pedeset različni pjesama, (ako je za taj posao) njemu je lasno novu pjesmu spjevati*" ("If a man knows fifty different songs (provided he is for that sort of job), for him it is easy to compose a new song"; Slavica's translation). Cf. *Srpske narodne pjesme*, ed. V.S. KARADŽIĆ (Belgrade, 1976; original edition 1841-1862), 1 , p. 530.

A Formula Is a Habit Colliding with Life 85

Speaking of contexts, here is a confession: Miloš created the cartoon in Fig. 1 especially for this article, as a means of enabling translation into print of the joke that Slavica delivered orally / aurally back in 2019, at the conference that has given rise to this volume. On that occasion, Slavica did not write the pattern but rather performed / enacted it with the horizontal movement of a raised forearm, with the fist alternately opening and closing. Whether the ideograms in Fig. 1 reminded you a little of the cursive letter 'g' (with oddly placed '<' and '=' signs) or a tweeting bird, this, in fact, is their pre-history – the fist (opening and closing), the forearm and the elbow, moving from left to right. And yet, even there, in the conference room, Slavica did not tell the joke exactly as she had first heard it – from her husband, in Serbian rather than in English. But even if, in turn, we can trust Miloš to have at least repeated the verbal part of the joke exactly as he had heard it himself – long time ago, as a boy at some Belgrade playground – the context in which he told it to Slavica (and not 'Slavica, his wife', but rather 'Slavica, his debate opponent') was completely different, as indeed was his purpose at the time: not simply to amuse his audience and make them smile, but to illustrate the point he was making about formulas – just as we are both doing right now.

All this taken into account, one might well wonder if the above instances indeed amount to the same pattern / joke, and if not, at what point do the variations precipitate enough so as to constitute a different pattern / joke. What would be that difference that makes *the* difference? Or is this in a sense akin to the well-attested habit of the oral singers and storytellers who, as they re-perform (which is to say, recreate) their material, continuously adapt it to different contexts and audiences, while claiming (and often firmly believing) that they did not change a single word?[9] After all, whether told / performed orally or represented as a cartoon, whether featuring a graphic or a gestural pattern (the specific one described here or an entirely different one), enacted by children in a Belgrade playground or by scholars at the Tartu conference, time and again, in its various incarnations, the joke dutifully performs its 'here it comes again' trick. It therefore appears to be the same and a different joke / pattern all at once. In each case, something was definitely recognised as having 'come again', but if that something is not in the exact words of the joke, or in the particular (out-)lines of the pattern / gesture, then where is it? When is it? What is it?

---

[9] See, for example, the conversation (discussed below) between Milman Parry's interpreter / assistant, Nikola Vujnović and the singer Mujo Kukuruzović.

This non-literary example, purposefully chosen for the estrangement effect, reflects the kind of difficulties that arise in an attempt to define the formula, whether in poetry or in prose: no sooner than a pattern / rule is identified, then the number of variations, exceptions, nested structures, as well as the complex relationships that arise between the instances seem to proliferate beyond anything that can be usefully generalised. That is why, in our work so far, we have been more inclined towards analogies and metaphors, ways of envisioning formulas and how they work in a given text, rather than to proffering definitions.[10] Another, related reason why we have been wary of definitions is that they have a way of acquiring a life of their own, becoming a force of gravity and inertia beyond the contexts in which they have originally arisen. When it comes to the formula, the one by Milman Parry must be the most famous case in point (not least judging by the number of times it was quoted at the Tartu conference and, hence, likely to be referenced in this volume too): "The formula in the Homeric Poems may be defined as a group of words which is regularly employed under the same metrical conditions to express a given essential idea".[11] And no wonder. After all, along with his student, Albert B. Lord, Parry is considered to be the father of the oral-formulaic theory which, whether adhered to or criticised, has become an obligatory point of passage for all scholars dealing with oral or orally derived literatures. Although Parry was not the originator of the term 'formula',[12] he was nevertheless the one who made it an object of study in its own right and strove to generalise its use beyond the confines of Homeric epic. And yet, in using his definition as the customary point of departure, we fear that we not only do Parry a great honour, but also a great

---

[10] See, for example, RANKOVIĆ, "The temporality of the (immanent) saga", p. 160, where a thorough examination of the 'blue-black clothes' formula instances in the sagas of Icelanders has led Slavica to a following conclusion: "[...] instead of a sharply defined entity, a picture of the formula that emerges is something resembling a cloud, with a tentative, burgeoning core [of most typical instances] and smaller or larger masses that diverge (as variations themselves show common characteristics and group) to the point of tearing themselves away from the fuzzy fringes (of usage), on their way to fusing with a neighbouring bulk or becoming another cloud, another formula. The sense of direction and purpose implied in this metaphor, i.e. that the 'cloud' and its separating 'masses' are somehow 'on their way' to become this or that, is something that can, like in the case of biological speciation, be identified and speculated in retrospect only".

[11] M. PARRY, "Studies in the epic technique of oral verse-making, I, Homer and Homeric style", *Harvard Studies in Classical* Philology 41 (1930), pp. 73-148, at p. 80.

[12] The term was already in use at the time, among others by Parry's mentor at the Sorbonne, Antoine Meillet, who also pointed to the formula's oral origins in Homer: "Homeric epic is entirely composed of formulas handed down from poet to poet". Cf. A. MEILLET, *Les origines indo-européennes des mètres grecs* (Paris, 1923), p. 61, as quoted in M. PARRY, *The Making of Homeric Verse: The Collected Papers of Milman Parry*, ed. A. PARRY (Oxford, 1971), p. 9.

injustice. We quote it (if anything, unlike analogies, definitions tend to be pithier, more quotable), but then usually proceed to dismantle it, listing all the ways in which it fails to relate to our particular (often non-Homeric) examples, faulting Parry for being too insistent upon either the lexical fixity, or the importance of the metre (especially if we are dealing with formulaic prose), or conceiving of the formula too narrowly by not taking into account larger bits of text (motifs, themes, scenes) rather than just "groups of words", not to mention his notion of "essential idea" which some scholars find too specific, (even "banal"),[13] others, on the other hand, too vague and ambiguous.[14]

Of course, it is not the fact that we query and criticise Parry's definition that is bothersome, but that we should insist upon doing so even after the author himself had, since first publishing these words in his 1928 doctoral dissertation (as a twenty-six-year-old), undergone a transformative experience during his fieldwork in the Balkans and had invested an extraordinary effort in refining his preconceived notions about oral traditions and the function of formulas. Parry's notes, taken between 1933 to 1935, testify to this effect: "It was only when the South Slavic poetry showed me the actual practice of a sung poetry that I saw how foolish my notions had been".[15] Still, even in that same doctoral thesis, some finer and more complex notions such as "formula types" and "systems" were already introduced, but scholars have seldom engaged with them in any greater depth.[16] However, the notes Parry made on his research of South Slavic singers' practices in preparation for the book he was planning to write before his life was tragically cut short at the age of thirty-three,[17] bear witness to far more nuanced views on oral culture in general and formulas in particular. By this time Parry had given up on modern, post-print notions of "fixity", noting

---

[13] Cf. Daniel Sävborg's discussion of John Miles Foley's criticism of Parry's definition in: SÄVBORG, "The formula in saga prose", p. 60.

[14] See, for example, M.W. EDWARDS, "Homer and Oral Tradition: The Formula, Part 1", *Oral Tradition* 1.2 (1986), pp. 171-230, at p. 190.

[15] PARRY, *The Making of Homeric Verse*, p. 455.

[16] For some notable exceptions and productive engagements with Parry's concept of formulaic systems, see, for example: D.K. FRY, "Old English formulas and systems", *English Studies* 48 (1967), pp. 193-204; or, more recently, FROG, "Formulaic language and linguistic multiforms: Questions of complexity and variation", in: *Formula: Units of Speech, 'Words' of Verbal Art*, ed. FROG (Helsinki, 2017), pp. 252-270.

[17] Milman Parry's short but fruitful life has long fascinated scholars of oral poetry and the general public alike. Most recently, his life and work have caught the attention of the biographer Robert Kanigel, best known as the author of *The Man Who Knew Infinity: A Life of the Genius Ramanujan*, which was made into a 2015 feature film, starring Dev Patel and Jeremy Irons. Cf. R. KANIGEL, *Hearing Homer's Song: The Brief Life and Big Idea of Milman Parry* (New York, 2021).

how, for example, "a singer who learns a song from another singer makes his own version more or less from the same themes (...) but almost altogether out of his own verses",[18] and when these verses actually happen to be identical, he lists a number of constraints (not only metrical and lexical, but semantic, contextual and cultural) that makes fixity (in our sense of the word) more likely – but still not a must. Parry also does not conceive of the formula any more as a necessarily small unit, a "group of words", but rather broadens the concept so as to include groups of verses, scenes, or themes, noting their differences as those of degree rather than of kind, i.e. fundamental:

> Indeed, it is obvious that the distinction between the verse and the simple theme is only one of degree, and that even as the verse and the theme might be called formulas, so the simple verse might be designated as one of the types of simple themes.[19]

What definition of the formula (if any) Milman Parry would have offered in his ill-fated book *Ćor Huso* will remain forever in the realm of speculation. What we do know is that the eponymous Bosnian bard Ćor Huso ('Blind Huso') eventually morphed into the more universally sounding *Singer of Tales*, the book published by Parry's assistant on the Balkan adventures and a formidable scholar in his own right – Albert B. Lord. And although the student has amply acknowledged his debt to the teacher, adopting and incorporating Parry's various insights, the last word on any matter in the *Singer of Tales* is, after all, Lord's own.[20] In fact, while he dedicates a whole chapter to the formula and discusses its role in oral composition in great detail, the actual definition that Lord offers is the familiar one he adopts from Parry's old thesis (with none of the subsequent refinements),[21] which might just be the reason why this definition became so familiar in the first place – owing to the great success of the *Singer of Tales* which was the first to perpetuate it. After all, nothing in Parry's later notes, or in Lord's own writing on the topic, was quite as pithy and quotable as that definition; nothing was, indeed, as 'formulaic'.

While, sadly, Milman Parry did not get to develop his later insights and ideas to the full, he has still left us something of exceptional value, a proper treasure-trove of insights yet to be fully quarried and which Harvard University

---

[18] PARRY, *The Making of Homeric Verse*, p. 442.

[19] PARRY, *The Making of Homeric Verse*, p. 446.

[20] A.B. LORD, *The Singer of Tales* (Cambridge, Massachusetts, 2000; originally published in 1960).

[21] LORD, *The Singer of Tales*, p. 30.

A Formula Is a Habit Colliding with Life 89

has so generously shared with us digitally: the 'Milman Parry Collection of Oral Literature'.[22] This collection not only features recorded poetry but also the recordings and transcripts of the interviews Parry and his native assistant / interpreter Nikola Vujnović conducted with the Balkan singers. During these interviews, the singers were often induced to 'theorise' about their own practices, including their usage of formulas. This resource, which Parry already envisaged would be valuable to scholars to come,[23] is, however, still woefully underused. Most likely, this is due to the language barrier which forces non-native scholars to either give up in advance or rely on the sparsely available, highly selective and, regrettably, not always reliable translations of the transcripts, not to mention all the important non-verbal aspects of the actual recordings that are usually left by the wayside – intonation, significant pauses, and such that sometimes speak volumes.[24]

Delving into this material first-hand has proven fruitful, not least to Lord's own former pupil, John Miles Foley. While in their pioneering efforts Parry and Lord had, understandably, focused more on the formula's utility and its role in the mechanics of oral composition,[25] Foley has, as the next step, paid more mind to the way formulas signify and create aesthetic effects through a specific kind of traditional intertextuality, or "traditional referentiality", as he has termed it.[26] Foley's work has gone a long way towards dispelling the past misconceptions about formulas being akin to literary clichés and has revolutionised the way we now read oral and orally-derived literature.[27] However, here we

---

[22] This resource is available at <https://mpc.chs.harvard.edu>. Last accessed 1 March 2021.

[23] Parry notes: "These volumes are in no way meant to be finished work, but first a source of material for the author for a work of a very certain sort, and then a source for other students who may either wish to use the material for their own ends or to better the conclusions which I myself have drawn" (PARRY, *The Making of Homeric Verse*, p. 439).

[24] Slavica addresses these issues in depth in S. RANKOVIĆ, "Managing the 'Boss': Epistemic violence, resistance, and negotiations in Milman Parry's and Nikola Vujnović's *Pričanja* with Salih Ugljanin", *Oral Tradition* 27.1 (2012), pp. 5-66, available online at <https://journal.oraltradition.org/wp-content/uploads/files/articles/27i/02_27.1.pdf>.

[25] This, however, does not mean that Parry and Lord were unaware of the special aesthetics of formulas. Consider, for instance, how in the following passage Lord anticipates some of the ideas that Foley will develop more fully: "[The singer's] oft-used phrases and lines lose something in sharpness, yet many of them must resound with overtones from the dim past whence they come. Were we to train our ears to catch these echoes, we might cease to apply the clichés of another criticism to oral poetry and thereby become aware of its own riches" (LORD, *The Singer of Tales*, p. 65).

[26] J.M. FOLEY, *Immanent Art: From Structure to Meaning in Traditional Oral Epic* (Bloomington and Indianapolis, 1991).

[27] It has since come to our attention that, coincidentally, the Russian scholar Olga A. Smirnitskaya has, in her own independent efforts to resolve the apparent 'mechanism' vs 'art'

would like to draw particular attention to an important further inroad into defining the formula that Foley made by directly drawing on the South Slavic singers' notion of *reč*, that is 'word', and recognising it, in a way, as the singers' own definition of the formula. Foley's point of departure is an interview Parry conducted with the Bosnian singer (*guslar*) Mujo Kukuruzović (through his Herzegovinian interpreter and assistant mentioned above, Nikola Vujnović). Asked about the way in which he learns a new song, Mujo is full of professional pride and so he utters the following 'boast', so frequently expressed by other South Slavic singers as well:[28]

> MK: So now, brother, you go ahead and find some song I do not know. Then, brother, read it to me twice and then give me the *gusle* [the musical instrument used for accompaniment], brother. If I make a mistake, I'll give you a finger off my hand.
> NV: And with everything just so?
> MK: Just so; I'll repeat every single *reč*.[29]

Of course, Mujo Kukuruzović was given a chance to make good on his boast, and although he did not repeat every single *word*, he sure did repeat every single *reč* – at least according to his own understanding of the word 'word' in this context, and so Nikola Vujnović and Milman Parry could not claim his finger after all. As John Foley explains:

dichotomy, come up with ideas very similar to Foley's, and at approximately the same time too. However, due to the language barrier and other external factors, Smirnitskaya's extensive work on Old Germanic literature still remains largely unknown in the West. Fortunately, this is to be rectified thanks to the dedicated efforts of her former student, Ilya V. Sverdlov, to whom we wish to express a deep gratitude for sharing with us, ahead of publication, his English translation of Smirnitskaya's seminal work on Old Germanic alliterative verse (originally published in Russian in 1994). Compare, for example, how the following passage from Smirnitskaya's work resonates with Foley's well-known concepts of traditional 'word power' and 'traditional referentiality': "(...) for a given listener, a word acquires semantic multi-dimensionality only when, and affects him / her emotionally only in the degree that, the said listener is able to position the line that this word occurs in inside a complex network of other similar lines, only if it triggers memories of concrete epic texts that the listener has stored in his memory. This, of course, means that a listener is, on one hand, a full participant in the given poetic tradition, and, on the other hand, that the epic *word* has a specific, peculiar role in re-creation, reinstatement, re-establishment of the epic wor*l*d (...)". Cf. O.A. SMIRNITSKAYA, *The Verse and Language of Old Germanic Poetry*, ed. and trans. I.V. SVERDLOV (Tempe, forthcoming), the author's emphases.

[28] See, for example, LORD, *The Singer of Tales*, pp. 26-27, where Nikola Vujnović asks the singer Sulejman Makić very similar questions to those he poses to Kukuruzović (cf. above), and receives a similar answer too.

[29] J.M. FOLEY, *How to Read an Oral Poem* (Urbana, 2002), p. 12.

A Formula Is a Habit Colliding with Life 91

> For the guslar a *reč* in a song is clearly not the same thing as a textual [graphical] word, defined like those you're reading now by the convention of white space on either side. Nor is it a lexical word certified by inclusion in a dictionary, nor some abstraction defined in linguistic terms. For Kukuruzović a word in oral poetry is a unit of utterance, an irreducible atom of performance, a speech-act. (...) [W]hether phrases, lines, multiple lines, or scenes, these *reči* function like whole integers – rather than fractions – in a verbal mathematics. (...) The scenes and motifs, with their narrative rather than metrical boundaries, are also the whole units and not fractions (...).[30]

It is in these terms of the whole (if variously sized) "integers of traditional meaning"[31] that Foley defines the formula. And so, he warns us, "the textually conditioned readers":[32] "If we insist on reducing the singer's *reči* [read: formulas], to our words, if we 'murder to dissect', we will blunt a finely honed instrument of expression that has long served as the prescribed channel for communication".[33]

Defining the Formula

Our own view of the formula comes very close to Foley's here, but takes this notion of not reducing the singer's *reči* to our words a step further through distinguishing between a formula and any specific strings of words expressing it, such as, for example, those that Foley quotes as *reči*: "miserable captive", or "Mustajbey of Lika was drinking wine", or entire blocks of verses describing, for instance, a hero arming himself for battle.[34] To account for various degrees of lexical flexibility within *reči*, Foley, as we have seen, defines formulas as "integers of traditional meaning", but in our view, traditional meanings are not much more stable than are the words in the 'post-print' sense comprising *reči*, i.e. the words in the singers' sense. When considering the meanings, we cannot simply pluck out formula instances from the surrounding narrative (formulas are not like Lego pieces) but must also carefully pay mind to how each instance plays out in its particular context of usage. For example, Slavica's research of the saga formula relating to a hero who is said to wear blue-black clothing

---

[30] FOLEY, *How to Read an Oral Poem*, pp. 13-14.
[31] Cf. J.M. FOLEY and P. RAMEY, "Oral theory and medieval studies", in: *Medieval Oral Literature*, ed. K. REICHL (Berlin, 2012), pp. 71-102, at p. 80.
[32] FOLEY, *How to Read an Oral Poem*, p. 14.
[33] FOLEY, *How to Read an Oral Poem*, p. 14.
[34] Cf. FOLEY, *How to Read an Oral Poem*, p. 13.

before setting off to kill (usually in revenge) has shown that, in different instances, even when the familiar formulation "X / he was in a blue-black cloak" ("*X / hann var í kápu blári*") is employed, the "traditional meaning" of the phrase can differ subtly or even vastly, depending on the specific context of application.[35] Thus, for example, when, clad in his blue-black cloak (*í kápu blári*),[36] Gísli Súrsson sets off to kill his brother-in-law in revenge, the hero's action and its outcome resemble more closely that of Skarphéðinn who, on his own revenge mission, wears a blue-black jacket (*í blám stakki*)[37] rather than the cloak, or Valla-Ljótr who is in blue-black tunic (*í blám kyrtli*),[38] or Hrafnkell who is simply said to wear blue-black clothes (*í blám klæðum*),[39] and so on, than another such instance in *Gisla saga* itself, where the hero is again said to be *í kápu blári*, but where he proceeds to gift this precious (if compromising) item to his cowardly slave as a part of a ruse, using the poor, witless fellow as a decoy. Despite the same wording being used in both instances, in the latter it is the wearer who ends up killed, and in circumstances meant to be comical rather than customarily solemn.[40] And what of the complex, meta-textual employment of the phrase in *Vatnsdœla saga*, in which Ingimundr the Old's appearance in blue-black cloak (*í blári kápu*) turns out to be an act of supreme self-sacrifice, his choice of clothes constituting a deliberate ploy meant to be misread by both his killer *and* the reader?[41] Even in these rare cases when, for once, the formula *wording* is rather stable,[42] its 'traditional *meaning*' appears to be shifting, drifting, mutating – in other words, it ever remains context-sensitive, as the habits of usage continuously collide with idiosyncrasies of life.

It is interesting that biologists, trying to define the gene (and later the culturologists trying to define the 'meme'[43]) have run into the same sort of

---

[35] Cf. RANKOVIĆ, "The temporality of the (immanent) saga", pp. 199-233.

[36] *Gísla saga Súrssonar*, in: *Vestfirðinga sögur*, ed. B.K. ÞÓRÓLFSSON and G. JÓNSSON (Reykjavík, 1943), p. 52.

[37] *Brennu-Njáls saga*, ed. E.Ó. SVEINSSON (Reykjavík, 1954), p. 231.

[38] *Valla-Ljóts saga*, in: *Eyfirðinga sögur*, ed. J. KRISTJANSSON (Reykjavík, 1956), p. 245.

[39] *Hrafnkels saga Freysgoða*, in: *Austfirðinga sögur*, ed. J. Jóhannesson (Reykjavík, 1950), p. 104.

[40] *Gísla saga*, pp. 64-65.

[41] *Vatnsdœla saga*, ed. E.Ó. SVEINSSON (Reykjavík, 1939), p. 60. The metatextual employment of this instance is discussed in more detail in RANKOVIĆ, "The temporality of the (immanent) saga", pp. 179-180 and EAD., "The performative non-canonicity of the canonical", pp. 267-268.

[42] We prefer this notion of stability (e.g. as opposed to the 'fossilisation' or 'crystallisation' which are sometimes used in relation to formulas), because it keeps the potential for change alive and open-ended, even if change is unlikely.

[43] While the term 'meme' (echoing 'gene') was coined by Richard Dawkins (cf. R.

problems that we are facing in conceptualising the formula, which is probably not very surprising, given that these phenomena all perform the same basic function as units of inheritance, only on different substrata. At the beginning, just as the groups of repeating words were quickly identified as formulas by the early proponents of the oral-formulaic theory, so were genes conceived of as particular strings of nucleotides that directly translate into particular phenotypic traits, such as, for instance 'blue eyes' or 'red hair'. Soon, however, such 'low hanging fruit' cases have proven to be an exception rather than the rule as, in the much larger number of cases, there is no such direct mapping between the genetic code and the resulting traits – for example, when it comes to height and weight, such mapping is much more complex. More often than not, it turns out that the same strings of nucleotides can be 'responsible' for more than one trait and, vice versa, one trait might come as a consequence of a complex interaction between different nucleotide sequences, not to mention the further complexities due to the important role of the environment (microscopic and macroscopic) in which the processes of inheritance take place, which has made 'epigenetics' as important an area of study to geneticists as genetics.[44]

The difference between a gene and a trait, and between the formula and its instance in a narrative is analogous (and here we are – back to analogies) to the difference between a recipe (as a series of instructions, or a chef's decisions, choices) and a cake. Some decisions, such as putting a cherry on top of the cake will have this one-to-one, local correspondence with the resulting effect, whereas the effects of the decision to, for example, stir the mixture rather than to shake it will be more distributed throughout the texture of the cake and therefore not as easy to point to locally, as it is to a cherry perching on its top. Furthermore, the same recipes will never produce exactly the same cakes because

DAWKINS, *The Selfish Gene* (Oxford, 1976); see also: ID., *The Extended Phenotype* (Oxford, 1982)), the memetic approach to studying culture has been popularised and further developed by Daniel C. Dennett (see in particular: D.C. DENNETT, *Darwin's Dangerous Idea: Evolution and the Meanings of Life* (New York, 1995)). For an attempt at application of the memetic theory to the formula, see M.D.C. DROUT, "A meme-based approach to oral traditional theory", *Oral Tradition* 21.2 (2006), pp. 269-294, available online at <https://journal.oraltradition.org/wp-content/uploads/files/articles/21ii/Drout.pdf>. For a critical view of the of the selfish gene / meme paradigm, see S. OYAMA, *Evolution's Eye: A Systems View of the Biology-Culture Divide* (Durham and London, 2000), especially pp. 44-76.

[44] In a way, the natural sciences are now themselves going through the transition from structuralism to super- or post-structuralism, and by similar means. Just as the old paradigm in the humanities was criticised for its 'logocentrism' so are current 'gene-centric' (and, consequently, 'meme-centric') intuitions challenged for their naive metaphysics of presence. See, for example: E. JABLONKA and M.J. LAMB, *Evolution in Four Dimensions: Genetic, Epigenetic, Behavioural, and Symbolic Variation in the History of Life* (Cambridge, MA, 2005).

of the intractable number of variables in the ecology of the kitchen (e.g. the temperature of the oven, the quality of the ingredients, the timing of each procedure, etc.), although the equally present constraints upon these variations (e.g. the same master-chef) will have a stabilising effect and make some outcomes more likely than others. As with the phenotypic traits and traditional meanings, cakes, too, are context-sensitive.

A formula is like a recipe or a gene, not like a cherry on a cake or the colour of one's eyes. It does not reside in any range of highlighted text (e.g. 'X was in a blue-black cloak'), however carefully chosen. Just as chefs do not inherit their parents' four eyes and their teacher's thousand cakes, singers and storytellers inherit no words, spoken or written. It is the wordsmith skills they inherit, the habits of composition they hold on to for their dear storytelling life. Formulas are the genes of traditional literature and the engines of communal memory. Whether in poetry or in prose, whether expressed as a phrase, a motif, a theme, or a larger narrative structure, a formula is both older and younger than the words expressing it, since composition is its legacy and reception is the time of its conception. It is a unit of skill, which is to say a mechanism by which the words are summoned. So, this time attempting a definition rather than an analogy:

> A formula is an evolving habit of composition and reception – a unit of poetic or narrative inheritance.

So What?

Even if this definition and its theory go some way to describing our field of research, what difference does it make? Indeed, it may be tempting to ask if it is far too general to be of any use, since a theory of everything – for here everything is a formula – is often not much better than a theory of nothing. Else, it may be suspected of being far too narrow by reducing a long and diverse research history to a singular perspective of cultural evolution.

In its defence, we could point out that many theories of everything have impressive records of motivating an abundance of very specific research. Or we could argue that this particular perspective is so intensely introspective, that it poses less risk of alienating us from past research than any known alternative. And, while these considerations do enter our thinking as criteria for a good theory, the real reason we are attracted to this particular one has to do with how enriching it has proven itself to be in the everyday practice of reading.

Throughout the century-old quest for a definition befitting the formula, and for all the evident difficulty, we may have yet been lacking ambition by merely looking to draw a Venn diagram around all the formula instances we care about, whilst at the same time betraying a familiar arrogance by assuming that those are instances of all the formulas that there are, or else worth caring about. Note how this evolutionary definition of the formula predicts not merely that we have not yet enumerated all the formula instances, but that there are many more formulas to discover, which is to say, many more fascinating skills of narrative and poetic composition encoded in the corpora we think we know very well.

An instance of a formula is like a member of a species. One will never be bitten by a species, but that will prove to be of little help if this particular member turns out to be of a species that bites. Just so, one will never be sent into a cold sweat by a formula, even though it is where its instances draw their nail-biting power. This is where the related notions of formulas, instances and meaning nevertheless diverge. The meaning of a bite is not in its wound or in its grim genre of harm, but in all that it had put at risk. Just so, no meaning is to be found in the formula or its instances. Like getting a device to animate by plugging it into the current of a live electrical charge, so do the formulas and their instances alternate in an animated series of recapitulation and diversification only when plugged into the current of life's investments.

This is what is so starkly made clear by GPT-2. As far as our expectations about machines go, its skill of composing new articles is truly impressive. Yet, we know that it has no facility to appreciate its own work, even while the very text it produces expresses appreciations of all kinds with such impressive eloquence and originality. Yes, originality. While the method of creating this machine (a machine learning algorithm) does involve a corpus of human-generated text, the machine itself does not store a single word of it. Nor does the machine consult the corpus it was trained on ever again. Now that GPT-2 is being replicated, shared, and used by thousands of researchers and businesses around the world, the corpus it was trained on does not come with it at all. When GPT-2 generates a new article, it does so without any reference to the corpus it was trained on. So where do the words come from? All those idioms? Turns of phrase? Knowledge of geography and awareness of social relations? Well, they do not 'come from' the machine just as a cake does not 'come from' its recipe. What Darwin, Derrida, and Dennett keep emphasising is that cakes, like animals and texts, are not 'there already' and then simply delivered whence they came from. They are cooked.

GPT-2 is a very large network of very simple formulas. Mathematicians would say that the output **y** is defined to be some function of the input **x**:

$$f(\mathbf{x}) = \mathbf{y}.$$

Mathematicians being the students of patterns, formulas are how they denote them. Equations in this general form, rigorously denoting a pattern, probably played a part in the initial motivation to use the word 'formula' to describe conspicuous patterns of narrative and poetic composition. Mathematicians have since discovered formulaic frameworks capable of capturing any pattern. Alan Turing, for example, invented universal computing machines (one instance of which is being used now to type this text) in order to prove that there are numbers without any pattern in their digits. He then went on to pioneer the study of formulaic networks such as GPT-2 as well.

We believe that these are not coincidences. Formulas, species, waves, and algorithms, all contribute to a general study of patterns. We likewise believe that GPT-2 represents a historical milestone in the study of narrative and poetic composition. Whether or not we today have the courage to cross the disciplinary boundaries, we believe that such departmental divisions will be of much less concern to the next generation of scholars who will discover that we have barely scratched the surface of our research domain.

Meaning is the purpose of skill. The meaning of dodging a bite is to survive, just as the meaning of inflicting a bite is to survive. But meaning is not 'in' the skill. It is distributed across evolutionary time and it is always provisional, as it co-opts existing skills into ever new arrangements. In natural selection, it is not just species that evolve over time, but also the selection pressures. For example, if being bigger is advantageous at present, then in the next generation being that big is no longer big enough to still be advantageous – hence, brontosaurus. And so, to emphasise the implications of this non-locality to reading, we have proposed a methodology of distributed reading, which attempts a concerted and rigorous response to Lord's challenge to "train our ears"[45] to catch the echoes and the riches of formula networks, i.e. to learn to read and relate to traditional poetry and narratives that come to us from times and cultures so different from our own.

---

[45] LORD, *The Singer of Tales*, p. 65. For the full quotation, see *supra*, note 25.

2. A Distributed Reading of Grettir's Temper

Introducing the Distributed Reading Project

Formulaic patterns, much like neuronal connections and memory traces, run across and thickly populate traditional texts we read, with each enactment of a particular expression, motif, or a theme being an occasion of both iteration and change of communal memories. From this perspective, the spaces or tensions between the more iterative and the more experimental employments of familiar expressions and narrative patterns potentially index for us moments of intense pondering, a dilemma, a community trying to make 'its mind' up about an issue, social practice, or aesthetic convention. The goal of the Distributed Reading project is just that: to map and analyse such spaces and tensions between individual formula instances in order to sensitise the reader to the semantic nuance and aesthetic abundance generated by their interplay in traditional narratives – in the present case, the sagas of Icelanders.[46] The project thus aims to develop a non-linear reading methodology that takes into account traditional narratives' distributed authorship, i.e. the network dynamics and evolutionary processes that give rise to oral and orally derived literature.[47] The distributed reading builds on the mentioned pioneering work by John Miles Foley on the aesthetics of traditional referentiality while also utilising the available (and developing novel) digital analytical tools that enable us to process large amounts of data, and, most importantly, keep track of, as well as garner new insights from, their complex interrelationships.[48] The project (still in its experimental stages) is hosted on GitHub, as this online repository and versioning system provides a particularly good platform for project management, enabling different (close and loose) modes of collaboration, as well as keeping track of different project branches and their historical developments. Our page, featur-

---

[46] Beyond saga research, it is hoped that, as a reading methodology, distributed reading will be applicable to other traditional narratives too.

[47] Slavica develops the concept of the 'distributed author' in S. RANKOVIĆ, "Who is speaking in traditional texts? On the distributed author of the sagas of Icelanders and Serbian epic poetry", *New Literary History* 38.2 (2007), pp. 239-307. More recently, she revisited and refined it in EAD., "Spectres of agency".

[48] For other digitally assisted reading practices (in particular, Franco Moretti's "distant reading" and Matthew L. Jockers' "macroanalysis") which focus on the larger-scale historical and / or aesthetic phenomena, spanning textual corpora (e.g. literary epochs, styles, genres); see: F. MORETTI, *Graphs, Maps, Trees: Abstract Models for Literary History* (London and New York, 2005). M.L. JOCKERS, *Macroanalysis: Digital Methods and Literary History* (Urbana, Chicago, and Springfield, 2013).

ing the branch dedicated to the present, modest-scale study of Grettir's temper, can be found at: <https://github.com/distributedreading/grettir>. The page provides full access to our data (i.e. our Evernote notes; still a work in progress), as well as links to the 'Dimension Browser' analytical tool (<https://distributedreading.github.io/grettir/>) and interactive visualisations of the data: 'Formula Tree' (<https://distributedreading.github.io/grettir/tree.html>) and 'Principal Component Analysis' (<https://distributedreading.github.io/grettir/pca/>).

Our distributed reading case study on this occasion will be the saga formula concerned with heroic restraint, or the 'no reaction' formula as we call it, relating to the instances in which offended heroes try to resist the temptation to react impulsively, instantly, but rather show initial self-restraint and act later, with a cool head and a clear mind. More specifically, we will focus on the particularly imaginative employment of this formula in *Grettis saga*, the way it subtly yet relentlessly contests the overt pronouncements about its hero's unbridled temper – whether narratorial, other characters', or even the hero's own.[49] Contrary to the raised expectations, we will see that the volcanic eruptions of anger turn out to be an exception rather than the rule, for, when faced with an actual provocation, Grettir, like so many worthy saga heroes, tends to show no immediate reaction to it. Rather, he too is often said to "*lætr sem hann sé / heyrði / viti / vissi ... ekki / eigi*" ("pretend as if he did not see / hear / know / take notice") or be aware of an offence at first. This deliberate discrepancy between Grettir's declared fiery nature and his ability to tame it when put to the test, has the effect of potentially raising this saga hero above any other, for such a self-conquest must be a feat far greater than when performed by a hero already blessed with an even temperament.

The visualisation in Fig. 2 will be the focus of the discussion to follow, as it represents the result of the analysis of the forty-one instances we identified in which Grettir's temper is challenged in the saga.[50]

---

[49] Slavica discusses this discrepancy (and Grettir's temper in general) in more detail in S. RANKOVIĆ, "The exquisite tempers of Grettir the Strong", *Scandinavian Studies* 89.3 (2017), pp. 375-412.

[50] This figure, along with a succinct discussion of the early results of this research was published in S. RANKOVIĆ, "Exploring memory spaces of the sagas' formulaic patterns: The case of Grettir's temper management", in: *Skandinavische Schriftlandschaften: Vänbok till Jürg Glauser*, ed. K. MÜLLER-WILLE et al. (Tübingen, 2017), pp. 315-318.

A Formula Is a Habit Colliding with Life 99

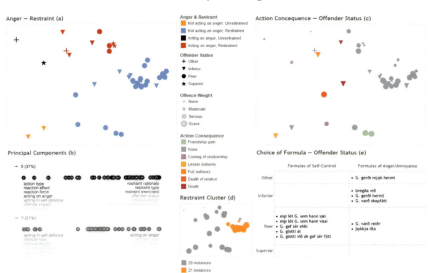

Fig. 2 "Grettir's Temper Management". Image by Miloš RANKOVIĆ, produced in Tableau.

Fig. 2 can thus be conceived of, at least according to *our* criteria, as the space of Grettir's temper management. Of course, for this image to make proper sense, it is necessary to take a closer look at how it was arrived at and what it is that it actually shows.

Identifying a Formula Instance

The distributed reading process begins by identifying an instance in which the hero's temper is provoked. Notice that, instead of only tracking the most familiar expressions tied to the 'no reaction' formula such as the already mentioned "*X lét / lætr sem hann sé / heyrði / viti / vissi ... ekki / eigi*" ("X pretends / pretended as if he did not see / hear / know / take notice"), or "*X gaf sér ekki / fátt*" ("X took no notice"), it was of the utmost importance that *all* instances that might call for heroic restraint were examined. In the echoic medium of the tradition, the absence of a particular formula where one is expected is rarely a neutral, arbitrary compositional decision but often speaks volumes, not to mention when the opposite happens – for example, the hero flies into a rage, thus failing to rise to the occasion and maintain his dignity.

Once a relevant instance is identified, a special note is dedicated to it. Fig. 3 represents a typical note of this kind.

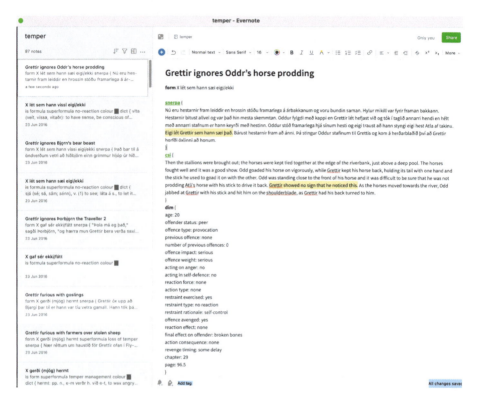

Fig. 3   "An instance note". Image by Slavica RANKOVIĆ, produced in Evernote.

This particular note is dedicated to the instance in which Grettir pretends not to see that Oddr the Pauper poet is trying to cheat the hero's brother Atli at a horse fight.[51] The note features relevant quotations (for our convenience, both in Icelandic and English translation), as well as the formulaic expression used (if any). To enable later computer processing, the tag 'form' (short for 'formula

---

[51] *Grettis saga*, ed. G. JÓNSSON (Reykjavík, 1936), p. 99.

instance') is placed in front of the noted formulaic expression,[52] in this case: "*X lét sem hann sæi eigi / ekki*" ("X pretended not to see anything").

Evaluating Formula Instances

Next, we proceed to evaluate each instance according to a number of criteria or dimensions (the tag 'dim' in Fig. 3 is the shorthand markup word for 'dimension') that span all the instances. In the case of the 'no reaction' formula, such are the dimensions: 'acting on anger', 'offence weight', 'offender status', 'restraint type', etc. (cf. Fig. 3). In fact, coming up with good dimensions or evaluation criteria is the most valuable and most difficult aspect of this reading practice, as you normally start with a few you set in advance, but once you try to view *all* the formula instances through their lens, you very soon find that the narrative is resisting certain categorisations and opening up to others. To give an example, as we started evaluating instances according to how heavy the offence committed against Grettir was ('offence weight'), we quickly realised that this requires two rather than just one parameter as, early into the evaluation process, a need arose to distinguish between the way Grettir's social milieu (as represented by the saga) judges a given offence, and the way it is experienced by the hero. Thus, the more objective sounding 'offence weight' dimension was retained to record the former and the more subjective 'offence impact' was introduced to keep track of the latter. This is just one of many such examples where the evaluation keeps turning on itself, as it were, making us refine our criteria. In the end, the most useful dimensions turn out to be those that evolve from the initial set, emerging as a result of the evaluation process itself – the distributed reading. The two of us often joke that the violence of our headache during these evaluations of the instances is the measure of success with which the sagas resist the violence that we are inflicting upon them by imposing our criteria. Then again, this is precisely what makes this process so rewarding – the feeling that the saga corpus can indeed 'fight back' and make itself heard over the noise of our scholarly assumptions.

---

[52] For example, when no familiar formulaic expression is used, but the hero still exercises a form of self-control (e.g. confronting his offender verbally rather than resorting to violence), then we mark the instance as 'self-control'.

Formula Family Tree

Apart from the 'instance notes', we also keep separate notes on specific formulaic expressions (if any). The one in Fig. 4 (also featured in Fig. 3): "*X lét sem hann sæi eigi / ekki*", we have marked as a sub-species of the larger, more complex formulaic pattern (or a 'superformula'): the 'no-reaction' formula in this case.

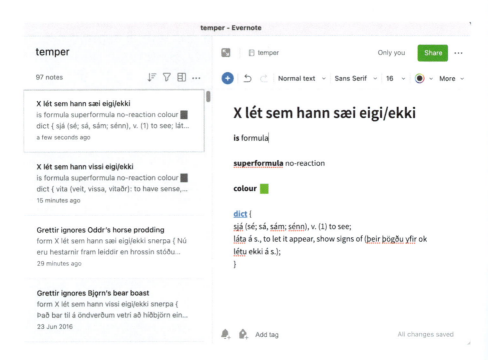

Fig. 4   "A note on the formulaic expression". Image by Slavica RANKOVIĆ, produced in Evernote.

Through this markup, our software keeps track of the relationships between the noted formulaic expressions belonging to the same formula family. As noted earlier, the project page features a link to the ever-evolving visualisation of the formula family tree (<https://distributedreading.github.io/grettir/tree.html>).

Types of Dimensions

We also make notes on each of our dimensions (i.e. the instance evaluating criteria) which include a rough, working definition of each. Thus far, we have come up with three basic types. The one in Fig. 5 is a simple 'yes or no' dimension and it marks whether the provoked party (Grettir in this case) actually acts on his anger or not.

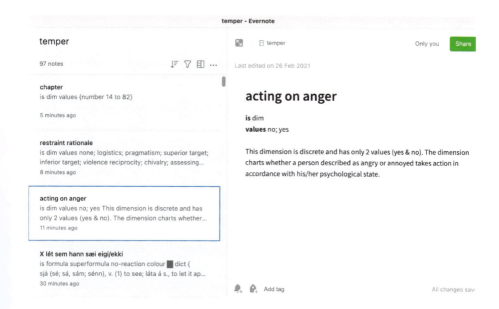

Fig. 5   "The 'yes or no' dimension". Image by Slavica RANKOVIĆ, produced in Evernote.

Fig. 6 is an example of a multiple value dimension, in this case, the 'restraint rationale', which offers a number of possible reasons for the offended party not to take immediate revenge. These range from the basest ones such as pure pragmatism (e.g. the hero is outnumbered) to the noblest of motivations such as deference to the innocent third party, or simply self-control as its own goal and reward.

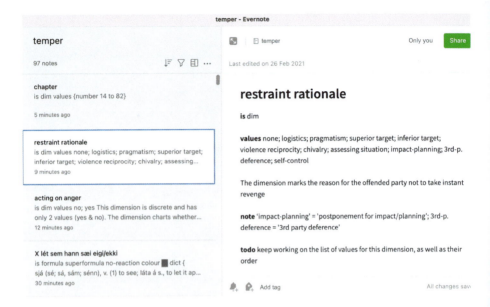

Fig. 6 "The multi-value dimension". Image by Slavica RANKOVIĆ, produced in Evernote.

The third kind of dimension (Fig. 7) is logistical, marking the chapter or page number in which a given instance occurs, and it therefore seems the most prosaic.

A Formula Is a Habit Colliding with Life   105

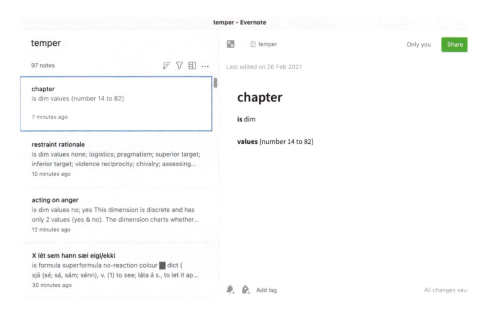

Fig. 7   "The logistical dimension". Image by Slavica RANKOVIĆ, produced in Evernote.

However, this dimension proves itself very useful if, for example, one wants to keep track of whether a character tends to lose or control his temper more easily at different stages of his life. Grettir, for instance, is more prone to loss of temper in his childhood and youth, whereas, as he reaches maturity, he also seems to be better at mastering his emotions, despite the fact that, after killing the revenant Glámr, this has, in fact, become much harder for him to do.[53]

Dimension Browser

Once we have collected and evaluated our data, we can (or indeed anyone can) proceed to 'play' with the results using the analytical tool we called 'Dimension Browser' (<http://distributedreading.github.io/grettir/>). At any one time, the tool allows us to pit two dimensions against one another by selecting them from the menu bars at the top right corner. In Fig. 8 we have crossed the 'offence type' (on the vertical, 'y' axis) and 'restraint exercised' (on the horizontal, 'x' axis). The former is the multi-value and the latter a 'yes or no' dimension.

---

[53] Cf. *Grettis saga*, p. 122.

Fig. 8   "Offence type vs. restraint exercised". Image by Miloš RANKOVIĆ.

Interestingly, this graph tells us not only that Grettir manages to restrain himself most of the time, but that even the gravest kind of offence such as the attempt on his life need not result in Grettir's loss of temper or the death of the offender.[54]

The graph in Fig. 9 shows the type of action (if any; y axis) that Grettir takes, pitted against the number of the previous offences his enemies perpetrated against him (x axis). While the top left corner marks the moments when Grettir acts most violently and impulsively (the top left dot is the poor goslings he kills as a child),[55] the bottom right shows his greatest feats of temper where he reacts minimally after maximal provocation, such as, for example, when he only gives an ominous grin to the brazen boaster Bjǫrn, after the latter provoked his temper more than six times.[56]

Principal Component Analysis: The Space of Grettir's Temper Management

While pitting two dimensions against one another in this way can be very rewarding and insightful, crossing all the dimensions at once would be likely to afford a fuller picture of Grettir's ability (or otherwise) to manage his temper. Of course, such a highly dimensional set of data is exceptionally difficult to

---

[54] Here we have in mind the attack on Grettir by Snorri *goði*'s unworthy son, Þóroddr. Cf. *Grettis saga*, pp. 219-222.
[55] *Grettis saga*, p. 37.
[56] *Grettis saga*, p. 78.

A Formula Is a Habit Colliding with Life

Fig. 9 "Action type vs. number of previous offences". Image by Miloš RANKOVIĆ.

understand as a whole (let alone represent), but luckily for us, mathematicians have come up with effective ways of coping with this complexity, and one that is found to be particularly effective is the so-called principal component analysis (PCA). Without going too much into technical detail on how PCA works,[57] the gist is that multidimensional data such as ours on Grettir's temper is processed by a dimension reduction algorithm whose purpose it is to identify principal components that best represent our data, affording the most informative and wieldy, yet the least violent view of the complex system of relationships that constitute what can be conceived of (at least according to our dimensions / criteria) as the space of Grettir's temper management (Fig. 10).

The link to the interactive version of the image in Fig. 10 is available on our GitHub page (<http://distributedreading.github.io/grettir/pca/>). If one hovers over each of the numbered dots (which follow the chronology of the saga), one will get a brief reference to the instance in question. Thus, for example, number 17 is when Grettir offers Bjǫrn that ominous smile mentioned above, and 32 is when he manages to fulfil his promise to Þorbjǫrg the Stout and does not retaliate against the farmers who had tried to hang him.[58]

---

[57] For a quick and easy introduction to the PCA principles, see, for example: G. DALLAS, "Principal Component Analysis 4 Dummies: Eigenvectors, Eigenvalues and Dimension Reduction", available at <https://georgemdallas.wordpress.com/2013/10/30/principal-component-analysis-4-dummies-eigenvectors-eigenvalues-and-dimension-reduction/>, or see the following YouTube video by R. BRO, available at <https://www.youtube.com/watch?v=9DPiXrN2pEg>.

[58] *Grettis saga*, pp. 169-170.

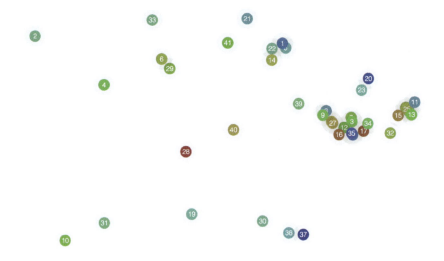

Fig. 10 "PCA analysis: The Space of Grettir's Temper Management". Image by Miloš RANKOVIĆ.

Fig. 11 (also Fig. 2(b)) shows the top two principal components or the X and Y axes that delineate the space of Grettir's temper management, with each listing our dimensions in the order of their contribution and overall impact on the component in question (expressed through greyscale). Thus the instances plotted to the right of the most influential principal component, the X axis (which wields 37% of the overall influence), are those where Grettir exercises restraint of the strongest and noblest kind, and where, though to a significantly lesser extent, the offender's social status is the highest, the offence the gravest, and preceded by the largest number of previous ones. Conversely, to the left of the X axis we find instances where Grettir is at his angriest, takes the most severe and forceful action, with the gravest consequences for the perpetrator. The next most influential principal component, the Y axis (21% of the overall influence), divides the instances almost solely according to the extent to which the hero is forced to act in self-defence (left), or, conversely, because he is driven by anger (right). A few other dimensions add further considerations into the mixture, but to an almost negligible degree (which is why you can barely discern them on the greyscale). While this method has certainly reduced some of the data complexity on one level, it has facilitated more of it on another, effectively empowering the narrative to use the vocabulary of our criteria merely as a starting point in deriving subtler terms to describe the ethic / aesthetic

A Formula Is a Habit Colliding with Life

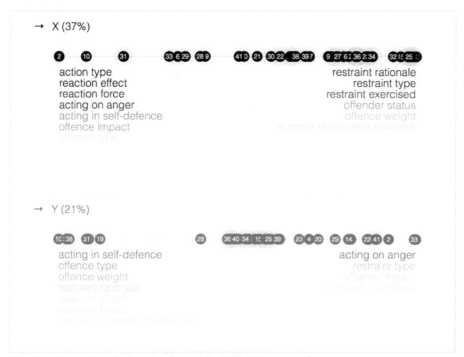

Fig. 11 "PCA, X and Y axes". Image by Miloš RANKOVIĆ.

tangents along which Grettir's behaviour can be fruitfully considered. As we have seen in Fig. 10, crossing the X and Y principal components delineates our research space of Grettir's temper management, with the instances plotted towards the bottom right being the ones where the hero reacts most wisely / nobly, despite being most intensely provoked (as when, out of deference for the cunning Snorri *goði*, Grettir spares the life of his son who had tried to kill him),[59] and the exact opposite pertaining to the instances in the upper left corner (e.g. the infamous killing of the goslings).[60]

The graph in Fig. 2(a) (a version of Fig. 10) in addition highlights Grettir's anger-restraint ratio, with the shapes indicating the social status of the offender with respect to the hero. Thus, the twenty-seven instances coloured blue are those where he does not react immediately upon provocation, with twenty-one forming a particularly tight cluster (the orange dots in Fig. 2(d)) and indicating the most stable / predictable behaviour. That these instances should constitute

---

[59] *Grettis saga*, pp. 219-222.
[60] *Grettis saga*, p. 37.

such a vast majority comes as a surprise, considering the overt assertions about the hero's hot-headedness. The two black instances in Fig. 2(a) are those where Grettir acts without any restraint (if only as a ten-year-old), while the two orange ones are the cases of self-defence where he neither restrains himself nor acts on anger. The nine red instances are perhaps the most interesting, as there he indeed acts on anger but still employs some form of restraint – be it to throw a barbed verse rather than a barbed spear at his opponent,[61] or to deflect his fury by sinking his axe into a log instead of his impudent thrall.[62]

The graph in Fig. 2(c) highlights the offender's social status with respect to Grettir (i.e. circle = 'peer', triangle = 'inferior', star = 'superior', cross = 'other') and the gravity of the offence (indicated by the size of the shapes), while also showing the consequence (if any) of the hero's action in a given instance (indicated by colour). What this graph makes immediately apparent (though not less surprising) is that it is not the dealings with his peers that breed fatal consequences for Grettir, but rather those with the socially inferior (orange and red triangles). Thus his killing of the farmhand Skeggi leads to an instance of lesser outlawry,[63] as boxing the insolent boy on the ear in the Trondheim church deprives Grettir of a chance to clear his name and effectively leads to the sentence of full outlawry,[64] while breaking the witch's thighbone[65] and hacking at her enchanted log while being blindly enraged by his servant leads to the self-inflicted wound that will be the death of him.[66] Elsewhere,[67] Slavica has argued at length that, in the two latter cases, the hero fails to rein in his temper not because he cannot do so, but because he does not think he is supposed to, which is precisely what the forces of evil (involved in both instances) count on happening. In other words, Grettir loses his life because he fails to read these situations correctly; that is, he fails to see that, regardless of the seemingly inadequate opponents, these instances, too, call for the formulaic heroic restraint.

The irony of the hero being laid low by such unworthy opponents adds to the overwhelming sense of *ógæfa* ('misfortune') that is said to plague him, yet there is something more down-to-earth to conclude from all this too, namely, that the hero might simply be better 'trained' within his tradition to handle con-

[61] *Grettis saga*, p. 77.
[62] *Grettis saga*, p. 251.
[63] *Grettis saga*, pp. 46-48.
[64] *Grettis saga*, p. 133.
[65] *Grettis saga*, p. 248.
[66] *Grettis saga*, p. 251.
[67] Cf. RANKOVIĆ, "The exquisite tempers of Grettir the Strong".

flicts with peers.[68] While he invariably shows some form of restraint towards them, this is not always the case with his social inferiors (or even superiors), where the behaviour seems to be less clearly regulated and socially codified. Thus, as we can see in Fig. 2(e), the typical 'no reaction' formulaic expressions are exclusively applied in the context of the hero's dealings with peers, whereas the strongest terms relating to his loss of temper are applied in connection to the people belonging to lower social strata.

To conclude, what excites us about the methodology behind all these graphs – the distributed reading – is not the promise of some scientific objectivity (after all, these remain our own readings of Grettir's temper management), but the possibility it opens for laying bare and rendering communicable the decisions that go on in any reading, yet normally remain hidden. When we engage in someone's interpretation of a text, we get all their overt reasoning (the rhetoric of persuasion), but not necessarily the expert intuition that underpins both their reasoning and their reading. What the methodology proposed here offers, is to enable us to document, reflect on, share, and compare, and thus learn from each other's reading practices. It also potentially opens up new and exciting avenues for collaboration – a 'hands-on' approach for a communal scholarly exploration and re-imagination of the formula.

---

[68] In fact, the same pattern applies to other saga heroes struggling with temper, such as Þorgeirr Hávarsson, who also shows heroic restraint towards his peers but is far less patient with the people of lower social strata. Slavica conducts a detailed comparison between Grettir and Þorgeirr in S. RANKOVIĆ, "Twisted mirror twins: Þorgeirr Hávarsson and Grettir the Strong", *Saga-Book* 44 (2020), pp. 81-138.

Chunks, Collocations, and Constructions: The Homeric Formula in Cognitive and Linguistic Perspective

CHIARA BOZZONE

Introduction

Homeric philology is the birthplace of the study of formularity, though also a domain in which oral-formulaic theory has received, over the past century, a mixed reception at best.[1] From the start, there was resistance to the idea that the greatness of Homer could be reduced to the mechanics of oral composition in performance (at least in the form in which it was first described).[2] To this day, many scholars want to view Homer as a somewhat non-traditional, exceptional figure standing at the end of a tradition, rather than as a proficient practitioner thereof.[3] But even for those who have more enthu-

---

[1] For a history of oral-formulaic theory, see J.M. FOLEY, *The Theory of Oral Composition: History and Methodology* (Bloomington and Indianapolis, 1988).

[2] For this type of attitude, see P. VIVANTE, *The Homeric Imagination* (Bloomington, 1970).

[3] Notable (and recent) examples are M.L. WEST, *The Making of the Iliad* (Oxford, 2011); ID., *The Making of the Odyssey* (Oxford, 2014); and Z. ČOLAKOVIĆ, "Avdo Međedović's post-

siastically embraced Parry and Lord's teachings, many aspects of oral-formulaic theory have proven hard to pin down: What exactly is a formula? How much of Homer is formulaic? And what can formulas truly tell us about the poems? These questions have occupied the field of Homeric studies for a few decades (with many important contributions appearing in the late 1960s and 1970s), but by the late 1980s, enthusiasm for Parry's revolution had largely deflated. Not only did formulas seem hard to define, it was unclear what they could do for us.[4] The aim of this paper is to address these questions in the light of recent advances in the fields of linguistics and cognitive studies, and to illustrate some novel applications that these new insights and methods allow. While the focus is on Homer, and all of the examples are drawn from the *Iliad* and the *Odyssey*, the goal is to inspire the application of these principles to other traditions as well.

From Formulas to Chunks: A Cognitive View

Studies of cognitive psychology have long established that the capacity of our working memory (WM) is rather limited, famously able to hold only between four and nine items at one time.[5] This is the part of our memory which is responsible for the processing of our attention (very roughly akin to a computer's RAM) and works as a bottleneck for our conscious processing. It is indeed surprising that we can carry out so many complicated cognitive and practical tasks despite these limitations.

One of the main strategies we can employ to bridge these limitations is called *chunking*: this is the process by which our mind can break up large pieces of information into smaller units, so as to better fit them to our working memory. If we have ever broken down a long phone number into shorter subsequences of digits in order to memorise it, we have employed chunking as a

---

traditional epics and their relevance to Homeric studies", *The Journal of Hellenic Studies* 139 (2019), pp. 1-48.

[4] A symptomatic title in this sense is J.M. BREMER, I.J.F. DE JONG, and J. KALFF, *Homer Beyond Oral Poetry: Recent Trends in Homeric Interpretation* (Amsterdam, 1987).

[5] The classic study here is G.A. MILLER, "The magical number seven, plus or minus two: Some limits on our capacity for processing information", *Psychological Review* 63.2 (1956), pp. 81-97. See more recently N. COWAN, "The magical number 4 in short-term memory: A reconsideration of mental storage capacity", *Behavioral Brain Science* 24 (2001), pp. 84-114. For an introduction to the workings of human memory (including long-term memory, short-term memory, and working memory), see A. BADDELEY, M.W. EYSENCK, and M.C. ANDERSON, *Memory* (London and New York, 2020³).

conscious strategy. But chunking works unconsciously as well: elements that often co-occur in our experience can become chunked together in our mind (i.e. treated as a single chunk, or unit), and then stored as such in our long-term memory (LTM). This is, effectively, one of the main ways we learn to master complex tasks (i.e. tasks that in themselves would overwhelm our WM capacity). Through repeated exposure and practice, we establish conventionalised chunks in our LTM, which can then be retrieved without conscious effort when needed, bypassing the limits of WM.[6] This is how we learn to, say, tie our shoes, brush our teeth, or drive a car: through repetition and practice, we chunk together many of the required operations, so that each necessary step now flows effortlessly into the next. Not only can we now execute these routines without conscious attention and while processing other information (say, while listening to the news or thinking about our day), these are now motor processes that we would likely struggle to break down into a sequence of discrete movements: they exist in our mind as indivisible units.

We employ the very same strategies when processing language. Here, chunking can work by grouping together words that co-occur often, and treat them as a single unit as opposed to many separate entries.[7] Many everyday linguistic interactions (e.g. at the check-out counter of a grocery store) rely almost entirely on these conventionalised chunks, where interlocutors can go through an entire exchange by simply pulling pre-made, multi-word chunks from their LTM.[8] If you have ever had a conversation with somebody while preoccupied with something else, to the point that you had no memory of what was discussed, you likely have chunking to thank for it.

This 'copy and paste' approach to language production is surprisingly widespread. Some corpus studies suggest that about half of the words (55%) that we speak or write are part of some larger chunk (prefabricated sequence) that we retrieve from LTM.[9] This of course is not to deny the creative and ana-

---

[6] In this case, one can talk about routinisation or automatisation, cf. D. WOOD, *Fundamentals of Formulaic Language: An Introduction* (London, 2015), pp. 54-55.

[7] See J. BYBEE, *Language, Usage and Cognition* (Cambridge, 2010), pp. 33-56, for an introduction to chunking in language.

[8] For a study of these 'formulaic genres', see K. KUIPER, *Formulaic Genres* (London, 2009).

[9] The figures come from B. ERMAN and B. WARREN, "The idiom principle and the open choice principle", *Text* 20 (2000), pp. 29-62, who looked at 'prefabricated sequences' in a (relatively small) corpus of spoken and written English. Specifically, Erman and Warren measured the proportion of slots (i.e. words) filled with parts of prefabricated expressions in their corpus vs. slots filled with words that are "freely chosen". They found little quantitative difference, in terms of formularity (i.e. reliance on prefabricated sequences), between spoken and

lytical capabilities of the human language faculty (which allow us to understand and process entirely novel linguistic sequences as needed), but rather to highlight that formularity, in a broad sense, is an extremely common and cognitively expected phenomenon in all realms of language usage.[10]

Homeric formulas (and formulas in other oral and written traditions) are then just a particular type of linguistic chunking, one that has been tailored to the particular necessities of oral epic performance. Imagine that you are an oral poet trying to compose a dialogue scene. It will be quite helpful to you that, in order to compose a basic verse meaning 'X replied to Y', you only need to bring up a couple of memorised chunks (i.e. formulas) and combine them, instead of having to mentally access each single word independently. This is how speech-introduction expressions in Homer arguably work.[11] Here, the line[12]

(1) Τὸν δ' ἀπαμειβόμενος προσέφη πόδας ὠκὺς Ἀχιλλεύς· (*Iliad* I. 58)
    "To him said in reply swift-footed Achilles"

is arguably made up of two independent chunks which recur elsewhere in the poems, namely:

(2) Τὸν δ' ἀπαμειβόμενος προσέφη (66×)
    "To him said in reply"

---

written texts (58% vs. 52% respectively). Qualitatively, spoken and written English simply made use of different *kinds* of prefabricated materials. These results should make us somewhat wary of simple quantitative approaches to determining orality of composition, such as establishing a cut-off point for formulaic density beyond which a given composition is to be regarded as oral; cf. C.O. PAVESE and F. BOSCHETTI, *A Complete Formulaic Analysis of the Homeric Poems* (Amsterdam, 2003). For a discussion, see C. BOZZONE, "New perspectives on formularity", in: *Proceedings of the 21st Annual UCLA Indo-European Conference*, ed. S.W. JAMISON, H.C. MELCHERT, and B. VINE (Bremen, 2010), pp. 27-44.

[10] Much recent work on formulaic language exists. A good introduction is WOOD, *Fundamentals of Formulaic Language*. Standard references are A. WRAY, *Formulaic Language and the Lexicon* (Cambridge, 2002), and EAD., *Formulaic Language: Pushing the Boundaries* (Oxford, 2008). For the role of formularity in language acquisition, see M. TOMASELLO, *Constructing A Language: A Usage-Based Theory Of Language Acquisition* (Cambridge MA, 2003).

[11] These are some of the best-known examples from Parry's work; cf. M. PARRY, *The Making of Homeric Verse: The Collected Papers of Milman Perry*, ed. A. PARRY (Oxford, 1971), pp. 15-16.

[12] All of the Greek examples have been obtained from the *Thesaurus Linguae Graecae* (<http://stephanus.tlg.uci.edu>). The editions used are *Homeri Ilias*, ed. T.W. ALLEN (Oxford, 1931) and *Homeri Odyssea*, ed. P. VON DER MÜHL (Basel, 1962).

and

πόδας ὠκὺς Ἀχιλλεύς (30×)
"swift-footed Achilles"

In this specific example, chunking gets the job done by using two formulas instead of seven words. In the context of oral performance, chunking facilitates the work of the audience as well: instead of parsing a completely novel sequence of words, the audience's task is lightened by recognising known and familiar strings.

But there is more: storage in LTM affords many additional advantages, which can be exploited in multiple ways for artistic effect. We know from psycholinguistic experiments that linguistic information is stored in the brain along with abundant non-linguistic information – from ambient sounds like car horns, or bird calls, to information about the people speaking and the circumstances.[13] In other words, linguistic chunks which are stored in the brain can acquire a number of *multimodal* associations, and thus the capacity to activate a number of connected memories in the mind: this is the cognitive basis for what Foley called "traditional referentiality".[14]

But how do we establish these useful chunks in our LTM? While frequency (i.e. encountering the same sequence over and over) is likely to cause memorisation of a chunk,[15] several strategies can be employed to increase the *memorability* of a linguistic sequence from the outset. As already mentioned, circumstantial cues (such as background noise or music that matches the original learning environment) can help with the retrieval of linguistic material.[16] Additionally, the work of David Rubin has shown that a combination of constraints (such as repeated sound pattens like rhyme, alliteration, rhythm, and metre) can

---

[13] J.B. PIERREHUMBERT, "Phonological representation: beyond abstract versus episodic", *Annual Review of Linguistics* 2 (2016), pp. 33-52, at p. 20.

[14] J.M. FOLEY, *Immanent Art: From Structure to Meaning in Traditional Oral Epic* (Bloomington, 1991). For the concept of multimodality see F. STEEN and M.B. TURNER, "Multimodal construction grammar", in: *Language and the Creative Mind*, ed. M. BORKENT *et al.* (Stanford, CA, 2013) <http://dx.doi.org/10.2139/ssrn.2168035ghgfdty>.

[15] For the role of frequency in language organisation and storage, see J. BYBEE, *Frequency of Use and the Organization of Language* (Oxford, 2007).

[16] Vedic memorisation, for instance, associates specific hand and head movements to each syllable that needs to be memorised. This can be seen in the movie *Altar of Fire,* dir. by R. GARDNER and J.F. STAAL (Documentary Educational Resources, 1976). For an account of modern practitioners of the oral tradition of the Vedas, see D.M. KNIPE, *Vedic Voices: Intimate Narratives of a Living Andhra Tradition* (Oxford, 2015).

boost memorability as well.[17] The fact that such constraints are particularly frequent in oral traditions should not surprise us: these traditions are exceptional laboratories for maximising the resources of memory. Yet, all of these strategies are rooted in human cognition, and examples of the same mechanisms can be observed in everyday language usage as well.

If chunks are a useful strategy for fitting more information into the limited slots of our WM, then using *larger chunks* should push our processing capacity even further. We know this to be the case for chess players: classic studies here have shown that expert players can handle much larger chunks of chess-related information than novices can.[18] In these experiments, master players were much better at recalling the position of pieces on a board after a very short exposure, but only if the arrangement of pieces represented a possible game configuration. In other words, master players were using their knowledge of the game to chunk information and store it more efficiently.[19] Since oral traditions, and especially those with some form of composition in performance, should be particularly interested in lowering the WM load of their performers, we might expect to find some particularly large chunks (i.e. particularly long linguistic expressions pulled directly from LTM) employed there. This seems to be the case for Homer, at least when it comes to a specific corpus measure: the presence of *long collocations*.[20]

All texts contain frequent collocations (i.e. text-based units formed by two or more orthographic words which tend to occur close to each other in a given corpus). It is reasonable to assume that many (if not all) collocations in a given corpus represent chunks that are stored in LTM, and are retrieved as such by language users. Of course, not all of these text-based units will match our definitions of formularity (see the discussion below). But for now, and for the purposes of a short experiment, this very rough measure will do.

In a typical language corpus, the count of collocations decreases sharply the longer the collocations become (i.e. it is very easy to find 2-word collocations;

---

[17] D. RUBIN, *Memory in Oral Traditions: The Cognitive Psychology of Epic, Ballads, and Counting-Out Rhymes* (Oxford, 1995).

[18] W.G. CHASE and H.A. SIMON, "The mind's eye in chess", in: *Visual Information Processing*, ed. W.G. CHASE (New York, 1973), pp. 215-281.

[19] See also T.W. ROBBINS et al., "Working memory in chess", *Memory and Cognition* 24 (1996), pp. 83-93.

[20] The values below have been obtained by using the software CasualConc 2.0 (<https://sites.google.com/site/casualconc/>) on the LOB corpus and the texts of Herodotus and Homer as they appear in the *Thesaurus Linguae Graecae* respectively.

5-word collocations are extremely rare). Fig. 2 for instance shows type and token counts for the Lancaster-Oslo-Bergen corpus of written English.[21]

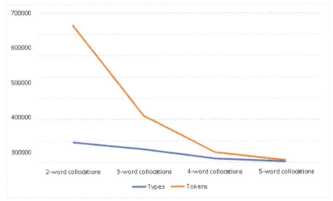

Fig. 1. Type and Token Counts of 2-, 3-, 4-, and 5-word collocations in the LOB corpus of written English.

We can observe how sharply the counts fall as the collocations become longer. For 2-word collocations, about 93% of all tokens are repeated more than twice, i.e. only 7% of 2-word collocations in our corpus are *singula iterata*. For 5-word collocations, only 16% of all tokens are repeated more than twice, i.e. 83% of 5-word collocations are *singula iterata*.

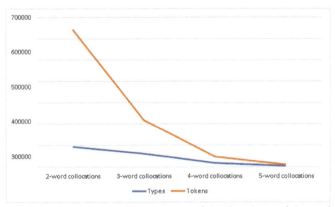

Fig. 2 Type and Token Counts of 2-, 3-, 4-, and 5-word collocations in Herodotus.

---

[21] Available at: <https://www1.essex.ac.uk/linguistics/external/clmt/w3c/corpus_ling/content/corpora/ list/private/LOB/lob.html>. For type and token counts, see *infra*, n. 63.

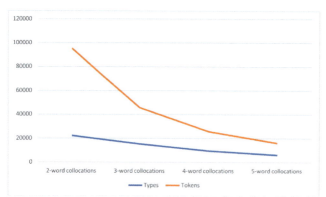

Fig. 3   Type and Token Counts of 2-, 3-, 4-, and 5-word collocations in Homer.

The same general pattern seems to hold for an ancient prose author like Herodotus (which is a better *comparandum* for Homer given its size and language).[22] If anything, the fall in the ratio of token to type frequency appears somewhat sharper than what we saw in the LOB corpus: at the 5-word collocation level, collocations repeated more than twice make up only 10% of our tokens, with *singula iterata* constituting 90% of the attested 5-word collocations.

Homer differs from Herodotus (and the LOB corpus) rather sharply, in that while the general tendency holds (collocation counts are inversely proportional to collocation length), the type and token lines in Fig. 3 never touch.

Already starting at the 2- and 3-word level, Homer displays more collocations than Herodotus. And at the 5-word stage, collocations repeated more than twice still make up 25% of all tokens, with *singula iterata* accounting for only 75% of the attested 5-word collocations. In other words, Homer seems to use more collocations overall, and significantly more 'longer' collocations than a regular prose author (and note that the trend is very likely to continue beyond 5-words, with some Homeric formulaic runs spanning several lines of text).

It is reasonable to interpret these facts as signs that Homer, likely through a long training process, has become able to manipulate linguistic chunks that are larger than chunks that most normal speakers (or writers) would employ. While this might not constitute direct quantitative proof of orality of composition of the sort that earlier versions of oral-formulaic theory might have hoped for, it can be taken as a strong indication that something peculiar (and out of the

---

[22] The LOB corpus contains 1,033,210 words. Herodotus contains *c.* 186,000 words. The *Iliad* and the *Odyssey* together contain *c.* 199,000 words.

ordinary) is going on with the memory optimisation of a speaker. In the context of Archaic Greece, it seems very reasonable to me to presume that the conditions that would necessitate such a level of optimisation would be found in the context of oral composition in performance. When looking at oral traditions outside of Homer, long collocations might be a first place to start in order to establish whether the language of a given genre or text might have been 'more formulaic' (i.e. more reliant on prefabricated linguistic materials) than elsewhere.

From Formulas to Constructions: A Linguistic View

So far, we have examined formulas as linguistic chunks that are stored in LTM and that can be called up with little effort when needed.[23] But we have not yet specified what these chunks might look like in practice, nor have we discussed how we might identify and classify them in a text.

Identifying Formulas: Textual and Psychological Approaches

Parry's famous definition of formula[24] is a good starting point for this discussion, since it already encapsulates the unique challenges in identifying formulaic sequences: it includes a text-based component ("A group of words which is regularly employed under the same metrical conditions") as well as a psychological or semantic one ("to express a given essential idea"). In practice, Parry's criteria are easily implemented: any meaningful expression involving content words (say, not a sequence of a conjunction and a preposition, but a recognisable unit like noun-phrase or a verb phrase), which recurs identically somewhere in the corpus, may be counted as a formula. Note that the metrical conditions are most often not telling: identical expressions (at least in a demanding metre like the hexameter) tend to occur in the same position in the line, with relatively few exceptions.

Contemporary corpus-linguistic approaches to formularity often rely on more stringent criteria: first, recurring multi-word expressions are considered

---

[23] This is also referred to as 'holistic processing' (as opposed to 'attended processing'). For a review of recent literature on the processing of formulaic sequences, see WOOD, *Fundamentals of Formulaic Language*, pp. 55-66.

[24] PARRY, *The Making of the Homeric Verse*, p. 272.

as candidates for formularity only above a given frequency cut-off point (this can range from 10 to 40 occurrences per million words).[25] Second, some mathematical tests can be employed to verify whether the expressions in question are particularly 'sticky' (i.e. whether their members seem particularly tied to one another). Several such tests are available.[26] Of these, the measure of 'mutual information'[27] is intended for use with two-word collocations.[28]

Third, much contemporary work on phraseology tends to focus on particular language genres and aims to identify formulaic sequences that are specific to these. For instance, research on 'lexical bundles' is typically concerned with academic English, and removes from consideration sequences that are not shared by at least three to five different texts, or 10% of the corpus.[29] When working on ancient corpora, we should ask from the outset whether we are interested in a given sub-set of formulaic sequences (i.e. sequences pertaining to the poetic register exclusively, or to a given poetic tradition, or to a given poet within that tradition), or whether we want to track *all* multi-word sequences that are likely to have been stored in LTM by a speaker. From the point of view of storage, poetic-sounding formulas like 'swift-footed Achilles' and the fixed greeting 'Catch you later!' are equally formulaic – the only difference is register. If needed, comparison with texts from other genres (when available) can be used to isolate formulaic sequences exclusive to a given register.

All of the operations outlined so far can be carried out relatively unproblematically on closed corpus languages as well. Implementing the psychological portion in the absence of native speakers, however, requires some slightly more sophisticated procedures.

First, we would want our formulaic sequences to represent a single idea (or at least a useful linguistic unit), while still being larger than a single word; one approach is to specify how many words our expression should contain (in studies of English phraseology, for instance, 4-words is the standard size for a *lexical bundle*).[30] But more important than size is morphological status: typically, we would not want to say that a trivial sequence like 'she said' is formulaic, no

---

[25] For Homer (*c.* 200,000 words), this would mean between 2 and 8 occurrences; cf. WOOD, *Fundamentals of Formulaic Language*, p. 21.

[26] They are set out in detail in C.D. MANNING and H. SCHÜTZE, *Foundations of Statistical Natural Language Processing* (Cambridge, MA, and London, 1999), pp. 151-189.

[27] *Ibid.*, pp. 178-183.

[28] This has been employed by N. SCHMITT, *Researching Vocabulary: A Vocabulary Research Manual* (London, 2010).

[29] WOOD, *Fundamentals of Formulaic Language,* pp. 122-123.

[30] *Ibid.*, p. 123. Note that linguistic typology will impact the size of formulaic sequences, as well as the criteria that should be used to identify them.

matter how frequently it is repeated, while we would want to say that 'unforeseen consequence' potentially is.[31] A first step then would be to exclude function words from our word count, so that 'unforeseen consequence' (containing two lexical words) would qualify, while any combination of pronoun plus verb (or preposition plus noun, or article plus noun) would not. Even better would be to say that our multi-word expressions, in order to be formulaic, must match some type of known linguistic constituent (such as a verb phrase, noun phrase, prepositional phrase, etc.).[32] This would exclude frequent but non-meaningful sequences such as 'all of the' or 'on the other' from our count (in some cases, this would also help us decide the appropriate size for a given formulaic sequence, and solve the problem of nesting sequences: this criterion would exclude the shorter sequence 'on the other', while repeated, while it would count the longer sequence 'on the other hand').[33]

Second, we would like formulaic sequences to enjoy some type of holistic storage in LTM. Testing this usually requires access to native speakers, who can either give native judgment on some features of the sequence (its conventionality and idiomaticity, its modifiability, its specificity), or can take part in psycholinguistic experiments of various kinds (such as measuring reaction times in silent reading or pauses in reading aloud).[34] Erman and Warren rely on native speaker judgment as to whether a given sequence exhibits restricted modifiability (e.g. it cannot be negated or pluralised without losing idiomaticity).[35] Many checklists for formularity developed for the purposes of language teaching similarly depend on native speaker decisions.[36] For ancient languages,

---

[31] Note that some of the "stickiness" tests mentioned above might already serve to resolve some of these issues.

[32] This approach was pioneered by P. KIPARSKY, "Oral poetry: Some linguistic and typological considerations", in: *Oral Literature and the Formula*, ed. B.A STOLZ and R.S. SHANNON III (Ann Arbor, 1976), pp. 73-106.

[33] Note that linguistic structure and frequency of co-occurrence are arguably related (J. BYBEE and P. HOPPER, *Frequency and the Emergence of Linguistic Structure* (Amsterdam, 2001)).

[34] Cf. WOOD, *Fundamentals of Formulaic Language*, pp. 60-64. Interestingly, N. SCHMITT, S. GRANDAGE, and S. ADOLPHS, "Are corpus-derived recurrent clusters psycholinguistically valid?", in: *Formulaic Sequences: Acquisition, Processing, and Use*, ed. N. SCHMITT (Amsterdam, 2004), pp. 127-151, come to the conclusion that "corpus data on its own is a poor indicator of whether those clusters are actually stored in the mind as wholes".

[35] ERMAN and WARREN, "The idiom principle".

[36] See, for instance, the checklist provided by A. WRAY and K. NAMBA, "Use of formulaic language by a Japanese-English bilingual child: A practical approach to data analysis", *Japanese Journal for Multilingualism and Multiculturalism* 9 (2003), pp. 24-51. For more checklists, see WOOD, *Fundamentals of Formulaic Language*, pp. 19-33.

the challenge is that most of the evidence in this sense will be negative in nature: typically, a text will not state "you can say X and Y, but not Y and X"; rather, one is only likely to find instances of "X and Y" and no instances of "Y and X". Some other cues, however, can still be leveraged.

While not all formulaic sequences are necessarily idiomatic (in corpus linguistic research, one typically distinguishes between idioms and non-idiomatic multi-word expressions), idiomaticity is a feature that is believed to require LTM storage. Thus, for our purposes, multi-word expressions that appear to have non-compositional meaning are strong candidates for formularity, and they can be identified even in the absence of native speakers. For Homer, we can think of the idiomatic expression ἔπεα πτερόεντα, 'winged words', as opposed to a relatively transparent sequence like δῖος Ἀχιλλεύς, 'divine Achilles'.[37]

Some additional features might indicate holistic storage: syntactic or morphological irregularity might reveal that a sequence is not being produced by the synchronic grammar of a speaker, but is instead a fragment of older language preserved as such because of its frequency (one can think of English expressions such as 'be that as it may' or 'I dare not say', which reflect older, non-productive syntactic patterns). In Homer, metrical irregularities often belie the same process (i.e. the expression was created before some changes in the phonology of the language rendered the metre imperfect). Consider the verse below:

(3) τὸν δ' ὁ γέρων Πρίαμος πρῶτος ἴδεν ὀφθαλμοῖσι (*Iliad*, XXII, 25)
"And the old Priam saw him first with his eyes"

The metre only scans correctly if the verb ἴδεν [íden] 'saw' is restored to its pre-form *[wíden] (from the Proto-Indo-European root *wid- 'know, see', Lat. *videō*, 'id.'). Ionic had lost word-initial [w] early in the first millennium BCE, and the sound was likely no longer pronounced in Homeric performances, but many formulaic sequences originally containing initial [w] were still in circulation in the poetic technique centuries later.[38] An expression of this type (containing a so-called linguistic archaism that is guaranteed by the metre) is most likely formulaic.

---

[37] Note that, based on frequency alone, both sequences are identified as formulas in Homer (the latter occurs 55× and the former 114×).

[38] For more examples, see O. HACKSTEIN, "The Greek of epic", in: *A Companion to the Ancient Greek Language*, ed. E. BAKKER (Malden, MA, 2010), pp. 401-423.

Phonological information can also point to the holistic storage of a sequence.[39] To begin, frequent sequences can show phonetic reduction due to frequency itself, and their constituents can over time blend into each other (i.e. become fused in a single word).[40] But additional features apply too: in English, formulaic sequences tend to display fixed stress placement, intonation, and tempo (which are usually different from what an identical sequence would display without conventionalisation).[41] In production, formulaic sequences typically contain no pauses, they are fluent (even if the surrounding discourse is not),[42] and they tend to align with intonational (i.e. prosodic) boundaries.[43] While most of this information would not typically be available for ancient corpora, in metrical texts the tendency for formulaic sequences to fit into given metrical constituents can be understood in this way (formulaic sequences will tend to fit the internal divisions of the metre, for instance by starting and ending at known caesuras). Aberrant accentual behaviour, or even the practice of running words together in spelling, might also be interpreted in this light.

Flexibility and Gradiency

The challenges discussed so far are just the beginning: while the multi-word sequences that we have observed up to this point are unchangeable (and they might even resist modification), formulaic phenomena are famously gradient, and one might encounter many linguistic sequences that look sort of formulaic though not entirely so. For instance, some expressions which are definitely fixed and idiomatic in meaning (thus, arguably stored) allow for some modification, like the verb phrase 'run the (whole / entire) gamut' and the noun phrase

---

[39] See P.M.S. LIN, "The phonology of formulaic sequences: A review", in: *Perspectives on Formulaic Language: Acquisition and Communication*, ed. D. WOOD (New York and London, 2010), pp. 174-193, and P.M.S. LIN, "Sound evidence: The missing piece in the jigsaw in formulaic language research", *Applied Linguistics* 33 (2012), pp. 342-347.

[40] Note that this is true of single words as well, not just multi-word expressions. For a discussion of the reducing effects on frequency, see J. BYBEE, *Language, Usage and Cognition* (Cambridge, 2010), pp. 37-44.

[41] M. ASHBY, "Prosody and idioms in English", *Journal of Pragmatics*, 38 (2006), pp. 1580-1597, is a study of the accentual patterns of idioms, which suggests that different levels of conventionalisation and fixedness exist.

[42] Indeed above-expected fluency is one of the main criteria to identify formulaic sequences in the speech of young children, as established already by A.M. PETERS, *Units of Language Acquisition* (Cambridge, 1983).

[43] LIN, "The phonology of formulaic sequences", p. 188.

'the (big / fat / big fat) elephant in the room'. Are all of these sequences equally formulaic? Where should we draw the line?[44] Additionally, there is creative reshaping of formulas, as in the expression 'God save the Queen' and its humorous modification 'God shave the Queen'. Is the latter to be considered formulaic in some way? There is a fixed sequence and there is manipulation, but not in the same way as in the previous examples.[45]

In many cases, these distinctions might be a matter of taste: let us say we can arrange linguistic expressions on a continuum going from entirely compositional (a new, never-uttered-before sequence) to entirely fixed (conventional, stored, etc.). It is likely that different scholars would draw the line for what counts as formularity at different points along this continuum.[46] That decision might in turn depend on the purposes of the study in question.

In fact, much of the debate on the Homeric formula has focussed on the problem of flexibility. The discussion goes all the way back to Parry, who, beyond formulas, introduced the (rather vague) concept of 'formulaic expression', "phrases which are of the same type as others".[47] In Parry's famous study of the first 25 verses of *Iliad* I,[48] formulas are marked with solid underlining, while formulaic expressions are marked with broken underlining. The same

---

[44] If we want to base our judgment on Google searches (cf. C.C. SHEI, "Discovering the hidden treasure on the internet: Using Google to uncover the veil of phraseology", *Computer Assisted Language Learning* 21 (2008), pp. 67-85), all of the sequences above do seem to qualify for formularity by reason of their absolute frequency. In relative terms, though, the modified versions are much less frequent than the unmodified ones. The number of hits for a search conducted on 8 March 2021 is as follows: 'run the gamut' (4,910,000 hits) / 'run the whole gamut' (228,000 hits) / 'run the entire gamut' (127,000 hits); 'the elephant in the room' (6,860,000 hits) / 'the big elephant in the room' (60,700 hits) / 'the fat elephant in the room' (17,300 hits) / 'the big fat elephant in the room' (11,000 hits).

[45] Formularity in Vedic poetry, for instance, often appears to belong to the 'artistically manipulated' category, which fits with the overall poetics of the genre (rather than improvised narrative poetry, this is lyric poetry that prides itself in its own sophistication). For an introduction to Vedic poetry, see S.W. JAMISON and J.P. BRERETON, *The Rigveda: The Earliest Religious Poetry of India* 1 (Oxford, 2014). A discussion of phraseological substitution in ancient Indo-European languages is given in E. MEUSEL, *Pindarus Indogermanicus* (Berlin, 2020), p. 79.

[46] In Homeric studies, as well as in linguistics, some scholars belong to the camp "everything is formulaic" (in some sense). For Homer, this view has been expressed most famously by Gregory Nagy (see for instance G. NAGY, "Introduction", in: *The Homer Multitext Project* (2010) <http://nrs.harvard.edu/urn-3:hlnc.essay:Nagy.The_Homer_Multitext_Project.2010>). For linguistics, we can think of the Construction Grammar motto "It's constructions all the way down", as discussed in A.E. GOLDBERG, *Constructions at work: The Nature of Generalization in Language* (Oxford, 2006), p. 18.

[47] PARRY, *The Making of the Homeric Verse*, pp. 301-302.

[48] Ibid.

practice is taken over by Lord.[49] As an example, we can compare the sequence πόδας ὠκὺς Ἀχιλλεύς, 'swift-footed Achilles' (30× in Homer) with the isometric and structurally similar phrase πόδας αἰόλος ἵππος, 'nimble-footed horse', occurring only once in *Iliad* XIX, 404. We could argue that the second expression is formulaic because it is 'of the same type' as the first one. But the criteria are not clearly established.

The most famous contribution on the flexibility of the Homeric formula is by Hainsworth,[50] who developed a constrained set of modifications formulas could undergo while still being considered as such (cf. Table 1). In a way that is very reminiscent of contemporary corpus linguistics, Hainsworth argues that what binds the formula together is a "mutual expectancy" between words, in the sense that "the use of one word created a strong presumption that the other would follow".[51] Hainsworth was ahead of his time in the crucial insight that flexibility and frequency of use where in an inverse relationship, and that flexibility, not fixity, accounts for most of the system: in his view, "highly schematized formula-types are then the consequence of ossification of more flexible systems at points of frequent use".[52]

Another important take on flexibility is that of Kiparsky, who introduced a principled distinction between the 'fixed formula' (a linguistic sequence stored in memory as such) and the 'flexible formula' (a well-formed linguistic constituent which is already partially lexically specified).[53] These categories are meant to reflect the linguistic concepts of 'fixed bound phrase' and 'flexible bound phrase' respectively. Kiparsky has recently revisited this distinction,[54] and now recognises only two categories: 'fixed formulas' (as above) vs. 'themes' (anything else in the technique that is flexible, including non-verbal material like plot sequences of different sizes). Later approaches to formularity like those of Visser[55] and Watkins[56] went even farther (though in different ways) in emphasising formal flexibility, to the point of almost dissolving the

---

[49] A.B. LORD, *The Singer of Tales* (Cambridge, MA, 1960), p. 143.
[50] J.B. HAINSWORTH, *The Flexibility of the Homeric Formula* (Oxford, 1968).
[51] *Ibid.*, p. 36.
[52] *Ibid.*, p. 113.
[53] KIPARSKY, "Oral poetry".
[54] P. KIPARSKY, "Formulas and themes", in: *Formula: Units of Speech, Words of Verbal Art*, ed. FROG (Helsinki, 2017), pp. 155-163.
[55] E. VISSER, *Homerische Versifikationstechnik: Versuch einer Rekonstruktion* (Frankfurt a.M., 1987), and ID., "Formulae or single words? Towards a new theory of oral verse-making", *Würzburger Jahrbücher für die Altertumswissenschaft* 14 (1988), pp. 21-37.
[56] C. WATKINS, *How to Kill a Dragon: Aspects of Indo-European Poetics* (Oxford, 1995).

textual side of the original Parrian formula. Table 1 below gives a short overview of some influential definitions of the Homeric formula.[57]

Table 1. Select definitions of the Homeric formula.

Parry	"An expression regularly used under the same metrical conditions to express an essential idea" (PARRY, *The Making of the Homeric Verse*, p. 13); "A group of words which is regularly employed under the same metrical conditions to express a given essential idea" (*ibid.*, p. 272). Group of words: πόδας ὠκὺς Ἀχιλλεύς, 'swift-footed Achilles' Metrical conditions: from the ephthemimeral caesura to the end of the line. Essential idea: Achilles.
Russo[1]	Structural formula $[-\smile]_V [\smile--]_N$ e.g.: τεῦχε κύνεσσιν, 'threw to the dogs'; δῶκεν ἑταίρῳ, 'gave to his companion'.
Nagler[2]	Pre-verbal Gestalt (true formula): idea of Achilles. Surface realisation (not really a formula): πόδας ὠκὺς Ἀχιλλεύς. In Nagler's conception, repeated occurrences of the same surface realisation are not really repetitions: the poet simply happens to realise the same pre-verbal Gestalt in the same way multiple times, because of various metrical and linguistic constraints.
Hainsworth[3]	Basic formula (the mutual expectation between two words: καρτερὰ δεσμά. Modifications: (a) dislocation, (b) modification (i.e. inflection), (c) expansion, (d) separation. e.g.: Expansion + modification: κρατερῷ ἐνὶ δεσμῷ 'in strong chains'. Separation + modification: δεσμοῖο – κρατεροῦ 'of strong ... chain'.
Kiparsky[4]	Fixed formula (a linguistic sequence stored in memory): Ἦμος δ' ἠριγένεια φάνη ῥοδοδάκτυλος Ἠώς ("As soon as early-born rose-fingered Dawn appeared").

---

[57] For a fuller discussion, see C. BOZZONE, *Constructions: A New Approach to Formularity, Discourse, and Syntax in Homer* (Ph.D. dissertation, University of California at Los Angeles, 2014), pp. 11-24. For a detailed history of the debate up to the mid-1980s, see M.W. EDWARDS, "Homer and oral tradition: the formula, part I", *Oral Tradition* 1.2 (1986), pp. 171-230, and ID., "Homer and oral tradition: the formula, part II", *Oral Tradition* 3.1-2 (1988), pp. 11-60.

	Flexible formula (a well-formed syntactic constituent with lexical items already specified): [[ἄλγος]$_{NP}$ παθ-]$_{VP}$ 'pain ... suffer'.
Visser[5]	[πόδας ὠκὺς]$_{PERIPHERY}$ [Ἀχιλλεύς]$_{NUCLEUS}$. Poets compose by words, not by formulas: first they place in the line the semantically necessary words (*nuclei*), then they fill the rest with "ornamental" items (*periphery*).
Watkins[6]	Reconstructible Indo-European formulas are "whole noun phrases or verb phrases, with wholly or partially reconstructable semantics, syntax, lexical expression, morphology, and phonology" (WATKINS, *How to Kill a Dragon*, p. 42). They work as the "vehicle of a semantic theme" (*ibid.*, p. 28). e.g.: HERO SLAY (*$g^{wh}en$-) SERPENT (with WEAPON/with COMPANION) English upper case is used to identify the semantics and lexical constituents of a reconstructed formula (conventionally, word order is English). In the example above, the semantic element SLAY is specified for realisation via the PIE verbal root $g^{wh}en$- 'strike, kill'. The other elements given in parenthesis are optional. "HERO" is given outside the box, since an overt subject is typically missing (*ibid.*, p. 302).

[1] J. RUSSO, "A closer look at Homeric formulas", *Transactions of the American Philological Association* 94 (1963), pp. 235-247; ID., "The structural formula in the Homeric verse", *Yale Classical Studies* 20 (1966), pp. 217-240.
[2] M.N. NAGLER, "Towards a generative view of the Homeric formula", *Transactions of the American Philological Association* 98 (1967), pp. 269-311.
[3] HAINSWORTH, *The Flexibility of the Homeric Formula*.
[4] KIPARSKY, "Oral poetry".
[5] VISSER, *Homerische Versifikationstechnik*.
[6] WATKINS, *How to Kill a Dragon*.

Formulas as Constructions

How can we reconcile the existing work on Homer with the more recent findings of linguistic theory? In my previous work,[58] I have proposed to borrow the concept of construction from *Construction Grammar* (C×G) in order to describe formulaic phenomena in Homer at different levels of fixity and abstraction. In C×G, constructions are generalisations that learners carry out over

[58] BOZZONE, "New perspectives on formularity"; EAD., "Constructions".

linguistic data: they are defined as pairings of form and function which are learned (i.e. stored in LTM). In this sense, constructions can span from general rules of morphology or syntax (e.g. the ditransitive construction) to specific fixed expressions (the 'kick the bucket' construction).[59]

In practice, many constructions will have a fixed part and a flexible part, combining elements that are simply retrieved from LTM and elements that need to be filled in and manipulated on the spot (such as the flexible idioms cited above). Similarly, Homeric constructions can exist at different levels of abstraction, depending on the availability of data or the granularity of the analysis. Unlike constructions in everyday language, they can contain metrical information. And their function, beyond their meaning, might entail some specific narrative or discourse task (i.e. introducing a new referent or signalling the beginning of a given thematic unit).

Let us look at a simple example. In language acquisition, children build constructions by conducting generalisations over expressions that share similarities in form and function. Similarly, an apprentice poet coming across the following expressions:

Τὸν δ' ὡς οὖν ἐνόησεν ἀρηΐφιλος Μενέλαος (*Iliad*, III. 21)
"And Menelaos dear to Ares noticed him"

Τὸν δ' ὡς οὖν ἐνόησεν Ἀλέξανδρος θεοειδὴς (*Iliad*, III. 30, *Iliad*, XI. 581)
"And Alexander similar to the gods noticed him"

Τὸν δ' ὡς οὖν ἐνόησε Λυκάονος ἀγλαὸς υἱὸς (*Iliad*, V. 95)
"And the splendid son of Lycaon noticed him"

Τοὺς δ' ὡς οὖν ἐνόησε θεὰ λευκώλενος Ἥρη (*Iliad*, V. 711)
"And the goddess Hera of the white arms noticed them"

Τοὺς δ' ὡς οὖν ἐνόησε θεὰ γλαυκῶπις Ἀθήνη (*Iliad*, VII. 17)
"And the goddess Athena of the grey eyes noticed them"

Τὸν δ' ὡς οὖν ἐνόησε Κόων ἀριδείκετος ἀνδρῶν (*Iliad*, XI. 248)
"And Coon, glorious among men noticed him"

τὸν δ' ὡς οὖν ἐνόησε ποδάρκης δῖος Ἀχιλλεὺς (*Iliad*, XXI. 49)
"And divine Achilles who runs to the rescue noticed him"

---

[59] Cf. GOLDBERG, *Constructions at work*, and A.E. GOLDBERG, *Explain Me This: Creativity, Competition, and the Partial Productivity of Constructions* (Princeton, 2019).

τὴν δ' ὡς οὖν ἐνόησε θεὰ λευκώλενος Ἥρη, (*Iliad*, XXI. 418)
"and the goddess Hera of the white arms noticed her"

τὸν δ' ὡς οὖν ἐνόησεν Ὀδυσσῆος φίλος υἱός, (*Odyssey*, XV. 59)
"and the son of Odysseus noticed him"

τὸν δ' ὡς οὖν ἐνόησε πολύτλας δῖος Ὀδυσσεὺς (*Odyssey*, XXIV. 232)
"and divine Odysseus who has much endured noticed him"

might notice their formal and functional similarities and capture them by learning the following construction:

[–]_Obj.Pr. **δ' ὡς οὖν ἐνόησε(ν)** [⏑ – – ⏑ ⏑ – ⏑ ⏑ – –]_Subj.NP

The bolded part is invariant, while the variable parts are specified for syntactic and metrical structure. The general discourse function of the construction might be switching to another referent, with specific thematic sub-functions (in most cases in the *Iliad*, this line is used when a character witnesses another character in distress on the battlefield and intervenes; the usage in the *Odyssey* is less specific).

Using the construction above, apprentice poets might then create new expressions that fit this mould but that they have not encountered before, such as:

*τὴν δ' ὡς οὖν ἐνόησε πολύτλας δῖος Ὀδυσσεὺς
"and much-enduring divine Odysseus noticed her"

The construction above centres around a finite verb and builds an entire sentence. But smaller constructions exist too, and they can effectively nest into larger constructions. For instance, the construction above calls for a Subj.NP (Subject noun-phrase) construction of a given metrical shape. Moulds for these types of construction can in turn be learned, such as:[60]

---

[60] While it is possible to write such a construction, one might question to what extent an apprentice poet would be likely to learn it, since it only captures two examples, and both have very high frequency (meaning that both expressions are likely to be stored in LTM as such). In the examples below, metrical information about the position of a given construction in the hexameter is given following the format foot number (1-6) + position within the dactylic foot (a, b, or c, where a is the *longum*, b is the first *brevis* in the *biceps*, and c is the last element in the *biceps*). Thus, 3c means: this construction starts in the third foot, with the second brevis of the biceps. This is the model proposed by M. JANSE, "The metrical schemes of the Hexameter", *Mnemosyne* (2003) pp. 343-348.

³ᶜ[˘ – ˘ ˘]_Subj.Adj. δῖος [˘ – –]_Subj.Noun

ποδάρκης δῖος Ἀχιλλεὺς (21×)
"divine Achilles who runs to the rescue"

πολύτλας δῖος Ὀδυσσεὺς (42×)
"divine Odysseus who has much endured"

This last construction in fact seems like an expansion of another much more popular construction, given below:

⁵ᵃδῖος [˘ – –]_Subj.Noun

δῖος Ἀχιλλεύς 'divine Achilles' (55x)
δῖος Ὀδυσσεύς 'divine Odysseus'(102x)
δῖος Ἀγήνωρ 'divine Agenor' (*Iliad*, XIV. 425, *Iliad*, XV. 340, XXI. 579)
δῖος Ἐπειός 'divine Epeios' (*Iliad*, XXIII. 689)
δῖος Ὀρέστης 'divine Orestes' (*Odyssey*, III. 306)
δῖος Ἐχέφρων 'divine Echephron' (*Odyssey*, III. 439)
(etc.)

It is important to maintain the terminological distinction between a construction (i.e. an abstract template stored in the LTM of a speaker) and the expressions (i.e. concrete instances of language) that it produces. In this sense, a given text will not contain a construction per se, but only expressions created by a construction.

Constructions and their Productivity

A constructional approach to Homeric formularity has another particular advantage: it allows us to study the *productivity* of a given construction, and thereby gain insight into which expressions are relatively newer vs. relatively older in the poetic technique, as well as into the evolution of the poetic language overall (note that productivity in this sense is very close to the flexibility of a formula discussed above).[61]

---

[61] The methodology for this type of study is detailed in C. BOZZONE, "Homeric constructions, their productivity, and the development of epic Greek", in: *Language Change in Epic Greek and other Oral Traditions*, ed. L. VAN BEEK (Leiden, forthcoming), and EAD., "Homeric formulas and their antiquity: A constructional study of ἀνδροτῆτα καὶ ἥβην", *Glotta* (2022), pp.

In short, productivity is a concept within the study of morphology which aims to explain why some morphological processes (either derivational or inflectional) can be readily extended to new items while some other cannot. In English, a ready example is the difference between strong verbs vs. weak verbs in the formation of the past tense. Here, strong verbs follow a non-productive pattern (i.e. changing the root vowel), which cannot (usually) be extended to new members, while weak verbs follow a productive pattern (i.e. adding the ending -*ed*), which can easily be extended to new members. Thus, the past tense of the recently-coined verb to *google* is *googl-ed* – not *gagle* or the like.[62] Interestingly, the productivity of a given process seems to reflect its antiquity within the language (in the sense that processes tend to become less and less productive over time): in the history of English, the productive pattern for the weak past tense (which goes back to Proto-Germanic) is indeed much more recent than the unproductive pattern for the strong past tense (which goes all the way back to Proto-Indo-European).

These insights can be leveraged for the study of phraseology (and in our case, traditional poetic phraseology) as well. Let us look at an example. In Homer, there are several expressions (both Parrian formulas and unique expressions) meaning 'suffer(ing) pains' which occupy the last two feet of the hexameter (in Parrian terms, we might call these equivalent formulas); these can be grouped into two constructions:

(1) [5a][πήματα πάσχ –]$_{\text{VP}}$

    1. [5a] πήματα πάσχων "suffering pains" (*Odyssey*, V. 33, XVII. 444, XVII. 524)

33-67. It is based on H. R. BAAYEN, *A Corpus-Based Approach to Morphological Productivity. Statistical Analysis and Psycholinguistic Interpretation* (Ph.D. dissertation, Vrije Universiteit Amsterdam, 1989), and ID., "Quantitative aspects of morphological productivity", in: *Yearbook of Morphology 1991*, ed. G.E. BOOIJ and J. VAN MARLE (Dordrecht, 1992), pp. 109-149. Note that Baayen's work was concerned primarily with derivational morphology, while here we are applying the same principles to the study of syntactic units. For an application of Baayen's work to historical linguistics, see R.P. SANDELL, *Productivity in Historical Linguistics: Computational Perspectives on Word-Formation in Ancient Greek and Sanskrit* (Ph.D. dissertation, University of California at Los Angeles, 2015). See also A. ZELDES, *Productivity in Argument Selection: From Morphology to Syntax* (Berlin, 2012), who has applied Baayen's quantitative measures to syntactic units in German, and shown that the measures can be sensibly applied and interpreted at the syntactic level.

[62] For productivity in morphology, see L. BAUER, *Morphological Productivity* (Cambridge, 2001). For a history of English strong verbs, see S. BRANCHAW, *Survival of the Strongest: Strong Verbs in the History of English* (Ph.D. dissertation, University of California at Los Angeles, 2010).

2. ⁵ᵃ πήματα πάσχει "s/he suffers pains" (*Odyssey*, I. 49)
3. ⁵ᵃ πήματα πάσχειν "to suffer pains" (*Odyssey*, 1. 190)
4. ⁵ᵃ πήματα πάσχεις "you suffer pains" (*Odyssey*, VIII. 441)
5. ⁵ᵃ πήματα πάσχω "I suffer pains" (*Odyssey*, VII. 152)

(2) ⁵ᵃ[ἄλγεα πάσχ –]_{VP}

1. ⁵ᵃ ἄλγεα πάσχων "suffering pains"(9×)
2. ⁵ᵃ ἄλγεα πάσχειν "to suffer pains" (*Iliad,* III. 157, *Odyssey*, xx. 221)
3. ⁵ᵃ ἄλγεα πάσχῃ "that s/he might suffer pains"(*Odyssey*, XIII. 418, *Odyssey*, XXII. 177)
4. ⁵ᵃ ἄλγεα πάσχει "s/he suffers pains" (*Iliad,* XX. 297)

The two constructions might look very similar, but their productivity is different. In particular, construction (1) is significantly more productive (i.e. more flexible) than construction (2). How can we tell? The productivity of a construction can be measured by looking at the *frequencies of types, tokens and hapax legomena* of the expressions created by each construction.[63] Specifically, the value *P* (i.e. Productivity, as defined by Baayen) can be measured as the ratio of hapaxes to tokens, where 1 is the highest productivity value. Construction (1) has five types and seven tokens; of these tokens, 4 are hapaxes. Its *P* value is thus 4/7=0.571. Construction (2), on the other hand, has 4 types and 14 tokens. Of these tokens, only 1 is a hapax. The P value is thus 1/14=0.07.[64] In other words, apprentice poets learning their technique from the *Iliad* and the *Odyssey* would have had more evidence for the flexibility of construction (1) than for construction (2). If they wanted to create a new, unique expression following one of these constructions, they would more likely have reached for (1) than (2).

Another way of thinking about productivity of a construction is thinking about its life cycle. As mentioned above, the productivity of a construction (i.e. flexibility) usually decreases over time; young constructions start out as very

[63] The difference between 'type (class) and 'token' (instance) is easily exemplified: say we have a bowl of fruit, containing two oranges and five pears: the bowl contains two types of fruit (oranges and pear), as well as seven tokens. Specifically, the type 'orange' has two tokens and the type 'pear' has five tokens. When we talk about a construction, each different expression produced by the construction is a type; if a given expression is repeated multiple times, then we say that that type has multiple tokens.

[64] Note that it only makes sense to compare *P*-values for constructions that are of the same size, and that specifically have the same number of open slots. *P*-values (especially when applied to syntactic constructions) should not be seen as absolute, or treated as a magical number for telling us how old a construction is.

productive, only to become increasingly fixed (and even fossilised) as they age. Eventually, newly created constructions replace the old ones, and the cycle begins anew (this is ultimately what we predict for the strong past tenses in English, though their high token frequency is likely to preserve them for a few more centuries).[65] Typically, young, productive constructions will produce many expression types, each with relatively few (or often just one) token. Thus hapaxes, i.e. types that only have one token, are a hallmark of productive constructions (as measured by Baayen's P measure above). Old, fossilised constructions will usually have just one type hoarding all of the tokens. In a forthcoming study I show that speech-introduction constructions appear to 'age' between the *Iliad* and the *Odyssey* (while new constructions are created as well), confirming the scholarly consensus that the textualisation of the *Iliad* predates the textualisation of the *Odyssey* by at least one or two generations.[66]

This method can also be used to verify whether a given expression is likely to be very old in the technique. I have argued elsewhere that Homeric expression λιποῦσ' ἀνδροτῆτα καὶ ἥβην, "leaving behind manliness and youth" (*Iliad*, XVI. 858, XXII. 363), usually recognised as a deep archaism within the technique, dating back to the second millennium BCE, belongs instead to a recent layer in the poetic composition, and was created by a construction that was still young and flexible at the time of the textualisation of the *Odyssey*.[67]

From Constructions to Collocations and Themes

Constructions can help us capture a large swathe of formulaic phenomena in Homer's diction, but they are, in many ways, just the tip of the iceberg. Many more regularities can be found in a poetic language that cannot be described as syntactic or metrical templates. In some cases, these regularities simply reflect the collocational habits of given lexical items, which are not tied to a given metrical position or syntactic construction. In other cases, we might come across a traditional association of ideas which, however, does not have a fixed lexical realisation. All of these phenomena are closer to Lord's concept of

---

[65] Interestingly, this life cycle is also in part driven by the balance between LTM and WM in language processing, as regulated by frequency of usage; see the discussion in BOZZONE, "Homeric formulas and their antiquity".

[66] C. BOZZONE, "Homeric constructions, their productivity, and the development of epic Greek".

[67] BOZZONE, "Homeric formulas and their antiquity".

the 'theme'[68] than to Parry's concept of the formula. In the past, some of these phenomena have been described as flexible formulas (or formulaic expressions), but I think it would be useful to introduce a more granular terminology.

Many expressions in Homer arise from the combination of the lexemes ἀλγ- 'pain' + παθ- 'suffer' (here given in their root form). Only some of these expressions are formulas in Parry's definition, and only some can be notated as constructions. Others are unique expressions that do not follow any traditional pattern (i.e. they are potentially individual creations of single singers). In this sense, one might talk of the *collocation* ἀλγ- 'pain' + παθ- 'suffer', and the expressions that reflect it. Some examples of the different types are given below, sorted by whether the expression is repeated or unique in the Homeric corpus. Note that, of course, 'unique' does not necessarily mean "entirely non-formulaic", since some constructions might be written grouping together some of the unique examples (these, such as πῆμα πάθῃσι and πῆμα παθόντες, are marked with broken underlining in the tables below).

Table 2. Some unique and repeated expressions reflecting the collocation ἀλγ- 'pain' + παθ- 'suffer' in Homer.

collocation	repeated expressions	unique expressions
ἀλγ- 'pain' + παθ- 'suffer' (32×)	ἄλγεα πάσχων "suffering pains" (9×) ἐπεὶ πάθον ἄλγεα θυμῷ "after I suffered pains in my heart" (*Iliad,* IX. 321, *Iliad,* XVI. 55) ὅθι πάσχομεν ἄλγε' Ἀχαιοί "where we Achaeans suffered pains" (*Odyssey,* III. 220, *Odyssey,* XXIV. 27)	ἄλγεα πολλὰ πάθοιμεν "so that we would suffer many pains" (*Odyssey,* IX. 53) ἄλγεα πάσχουσιν "they suffer pains" (*Odyssey,* IX. 121) πάθετ' ἄλγεα "you guys suffered pains" (*Odyssey,* X. 457)

And we can go further. The collocation ἀλγ- 'pain' + παθ- 'suffer' is only one of the ways one might express the *conceptual association* SUFFER+PAIN in Homer.[69] At least three more collocations cover this semantic space, namely:

---

[68] Cf. also WATKINS, *How to Kill a Dragon*, and KIPARSKY, "Formulas and themes".

[69] We might properly call this a (micro-) theme, in Lord's sense: "the groups of ideas regularly used in telling a tale in the formulaic style of traditional song" (LORD, *The Singer of Tales*, p. 68).

Table 3 Some unique and repeated expressions reflecting the collocations πηματ- 'misery' + παθ- 'suffer', κακ- 'bad, ill'+ παθ- 'suffer', and αιν- 'terrible' + παθ- 'suffer' in Homer.

collocation	repeated expressions	unique expressions
πηματ- 'misery' + παθ- 'suffer' (13×)	δήμῳ ἔνι Τρώων, ὅθι πάσχετε πήματ' Ἀχαιοί· "in the land of Troy, where you, the Achaeans, suffered pains" (*Odyssey*, III. 100, *Odyssey*, IV. 243, *Odyssey*, IV. 330)	μηδέ τι μεσσηγύς γε κακὸν καὶ πῆμα πάθῃσι "that you might not suffer any pain or ill during your trip" (*Odyssey*, VII. 195) ἢ ἁλὸς ἢ ἐπὶ γῆς ἀλγήσετε πῆμα παθόντες. "that you guys will be tormented, suffering pains by land or sea" (*Odyssey*, XII. 27)
κακ- 'bad, ill'+ παθ- 'suffer' (30×)	κέκλυτέ μευ μύθων, κακά περ πάσχοντες ἑταῖροι, "listen to my words, oh companions, even if you are suffering ills" (*Odyssey*, X. 189, *Odyssey*, XII. 271, *Odyssey*, XII. 340) ἔτ' εἰς Ἰθάκην, κακά περ πάσχοντες, ἵκοισθε· "so that you might reach Ithaca, even after suffering illls" (*Odyssey*, XII. 138, *Odyssey*, XI. 111) κακὰ πολλὰ παθών "suffering many ills" (*Odyssey* 4×)	ἆ δειλοί, τί κακὸν τόδε πάσχετε "oh , what ill are you guys suffering?" (*Odyssey*, XX. 351) ὤ μοι ἐγὼ τί πάθω; μέγα μὲν κακὸν αἴ κε φέβωμαι "Oh my, what am I suffering? It is a terrible ill if I run away" (*Iliad*, XI. 404)
αιν- 'terrible' + παθ- 'suffer' (2×)	–	αἰνὰ παθοῦσα "suffering terrible things" (*Iliad*, XXII. 431), αἰνοπαθής "terribly-suffering" (*Odyssey*, XVIII. 201)

A few observations may be added: most of the expressions reflecting the collocations above maintain a fixed grammatical relationship between the two lexical items in question (in this case, παθ- is the verb and the other item is its direct object), but this is not necessary: the collocates might simply appear in adjacent clauses, without sharing any syntactic relation (as in ὤ μοι ἐγὼ τί πάθω; μέγα μὲν κακὸν αἴ κε φέβωμαι "Oh my, what am I suffering? It is a terrible ill if I run away" (*Iliad*, XI. 404); at the other extreme, the collocates might constitute the two members of a compound, as in the adjective αἰνοπαθής 'terribly-suffering' (*Odyssey*, XVIII. 201).

We can also investigate the relative chronology and register of our different collocations. In expressing the *conceptual association* SUFFER+PAIN, the collocation κακ- + παθ- appears to belong to the general, non-poetic register of the language, and as such is found in later prose authors (it is attested, for instance, in Herodotus, Thucydides, and Plutarch, though it also appears in the poetry of Theognis and Euripides). The other collocations are limited to poetry, with ἀλγ- + παθ- arguably representing the older layer of the technique,[70] πηματ- + παθ- a newer development specific to the *Odyssey*,[71] and αἰν- + παθ- representing an even more marginal usage.[72]

Table 4 below summarises all of the terminology employed so far:

Table 4 From Themes to Formulas.

	same ideas	same lexical item(s)	same syntax	same metre
conceptual association (*mini-theme*)	✓			
collocation	✓	✓		
construction (properly a *lexically filled construction*)	✓	✓	✓	
metrical construction (formula)[1]	✓	✓	✓	✓
structural formula (à la Russo)			✓	✓

---

[70] Of 32 attestations, only 3 expressions appear to be unique, all others being more or less fixed.

[71] The collocation is found once in *Iliad*, V. 886, but in a clearly non-formulaic usage.

[72] This collocation, at least judging from its distribution, might have been tied to the genre of lamentation specifically, and thus its limited attestation might just be an effect of the nature of our corpus. For the genre of the funerary lament in Indo-European, see C. BOZZONE "Weaving songs for the dead in Indo-European: Women poets, funerary laments, and the ecology of **kleu̯os*", in: *Proceedings of the 27th Annual UCLA Indo-European Conference*, ed. D.M. GOLDSTEIN, S.W. JAMISON, and B. VINE (Bremen, 2016), pp. 1-22.

¹ In this group we put fixed formulas and (most) flexible formulas alike: fixed formulas are instances of metrical constructions that recur without variation; flexible formulas are metrical constructions that admit of some variation. Admittedly, some of Hainsworth's flexible formulas are independent from metre (e.g. in the case of separation and dislocation). These would better be described as collocations (or even constructions without metrical specification), but not formulas).

We can illustrate these concepts once more as follows:

- conceptual association: SUFFER + PAIN
- collocation: ἀλγ- 'pain' + παθ- 'suffer' (in any syntactic relationship)
- (lexically filled) construction:[73] [ἀλγ-$_{Obj.NP}$ + παθ-$_V$]$_{VP}$
- metrical construction: ^{5a}[ἄλγεα πάσχ–]$_{VP}$
- structural formula: ^{5a}[[– ⏑ ⏑]$_{Obj.NP}$ [– –]$_V$]VP

Conclusion: Formulas Beyond Homer

Oral-formulaic theory started to grapple with some basic questions about language production and the human mind long before the fields of contemporary linguistics and cognitive studies turned their attention to these questions. In fact, some of difficulties it encountered might be explained by the fact that so little was known at the time about these phenomena in natural language production – let alone the exceptional circumstances that oral traditions afford. Even as the debate continued in the 1970s and 1980s, few were the scholars who leveraged contemporary linguistic notions in order to make sense of the phenomena observed in Homer. We are much more fortunate nowadays, in that we can rely on concepts and methodologies coming from a number of neighbouring disciplines (cognitive psychology, psycholinguistics, corpus linguistics, language-acquisition studies, usage-based linguistics, etc.) in order to inform our work on oral traditions. In this paper, I have given a short survey of some of the insights and tools that I have employed in my work on Homer over the last decade. My hope is that some of these examples may prove useful to scholars working on other traditions as well.

---

[73] In studying the relationship between given syntactic constructions and given lexical items, methodology from *collostructional analysis* might be employed as well. See A. STEFANOWITSCH and S.T. GRIES, "Collostructions: Investigating the interaction between words and constructions", *International Journal of Corpus Linguistics* 8 (2003), pp. 209-243.

A Further History of Orality and Eddic Poetry

PAUL ACKER

In my monograph from 1998, *Revising Oral Theory*,[1] I included a survey of oral-formulaic critical theory as applied to Eddic poetry. In a section titled "Before Theory", I first discussed what I called the "formula *collecting*" of nineteenth-century German scholars, most notably Richard Meyer's work from 1889, *Die altgermanische Poesie nach ihren formelhaften Elementen beschrieben*.[2] For this update to that survey, I will start even further back, with the medieval manuscripts themselves.

While modern editions of the Edda scarcely take notice of the phenomenon, a few scholars, including Joseph Harris, Frog, Scott Mellor, and Heimir Pálsson, have mentioned the presence of a distinctive form of scribal abbreviation to indicate repeated lines in the poems. A typical example is found on f. 19v of the Codex Regius (MS GKS 2365 4to, henceforth **R**), where the poem *Alvíssmál* begins with a greenish-blue capital letter. From stanza 9 onward, Thor asks the

---

[*] I delivered a version of this paper as a keynote lecture at a conference on "The Formula in Oral Poetry and Prose," organised by Daniel Sävborg in Tartu, Estonia in December, 2019.

[1] P. ACKER, *Revising Oral Theory: Formulaic Composition in Old English and Old Icelandic Verse* (New York, 1998).

[2] R. MEYER, *Die altgermanische Poesie nach ihren formelhaften Elementen beschrieben* (Berlin, 1889).

dwarf Alvíss to tell him how to name various concepts in the different 'worlds' of Old Norse cosmogony. Thor's stanzas are quite repetitive or formulaic, differing only in the particular concept Thor asks about, followed by a half-line to alliterate with it.[3] Hence Thor asks in stanza 9 (**R**, f. 19v):

> *Segðu mér þat, Alvíss*[4] *– öll of röc fira*
> *voromc, dvergr, at vitir –*
> *hvé sú iörð heitir, er liggr fyr alda sonom,*
> *heimi hveriom í.*[5]

Tell me, Alviss, all the fates of men
I think, dwarf, that you know –
how is the earth called, which lies before the sons of men,
in each of the worlds.

Alvíss in stanza ten tells Thor what the earth is called among the Æsir, Vanir, giants, elves, and powers. In stanza eleven, Thor next asks for the names of 'heaven', and thereafter the names for the moon, sun, clouds, wind, and so on. But the repeating parts of Thor's stanzas are abbreviated in the Codex Regius in an unusual way, with the first letters of words, or rather some of the words. Hence stanza eleven reads "*Segðu mér þ. a. v.*".

The abbreviation letters begin with *þ. a.* for *þat, Alvíss*, then skip over the words "*öll of röc fira / Voromc, dvergr, at*" and then provide a letter *v* for the final word of the first half stanza, "*vitir*". The next line with the new material is written out: "*hvé sá himinn heitir erakendi*" ("what heaven is called [obscure]") and then the closing full line "*heimi hveriom í*" is abbreviated "*h. hi.*" In their edition, Neckel and Kuhn indicate in their textual notes at the foot of the page that "*sind viele der wiederkehrenden wörter abgekürzt*" ("many of the repeated words are abbreviated")[6], without specifying exactly which words are abbreviated. This scribal technique of abbreviation by first letters (a more ex-

---

[3] I examine the repetition and variation in these stanzas in detail in ACKER, *Revising Oral Theory*, pp. 61-66; see also FROG, "*Alvíssmal* and orality I: Formula, alliteration and categories of mythic being", *Arkiv för nordisk filologi* 126 (2011), pp. 17-71 (online at <academia.edu>).

[4] S. MELLOR, *Analyzing Ten Poems from the Poetic Edda: Oral Formula and Mythic Patterns* (Lewiston, 2008), p. 121, lists comparable versions of the first half-line from a number of other Eddic poems, with the name of the person addressed carrying the alliteration, as in *Fáfnismál* h14.1, *Segðu mér þat, Fáfnir.*

[5] *Edda: Die Lieder des Codex Regius nebst verwandten Denkmälern*, ed. G. NECKEL and H. KUHN, 4th edn. (Heidelberg, 1962), p. 125.

[6] *Edda*, ed. NECKEL and KUHN, *ibid.*

A Further History of Orality and Eddic Poetry 143

tended, text-specific version of 'suspension') continues through stanza 33, Thor's final question about the names for beer. In two of these question stanzas, numbers 15 and 17, the abbreviation for the half stanza is reduced even further to just *"s.m.þ."*, for *"segðu mér þat"*.

Joseph Harris commented that this type of abbreviation "is frequent in the Codex Regius where obvious and extensive repetitions occur (e.g. in *Alvíssmál*) and is, of course, to be distinguished from ordinary abbreviation".[7] Harris then examined this feature in the Codex Regius transcription of the heroic Helgi poems, where the second Helgi Hundingsbani poem abbreviates lines from the first, especially in a repeated *flyting* or contest of words. Harris reprints stanzas 23 and 24 (**R** f.25v) of *Helgakviða Hundingsbana önnur* from Sophus Bugge's diplomatic edition, which reproduces the abbreviations without expanding them (I have boldfaced some of the points of difference):[8]

HH	HH II
45 *Væri ycr, Sinfiotli .q.*	23 *"Þer er, Sinfiotli*
sæmra myclo	*sæmra myclo*
gvnni at heyia	*gvnni at heyia*
oc glaþa orno	*oc glaþa orno,*
en se onytom	*enn onytom*
orþom at bregdaz,	*o. a. d. [**deila**]*
þot hringbrotar	*þott **hilldingar***
heiptir deili.	*heiptir **deili**.*
46 *Þicciat mer godir*	24 *Þiccit mer goþir*
Granmars synir,	*gran. s.*
þo dvgir siklingom	*þo d. s.*
satt at mæla	*s. a. m.*
þeir hafa marcat	*þeir mærcþ h.*
a Moinsheimom	*a. m. r.*
at hvg hafa	*at hvg hafa*
hiorom at bregda.	*hior. a. b.*
	ero. hildingar

---

[7] J. HARRIS, "Eddic poetry as oral poetry: The evidence of parallel passages in the Helgi poems for questions and performance", in: *Edda: A Collection of Essays*, ed. R. GLENDINNING and H. BESSASON (Winnipeg, 1983), pp. 210-242, at p. 236, n. 21; the article is reprinted in: ID., *"Speak Useful Words or Say Nothing": Old Norse Studies by Joseph Harris*, ed. S.E. DESKIS and T.D. HILL (Ithaca, 2008), pp. 189-225.

[8] The 2019 diplomatic edition, *The Codex Regius of the Poetic Edda: Konungsbók Eddukvæda GKS 2365 4to*, ed. G.M. GUNNLAUGSSON, H. BERHARÐSSON and V. ÓLASON (Reykjavík, 2019), expands the abbreviations with italics, e.g. or*ðom at* deila (st. 28, p. 124).

haullzti sniallir.

For you, Sinfjotli, it would be more fitting / to give battle and to gladden eagles / than to taunt / **contend** with useless words, even if the ring-breakers / **warlords** engage in hateful deeds.

I do not expect good from Granmar's sons, though it befits princes to tell the truth. They have shown at Móinsheimr (that they) have temperament to draw swords [the warlords are far-too bold].

For Harris, one question posed by these abbreviations has to do with textual identity: which lines did the scribe consider identical, and thus could be heavily abbreviated?[9] The scribe started abbreviating in stanza 23.6 with the half-line *orþom at bregdaz* abbreviated *o.a.d.* instead of *o.a.b.*, with *d.* for ***deila*** either as a variant or an error influenced by the following line. The scribe also abbreviates the half-line in 24.4, with *s.a.m.* for *satt at mæla*. Generally the scribe's abbreviations cover half-lines or whole-lines, which indicates that the scribe thinks of the poetry in those groups, in formulas, not just in repeated individual words. Since the poetic lines in the Codex Regius and elsewhere are written out as continuous prose, which editors then divide into lines according to metre and alliteration, it is good to have this indication that scribes also recognised lines and half-lines. The scribe had to write out line 23.7 without abbreviation because it had a variant word, ***hilldingar*** ('warlords') for *hringbrotar* ('ring-breakers') in *Helgakviða Hundingsbana in fyrri*. The scribe also felt the need to record the inversion in 24.5.

In stanza 19, from a bit earlier in the poem, Harris thinks the scribe is trying to quote from memory, but substitutes a different alliterating line: (HH II 19) "*hverr er fylkir / sá er flota stýrir*" ("who is the prince who steers the ships") for (HHI 32) "*Hverr er landreki, sá er liði stýrir*" ("who is the land-protector [king] who guides the troop [on a ship]"). Overall, Harris considers that the treatment of repetitions indicates deliberative composition and memorial transmission, rather than improvisational composition and transmission as per the Parry / Lord model for South Slavic oral epic.[10] Arguably, however, one could say the Codex Regius scribe is here improvising, with pen in hand, a different line for the one he misremembers. In a recent survey, Harris cites Katherine O'Brien O'Keefe in a similar vein, that the scribes sometimes varied their copy "poetically in something like composition in (writing) performance".[11]

---

[9] HARRIS, "Eddic poetry as oral poetry", p. 216.
[10] HARRIS, "Eddic poetry as oral poetry", p. 211.
[11] J. HARRIS, "Traditions of Eddic scholarship", in: *A Handbook of Eddic Poetry: Myths and*

A Further History of Orality and Eddic Poetry

To continue this discussion begun by Harris, I will examine other line abbreviations in the Codex Regius with an eye toward formulas and scribal transmission, beginning with the first poem, *Völuspá*, and its first repeated half-stanza. Stanza 6, lines 1-4 reads on page one of the manuscript thus:

Þa gen gengo regin oll arǫk stola giNhęilog god oc vm þat gęttvz,

or as edited by Neckel and Kuhn:

Þá gengo regin öll á röcstóla,
ginnheilog goð, oc um þat gættuz:[12]

Then all the powers went to their judgment-seats,
most holy gods, and deliberated about it.

Stanza nine begins with the same two lines, but now they are abbreviated:

Þa g. r. a. ar.[13]

The abbreviation covers only the first whole line of the repeated two lines; the reader is expected to supply the rest ("*ginnheilog goð, oc um þat gættuz*"), either by rereading stanza 6, or from memory, from previous acquaintance with the (presumably) well-known poem. The opening word, *Þá*, is not abbreviated but written in full; the next word *gengo* is abbreviated with the letter *g.*; *öll* is abbreviated with *a.*, probably for the alternative spelling *aull* (see *rauk-* in st. 6 for *rök*[14]). The preposition *a* is conjoined with its following noun, abbreviated as *ar.*

The line is not abbreviated in the text of *Völuspá* in MS **H**, *Hauksbók*, which seldom employs this type of abbreviation (extended suspension). But an abbreviation does occur where stanza 9 from *Völuspá* is quoted in *Snorra Edda*, in MS **U** (the Uppsala Codex, DG 11 4to, *ca.* 1300, p. 8):

Legends of Early Scandinavia, ed. C. LARRINGTON, J. QUINN, and B. SCHORN (Cambridge, 2016), pp. 33-57, at p. 38.

[12] *Edda*, ed. NECKEL and KUHN, p. 2.

[13] *The Codex Regius of the Poetic Edda*, ed. GUNNLAUGSSON et al., p. 20: "Þa gengo regin avll ar k ſtola". Note *oll* from st. 6 is spelled *avll*, and *ar k stola* is abbreviated *ar*. In his section on palaeography, Guðvarður mentions this instance and another from the end of *Skírnismál* as examples of suspension to indicate repeated words or lines (p. 439). He then adds that there are 94 such examples in *Alvíssmál*, 44 in *Völuspá*, and 41 in *Hávamál*.

[14] Or the editorial expansion, p. 125, of **U** p. 23 below.

Þa gengv v. A. s. g. h. g. & vm þat g.'

The editors of the diplomatic transcription of this manuscript, Anders Grape *et al.*, expand the line thus:

[v]regin a [rauk]stola giNheilog gvþ og ok vm þat getuz[15]

noting that the scribe miswrites *v*. for *r*. (which it can resemble graphically) and omits the compound word element *rauk-* from *raukstola*. Further, a later scribe expanded the abbreviations (or copied the line from elsewhere) in the margin below as "*Þa* gen*go reghin oll ā raukstola ginnheilug goð & vm þat gietuz*".

The recent editor of the Uppsala *Snorra Edda* for the Viking Society, Heimir Pálsson, takes note of these "strange abbreviations", made stranger still in this case because the stanza had not appeared earlier in Snorri's text, in *un*abbreviated form. Heimir suggests that the scribe, and perhaps Snorri himself in an earlier manuscript, "abbreviated the lines as an *aide-mémoire* and relied on his memory to recall the full text".[16] In a previous article in *Scripta Islandica*, Heimir Pálsson and Lasse Mårtensson had discussed a total of six such abbreviations in the Uppsala *Snorra Edda*, suggesting they had been abbreviated from a full transcription in their source manuscript.[17]

Returning to the Codex Regius, Stanza 23 of *Völuspá* begins again with the same two memorable lines, as does st. 25, and they are abbreviated thus (**R**, page 2):

St. 23 *Þa g. r. a. a.*
St. 25 *Þa g. r. a.*

---

[15] *Snorre Sturlassons Edda Uppsala-Handskriften DG 11*, ed. A. GRAPE *et al.*, 2, *Transkriberad text och Paleografisk kommentar av Anders Grape†, Gottfried Kallstenius† och Olf Thorell* (Uppsala, 1977), Comm. p. 117.

[16] Snorri Sturluson, *The Uppsala Edda* (DG 11 4to), ed. H. PÁLSSON, trans. A. FAULKES (London, 2012: *Viking Society for Northern Research*), p. XLVI.

[17] L. MÅRTENSSON and H. PÁLSSON, "Anmerkningsvärda suspensioner i DG 11 4to (Codex Upsaliensis av Snorra Edda): Spåren av en skriven förlaga?", *Scripta Islandica* 59 (2008), pp. 135-155.

A Further History of Orality and Eddic Poetry

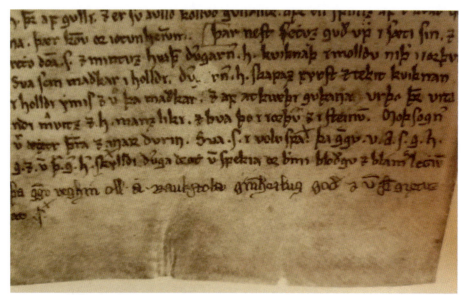

Fig. 1   MS U, p. 8, bottom margin.

The abbreviation has been abbreviated further, with the half-line's final abbreviation *ar.* shortened to *a.* in st. 23 and then omitted in st. 25. St. 25 is also abbreviated in Snorra Edda (MS U, p. 23), as:

> *þ. g'. c. a. A. r. s. [gin h. Gvþ ok v. þat g.]*

expanded by Grape *et al.* as: "*þa gengv [c]regin avll á ravk stola*", with again an error, *c.*, for the *r* of *reginn*.

This is actually the fullest abbreviation of the lines, since it adds an s. for *stóla* in the compound *raukstola*, although the scribe again makes an error, *c.* for *r.*, as if perhaps copying a prior abbreviation rather than rendering it on his own.

This form of extensive abbreviation picks up again in the Codex Regius, f. 1v with a well-known, stanza-final half-line from *Völuspá*, "*vitoð ér enn, eða hvat?*", which translates "would you know more, or not?", or, if you can tolerate a Brooklyn dialect, the verbally closer "you wanna know more, or what?" The refrain is partly spelled out at the end of stanza 27, where it first occurs, as "*uitoþ ē ē e. hvat*" but abbreviated by initials soon and always thereafter, as in stanza 28 and following:

28 MS *v. e. e. h.*
33 MS *v. e. e. e. h.*
35 MS *v. þ. e. h.*
39 MS *v. e. e. e. h.*
41 MS *v. e. h.* (also **U**: *e. h.*)
51a (48) *v. e. e. h.*
62 *v. e e. h.*
63 *v. e. e. h.*

The most frequent abbreviation is *v.e.e.h.*, probably for *vitoðér enn eða hvat*, (or *vitoð ér [enn] eða hvat*). All three e's occur in two other instances, for *ér, enn, eða*, and thorn appears for *þér* in st. 35, and st. 41 with v.e.h. apparently skips from the first word to the last two. In all cases, though, the scribe is thinking of the half-line as a unit to be abbreviated with suspensions.

One other repeated and abbreviated stanza from *Völuspá* is first written out in full in stanza 44:

Geyr Garmr mioc fyr Gnipahelli,
Festr mun slitna, enn freki renna
Fiöld veit hon fræða, fram sé ec lengra
Um ragna röc, römm, sigtýva.

Garmr howls much before Gnipahell,
Bond will be torn, and the wolf run
She knows much lore, I see further ahead
About fate of gods, mighty battle-gods.

The same four lines are repeated as stanzas 49 and 58, where the Codex Regius abbreviates them thus (f.2v):

49 *Geyr nv g.*
58 *Geyr n.*

In other words, the reader is expected to be able to reproduce the whole stanza based on its first two or three words (with the adverbial *nú* meaning 'now' added); the abbreviation means little more than 're-insert the 'Geyr' stanza", where the word *geyr* ('howls') would be suitably distinctive.

This type of abbreviation continues throughout the Codex Regius, as for instance in the Loddfáfnismál section of *Hávamál*, stanzas 125-137, where the initial words *Ráðomc þér Loddfáfnir* and so on are abbreviated. Reading on through the mythological portion of the Codex Regius and some of its well-known repeated passages, we find next in *Vafðrúðnismál* (f.8) a numbered sequence where Odin asks information of the giant Vafðrúðnir.

Vfþ 20 *Segðu þat iþ eina, ef þitt œði dugir / oc þú, Vafðrúðnir, vitir*
Vfþ 22 *Segðu þat ii e. þ. e. d. & þ. v.*
Vfþ 22 MS A *Sæg þu þat ii e. þ. e. d.*

Stanza 20 reads "*Segðu þat iþ eina, ef þitt œði dugir / oc þú, Vafðrúðnir, vitir*"; stanza 22 is written out "*Segðu þat ii*" (with roman numeral II for *annat*, 'second'), followed by the initials "*e. þ. e. d. & þ. v.*". This poem is also preserved in MS AM 748 4to, which abbreviates stanza 22 a little more heavily, with "*Sæg þu þat ii e. þ. e. d.*", omitting abbreviations for line 22.3, the full line "*oc þú, Vafðrúðnir, vitir*". At the end of the poem, Odinn's repeated half-stanzas "*Fjölð ec fór*", "*fjölð ec freistaðac*", "*fjölð ec reynda regin*" are also abbreviated in five stanzas (44; 46, 48, 50, 52, 54).

The poem *Skírnismál*, likewise written in *ljóðaháttr* metre, abbreviates many of its half stanzas as part of the incremental repetition of its dialogue, as in stanzas 2.5-6 (cf. 1.5-6) and 25.1-3 (cf. 23.1-3; st. 25 is also abbreviated in MS A). In stanza 39, the giantess Gerðr tells Skírnir about the grove named Barri, where she will meet Freyr. In stanza 41, Skírnir repeats that information to Freyr, and the entire stanza is abbreviated:

Skm 39 *Barri heitir, er við bæði vitom,*
              lundr lognfara;
       Enn ept nætr nío þar mun Njarðar syni
              Gerðr unna gamans.

Skm 41 *Barri h. l. e'. vi. l. l. e. e. n. n. þ. m. n. s. g. u. gaman*s.

The abbreviation for line 41.2 adds a letter *l*, perhaps anticipating the word *lundr* ('grove'), in the full line 41.3. It also seems to omit the abbreviating letters for the end of 41.2, *bæði vitom*. Getting all the letters right must have been a bit difficult, whether the scribe was compiling the string of letters or copying a previously made string in the exemplar. In any case, the rest of the stanza's abbreviations run smoothly (MS A ends at st 27).

In *Hárbarðsljóð*, the question "*Hvat vanntu þá meðan*" ("What did you do meanwhile") from st. 15.7 and 18.13 is abbreviated in stanzas 19 (*h. v. m.*), 22, 23, 28, 36 and 39. Thor's foul retort to Loki in *Locasenna* stanza 57, "*Þegu þú rög vættr*" ("Shut up, faggot") and its following threat is abbreviated in stanzas 59 ("*Þegi þ. r. v. þ.*"), 61, and 63.

Lastly, among the mythological poems, *Þrymskviða* also has some long, incrementally repeated passages, such as in stanza 15 when Heimdallr says "Let us bind up Thor in bridal linen", and then in stanza 19 (f.17v) the narrative says they did just that. The verb and pronoun change and have to be written out, but the rest is abbreviated:

15 *Bindo vér Þór þá brúðar líni*
Hafi hann iþ micla men Brísinga!

16 *Látom und hánom hrynja lucla*
Oc qvennváðir um kné falla,
Enn á briósti breiða steina,
Og hagliga um höfuð typpom!

19 *Bu*ndo þar Þor þ. b. l. & e. m. me*n B. l. v. h. h. l. & k. v. v*m kne f. en*n a. b. b. s. & h. v. h. t.*

"*Hafi hann*" from 15.3 is omitted in a legitimate variant and some short ordinary abbreviations are employed (such as v̄ for v*m*). The word *kne* is written out, perhaps because k. for *kven* precedes it. 16.1 begins with an initial l. although the verb changes from first person *látom* to third person *létu*. But otherwise that is the longest Eddic sequence to be abbreviated with initial letters. That unusual method of indicating repetition is employed here as elsewhere for a passage in a single poem rather than for a compositionally useful formula employed across the corpus. Such poem-specific repetition is common in Eddic poetry and should perhaps be distinguished from the type of repetition accounted for by oral-formulaic theory.

After the Helgi poems, the heroic poems in the Codex Regius exhibit rather less of the extended suspension abbreviations, perhaps because there are fewer repeated stanzas. *Fáfnismál* 20.4-6 repeats a *ljóðaháttr* full line from 9.4-6. *Sigrdrífomál* contains a section on various types of runes, beginning with 6.1, "*Sigrúnar þú scalt kunna*". Subsequently the types of runes are written out, followed by the abbreviation "*s. k.*" or "*r. s. k.*" (for *rúnar scaltu kunna*", "runes you must know") in stanzas 9.1, 11.1, 12.1, and 13.1 (st. 10 has "*Brim r. s. r.*" (for "*Brimrúnar scaltu rista*", "runes you must carve"). A numerical sequence beginning in st. 22 with "*Þat ræð ec þér iþ fyrsta*" ("I advise you first") becomes "*Þ. r. e. þ' a.*" ("I advise you second") in st. 23 and so on through "sixth" in st. 29 (after which the Codex Regius text breaks off in the 'great lacuna').

In *Guðrúnarkviða* I, two lines from st, 5.1-4 are abbreviated in 11.1-4, and one halfline in 20.4 is abbreviated, unusually, in the very next repeated half-line, 20.5 (*"valda megir Giúca"*). *Atlakviða* makes no abbreviations, despite some repeated half-lines such as *"vín í valhöllo"* in 2.3 and 14.11. Nor does *Atlamál* abbreviate the repeating parts of sts. 15.1, 17.1, 19.1, 22.1, 24.1, and 26.1 (*"hugða ec hér inn"*). *Hamðismál* abbreviates 4.4-6 (three half-lines), but from the *preceding poem*, *Guðrúnarhvöt* 4.4-6.

This type of abbreviation by a string of initial letters (which we may call 'extended suspension') is not often parallelled in manuscripts from elsewhere in medieval Europe.[18] It is a distinctive, extended form of the ordinary method of abbreviation by suspension. In Iceland, it is found earliest in legal manuscripts from the twelfth century, where so-called 'legal formulas' are heavily abbreviated, such as *f.g.v.* for *"fjörbaugsgarð varðar"*, "punishable by lesser outlawry", in the law code *Grágás* (MS AM 315 d fol., f. 2r).[19] The practice in Iceland thus may have begun in legal manuscripts and was extended to long, repeated passages in poetic manuscripts.

Not surprisingly, given their repetitive refrains, this type of abbreviation continues on into ballad manuscripts, which first appear in the seventeenth century with Gissur Sveinsson's codex (AM 147 8vo).[20] The best known ballad in Iceland is the "Ballad of Olafur Lilyrose", which in this earliest version begins *"Olafur reið með björgum fram"*, and then the refrain begins *"rauður login brann"* ("the red fires burned"), abbreviated after its first instance as "*R. L. B.*" (f. 12v).The mention of ballads is apt, since Eddic poems, unlike Old

---

[18] On the listserv medtextl, William Schipper asked about this type of abbreviation as seen in glossed Bibles, where a long phrase from a psalm was abbreviated by initial letters. Mark Williams remarked that he had seen the practice in classical letter writing, and Anna Kirkwood Graham and William Flynn had seen it for Biblical passages in preacher's aids (June 23-24, 2020).

[19] H. BENEDIKTSON, *Early Icelandic Script as Illustrated in Vernacular Manuscripts from the Twelfth and Thirteenth Centuries* (Reykjavík, 1965), 3: 27.

[20] The abbreviated passages in ballad manuscripts are indicated in Jón Helgason's editions (*Íslenzk fornkvædi: Islandske folkeviser*, ed. J. HELGASON, 1 (Copenhagen, 1962). I am grateful to Vésteinn Ólason for pointing out to me this feature. The refrains can be reduced to a single letter, as in *Tófu kvæði,* where *"og dans vill hun heyra"* ("and she wants to hear a dance") can be rendered *"og d. v h h"* or just *"og d."* (p. 1.236). Gissur's ballad manuscript can be seen on <handrit.is>, a website with digital facsimiles of Icelandic manuscripts, such as the Codex Regius (<https://handrit.is/manuscript/view/is/GKS04-2367/9?iabr=on#page/3v/mode/ 2up>).

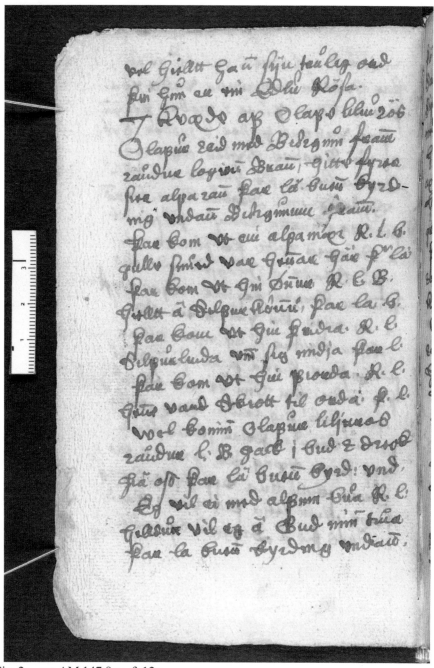

Fig. 2   MS AM 147 8vo, f. 12v.

English alliterative poems, are composed in stanzas, and have often been compared to ballads, most recently in a study by Joseph Harris.[21] He mentions their shared stanzaic form, incremental repetition and "leaping and lingering" narrative,[22] and considers that older Eddic poetry may have influenced a younger ballad genre in Norway in around the year 1300.[23] Formulas in Old English poetry are usually half-lines, or systems of related half-lines, that facilitate composition. Such lines occur sometimes in Eddic poetry, but more often the repetition takes the form of whole lines and even whole stanzas within individual poems, which as we have seen are picked out in the manuscripts with lengthy sequences of abbreviations by initial-letter suspension.

Studies of Eddic Poetry and Formulas Since 1995

To turn now to an update of scholarship on orality,[24] the final article I discussed in my monograph survey chapter was by Judy Quinn from 1992, "Verseform and voice in Eddic poems: The discourses of *Fáfnismál*".[25] I commented that her study was "representative of a more broadly-based oral theory that incorporates related approaches such as speech-act theory and discourse analysis". Proceeding chronologically I would next have gone on to Terry Gunnell's monograph from 1995, *The Origins of Drama in Scandinavia*,[26] portions of which he drew on in chapters published more recently in McTurk's 2005 *A Companion to Old Norse Literature and Culture*[27] and Larrington, Quinn and Schorn's 2016 *A Handbook to Eddic Poetry*.[28] Gunnell maintains that the dialogic Eddic poems in the *ljóðaháttr* metre, such as *Skírnismál*, *Lokasenna*, *Fáfnismál*, and *Hárbarðsljóð* "existed in oral tradition long before [they] came

---

[21] J. HARRIS, "Eddic poetry and the ballad: Voice, vocality and performance, with special reference to DgF 1", in: *Child's Children: Ballad Study and its Legacies*, ed. J. HARRIS and B. HILLERS (Trier, 2012), pp. 155-170.
[22] *Ibid.*, p. 160.
[23] *Ibid.*, p. 164.
[24] A few recent publications regarding orality and Eddic poetry are discussed by HARRIS, "Traditions of Eddic Scholarship".
[25] J. QUINN, "Verseform and voice in Eddic poems: The discourses of *Fáfnismál*", *Arkiv* 107 (1992), pp. 100-130.
[26] T. GUNNELL, *The Origins of Drama in Scandinavia* (Cambridge, 1995).
[27] T. GUNNELL, "Eddic poetry", in: *A Companion to Old Norse-Icelandic Literature and Culture*, ed. R. MCTURK (Oxford, 2005), pp. 82-100.
[28] T. GUNNELL, "Eddic performances and Eddic audiences", in: *A Handbook of Eddic Poetry*, ed. LARRINGTON, QUINN, and SCHORN, pp. 92-113.

to be recorded" and were "originally meant to be received orally and visually in performance rather than read privately".[29] As evidence, he points to the "speaker notation found in the margins of both the Codex Regius and the AM 748 manuscripts alongside the texts of at least four of the dialogic *ljóðaháttr* works".[30] These notations have mostly been trimmed away but can be glimpsed for instance in a leaf from *Hárbarðsljóð* (f.13v), where *q*. stands for *qvað*, *Hárbarðr qvað*, *Thor qvað* and so on. In a narrative poem in *fornyrðislag* metre, however, such as *Þrymskviða*, the speakers are indicated within the poem, sometimes in a formulaic set of lines (part of a formulaic system of lines, varied only in the name of the speaker), followed by a characterising half-line:

Þrym 15 Þá kvað þat Heimdallr, hvítastr ása
Þrym 17 Þá kvað þat Þórr, þrúðugr áss
Þrym 18 Þá kvað þat Loki, Laufeyjar sonr
Þrym 22 Þá kvað þat Þrymr, þursa dróttinn

Often it seems that Eddic lines repeat only within individual poems, as I mentioned above, but this particular formulaic strategy is found widely across the corpus, as shown in two lines from *Sigurðarkviða* and elsewhere:

Sgk I 12 Þá kvað þat Brynhildr, Buðla dóttir
Sgk I 15 Þá kvað þat Guðrún, Gjúka dóttir

This focus on speakers in relation to oral performance is also investigated by Bernt Øyvind Thorvaldsen, in a full analysis of the Codex Regius *Völuspá*, published in *Maal og Menne* in 2013. Referring to the "double scene" as Lars Lönnroth characterised it, Thorvaldsen proposes that "the immediate proximity between speaker and audience enables effects which are documented in oral storytelling from other contexts".[31] Specifically, his approach helps to explain the otherwise puzzling switches between the pronouns used for the speaking prophetess, *ek* and *hon*".[32] Gísli Sigurðsson has also written about *Völuspá* and

[29] GUNNELL, "Eddic poetry", p. 83.
[30] GUNNELL, "Eddic poetry", p. 96.
[31] B.Ø. THORVALDSEN, "Deictic traces of oral performance in the Codex Regius version of *Völuspá*", *Maal og Minne* 103.2 (2013), pp. 97-131, at p. 97.
[32] THORVALDSEN, "Deictic traces of oral performance", p. 122. Thorvaldsen has also written about whether an Eddic poem like *Þrymskviða* borrows from other poems or is composed with traditional expressions, motifs and formulas (B.Ø. THORVALDSEN, "Om Þrymskiða, tekstlån og tradisjon", *Maal og Minne* 100.2 (2008), pp. 142-166, and ID., "The Eddic author: On distributed creativity in The lay of Þrymr and Skírnir's journey", in: *Modes of Authorship in the Middle Ages*,

orality, suggesting that the poem was performed by women taking on the role of prophetess, but that versions would have changed constantly, even while "keeping the old knowledge alive".[33] Else Mundal compares the Codex Regius and *Hauksbók* versions of *Völuspá* and suggests which differences seem due to oral and which to scribal variation. She concludes

> that the characteristics of oral literature may vary from one culture to another, and that even the main characteristic of oral literature according to the oral-formulaic theory, namely the formulas, is characteristic of this oral literature only to a certain degree.[34]

Judy Quinn also examines the witnesses of *Völuspá* and casts "some doubt over the methodological appropriateness of stemmatic method for the transmission context of oral poetry".[35] For instance, Eddic scribes "may have been influenced during the process of writing by their independent knowledge of the oral traditions from which the poem was derived".[36]

A number of recent chapters in essay collections have addressed the transition from orality to literacy, with a more limited *runic* literacy along the way. Judy Quinn wrote on the subject in the year 2000 in a chapter for the Cambridge collection *Old Icelandic Literature and Society*, edited by Margaret Clunies Ross.[37] Quinn collects references in later writings to oral texts, including laws, heathen rituals, genealogies, lists and poems. Of runes, she states that

---

ed. S. RANKOVIĆ (Toronto, 2012), pp. 251-263). He opts for the latter, while specifying a difference from "the South Slavic poetry studied by Lord" in that the Eddic poems are shorter and the Old Norse community "knew verbatim oral transmission (in skaldic poetry" (2012, p. 255).

[33] G. SIGURÐSSON, "Völuspá as the product of an oral tradition: What does that entail?, in: *The Nordic Apocalypse: Approaches to Völuspa and Nordic Days of Judgement*, ed. T. GUNNELL and A. LASSEN (Turnhout, 2013), pp. 45-62 (online at <academia.edu>), at p. 58. ID., "On the classification of Eddic heroic poetry in view of the oral theory", in: *Poetry in the Scandinavian Middle Ages: The Seventh International Saga Conference* (Spoleto, 1990), pp. 245-255 (online at <academia.edu>) makes some of these same observations, while also contrasting the different versions of poems about Helgi, Atli and Guðrún.

[34] E. MUNDAL, "Oral or scribal variation in Völuspá: A case study in Old Norse poetry", *Oral Art Forms and their Passage into Writing*, ed. E. MUNDAL and J. WELLENDORF (Copenhagen, 2008), pp. 209-227, at p. 225.

[35] J. QUINN, "The principles of textual criticism and the interpretation of Old Norse texts derived from oral tradition", in: *Studies in the Transmission and Reception of Old Norse Literature: The Hyperborean Muse in European Culture*, ed. J. QUINN and A. CIPOLLA (Turnhout, 2016), pp. 47-78, at p. 73.

[36] QUINN, "The principles of textual criticism", p. 49.

[37] J. QUINN, "From orality to literacy in medieval Iceland", in: *Old Icelandic Literature and Society*, ed. M. CLUNIES ROSS (Cambridge, 2000), pp. 30-60.

inscriptions were made "widely, though perhaps not generally, throughout Scandinavia", primarily for the "discourses of memorializing, ownership and magic".[38] A few verses in Eddic measures were written down in runes,[39] including one carved on the Rök stone in about the year 810 (and so well in advance of the Christian literate period) in Östergötland, Sweden.[40] It is not clear how much of the overall inscription is carved in verse, but one stanza clearly is, composed in alliterating *fornyrðislag* metre[41] (the language here as I quote it has been converted into Old West Norse):

Réð Þjóðríkr hinn þormóði,
stillir flotna, strǫndu Hreiðmarar.
Sitr nú gǫrr á gota sínum,
skildi umb fatlaðr, skati Mæringa.[42]

Þjóðríkr the bold, chief of sea-warriors, ruled over the shores of the Hreiðsea. Now he sits armed on his Goth(ic horse), his shield strapped, the prince of the Mærings.

The stanza is set apart visually at the bottom of the stone's inscriptions.

---

[38] QUINN, "From orality to literacy in medieval Iceland", p. 30.

[39] QUINN, "From orality to literacy in medieval Iceland", p. 43.

[40] Rök Stone, Östergotland, Sweden (Ög 136). Harris dates the inscription 810-820 (J. HARRIS, "The Rök stone through Anglo-Saxon eyes", in: *The Anglo-Saxons and the North: Essays Reflecting the Theme of the 10th Meeting of the International Society of Anglo-Saxonists in Helsinki, August 2001*, ed. M. KILPIÖ, L. KAHLAS-TARKKA, J. ROBERTS, and O. TIMOFEEVA (Tempe AZ, 2009: *Medieval and Renaissance Texts and Studies*), p. 11). Other such verses on rune stones are collected and translated in S.B.F. JANSSON, *The Runes of Sweden*, trans. P.G. FOOTE (New York, 1962) and in P. LARSSON, "Runes", in: *A Companion to Old-Norse Icelandic Literature and Culture*, ed. MCTURK, pp. 403-426, and analysed in F. HÜBLER, *Schwedische Runendichtung der Wikigerzeit* (Uppsala, 1996: *Rünron* 10); one stanza is discussed in B.Ø. THORVALDSEN, "The Eddic form and its contexts", in: *Oral Art Forms and their Passage into Writing*, ed. MUNDAL and WELLENDORF, pp. 151-162, at p. 153, and another in J. JESCH, "Poetry in the Viking age", in: *The Viking World*, ed. S. BRINK and N. PRICE (New York, 2008), pp. 291-298, at p. 292.

[41] The first half-line may be in the shortened *kviðuháttr* metre (HARRIS, "The Rök stone through Anglo-Saxon eyes", p. 32). For competing transliterations and interpretations of the stanzas, see P. HOLMBERG *et al.*, "The Rök runestone and the end of the world", *Futhark* 9-10 (2018-2019), pp. 7-38, online at <uu.diva-portal.org>.

[42] J. JESCH, "Runes and verse: The medialities of early Scandinavian poetry", *European Journal of Scandinavian Studies* 47.1 (2017), pp. 81-202 (online at <Nottingham-repository-worktribe.com>, pp. 1-17, at pp. 5-6.

Fig. 3   Rök stone. Photo provided by the author.

Judith Jesch, in an article from 2017 concerning verse in runes, considers this portion of the Rök inscription to be a quotation of an orally composed stanza, rendered in runes. She concludes, "The written medium of runes, paradoxically, gives us some of the most useful insights into the uses and contexts of the lost medium of orality".[43]

Stefan Brink, writing about oral society in a collection from 2005 titled *Literacy in Medieval and Early Modern Scandinavia* (ed. Pernille Hermann), considers much of the surrounding sequences in the Rök stone text to have been spoken by a specialist in speech-making and memory, a figure otherwise known as a *þulr*.[44] Stephen Mitchell in 2013 emphasises the performative aspect of the Rök inscription, that such memorial stones "are meant as lasting elegiac performances, acts to honor the dead".[45] Other contributions about orality and runic literacy, or 'runacy', have been made by Spurkland, Zilmer, Harris, and Schulte.[46] For my part, I am struck by how the Rök stanza employs variations on Theodoric's name, in a manner more usual in Anglo-Saxon verse than in Old Norse Eddic verse.[47]

---

[43] JESCH, "Runes and verse", p. 15.

[44] S. BRINK, "*Verba volant, scripta manent*? Aspects of early Scandinavian society", in: *Literacy in Medieval and Early Modern Scandinavian Culture*, ed. P. HERMANN (Odense, 2005), pp. 77-135, at p. 106.

[45] S.A. MITCHELL, "Memory, mediality, and the 'performative turn': Recontextualizing remembering in medieval Scandinavia", in: *Memory and Remembering: Past Awareness in the Medieval North*, ed. P. HERMANN and S.A. MITCHELL = *Scandinavian Studies* 85.3 (2013), pp. 282-305, at p. 283.

[46] T. SPURKLAND, "Scandinavian medieval runic inscriptions – An interface between orality and literacy?", in: *Roman, Runes and Ogham*, ed. J. HIGGIT *et al.* (Donnington, 2011), pp. 121-128; ID., "'Literacy' and 'runacy' in medieval Scandinavia", in: *Scandinavia and Europe 800-1350*, ed. J. ADAMS and K. HOLMAN (Turnhout, 2004), pp. 333-344; K. ZILMER, "Viking age runestones in Scandinavia: The interplay between oral monumentality and commemorative literacy", in: *Along the Oral-Written Continuum: Types of Texts, Relations and Their Implications*, ed. S. RANKOVIĆ, with L. MELVE and E. MUNDAL (Turnhout, 2010: *Utrecht Studies in Medieval Literacy* 20), pp. 135-162; J. HARRIS, "Old Norse memorial discourse: Between orality and literacy", in: *Along the Oral-Written Continuum*, ed. RANKOVIĆ *et al.*, pp. 119-133; M. SCHULTE, "Memory culture in the Viking ages: The runic evidence of formulaic patterns", *Scripta Islandica* 58 (2007), pp. 57-74 (online at <uu.diva-portal.org>). Terry Gunnell (T. GUNNELL, "*Blótgyðjur, goðar, mimi*, incest, and wagons: Oral memories of the religion(s) of the Vanir", in: *Old Norse Mythology: Comparative Perspectives*, ed. P. HERMANN (Cambridge MA, 2018; online at <chs.harvard.edu>), pp. 113-137) and Pernille Hermann (P. HERMANN, "Methodological challenges to the study of Old Norse myths: The orality and literacy debate reframes", in: *Old Norse Mythology*, ed. HERMANN, pp. 29-52) have written about orality and literacy in relation to available sources for the study of Old Norse myth.

[47] The runic verse discussed in THORVALDSEN, "The Eddic form and its contexts", p. 153,

The scholar named Frog has written about Eddic poetry from various approaches, including register, multiform theory, and parallelism (see his page on academia.edu). In an article from 2012 in *Arkiv för nordisk filologi*, Frog analyses a poem which I mentioned at the outset of this lecture, namely *Alvíssmál*. Frog reveals in great detail the recurrent formulaic strategies from stanza to stanza, and from the Codex Regius version to the excerpts in *Snorra Edda*. He takes issue with Harris's binary of memorisation vs. improvisation and adopts the term 'crystallisation', where "more frequently recurring lines in the stanza exhibit a higher degree of crystallization in the memory of the performer".[48]

Scott Mellor's principal focus is a syntactic analysis of ten Eddic poems, documenting for instance half-lines beginning with a nominal followed by a prepositional phrase, such as *allar á þingi,* followed by the nearly synonymous *allar á máli* in *Þrymskviða* stanza 14.[49] Thus syntactic frames can sometimes work in tandem with lexical formulaic systems. Mellor also follows Kellogg's *Concordance to Eddic Poetry* (1988) in documenting some verbatim repetition of two successive whole lines or three successive half-lines in a *ljóðaháttr* stanza, which only happens within single poems. He then proceeds to document repetition of whole lines and variable half-lines, before moving on to the levels of systems, themes and mythic patterns. As a theme he selects "the sending of messengers", found in a number of Eddic heroic poems, which he judges to be more of a semantic theme that does not involve formulaic repetition.[50]

Marina Mundt addresses Eddic themes in an article from 1997, drawing comparisons with heroic themes in South Slavic poetry, which is more comparable in length than is Homeric epic poetry.[51] Albert Lord had itemised some fourteen steps in a South Slavic theme of assembly leading to a final battle. Mundt finds a portion of these narrative steps parallelled in the poem *Hlöðskviða* or "The Battle of the Goths and Huns", found in the legendary-heroic *Hervarar saga ok Heiðreks*. She asserts briefly that the narrative 'scheme' may also be found in heroic poems from the Codex Regius, namely *Atlakviða, Hamðismál* and the second lay of Helgi Hundingsbani.

---

also employs variation in its final lines: *liðs forungi, landmanna bæstr,* 'host's captain, of landmen the best'.

[48] FROG, "*Alvíssmal* and orality I", p. 52.
[49] MELLOR, *Analyzing Ten Poems from the Poetic Edda*, p. 171.
[50] *Ibid.*, pp. 131-139. In my 1997 monograph, I detect verbal repetition in Eddic themes of prophecy, arrival and welcoming (pp. 71-80).
[51] M. MUNDT, "A basic scheme of oral poetry as found in ancient Scandinavia", *Tijdschrift voor Scandinavistiek* 18.2 (1997), pp. 29-38.

Just as I was preparing my 1998 monograph for press, I started to investigate whether there were formulas shared by Old English and Old Norse Eddic poetry, which one might expect if the two traditions descended from a common Germanic alliterative tradition. I wrote Old English cognates alongside (some of) the Norse lemmata in Kellogg's *A Concordance to Eddic Poetry* (1988),[52] such as *dróttinn*: dryhten; *gull*: gold. We might for instance think the half-line "*í árdaga*" ("in the old days") from *Völuspá in skamma* 7 is a formula, especially since it is cognate with Old English *in geardagum*, familiar from the first line of *Beowulf*. In a recently published lecture, Matthew Townend calls these two phrases – shared examples from Old English and Old Norse – poetic formulas and half-lines,[53] but in fact the Old Norse phrase occurs as a separate half-line only once (Vsk st. 7). In the word's thirteen occurrences in Eddic poetry (gleanable from Kellogg's *Concordance*), *árdaga* always appears as part of a longer half-line (at the end), such as *hvat þú í árdaga* ('what you in the old days') from *Vafþrúðnismál* st. 55. One might hesitate to call strictly formulaic a phrase that just means 'in the old days' as preceded by non-repeating, non-synonymous words and elements (and so not part of a slot-filler system). It seems to operate more as a *cheville* or line-ending filler. (Lines marked c below are full lines in *ljóðaháttr*, with internal alliteration.)

Vsp 61a *þærs í árdaga*
Vfþ 28c *yrði í árdaga*
Vfþ 55b *hvat þú í árdaga*
Grm 5b *gáfu í árdaga*
Grm 6c *áss í árdaga*
Grm 43b *gengu í árdaga*
Skr 5b *várum í árdaga*
Skr 7c *ungum í árdaga*
Lks 9b *er vit í árdaga*
Lks 25b *drýgðuð í árdaga*
Lks 48b *þér var í árdaga*
Rgn 2b *scóp oss í árdaga*
Vsk 7b *í árdaga*

Taking the simplex *ár*, meaning 'early', it is true that two different poems begin with the same construction, *Ár var, þats Guðrún (Gðk 1 1)* and *Ár var, þats*

---

[52] R. KELLOGG, *A Concordance to Eddic Poetry* (East Lansing, 1988).
[53] M. TOWNEND, *Antiquity of Diction in Old English and Old Norse Poetry* (Cambridge, 2015: Quiggin Memorial Lecture 17), p. 14.

Sigurðr (Sgk II *1)*. In any case, formulas between Old English and Old Norse have yet to be sufficiently demonstrated, although Townend has listed some shared poetic compounds.[54] Some of these, such as Old English *þēodcyninga* ('of nation-kings') make up entire half-lines, as in *Beowulf* line 2a; so does the cognate Old Norse *þjóðkonunga*.[55]

I have not treated orality and saga prose in this survey, which is the focus of a new project by Daniel Sävborg. For my own part I have always thought it would be useful to have an internal motif-index of the sagas (rather than the comparative folkloric one by Boberg), so that one could for instance find out in which sagas feuds broke out over contested legal rights to beached whales, or what saga characters wore scarlet clothes, or how many characters were considered the most famous men with wooden legs, and so on. Such a project would be facilitated by the completed or ongoing publication of the entire corpus of family sagas translated into English,[56] Danish, Norwegian, Swedish, and German.

Some conclusions regarding Eddic poetry and oral-formulaic theory, formulated while I have been compiling this bibliographic survey, are as follows:

Albert Lord, following Milman Parry, defined a formula as "a group of words which is regularly employed under the same metrical conditions to express a particular essential idea".[57] The metrical conditions applying to Eddic half-lines, however, are not as rigorous as those in Homeric verse. There are roughly five types of lines, as defined by Eduard Sievers and more recently by Geoffrey Russom;[58] they range from trochaic, iambic, to iambic-trochaic, plus lines incorporating secondary stress from compound words. Within a pair of half-lines or the full line in *ljóðaháttr* metre, the formulas must also accommodate alliteration.[59] To count as an Eddic formula, I would argue, the half-line should be a) strictly repeated in another Eddic poem; or b) repeated with only minor differences (such as change of a verb tense) in another Eddic poem; or c) repeated as part of a slot-filler system in another Eddic poem, such as "*Ár var, þats Guðrún*" (Gdk I 1) and "*Ár var, þats Sigurðr*" (Sgk II 1) cited above. Repe-

---

[54] TOWNEND, *Antiquity of Diction*, pp. 13-14.
[55] TOWNEND, *Antiquity of Diction*, pp. 2-3.
[56] *The Complete Sagas of Icelanders*, ed. V. HREINSSON (Reykjavík, 1997).
[57] A.B. LORD, *The Singer of Tales* (Cambridge, MA 1960), p. 4.
[58] G. RUSSOM, *Beowulf and Old Germanic Metre* (Cambridge, 1998).
[59] For a preliminary study of alliterative collocations, see M.E. RUGGERINI, "Alliterative lexical collections in Eddic poetry", in: *A Handbook of Eddic Poetry*, ed. LARRINGTON, QUINN, and SCHORN, pp. 310-330.

tition of only part of a half-line, as in *í árdaga* discussed above, might count as a *cheville* (line-filler) within an aspect of oral composition, but would not strictly count as oral-formulaic repetition under the Lord model. Repetitions within a single Eddic poem, such as the repeated stanzas discussed above, would not count as oral formulas, and should be categorised separately.[60] Such stanzas are sometimes scribally recorded in an extended form of suspension abbreviation (as shown above) and are clearly a part of Eddic oral (or oral-derived) composition (not unlike repeated stanzas with incremental repetition in ballads), but they do not function to facilitate composition in the same way as oral formulas do under classic oral-formulaic theory. Indeed, as I discussed in my monograph, Eddic oral composition operates on a number of levels beyond the Parryite oral formula.

---

[60] I only know one whole stanza that is repeated (with slight variation) from one poem to another, namely the stanzas beginning "Senn vóro æsir" in *Þrymskviða* 14 and *Baldrs draumar* 1.

Formulas in Scottish Traditional Narrative: Finding Poetry in the Prosaic

WILLIAM LAMB

From early childhood, cradle songs, nursery rhymes, and the *fi-fo-fums* of fairy tales prime us to recognise poetic language. Paraphrasing Orwell, Allen states that poetry is "like speech, only more so" and that "[p]oets use naturally occurring phenomena to their artistic advantage".[1] This suggests that poetry, rather than being isolated from everyday speech, exists on a continuum that includes it. In school, however, most of us are taught that poetry and prose are fundamentally different and this division is reified by standard editing practices. Non-metred 'prose' occurs in sentences and paragraphs, while 'poetry' occurs in blocks of lines, or sometimes other structures[2] according to genre, authorial whim, and even certain linguistic traditions.[3] A more subtle view conceives prose as organised by syntax and prosody, and poetry organised by features such as periodic metre and phonic parallelisms (e.g. rhyme, asso-

---

[1] G. ALLEN, "The location of rhythmic stress beats in English: An experimental study I", *Language and Speech,* 15 (1972), pp. 72-100, at p. 72.
[2] cf. FROG, "Fee, fi, fo, formula: Getting to grips with the concept and deciding on a definition", in this volume, pp. 15-56.
[3] K. O'BRIEN O'KEEFE, *Visible Song: Transitional Literacy in Old English Verse* (Cambridge, 1990).

New Light on Formulas in Oral Poetry and Prose, ed. Daniel SÄVBORG and Bernt Ø. THORVALDSEN, *Utrecht Studies in Medieval Literacy*, 57 (Turnhout: Brepols, 2023), pp. 163-189.

nance and alliteration).[4] On the basis of intuition and distinctions like these, we usually can draw confident distinctions between poetry and prose. Yet, when we move away from literature and turn to the varieties of oral tradition presented in this volume, the boundaries begin to blur.[5]

In wide survey of oral epic, Carol Glover found that prose was rare.[6] Notably, the longer the form, the more likely it was to be in verse, or an admixture of prose and poetry known as *prosimetry*.[7] Glover notes the long prose traditions of Ireland and Scandinavia as exceptions, but not all Irish epic occurs in prose: character dialogue and other formulaic language, for example, often occurs in verse.[8] So, at least for longer forms of oral narrative, the dichotomy of prose and poetry is dubious.

Scholes and Kellogg went further than Glover and declared that "oral prose" cannot even develop in the first place: the logical and syntactic challenges associated with creating it obviate this.[9] While the corpus of European folktales collected from the Grimms' time onwards might seem to belie their view, perhaps we are misdirected by typesetting conventions and a limited appreciation of what constitutes poetry. Hymes, for example, argued that, while Native American folktales are typically set as sentential prose, many are better represented as verse.[10] His reasoning rests upon a broader, bifurcated definition of poetry.

According to Hymes, two types of poetry exist: metrical and measured.[11] Integral to both are parallelisms across all linguistic levels. These are the co-occurring elements that Jakobsen termed "recurrent returns" and "the essence of poetic artifice".[12] In *metrical* poetry, parallelisms exist at the level of the line,

---

[4] N. FABB, *What Is Poetry? Language and Memory in the Poems of the World* (Cambridge, 2015), pp. 9, 20.

[5] R.G.G. COLEMAN, "Poetic diction, poetic discourse and the poetic register", *Proceedings of the British Academy,* 93 (1999), pp. 21-93, at p. 24.

[6] C.J. GLOVER, "The long prose form", *Arkiv för nordisk filologi,* 101 (1986), pp. 10-39.

[7] GLOVER, "The long prose form", p. 16.

[8] A. BRUFORD, "Gaelic folk-tales and mediæval romances: A study of the early modern Irish 'romantic tales' and their oral derivatives", *Béaloideas* (1966), pp. 1-285, at pp. 34-35.

[9] See GLOVER, "The long prose form", p. 11.

[10] D. HYMES, "Discovering oral performance and measured verse in American Indian narrative", *New Literary History* 8.3 (1977), pp. 431-457; ID., "Ethnopoetics, oral formulaic theory, and editing texts", *Oral Tradition,* 9 (1994), pp. 330-370.

[11] See FROG, "Parallelism and orders of signification (parallelism dynamics I)", *Oral Tradition,* 31.2 (2017), pp. 425-484, and ID., "Metrical entanglement: The interface of language and meter", in: *Versification: Metricsin Practice,* ed. M. FROG, K. KALLIO, and J. NIEMI (= *Studia Fennica Litteraria* 12) <https://doi.org/10.21435/sflit.12>.

[12] R. JAKOBSON, "Grammatical parallelism and its Russian facet", in: ID., *Selected Writings,*

between "syllables, stresses, alliterations, tones [and] conventional feet".[13] These are the rhymes, rhythms, melodies, and alliterations that impart form and coherence to any typical song – although metrical poetry need not be tonal, of course. In *measured* poetry, parallelisms exist as "relations among lines"[14] or verses. Structures are set out by intonational patterns and the placement of discourse particles, as well as parallels of morphology, lexicon, syntax, and semantics. The two types of poetic parallelisms are summarised in Table 1. Those not accustomed to ethnopoetics[15] may view traditional narrative appearing in lines and stanzas to be bizarre. On the other hand, the approach is more isomorphic to spoken language than standard written representation. For instance, it jettisons artificial full-stops and better captures the careful staging of spontaneous speech.[16]

Table 1: Parallelisms in metrical and measured poetry

Metrical Parallelisms	Measured Parallelisms
alliteration	morphology
assonance	lexemes
metre	syntax
rhyme	semantics
tone	

Whether or not we view prose and poetry as discrete categories, or construe traditional narrative to be one or the other, metrical and measured parallelisms are common in traditional storytelling. Furthermore, where they occur, they typically have been *invoked before* in the tradition. In other words, it is in the prefabricated phrases of formulaic language that we find the greatest density of poetic features in narrative 'prose'.[17] Of course, this is hardly surprising: parallelisms in verbal art function, in part, as mnemonic wrapping and help to ensure its durability over time.[18] Those parts of oral tradition – or indeed, hu-

3, *Poetry of Grammar and Grammar of Poetry*, ed. S. RUDY (The Hague, 1981 [1966]), p. 98.

[13] HYMES, "Ethnopoetics", p. 331.

[14] *Ibid.*

[15] These types of reconsiderations flourished within the ethnopoetic school: see J.M. FOLEY, *How to Read an Oral Poem* (Urbana, 2002).

[16] See: K. LAMBRECHT, *Information Structure and Sentence Form* (Cambridge, 1994); M.A.K. HALLIDAY, *Spoken and Written Language*, 2nd edn. (Oxford, 1989); J.E. MILLER and R. WEINERT, *Spontaneous Spoken Language: Syntax and Discourse* (Oxford, 1998).

[17] A. WRAY, *Formulaic Language and the Lexicon* (Cambridge, 2002), p. 9.

[18] D.C. RUBIN, *Memory in Oral Traditions: The Cognitive Psychology of Epic, Ballads, and Counting-out Rhymes* (Oxford, 1995), p. 90; W.J. ONG, *Orality and Literacy the Technologizing of the Word* (London, 1982: New Accents), p. 34.

man language at large – that are packaged most memorably are more likely to endure. Yet, few authors have considered the ways that poetic features coalesce in the formulas of prose narrative. Furthermore, while much attention has been given to the longer, enregistered formulas of traditional narrative, few have considered the place and effect of more 'mundane' formulaic language in storytelling. My intention here is to discuss these topics from the perspective of the Scots and Gaelic traditions.

The outline of the paper is as follows. In the remainder of this introduction, we will briefly consider the definition of formula, as applied to prose narrative. Following this, in Part I, we will consider metred and measured poetic features in three narrative excerpts: two in Gaelic and one in Scots. These are arranged in increasing fixity and formality, to isolate some of the differences between formulas and poetic features at contrasting levels of vernacularity. Finally, in Part II, we will consider the results of a short, corpus-based study of Gaelic binomials. Binomials (a.k.a. 'couplets') are formulas of two coordinated nouns, which are closely associated with Gaelic *Märchen* and other international tales.[19] Here, we will examine assonance and alliteration in these formulas, as well as a linguistic constraint that is ubiquitous in formulaic language, but rarely discussed in relation to verbal art: prosodic end-weighting.

Defining 'Formula' for Traditional Prose

As applied to oral tradition, the term 'formula' is rooted in Milman Parry's work on the origins of Homeric verse.[20] Parry had noticed that much of the *Illiad* and *Odyssey* consisted of recurring epithets and other phrases embedded within the works' complex hexameter rhythms. He reasoned that these regularly occurring phrases functioned as semi-malleable building blocks, and explained how the poems' author(s) could have composed them at a time of scant literacy. His epiphany occurred after locating a parallel in the living tradition of epic poetry found in Yugoslavia at the time.[21] Trained poet-singers known as *guslars* were able to extemporise long performances by deploying a repertoire

---

[19] See W. LAMB, "From motif to multiword expression: The development of formulaic language in Gaelic traditional narrative", in: *Weathered Words: Formulaic Language and Verbal Art*, ed. by FROG and W. LAMB (Cambridge MA, 2022), pp. 193-220, at pp. 213-214.

[20] M. PARRY, "Studies in the epic technique of oral verse-making I.: Homer and Homeric style", *Harvard Studies in Classical Philology* 41 (1930), pp. 73-147.

[21] A.B. LORD, *The Singer of Tales*, 2nd edn., ed. S.A. MITCHELL and G. NAGY (Cambridge MA and London, 2000: *Harvard Studies in Comparative Literature*), p. 43.

of similar stock phrases. Lord's popularising of Parry's work caused a seismic shift within Homeric studies and stimulated a wide body of research on verbal art, under what became known as Oral-Formulaic Theory.[22]

Of course, Parry's definition of *formula* is a product of its original context and purpose: "a group of words (...) regularly employed under the same metrical conditions to express a given essential idea".[23] Since well before Parry's time, however, scholars noticed regularly-occurring phrases in non-metred traditional narrative too. For instance, the Gaelic folklore pioneer John Francis Campbell observed the following in the 1860s in *Popular Tales of the West Highlands*:

> One story grows out of another, and the tree is almost hidden by a foliage of the speaker's invention. Here and there comes a passage repeated by rote, and common to many stories, and to every good narrator.[24]

Notwithstanding such observations, most of the research to date on formulas in oral tradition has focussed on metred epic poetry[25] and on their importance for "composition in performance".[26] As I discuss elsewhere, formulas in non-metred narrative may diverge from metred ones somewhat in their function and form.[27] Except for inherently formulaic tales,[28] there is no suggestion that they are used, for example, as compositional devices. So, to what extent is it appropriate to discuss the stock phrases of non-metred narrative as 'formulas' in the first place?

When working on non-metred narrative, some scholars simply excise Parry's 'metred' criterion and carry on. Doing this leaves a serviceable definition,

---

[22] FROG and W. LAMB, "A Picasso of perspectives on formulaic language", in: *Weathered Words: Formulaic Language and Verbal Art*, ed. FROG and LAMB, pp. 5-17, at pp. 5-6.

[23] PARRY, "Studies in the epic technique", p. 80; cf. LORD, *The Singer of Tales*, p. 4.

[24] J.F. CAMPBELL, *Popular Tales of the West Highlands*, new edn., 4 vols. (Paisley, 1890), 1, pp. XLIX-L.

[25] D. SÄVBORG, "The formula in Icelandic saga prose", *Saga-Book* 42 (2018), pp. 51-86; see also B. GRAY, "Repetition in oral literature", *The Journal of American Folklore* 84 (1971), pp. 289-303.

[26] A.B. LORD, "The nature of oral poetry", in: *Comparative Research on Oral Traditions: A Memorial for Milman Parry*, ed. J.M. FOLEY (Columbus, 1987), pp. 313-350, at pp. 335-336.

[27] W. LAMB, "Verbal formulas in Gaelic traditional narrative: Some aspects of their form and function", in: *Registers of Communication*, ed. A. AGHA and FROG (Helsinki, 2015), pp. 225-246.

[28] See H.-J. UTHER, *The Types of International Folktales: A Classification and Bibliography Based on the System of Antti Aarne and Stith Thompson, Part II., Tales of the Stupid Ogre, Anecdotes and Jokes, and Formula Tales* (Helsinki, 2004).

of course: a sequence of words that is regularly invoked (e.g. within a particular register) to denote an important idea (e.g. to a tradition). This reframing is closely aligned to the concepts of 'formulaic sequence' and 'multiword expression', which emanated more or less independently from linguistic research. Yet, in contrast to detailing the 'specialness' of formulas in verbal art, linguists often recognise, instead, their ubiquity in human language.[29] These two observations are far from antithetical, however, and can be usefully synthesised by considering the psycholinguistic nature of formulas and the degree to which they are associated with extralinguistic factors.

The linguist Alison Wray provides evidence that formulaic sequences are like words themselves – entries in our internal lexicons and recalled as such:

> [A formula is] a sequence, continuous or discontinuous, of words or other elements, which is, or appears to be, prefabricated: that is, stored and retrieved whole from memory at the time of use, rather than being subject to generation or analysis by the language grammar.[30]

As communicators, we adapt our linguistic output to extralinguistic factors such as mode, purpose, and situation. When a set of linguistic features co-occurs with particular extralinguistic features, it is known as a *register*.[31] Each register is defined, in part, by its lexicon. Accordingly, once formulas are viewed as lexical items, we can discuss them in terms of how *enregistered* they are. For instance, some formulas are so enregistered that they are capable, on their own, of evoking the contexts with which they are associated. In some cases, they can even summon particular traditions or belief systems.[32] The longer formulas of Gaelic hero tales are a case in point.[33] We can think of formulas like these as specialists, and of other more prosaic formulas as generalists – entries in a language's common, vernacular lexicon. An example of the latter is the formulaic template 'PUT [NP] on [NP]', as in 'putting on his shoes', along with 'putting his shoes on'. Such phrases are no less formulaic than enregistered examples

---

[29] J. BYBEE, "From usage to grammar: The mind's response to repetition", *Language*, 82 (2006), pp. 711-733, at pp. 712-713.

[30] WRAY, *Formulaic Language and the Lexicon*, p. 9. See also EAD., *Formulaic Language: Pushing the Boundaries* (Oxford, 2008).

[31] D. BIBER, "An analytical framework for register studies", in: *Sociolinguistic Perspectives on Register*, ed. D. BIBER and E. FINEGAN (Oxford and New York, 1994), pp. 31-56, at p. 32.

[32] J.M. FOLEY, *Immanent Art: From Structure to Meaning in Traditional Oral Epic* (Bloomington, 1991), p. 60; ID., *How to Read an Oral Poem*, p. 113.

[33] LAMB, "Verbal formulas", p. 234.

like 'swift-footed Achilles' or 'grey-eyed Athena', but they receive little attention in studies of verbal art.

Certainly, non-metred traditional narrative is less replete with special formulas than metred oral poetry, but formulaicity is still important to it. Few have considered the place of vernacular formulas in narrative traditions, yet perhaps their role is more central than we have realised. As metrical parallels may lurk in the background when measured parallels collide,[34] it may be that vernacular formulas in traditional 'prose' provide a seedbed for more enregistered ones. One of the aims of this paper is to consider this possibility. So, we will distinguish between *enregistered formulas*, which are more restricted to and, hence, evocative of particular registers, and *vernacular formulas*, which cross the (extra-)linguistic landscape.[35]

Having set out some of the background of formulas in traditional 'prose', we will now examine the two types of poetic parallelisms in the formulas and surrounding text of three excepts of Scottish narrative, moving in decreasing vernacularity.

Part I: Metred and Measured Parallelisms in Scottish Narrative

How the Fairies Gave a Man a Hump (ATU 503)

The international folktale, 'The Gifts of the Little People' (ATU 503),[36] is one of the most popular narratives collected from Scots,[37] Irish[38] and Gaelic

---

[34] See FROG, "A preface to parallelism", in: *Parallelism in Verbal Art and Performance*, ed. FROG (Helsinki, 2014), pp. 7-28, at p. 20: "It is important to acknowledge parallelism at the level of sounds or signals because these are subtly in the background of many of the types of parallelism discussed, especially where several different types of parallelism may be used in combination with one another in complex ways".

[35] In the Gaelic tradition, it is also possible to distinguish between idiolectic formulas, which are apparent from one person's usage, and those that are shared between tradition bearers, often at a wide geographic remove. See LAMB, "Verbal formulas", and cf. C.S. ZALL, "Variation in Gaelic storytelling", *Scottish Studies* 35 (2007-2010), pp. 210-244.

[36] For ATU, see: H.-J. UTHER, *The Types of International Folktales: A Classification and Bibliography, Based on the System of Antti Aarne and Stith Thompson*, 3 vols. (Helsinki, 2004).

[37] Cf. B. HIGGINS, "The humph at the fit o the glen and the humph at the head o the glen", in: *Scottish Traditional Tales*, ed. A.J. BRUFORD and D.A. MACDONALD (Edinburgh, 2003), pp. 362-365.

[38] See S. Ó SÚILLEABHÁIN and R.T. CHRISTIANSEN, *The Types of the Irish Folktale*, (Helsinki, 1963: *FF Communications*), pp. 101-102.

speakers over the past 150 years. The following is a precis of the commonest ecotype in the UK and Ireland:

A humpbacked man encounters a group of fairies who are singing a song featuring the days of the week. (The days sung can vary, but the fairies often repeat, 'Monday and Tuesday'.) The humpbacked man interjects 'Wednesday' (or further days) to the fairies' delight. As a reward for improving the song, they remove the man's hump. He returns home and, soon after, encounters another humpback who inquires how he got rid of his hump. The first man relates his tale and encourages the second to visit the fairies himself. The second man successfully locates the fairies, who are singing their revised song. The second man interjects 'Thursday' (or sometimes the days up to 'Sunday'[39]). The fairies complain that he has ruined their song. As a punishment, they lump the first man's hump on the second, and he returns to the village even more disfigured.

One version of the tale from Gaelic tradition is transcribed below using lines and stanzas, to bring the underlying parallelisms and formulaic language into sharper focus.[40] Formulas are marked using curly brackets, with fixed elements in bold, and facultative ones left unmarked. Measured parallelisms are marked with underlining and subscript references. A close English translation follows the original Gaelic version:

Ò fear a bha san àite <u>air an robh croit uabhasach</u> $_A$
    {anns an t-seann aimsir}
    ri linn nan sìthichean
    <u>air an robh croit uabhasach</u> $_A$'s
Bha e an latha seo dol seachad air <u>na creagan far an robh na sìthichean</u> $_B$ a' fuireach,
    is chual' e iad
    <u>bha iad a' maistreadh</u> $_C$'s
    bha iad a' gabhail rann
    {'Diluain 's Dimàirt} 's
Chaidh e a-staigh far a robh iad 's
    thuirt e: *{'Diluain 's Dimàirt, Diciadain'}* [....]

---

[39] Some Gaels believed the fairies to be fallen angels who were offended by the mention of Sunday.

[40] A. MACDONALD, "Mar a thug na sìthichean croit do dhuine" ["How the fairies gave a man a hump"], School of Scottish Studies Archives, SA1968.134.6. Recorded in July 1968 by Morag MacLeod; translation and transcription by the current author. Recording available at <https://www.tobarandualchais.co.uk/track/45616>.

Rinn e beat <u>*na bu luaith' air*</u> _D *'s*
  thàinig an tìm air an uair sin <u>*na bu luaith' air*</u> _D
Dh'fhaighnich iad dhe gu dè dhèanadh iadsan air a shon 's
  is ò thuirt e
  an toireadh iad dhe <u>*a' chroit a bh' air*</u> _E
Rinn iad sin a chur dhe,
  <u>*a' chroit a bh' air*</u> _E

Tha e coltach gu robh fear eile a's an àite cuideachd <u>*air a robh croit*</u> _F *e fhèin 's*
...
  thachair e ris
Dh'fhaighnich e dhe ciamar a fhuair e a chroit dhe 's
  dh'innis e dha 's
Chaidh am fear sin chun <u>*nan creagan rithist far a robh na sìthichean*</u> _B
  is <u>*bha iad a' maistreadh*</u> _C *an latha sin cuideachd*
  *is iad ag ràdh {"**Diluain 's Dimàirt, Diciadain**"}*
  mar a dh'innis am fear eile dhaibh 's
Is an uairsin thuirt esan
  *{"**Diluain 's Dimàirt, Diciadain 's Diardaoin**"} 's*
  mhill e an rhythm *aca*
Hà 's rinn iad an uair sin
  a' chroit a thug iad far an fhir eile
  chaith iad air ... a' chroit aige
  còmhla ris <u>*a' chroit a bh' air*</u> _E *fhèin i*
'S chaidh e dhachaidh 's an dà chroit air

Oh there a man in [this] place <u>on whom there was a terrible hump</u> _A
  {**in the old days**}
  in the age of the fairies
  <u>on whom there was a terrible hump</u> _A and ...
He was on this day going past <u>the crags where the fairies</u> _B lived
  and he heard them
  <u>they were churning</u> _C [i.e. milk] and
  they were singing a verse {"**Monday, Tuesday**"} and
He went in to where they were [i.e. the fairy crag], and
  he said, {"**Monday, Tuesday, Wednesday**"}
He made the beat go <u>faster on it</u> _D and
  then the timing came <u>faster on it</u> _D
They asked him what he wanted for it, and
  oh, he said
  would they take off <u>the hump that was on him</u> _E
They took that off of him
  <u>the hump that was on him</u> _E

It seems that there was another man in the place <u>on whom was a hump</u> _F too ...
   he met him
He asked him how he got rid of his hump and
   he told him
That man went to the <u>crags again where the fairies</u> _B were
   and <u>they were churning</u> _C that day too
   and they [were] saying {"**Monday, Tuesday, Wednesday**"}
   as the other man had told them [to do]
And he then said,
   {"**Monday, Tuesday, Wednesday, Thursday**"} and
   he ruined their rhythm
Well and then they went and
   the hump that they took off of the other man
   they threw it on him ... his lump
   along with <u>the hump on him</u> _E himself
And he went home with the two humps on him

According to information on Tobar an Dualchais / Kist o Riches,[41] the narrator (Alasdair MacDonald from Dìricleit, Harris) provided only a small number of tracks to the School of Scottish Studies Archives. These appear to be limited to eight items: one international tale (ATU 503), two supernatural legends, and five accounts of oral history. On this basis, he appears to be a less practised tradition bearer than many contemporaries who provided material to the School of Scottish Studies. Despite this, his narrative is instructive for three key questions: 1) Can parallelism be found even in a very demotic narrative? 2) When does a vernacular formula become an enregistered one? And 3) What poetic aesthetics help to constrain formulaic language in Gaelic tradition?

As discussed in the Introduction, measured parallels operate across lines and verses, and can form between morphemes, words, syntax, and semantics. In this narrative, we see six repetitive phrases (underlined and noted with subscript A-F), which provide a lattice-like structure to the tale. Phrase A – "*air an robh croit uabhasach*" ("on whom there was a terrible hump") – repeats in the first stanza. Following this, "*a' chroit a bh' air*" ("the hump on him") (E) picks up the refrain and recurs through the rest of the tale, along with the syntactic variant (F), "*air an robh croit*" ("on which there was a hump"). Together, these phrases build up momentum towards the final reveal: "*chaidh e dhachaidh 's an dà chroit air*" ("he went home and the two humps on him" (emphasis added)).

[41] See <https://www.tobarandualchais.co.uk>.

The bi-episodic structure of the tale is framed by three key parallelisms: phrase B – providing the fairies' location; phrase C – providing their activity (i.e. singing whilst churning); and the song itself – a formulaic phrase comprised by the days of the week. There can be no more vernacular a formula than the days of the week, but here it is elevated to metred poetry by being incorporated in a song.

Although this contributor does not sing the song himself or even provide its rhythm, some renditions of the tale are in the style of a *chantefable*,[42] where the non-metred performance alternates with song. Usually, in these renditions, the song is characterised as a *luinneag* or movement song – a piece sung while dancing or working.[43] Falzett discussed several of these renditions and stated that the tale is essentially about metricity: "the rhythmic nuances and metrical relationships between the language and (...) music".[44] We may ask, on what basis do the fairies reward the first humpback and punish the second? The simplest answer is the contrasting rhythmic effects of the additions. This is obvious in the few sung versions of the tales, where *Diciadain* is consonant with the rhythm, while *Diardaoin* fights against it:

```
     -  1 (e &) a  2 (e &) a  3(e &)   a  4
A.  Di-LUAIN     Di-MÀIRT    Di-LUAIN     Di-MÀIRT
    juh-looain   juh-marsht  juh-looain   juh-marsht
    Monday       Tuesday     Monday       Tuesday


     -  1 (e &) a  2 (e &) a  3 e &a)  4
B.  Di-LUAIN     Di-MÀIRT    Di-CI-A-    DAIN
    juh-looain   juh-marsht  juh-cee-a-  dayn
    Monday       Tuesday     Monday      Wednesday
```

The fairies' initial rendition of the song fits a 4/4 bar of music in strathspey rhythm. So does the addition of *Diciadain* ('Wednesday'). *Diardaoin*, on the other hand, ruins the rhythm. While this seems to explain the fairies' grievance, the *chantefable* version of the tale could have originated *after* the trope of sing-

---

[42] H. SHIELDS, *Narrative Singing in Ireland: Lays, Ballads, Come-All-Yes and Other Songs* (Dublin, 1993), pp. 58-59.

[43] See W. LAMB, "Reeling in the strathspey: The origins of Scotland's national music", *Scottish Studies* 36 (2013), pp. 66-102.

[44] T.F.M. FALZETT, "Cuir dhachaigh e ('Send it home'): The gifts of the little people, the bob of fettercairn and the aesthetics of a tale and a tune", in: *Rannsachadh Na Gàidhlig* 6, ed. C. Ó BAOILL and N. MCGUIRE (Aberdeen, 2013), pp. 93-120.

ing had formed. If that is true, it is less obvious why the fairies would object to *Diardaoin*, or any other day being added after *Diciadain*. If we examine syllabic structure, however, a definite pattern emerges:

Diluain	1 short syllable + 1 short syllable
Dimàirt	1 short syllable + 1 long syllable
Diciadain	4 short syllables
Diardaoin	1 short syllable + 1 long syllable

While the sequence *Diluain, Dimàirt, Diciadain* shows a syllabic increase with each word, *Diardaoin* presents a decrease. This violates the principle of end-weighting,[45] the tendency for non-verb-final languages to present longer and phonologically heavier syntagms at the end of utterances. While end-weighting is a scalar device rather than parallelism per se, its ubiquity in human language suggests that it may play an important part in the formation and continuity of formulas in oral tradition. This is the focus of Part II. In the meantime, let us examine the confluence of vernacular formulas in an excerpt of Scots narrative, and consider how they exert influence on the surrounding text through parallelisms.

The Three Feathers (ATU 402)

The narrative under consideration in this sub-section is "The Three Feathers", a Scots ecotype of ATU 402 ("The Animal Bride"). When closely examined, it reveals features similar to those that Hymes located for Native North American storytelling. In contrast to the previous narrator, the current one (Andrew Stewart) was a practised raconteur. Indeed, he was a member of a family of tradition bearers often referred to as "The Stewarts of Blair".[46] Here is a brief summary of this twenty minute tale:

A dying king sets his three sons three tasks in succession: to find the best tablecover, to find the most beautiful ring, and to find the nicest wife to wear the ring. He who succeeds will inherit his kingdom. Each brother is given a feather to throw to the wind and is told to follow its direction to begin his quest. The first son's feather drifts north and the second son's drifts south. The feather

---

[45] K.M. RYAN, "Prosodic end-weight reflects phrasal stress", *Natural Language & Linguistic Theory* 37 (2019), pp. 315-356, at p. 315.

[46] *Scottish Traditional Tales*, ed. BRUFORD and MACDONALD, pp. 485-486.

of the third son, Jack, flies to the back of the castle and he is ridiculed for it. The first two sons promptly set off on their quests. Jack procrastinates. With little time before the deadline, he encounters a helpful frog who lives under the castle. The frog provides the items for the first two tasks, and then turns into a beautiful princess, fulfilling the final task.

The following short excerpt occurs soon after Jack seeks his first feather. It is presented in a similar fashion to the previous narrative, but marks metred parallelisms on view with italicisation (e.g. rhyme and alliteration):

an here when Jack went in
he {***sut* doon on** this *stool*}
an the frog saw
    {***speaking* tae** him}, ye *see*
an one frog {***jumpit* on tap**} o *Jack's knee*

an *Jack's*
    clapping the *wee* frog _A like this
an it's
    {**lookin up**}_B wi its *wee* golden eyes
    {**lookin up**} at Jack's face
an *Jack's*
    clappin the *wee* frog _A
    {***pattin*** him **on** top of **the *back***}
an it's
    {***looking* up**}_B at him
    an {***laughin*** at him **in his face**}[47]

To begin with measured parallelisms, we see a repeated clause ("an Jack's clapping the wee frog [like this]"), a series of gerunds – "speaking", "clappin(g)", "looking", "patting", "laughin" – and parallel prepositional phrases ("on this stool", "tae him", "tap of Jack's knee", "on top of the back", "up at him", "at him in his face"). We can also mention two block sequences: "an Jack's clapping ... and it's lookin"; "an Jack's clapping / patting ... and it's lookin up / an laughin". These parallelisms all operate at a structural level.

Metred features in this excerpt include rhyme (see~knee~wee), assonance ("Jack's~clapping"; "tap~Jack's"; "pattin~back"), alliteration ("sut~stool"; "wi~wee"; "jumpit~Jack"; "looking~laughin") and chiasmus alliteration – when sounds repeat in reversed order ("jum*pit*~*tap*"). Metrical features such as

---

[47] A. STEWART, "The three feathers", in: *Scottish Traditional Tales*, ed. BRUFORD and MACDONALD, pp. 79-80. Audio at: <https://www.tobarandualchais.co.uk/track/3999>.

these might not be expected in an informal prose tale, but – again – we should keep attentive for them when measured features coalesce in the way observed here.

Although no enregistered formulas appear in this excerpt, five vernacular formulas are marked in curly braces. They are *sut doon on, jumpit on top, speaking tae, lookin up, pattin ... on ... the back*, and *laughin ... in his face*. Of course, these Scots expressions are shared with English. What is notable here is how the phonic and morphological features of their fixed elements resound in the surrounding narrative. It is unlikely to be a coincidence, for example, that a *stool* was chosen for Jack to *sit* upon, instead of a non-alliterative surface like a bench or a chair. Nor does it seem accidental that Jack was *clapping* and *patting* the frog on the *back*, rather than on his head. These lexical choices are seeded in the formulas themselves. Despite being 'generalists', they exert important influence upon the surrounding narrative.

A Hero Tale 'Run'

Finally, we consider poetic features in an extended formula from a more formal register of traditional narrative: Gaelic hero tales. Alan Bruford, in his classic work on the intertextuality of Gaelic oral and literate hero tales,[48] mentions the importance of parallelism for *runs*,[49] the longer formulaic phrases that are typical of the register: "[t]he main development in runs (...) is a matter of adding rhyme or assonance of some sort and extra alliteration".[50] Runs with these qualities are plentiful within the Gaelic hero tales.[51] Consider this excerpt of a sailing run from the tale "*Fear na h-Eabaid*" ("Man of the Cassock"),[52] as

---

[48] BRUFORD, "Gaelic folk-tales".

[49] LORD, *The Singer of Tales*, p. 58, defines 'runs' as "larger groups of lines which the [performer] is accustomed to use often, and through habit they are always found together. The repetition of these groups is sometimes [verbatim], sometimes not". It seems that the concept of the 'run' appears first in: A. NUTT, "Notes", in: *Waifs and Strays of Celtic Tradition*, ed. D. MACINNES and A. NUTT, 2 vols. (London, 1890), 2, pp. 448-450, 456-457, 487, and the Index at p. 497.

[50] BRUFORD, "Gaelic folk-tales", p. 201.

[51] Practically any hero tale is replete with them. See CAMPBELL, *Popular Tales*, and D. MACDHÒMHNAILL and K.C. CRAIG, *Sgialachdan Dhunnchaidh* (Glasgow, 1950).

[52] D. MACDONALD, DUNCAN, "Fear na h-Eabaid", MS JLC1953_Storn (pamphlet), transcribed by D. THOMSON and A. MATHESON (Glasgow, 1950). Translation taken from *Scottish Traditional Tales*, ed. BRUFORD and MACDONALD, p. 178.

narrated by the expert twentieth-century storyteller Duncan MacDonald.[53] In contrast to the examples given so far, the entire stretch can be viewed as one long macro-formula.[54] Like other similar passages, it recurs with some consistency across time, narrators, modes (oral and literate) and languages (Irish and Scottish Gaelic). The annotation below is as before, although the marking of individual formulas would be redundant; the whole passage is formulaic:

'S thug mi a <u>toiseach a mhuir</u> $_A$ agus <u>a deireadh a thìr</u> $_A$
thog mi na siùil *bhreaca bhaidealacha*
an aghaidh nan <u>crann</u> $_B$ *fada fulangach*
a fiù 's nach robh <u>crann $_B$ gun lùbadh</u> $_C$ na <u>seòl gun reubadh</u> $_C$
a' caitheamh a' *chuain chuannaich bhàin*

Le linne bruach a' *bogarta*
's e bu cheòl cadail agus tàmha [dhomh]
<u>glocadaich</u> $_D$ *fhaoil* agus *lùbadaich easgann*
a' <u>mhuc bu mhotha</u> $_{E1}$ ag ithe na <u>muice bu lugha</u> $_{E2}$
's a <u>mhuc bu lugha</u> $_{E2}$ a' dèanamh mar a dh'fhaodadh i

Faochagan *croma ciara* an aigeil
a' <u>glagadaich</u> $_D$ a-staigh air a h-ùrlar
aig feabhas a bha e ga stiùireadh
gun dèanadh e <u>*stiùir* na toiseach</u> $_F$ <u>iùil na deiredh</u> $_F$
gum <u>fuasgladh e am ball a bhiodh ceangailte innte</u> $_G$
agus gun <u>ceangladh e am ball a bhiodh fuasgailte innte</u> $_G$

Translation:

And I set <u>her stem to the sea</u> $_A$ and her <u>stern to the shore</u> $_A$
and I raised the *dappled, flapping* sails
against the tall, tough <u>masts</u> $_B$
so that there was no <u>mast</u> $_B$ <u>unbent</u> $_C$ nor <u>sail untorn</u> $_C$
weathering the *white wallowing* ocean

Splashing of the sea-pool's shore
was music to soothe me to sleep

---

[53] For background, see: W. LAMB, "The storyteller, the scribe, and a missing man: Hidden influences from printed sources in the Gaelic tales of Duncan and Neil Macdonald", *Oral Tradition*, 27 (2012), pp. 109-160.

[54] FROG, "Multiform theory", in: *Weathered Words*, ed. FROG and LAMB, pp. 115-146, at p. 133.

<u>screaming</u> _D *of sea-gulls, coiling of eels*
<u>the greater whale</u> _{E1} eating <u>the lesser whale</u> _{E2}
and <u>the lesser whale</u> _{E2} doing as best it could

The *bent brown* buckies of the deep, <u>rattling</u> _D in on to her bottom boards
so surely was [he] steering her
[he] was <u>steersman in the stem</u> _F <u>pilot in the prow</u> _F
[he] would <u>loose the rope that was fast in her</u> _G
and make <u>fast the rope that was loose in her</u> _G

Bruford and MacDonald deftly convey some of the Gaelic alliteration and assonance in English, but no translation could capture all of the parallelism present. One metred feature cannot even be captured in the original transcription: its rhythm. Duncan MacDonald's delivery abounded in rhythm (not to mention tone). During formulaic sequences, especially, he punctuated each phrase as if reciting verse. Bill Innes, in a recent radio broadcast, describes one fieldworker's reaction to Duncan's narrative style:

Bha Calum [MacIllEathain] air a bheò-ghlacadh gu h-àraid leis an stoidhle a bh' aig Donnchadh. Agus mhothaich e, nuair a bhiodh e ag innse na sgeòil gum biodh a chas a' bualadh an làir a cheart cho math 's ged a biodh e a' gabhail òran

Calum [Maclean] was entranced especially with Duncan's style. And he noticed, when he'd be telling stories, that his foot would beat the floor just as solidly as if he had been singing a song[55]

Considering what we can gather from the text of the sailing run itself, we can observe the density of the poetic features on display and the economy of language. Every line except 7 and 13[56] embeds parallelism of some sort. Regarding measured features, we see repetitions at the level of syntactic frames and short phrases, in a fiery display of chiasmus and antimetabole:[57] "*toiseach a mhuir agus deireadh a thìr*" ("stem to sea and stern to land") in line 1, "*crann gun lùbadh na seòl gun reubadh*" ("no mast unbent nor sail untorn") in line 2, "*a'*

---

[55] B. INNES, "Donnchadh dòmhnallach, peighinn nan aoireann", in: *Sgaoileadh an Eòlais*, BBC Radio nan Gàidheal, 18 Oct. 2021, 20:15-20:26. Translation by the present author.

[56] At a push, one could say that line 14 shows a repetition of *stiùir-* from line 13.

[57] Antimetabole is when words repeat in successive clauses, but in reversed order, e.g. "Ask not what your country can do for you; ask what you can do for your country" (John F. Kennedy). It is contrasted to chiasmus, when structures repeat, but not the words themselves, e.g. "By day the frolic, and the dance by night" (Samuel Johnson).

mhuc bu mhotha ag ithe na muice bu lugha" ("the greater whale eating the lesser whale") in line 9, "*stiùir na toiseach, iùil na deireadh*" ("steersman in the stem, pilot in the prow") in line 14, and the last two lines, which contain "*gum fuasgladh e am ball a bhiodh ceangailte innte / agus gun ceangladh e am ball a bhiodh fuasgailte innte*" ("[he] would loose the rope that was fast in her / and make fast the rope that was loose in her"). Interlaced within these syntactic parallelisms are the semantic oppositions: stem vs. stern; sea vs. land; greater vs. lesser; and loose [unravel] vs. fast [tie].

On the metred level, the alliteration mentioned by Bruford is on full display: *bhreaca bhaidealacha* ('dappled flapping'); *fada fulangach* ('tall tough'); *mhuc ~ mhotha* ('whale ~ greater') and *croma ciara* ('bent brown'). The sailing run also deploys Gaelic's morphology for consonantal rhyme: e.g. the verbal nouns *lùbadh* / lʸuːpəɣ / ~ *reubadh* / rʸeːpəɣ / , *glocadaich* / klʸɔxkətix / ~ *lùbadaich* / lʸuːpətix / , and *fuasgladh* / fuasklʸəɣ / ~ *ceangladh* / kʰẽəlʸəɣ / , as well as the verbal adjectives *ceangailte* / kʰẽəlʲtʲə / ~ *fuasgailte* / fuaskilʲtʲə /.

It is in the runs of more formal[58] traditional 'prose' that we see the greatest convergence of poetic features. Given that several editors have set them as verse when printing them indicates that viewing them as poetry is uncontroversial. As impressive as they are, not to mention the memories of those who transmitted them, perhaps it is time for us shine our light elsewhere as well. In concentrating on specialist formulas, we may overlook the important contributions of more vernacular stock phrases in oral tradition. As we saw in the first and second narratives presented in this section, when measured parallelisms transect, they can lay seed for metred ones. Thus, with non-metred traditional narrative, it is possible to locate poetry even in the prosaic.

In Part II, we will consider parallelisms in a type of formulaic language that straddles the spectrum of vernacularity and en-registerment: the binomial.

---

[58] See LAMB "Verbal formulas", pp. 233-244; cf. LAMB "From motif to multiword expression", pp. 208-209.

Part II: Weighting and Alliteration in Narrative Binomials

As part of a recently funded project,[59] my colleagues and I are digitising and transcribing roughly 80k manuscripts of traditional narrative from the School of Scottish Studies Archives (University of Edinburgh) and the National Folklore Collection (University College Dublin). One of our objectives is to automatically identify and compare formulas within the Gaelic and Irish traditions. If successful, we will advance our understanding of their form, function, context, and historical transmission. In Part II, I report on an initial survey of 1.5M words of Gaelic data. This was restricted to binomials, a type of short formula associated with *Märchen* and other international tales,[60] and it attempted to uncover the most common metrical constraints associated with them. It was hoped that by elucidating this, it will help us to automatically detect a broader range of formulas in the future.

As mentioned in the Introduction, a binomial (or 'couplet') is a sequence of two conjoined words (usually nouns or adjectives) that tend to appear in a proscribed order. For this survey, I examined binomials conjoined by the following words:

Type	Forms	Gloss	Example	Gloss
Additive	*'s, is, agus*	'and'	*sgoil is ionnsachadh*	'school and learning'
Disjunctive	*no, neo*	'or'	*sileadh no stoirm*	'rain or storm'
Subtractive	*gun*	'without'	*gun bhean gun leanabh*	'without wife or child'

Binomials were chosen for two reasons. First, they have been extensively studied in English and in other languages. Secondly, it was hoped that their relative commonality and well-defined structure would lend themselves to automatic detection.[61] To help find binomials in the corpus, a tag ('_N') was added automatically to all the nouns and another tag ('_A') to all the adjectives. Candidate binomials were located using the following regular expression (REGEX) patterns, which were implemented using Python scripts:

---

[59] "Decoding Hidden Heritages in Gaelic Traditional Narrative with Text-mining and Phylogenetics", funded by the Irish Research Council (IRC) and the Arts and Humanities Research Council (AHRC). See: <https://www.gaois.ie/ga/about/hidden-heritages/>.

[60] LAMB, "From motif to multiword expression", pp. 213-214.

[61] The pilot corpus contained 380k words of narrative transcriptions from the School of Scottish Studies Archives, and a further 1.1 million words of transcriptions made by the fieldworker Calum Iain Maclean, while he was employed by the Irish Folklore Commission (see <https://www.calum-maclean.celtscot.ed.ac.uk/calmac/background.htm>).

Formulas in Scottish Traditional Narrative 181

```
1. (?i)(gun) (\w+_N)\W*,* (gun) (\w+_N)
2. (?i)(\w+_N) (is|agus|\'s|no|neo) (\w+_N)
3. (?i)(\w+_A) (is|agus|\'s|no|neo) (\w+_A)
```

Pattern 1 retrieved:

> *gun* Noun *gun* Noun
> *gun* Noun, *gun* Noun

Pattern 2 retrieved:

> Noun *is* Noun
> Noun *agus* Noun
> Noun *'s* Noun
> Noun *no* Noun
> Noun *neo* Noun

Pattern 3 retrieved:

> Adj *is* Adj
> Adj *agus* Adj
> Adj *'s* Adj
> Adj *no* Adj
> Adj *neo* Adj

Over 1,100 candidate binomials were found. After manual examination and consideration of context (in some cases), the list was winnowed to 336 items. The sums and percentages of items retrieved by each pattern are as follows: Pattern 1: 17 (5.06%); Pattern 2: 306 (91.07%); Pattern 3: 13 (3.87%). The first ten items from each pattern are provided below for illustration:

Pattern 1 (Nouns)

gun aighear gun bhrògan	'without joy without shoes'
gun aogas gun tlachd	'without countenance without joy'
gun Bheurla gun Ghàidhlig	'without English without Gaelic'
gun bhròg gun aodach	'without shoe(s) or clothes'
gun bhròig gun stocainn	'without shoe(s) or sock(s)'
gun duine gun laogh	'without a man or calf'
gun ghaoith gun uisge	'without wind or rain'
gun ghaoth gun turadh	'without wind or dry weather'

gun leanabh gun teine	'without an infant or fire'
gun ràmh gun seòl	'without an oar or sail'

Pattern 2 (Nouns)

aighean is beothaichean	'small heifers and animals'
aighear is ceòl	'joy and music'
aimhreit agus trod	'quarrelling and scolding'
airgid is òir	'silver and gold'
aodach no airgiod	'clothes or money'
aodaich agus brògan	'clothes and shoes'
aran agus càise	'bread and cheese'
aran agus tì	'bread and tea'

Pattern 3 (Adjectives)

anamoch is moch	'late and early'
coibhneil 's càirdeil	'kind and friendly'
duilich agus muladach	'sorry and sorrowful'
fada no goirid	'long or short'
fann agus sgìth	'weak and tired'
fireann is boireann	'male and female'
moch is anamoch	'early and late'
sàbhailte agus slàn	'safe and healthy'
teth is fuar	'hot and cold'
toilichte no diombach	'pleased or displeased'

To my knowledge, this is the first time that a list of binomials has been compiled or investigated linguistically for the Gaelic language. One will notice that some of the above items occur in both of the possible orders: A + B and B + A (e.g. *moch and anamoch* 'early and late' and *anamoch is moch* 'late and early'). Also noticeable – at least to Gaelic speakers – is that they run the gamut between generic phrases and ones closely associated with traditional narrative (e.g. *aighear is ceòl* ['joy and music'],[62] *rìgh is ridire* ['king and knight'], *latha is bliadhna* ['a day and a year'], and *sgoil is ionnsachadh* ['school and learning']). Some of these expressions can be figurative. For example, *gun bhròg gun aodach* ('without a shoe or clothes') communicates a state of destitution. Semantically, most of the paired elements are antonyms (*teth is fuar* ['hot and cold']), synonyms (*duilich agus muladach* ['sorry and sorrowful']) or hyponyms (*aran is càise* ['bread and cheese']).

---

[62] More commonly, "*ceòl is aighear*" ("music and joy").

Two sets of features were examined: metred parallelisms (assonance and alliteration) and end-weighting. Assonance (both vowel harmony and consonance) could be found in 13.99% of the returns. In many cases, the phrases showed parallels in their derivative and inflectional morphology; Gaelic morphology is fairly regular. Some examples of assonance follow:

bàthach no stàball	'a byre or stable'
coibhneil 's càirdeil	'kind and friendly'
gun bhean gun leanabh	'without a wife, without an infant'
sgoltaidhean is sgàinidhean	'cleaving and splitting'

Below are some examples of alliterative binomials, which had a similar incidence (13.69%):

crodh is caoraich	'cattle and sheep'
fuath agus falach	'aversion and concealment'
gun fhuil gun fheòil	'without blood, without flesh'
taigh agus teine	'a house and a fire'

Altogether, roughly one quarter of the sample (24.11%) showed either assonance or alliteration. Thus, while these features are not pervasive, they do occur regularly. In a sense, since binomials inherently have tightly associated semantics, one again observes: where measured features lead, metred features soon follow. We will turn our attention now to the second bundle of features: phonological weighting.

Previous research has indicated that binomials in English and other non-verb-final languages show distinct patterns of phonological weighting. In general, second elements pattern as 'heavier' by exhibiting at least some of the following features:[63]

1. longer vowels ('rain or shine');
2. lower vowels ('rhythm and blues');
3. longer and / or more sonorant codas ('thick and thin');
4. longer or more complex onsets ('meet and greet');
5. more obstruent onsets ('hue and cry');
6. more syllables ('kit and kaboodle').

---

[63] RYAN, "Prosodic end-weight reflects phrasal stress", p. 316.

Each of these features was investigated for the Gaelic binomial data. Before examining the results, it is important to state one limitation of the automatic detection method used here: only the first word after the conjunction or preposition was returned. So where the second element was a phrasal constituent (e.g. *eun no <u>creutair eile</u>* ('a bird or <u>another creature</u>')), it was truncated to its noun head only (e.g. *eun no <u>creutair</u>* ('a bird or <u>creature</u>')). The confound that this introduced was that it sometimes attenuated the syllable counts of the second element. In the future, this problem could be avoided or limited by using a syntactic parser, which would capture the full noun phrase.

We will now take the features in turn. Beginning with Features 1 and 2, no statistical support was found in this sample of Gaelic binomials for the second elements having longer or lower vowels.[64]

Regarding Feature 3, a *coda* is the consonant or consonant cluster at the end of a word. *Sonorants* are resonant consonants or glides that are produced with an open vocal tract. In Gaelic, sonorants include laterals (*l*-sounds), nasals (*n*- and *m*-sounds), rhotics (*r*-sounds) and vowels. Past research has found that the second elements in binomials tend to show longer and more sonorant codas. For this pilot, I coded only the coda types, distinguishing between sonorants, affricates,[65] fricatives,[66] sibilants[67] and plosives.[68] Raw counts for the coda types per position are provided in Table 2 and visualised in Fig. 1:

Table 2: Coda types per position (raw counts)

	SONORANT	AFFRICATE	FRICATIVE	SIBILANT	PLOSIVE	TOTAL
CODA 1	213	11	69	12	30	335
CODA 2	224	10	59	15	27	335

---

[64] But see the post-hoc analysis for Feature 6 below.

[65] Affricates are sounds that close the vocal tract with a stop consonant, and then release it with a fricative or sibilant in the same place of articulation, like the *j* sound on 'ajar' or the *ch* sound in 'choose'.

[66] Fricatives are consonants that narrow the vocal tract so that there is friction, but do not fully close it, like *f* in 'feet', or *ch* in 'loch' /lʸɔx/.

[67] Sibilants are *s*-sounds.

[68] Plosive fully obstruct airflow in the vocal tract, like *p* in 'paper' and *ck* in 'tack'.

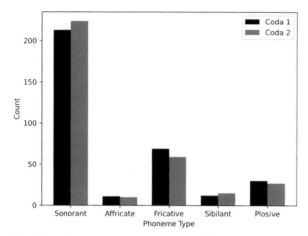

Fig. 1 Coda phoneme type per position.

As can be seen in Table 2, the sonorant counts were in the expected direction, with Position 2 showing 224 sonorants, while Position 1 had 213. These categorical data were analysed with a Fisher's Exact test, which produced a non-significant result: $p_{one\text{-}sided}=0.209$. Thus, no support was found for Feature 3 in these data; sonorance does not seem to be strongly associated with binomial weighting in Gaelic.

To examine Feature 4, I tabulated the number of initial consonants for each binomial. It was predicated that second elements, on average, would show more initial consonants than first elements. A random sample of 150 binomials was generated and the initial consonants were counted for each binomial word (e.g. *crodh is caoraich*: Onset 1 = /kʸrʸ/ = 2, Onset 2 = /kʸ/ = 1). After establishing that the data had a normal distribution using a Shapiro-Wilk test, the two groups were evaluated with a one-sided, related t-test. No significant difference was found between them the at the 0.05 level ($p_{one\text{-}tailed}=0.0585$). Yet, the direction of travel was as expected (i.e. the second elements showed slightly more consonant cluster onsets) and a larger sample might have provided more statistical power. The data are visualised with a bar plot in Fig. 2.

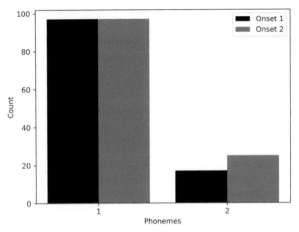

Fig. 2   Onset density per order.

Past research has indicated that although the second elements of binomials tend to have more sonorant codas, they have more obstruent onsets (Feature 5). The same random sample used to evaluate Feature 4 was coded for the presence of obstruent onsets. As with the previous features, no statistically significant support was found for Feature 5: a Fisher's Exact test produced a *p*-value of 0.320. As indicated in Fig. 3, Onset 1 was obstruent in 62/150 cases (41.33%), while Onset 2 was in 67/150 cases (44.67%). Although a larger sample might have produced a stronger result, we cannot conclude that the second elements of Gaelic binomials have more obstruent onsets based upon these data.

Table 3:   Coda obstruence per binomial position

	CODA1	CODA2	TOTAL
OBSTRUENT	62	67	129
NOT-OBSTRUENT	88	83	171

The tendency for later elements in conjoined words and phrases to have more syllables (or constituents) was first recognised in ancient times by the Sanskrit scholar, Pāṇini. It was also observed by the German linguist Behaghel, and so is referred to alternatively as "Pāṇini's Law" or "Behaghel's Law of Increasing Terms".[69] Unlike the previous features, syllable counts (Feature 6) do appear to be implicated in Gaelic binomial ordering. After establishing that the syllable

---

[69] See RYAN "Prosodic end-weight', p. 325.

Formulas in Scottish Traditional Narrative

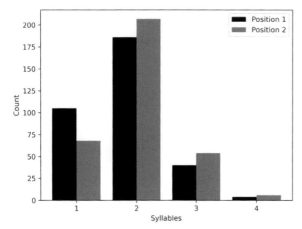

Fig. 3   Binomial element syllable counts per position.

data were normally distributed using a Shapiro-Wilk test, they were subjected to a one-sided, related t-test. This produced a significant result: $p_{one\text{-}tailed} < 0.001$. So, second binomial elements tended to have more syllables (mean = 1.994) than first elements (mean = 1.83). Bearing in mind the limitation mentioned above (i.e. that phrases in Position 2 were truncated to the noun head), this finding is probably more modest than it might have been. The data are visualised in Fig. 3.

Inspecting the binomials further revealed an interesting pattern: on average, when the first element had a higher syllable count than the second, the second element was more likely to display a long stressed vowel (i.e. a long nucleus) than a short one. This is visible in Table 4. It is possible that the lengthening of the second element acts as a compensatory mechanism. Some examples of this phenomenon follow:

Binomial	Syl1	Syl2	Translation
briosgaidean is ìm	3	1	'biscuits and butter'
iarratas is dùrachd	3	2	'desire and intention'
gille agus cù	2	1	'a boy and a dog'
dannsa is ceòl	2	1	'dance and music'

Table 4: Stressed vowel length in Element2, where $SYL_1 > SYL_2$

Long	36	59%
Short	25	41%

To conclude this section, it is possible to locate binomials in a large corpus of traditional narrative semi-automatically. The method followed here could be improved by using a statistical parser instead of basic part-of-speech tagging. This would capture the full extent of phrasal second elements, rather than truncating them to their first constituent (i.e. the NP head). By nature, binomials feature tight semantic relations. Thus, they are inherently measured constructions. Unsurprisingly, roughly one quarter of the binomials located for this study also showed metred parallelisms: alliteration and assonance. They also demonstrated a tendency to have a syllabically heavier second element. This is known as phonological end-weight. Although end-weight has been observed in human language since Antiquity, its potential as a constraining device has received little attention in studies of verbal art. At the same time, this particular dataset did not provide strong support for any of the other features associated in the literature with prosodic end-weighting. Nevertheless, given the relatively small sample gathered here, they could be considered again in the future using a larger, more comprehensive corpus.

Conclusion

We began by considering the nature of poetry vis-à-vis prose, and definitions of 'formula' for non-metred domains. Some scholars have averred that prose, in oral tradition, is unlikely or even an impossibility. Others, notably Hymes and others from the ethnopoetic school, have taken a broad view of poetry, locating it on a continuum with everyday speech. Accordingly, they have considered how non-metred verbal art may be better classified as poetry than 'prose'.

In Part 1, applying Hymes' concepts of measured and metred parallelism, we examined three contrasting narrative texts in Scots and Gaelic. Where measured parallelisms in them intersected, in some cases they seemed to lay the ground for metred ones. It was noted that, although the greatest coalescence of poetic features occurred in the longer formulas of formal storytelling (e.g. in

Gaelic hero tales), occasionally rich parallelisms are perceptible even in vernacular narratives.

Part 2 of the paper reported on a pilot study of Gaelic binomials, which used a large corpus of traditional narrative and semi-automatic retrieval methods. Binomials run the gamut between being vernacular phrases common to the language at large and enregistered expressions specific to traditional narrative. With their intrinsically tight semantic bonds, it is not surprising that they display relatively frequent metred parallelisms, such as assonance and alliteration. In addition, they also regularly display at least one aspect of prosodic end-weighting, a constraint that has been examined only rarely for formulas in traditional narrative.

In sum, it is clear that a broader view of poetry can be beneficial for how we view and represent traditional narrative. Likewise, a more inclusive consideration of formulaicity in verbal art – one that includes both vernacular and enregistered formulas – may lead to a better understanding of both performers' creativity and the durability of expression. Undoubtedly, it is possible to find poetry even in the most prosaic forms of traditional narrative.

Towards a Typology of Runic Formulas, with a Focus on the One-Word Formula in the Older Runic Inscriptions[*]

MICHAEL SCHULTE

Introduction

In this paper I offer a new typology of runic formulas, based on the minimal one-word formula and its extensions. The formula is a key notion in linguistics, stemming from idiomatics. It denotes sequences of words that are lexically and syntactically very stable or even unchangeable, that form complete utterances, and that can be subclassed according to their pragmatic func-

---

[*] A revised and expanded version of this paper appears in German: M. SCHULTE, "Bauprinzipien runischer Formeln: Zur Lexis und Morphosyntax urnordischen Formeln", *Beiträge zur Geschichte der deutschen Sprache und Literatur* 145.1 (2023), pp. 1-34. I am indebted to Michael Barnes for raising my level of caution as to the interpretation of the bracteate inscriptions. I owe thanks to Þorhallur Eyþórsson (University of Iceland), Marc Pierce (University of Texas at Austin), Patrick Stiles (University College London), Henrik Williams (University of Uppsala), and Gaby Waxenberger (Ludwig Maximilian University of Munich and Göttingen Academy of Sciences and Humanities) for a careful reading and feedback on the first version of this paper. Their incisive comments and corrections are greatly appreciated. The usual disclaimers apply.

New Light on Formulas in Oral Poetry and Prose, ed. Daniel SÄVBORG and Bernt Ø. THORVALDSEN, *Utrecht Studies in Medieval Literacy*, 57 (Turnhout: Brepols, 2023), pp. 191-225.

tions – compare modern greetings and formulas of politeness: Mod.E *Good afternoon, Take care,* Mod.G *Grüß Gott, Zum Wohl,* Mod.Fr. *Bonjour, À votre sainté.*[1]

The approach taken in this paper acknowledges the fact that the runic formula can be extremely short: it may consist of mono-lexemes, or one-word formulas, such as *alu* 'luck, hail!' and *laþu* 'invocation, summons', which can stand completely on their own. Compare the runestone from Elgesem (KJ 57) which exclusively features the formulaic key word *alu* (see Fig. 5 below).[2] In fact, the minimal formula, as I dub it here, may be shortened to the extreme, e.g. the *l*-rune, ᛚ, may stand for *līna* 'linen / flax' or *laukaR* 'leek', which are healing words (e.g. IK 128, see the discussion of the *līna laukaR* formula below), or alternatively, the *l*-rune may represent its ideographic value which is *laguR* (= ON *lǫgr*, OE *lagu*) 'sea, liquid'.[3] Taking one-word inscriptions as its point of departure, this study moves on to more complex formulas, particularly twin formulas, reduplication formulas and combined formulas, to explore their semantic value and functional use. Criteria of formulaicity deployed in this typology include frequency, lexical semantics and etymology, the fixedness of serial strings (i.e. Behaghel's Law), metricality and alliteration, and different degrees of condensation of the runic formula.

The present approach includes runic formulas on different objects such as bracteate amulets and runestones from the older runic period (up to 750 AD).

---

[1] This standard definition of the 'formula' is based on H. BUSSMANN, *Routledge Dictionary of Language and Linguistics* (London and New York, 1996), p. 171b. Abbreviations of languages used in this paper are as follows: G = German, MHG = Middle High German, Mod.E = Modern English, Mod.G = Modern German, Mod.Fr. = Modern French, Norw. = Norwegian, OE = Old English, OHG = Old High German, OInd. = Old Indic, OIr. = Old Irish, ON = Old Norse, PGmc = Proto-Germanic.

[2] KJ plus inscription number = W. KRAUSE, with H. JANKUHN, *Die Runeninschriften im älteren Futhark* (Göttingen, 1966: *Abhandlungen der Akademie der Wissenschaften in Göttingen: Phil.-hist. Klasse* 3, Nr. 65).

[3] On these three possible values, see W. KRAUSE, "Untersuchungen zu den Runennamen, I", in: *Nachrichten der Akademie der Wissenschaften zu Göttingen: Philologisch-Historische Klasse*, 1946-1947 (Göttingen, 1948), pp. 60-63, at p. 63; reprinted in ID., *Schriften zur Runologie und Sprachwissenschaft*, ed. H. BECK et al. (Berlin and Boston, 2014: *Ergänzungs-Bände zum Reallexikon der Germanischen Altertumskunde* 84), pp. 218-222; cf. the consent of W. HEIZMANN, "Die Formelwörter der Goldbrakteaten", in: *Die Goldbrakteaten der Völkerwanderungszeit – Auswertung und Neufunde*, ed. W. HEIZMANN and M. AXBOE (Berlin and New York, 2011: *Ergänzungs-Bände zum Reallexikon der Germanischen Altertumskunde* 40), pp. 525-601, at pp. 555-556. IK plus inscription number = M. AXBOE et al., *Die Goldbrakteaten der Völkerwanderungszeit: Ikonographischer Katalog*, 1-3 (Munich, 1985-1989: *Münstersche Mittelalter-Schriften* 24).

My linguistic typology of the *runic formula* in the older period (*c.* 50-750 AD) is as follows:

1. Charm word formulas, e.g. *alu*
2. Reduplication formulas, e.g. *salu-salu*
3. Twin formulas, e.g. *līna laukaR*
4. Alliterative non-twin formulas, e.g. *rūnō raginaku(n)dō*
5. Tandem and combined formulas, e.g. *laukaR alu*
6. Riddle-like, disguised and shortened formulas, e.g. *lua* for *alu*

This approach suggests a fundamental difference between the runic formula on the one hand and the Eddic formula and the literary poetic formulas more broadly on the other: the runic formula does not need to be metrical or alliterative, whereas metricality is a basic criterion of the Eddic formula, in particular the Eddic twin formula. A case in point is the Old Scandinavian *iǫrð / upphiminn* formula addressed below, e.g. "*iǫrð fannz æva | né upphiminn*" ("the earth was not there, and no upper heaven") in *Vǫlospá* 3,5-6. The runic formula proper has a much narrower range than the alliterative formula which is not restricted to a particular genre, medium, or text type.[4]

Ritualistic language is fixed and formulaic by nature because it must be accurately performed to fulfil its purpose, e.g. in a healing ceremony.[5] As to style and pragmatic choice, however, it has long been noted that formulas and formulaic sequences do not primarily constitute a device of elevated style in poetry, ritualistic texts, or narrative literature, but are a central feature of everyday language, fairy tales, and stories for children, among other things.[6] As Schmitt and Carter, among others, note, these "formulaic sequences / expressions" are ubiquitous in language use and almost synonymous with "idioms".[7] Thus, names – in particular 'magico-poetic' weapon names, such as **raunijaʀ**

---

[4] On the Eddic formula, see: P. ACKER, "A further history of orality and Eddic poetry", in this volume, pp. 141-162, and S.A. MELLOR, "Revisiting the formula and mythic patterns and the interplay between the *Poetic Edda* and *Vǫlsunga saga*", in this volume, pp. 227-258.

[5] See M. SCHULTE, "Literacy in the looking glass: Vedic and Skaldic verse and the two modes of oral transmission", *Scripta Islandica* 59 (2008), pp. 181-199.

[6] A. WRAY, "Identifying formulaic language: Persistent challenges and new opportunities", in: *Formulaic Language*, 1, *Distribution and Historical Change*, ed. R. CORRIGAN *et al.* (Amsterdam and Philadelphia, 2009), pp. 27-51, at p. 29.

[7] N. SCHMITT and R. CARTER, "Formulaic sequences in action: An introduction", in: *Formulaic Sequences: Acquisition, processing and use*, ed. N. SCHMITT (Amsterdam and Philadelphia, 2004), pp. 1-22, at p. 1.

'prober, tester' on the Øvre Stabu lance-head KJ 31 – are excluded from this study.

Moreover, two further types of Early Runic formula are excluded from this typology: first, the rune-row of the older *fuþark* interpreted as a fixed formula,[8] and secondly, the *ek erilaR / irilaR* formula, which presents the runemaster, or *erilaR*, in a sort of self-predication; compare the following formulaic phrase which very often highlights the writing skills of the *erilaR*: *I, the erilaR / irilaR [am called] N.N. [or, write (or, wrote) the runes]*.[9] The patently formulaic character of the older runic inscriptions can be illustrated by the use of this formula, which features prominently in the Early Runic corpus. These two types of formulas, the *fuþark* itself and the *ek erilaR* formula, are excluded from the following account because they are not built on the one-word formula, the cornerstone of the present approach. Larger formulaic expressions such as the curse formulas of Stentoften and Björketorp (Blekinge, KJ 96-97) are outside the range of this study as well.[10] Other runic formulas, such as **sakumukmini** on the Swedish Rök stone (suggested translation "I / we say the folk-mem-

---

[8] See in particular K.F. SEIM, *De vestnordiske futhark-innskriftene fra vikingtid og middelalder – form og funksjon* (PhD thesis, Trondheim, 1998); K. DÜWEL and W. HEIZMANN, "Das ältere Fuþark: Überlieferung und Wirkungsmöglichkeiten der Runenreihe", in: *Das Fuþark und seine einzelsprachlichen Weiterentwicklungen*, ed. A. BAMMESBERGER et al. (Berlin and New York, 2006: *Ergänzungs-Bände zum Reallexikon der Germanischen Altertumskunde* 51), pp. 3-60.

[9] See Th. BIRKMANN, *Von Ågedal bis Malt: Die skandinavischen Runeninschriften vom Ende des 5. bis Ende des 9. Jahrhunderts* (Berlin and New York, 1995: *Ergänzungs-Bände zum Reallexikon der Germanischen Altertumskunde* 12), pp. 151-159; K. DÜWEL, "Runenkenntnis als Oberschichtenmerkmal (mit bes. Berücksichtigung methodischer Aspekte)", in: *Archäologie und Runen: Fallstudien zu Inschriften im älteren Futhark*, ed. O. GRIMM and A. PESCH (Kiel and Hamburg, 2015: *Schriften des archäologischen Landesmuseums, Ergänzungs-Reihe* 11), pp. 265-290, at pp. 274-275; O. SUNDQUIST, "Contributions of the oldest runic inscriptions to the reconstruction of ancient Scandinavian religion: Some methodological reflections with reference to an example of the phenomenological category of 'ritual specialists'", in: *Archäologie und Runen*, ed. GRIMM and PESCH, pp. 121-143, at pp. 125-126; L. IMER, *Jernalderens runeindskrifter i Norden* [1.] *Kronologi og kontekst* (Copenhagen, 2015: *Aarbøger for Nordisk Oldkyndighed og Historie* 2013), p. 114; cf. also M. SCHULTE, "Wain, wagon and wayfarer: Names of speed, agility and alertness in the corpus of the older runic inscriptions", *NOWELE* 73.2 (2020), pp. 276-298, at p. 288.

[10] See M. SCHULTE, "Stylistic variation in runic inscriptions? A test-case and preliminary assessment", *Arkiv för nordisk filologi* 123 (2008), pp. 5-22, *passim*; E. MAROLD, "Vers oder nicht Vers? Zum metrischen Charakter von Runeninschriften im älteren Futhark", *Futhark* 2 (2011), pp. 63-102, at pp. 85-88; cf. also H.-P. NAUMANN, *Metrische Runeninschriften in Skandinavien: Einführung, Edition und Kommentare* (Tübingen, 2018: *Beiträge zur Nordischen Philologie* 60), pp. 48-54.

ory"), which have spawned a broad spectrum of readings and cultural interpretations, also fall outside the scope of this project.[11] Finally, the world of Christian prayers and formulas does not pertain to the time frame addressed here and such evidence is therefore also not considered.

Socio-interactional Formulas Carved in Runes?

As mentioned, the present approach – in contradistinction to the standard approach – takes the minimal formula, or one-word formula, as its basic phonological, morphological, lexical, and phrasal unit. Fixed expressions and formulas may carry loaded messages to the addressee, either in a positive or negative way, so that there may be "a retreat or sheltering behind shared values which coerces agreement and pre-empts disagreement".[12] Earlier research has pointed out that it makes little sense to produce those word strings which we use so frequently from scratch, and we appear to use formulaic chunks to minimise the amount of new processing to only that which *has* to be new.[13] In this regard, formulaic language, whether oral or written, can be extremely effective in social interaction. As Alison Wray and her co-authors put it,

> The driving force behind the *socio-interactional formulas* is ensuring that the speaker [or, writer – M.S.] gets what he / she wants and is perceived as an individual within the group. Significantly, formulaic language is better suited to this than novel language is, because a hearer [or, more broadly recipient – M.S.] is more likely to understand a message if it is in a form he / she has heard [or, read – M.S.] before, and which he / she can process without recourse to full analytic decoding.[14]

Healing charms, such as the *Pater noster*, are grounded in 'speech acts'. In this vein, Lea T. Olsan has defined charms as "*spoken, chanted* and *written* formulas, derived ultimately from a traditional oral genre and circulated both by word

---

[11] On the 'sagum' formula, see in particular L. LÖNNROTH, *The Academy of Odin: Selected Papers on Old Norse Literature* (Odense, 2011: *The Viking Collection: Studies in Northern Civilization* 19), pp. 309-311, at pp. 330-337; M. SCHULTE, "Memory culture in the Viking Age: The runic evidence of formulaic patterns", *Scripta Islandica* 58 (2007), pp. 57-73, at pp. 67-68.

[12] R. MOON, "Textual aspects of fixed expressions in learners' dictionaries", in: *Vocabulary and Applied Linguistics*, ed. P.J.L. ARNAUD and H. BÉJOINT (London, 1992), pp. 12-27, at p. 24.

[13] Cf. A. WRAY and M.R. PERKINS, "The functions of formulaic language: An integrated model", *Language and Communication* 20.1 (2000), pp. 1-28, at pp. 15-16.

[14] WRAY and PERKINS, "The functions of formulaic language", p. 18 (my emphasis; M.S.).

of mouth and through manuscripts and amuletic texts".[15] The runic formulas under scrutiny are *socio-interactional formulas* in the broadest sense, as the addressee may be a human or non-human being, in particular a god, a helping spirit, or a *draugr / aptrgǫngumaðr* (commonly translated as 'ghost' or 'apparition'). This may explain why certain Old Scandinavian formulas, such as the *ráð rúnar* formula or the *þistill-mistill* formula, appear maximally shortened, or even disguised and distorted, in runic epigraphy.[16]

In sum, formulaicity is a short-cut both in *processing* and *decoding* linguistic messages as it ensures effective production on the side of the speaker / writer and achieves successful comprehension on the side of the hearer, or the recipient more broadly. Against this background, I present the basic runic formulas.

Runic Formula Type 1: Charm Words

Among the one-word formulas in the older runic inscriptions are several lexical items which lend themselves to more or less clear-cut etymologies and semantics, among other things *alu, laþu, salu, tuwa, auja*, and *laukaR*. Accordingly, single attestations of 'magico-poetic' names such as **raunijaʀ** ('the prober, the one who tests [the enemy]'; Øvre Stabu KJ 31), **ranja** ('the assailer'; Dahmsdorf KJ 32), and **tilarids** ('goal-rider, the rider toward the target'), all of which feature on lance-heads or spear-heads, lie beyond the scope of this study.[17] This is because names – including 'magico-poetic' weapon names – tend to be individual and hence do not belong to the stock of prototypical formulas, which by definition are common and almost synonymous with idioms (see the Introduction).

The one-word formulas in question, e.g. *alu, laþu*, and *laukaR*, have often been labelled 'charm words' or 'words of power', as they interact with, conjure up, or summon what may be classed as non-human powers, both gods and evil or good spirits.[18] These runic formulas are sometimes labelled 'magic formulas'

---

[15] See L.T. OLSAN, "Charms in medieval memory", in: *Charms and Charming in Europe*, ed. J. ROPER (New York, 2004), pp. 59-88, at p. 60 (my emphasis; M.S.); D.C. SKEMER, *Binding Words: Textual Amulets in the Middle Ages* (Pennsylvania, 2006), p. 9.

[16] See M. SCHULTE, "*Tistel-mistel*-formelen i vikingtid og nordisk middelalder – Form, funksjon og symbolverdi", *Maal og Minne* 112.2 (2020), pp. 97-126, at pp. 102-117.

[17] On these weapon names, see SCHULTE, "Wain, wagon and wayfarer", pp. 276-282.

[18] For a state-of-the-art report, see K. DÜWEL, "Zum Sitz im Leben: Runen und Magie", in:

(*Zauberformeln* and *Heilswörter*), which condense a spell or incantation into a short formula. It is important to note that the bracteate inscriptions engage in personal communication with individual gods, spirits, and goddesses, rather than invoking a general (and mechanistic) magic of healing and blessing.[19]

The lexical semantics of these word formulas reveal much of their functional use. According to H. Williams and E. Lundeby, *tuwa* is related to ON *tó* (cf. OE *tōw*, Mod.E *tow* /'təʊ/, especially as part of the expression *tow-headed* ('blond-haired')), a designation for the fibres of hemp, flax, and wool in a prefabricated state. Hence a direct semantic connexion with runic *līna* ('flax, linen') suggests itself; compare the twin formula **lina laukaʀ** ('flax and leek') on the Fløksand bone scraper KJ 37 (see below on twin formulas) and other frequent formulaic words such as *salu* (probably meaning 'offering, sacrifice') and *laukaR* (meaning 'leek'), which may occur on their own; cf. **laukaʀ** on the Års II bracteate (see Fig. 1 below).[20] The term *laukaR*, designating the "magic plant par excellence", is probably attested in at least eighteen runic inscriptions, mainly bracteates, for instance the Års II bracteate IK 8.[21] The word is cognate with ON *laukr*, OE *lēac*, OHG *louh*; this plant of the genus *allium* symbolises fertility, health, and prosperity *in nuce*.[22] On the bracteates, *laukaR* appears in the context of veterinary medicine, not least horse medicine: the healer, Óðinn as a healing god, or possibly a helping spirit in the shape of an animal, is curing a horse. Thus a clear connection to the Old High German Merseburg Charms

---

Die südgermanischen Runeninschriften, ed. K. DÜWEL, R. NEDOMA, and S. OEHRL (Berlin and Boston, 2020: *Ergänzungs-Bände zum Reallexikon der Germanischen Altertumskunde* 119), pp. CXIX-CXLVI, and M. SCHULTE, "Magie in den älteren und jüngeren Runeninschriften? – Zum Status magischer Konzepte in der Runologie", *Filologia Germanica – Germanic Philology* 13 (2021), pp. 307-327.

[19] See H. BECK and K. HAUCK, "Zur philologischen und historischen Auswertung eines neuen Drei-Götter-Brakteaten aus Sorte Muld, Bornholm, Dänemark (Zur Ikonologie der Goldbrakteaten, LXIII)", *Frühmittelalterliche Studien* 36 (2002), pp. 51-94, at p. 53; HEIZMANN, "Die Formelwörter der Goldbrakteaten", p. 548.

[20] See E. LUNDEBY and H. WILLIAMS, "Om Vadstenabrakteatens **tuwa** med et tillegg om Lellingebrakteatens **salu**", *Maal og Minne* 1992, pp. 10-26, based on E. LUNDEBY, "Urnordisk **salu**", *Maal og Minne* 1982, pp. 33-40.

[21] On the runic attestations of *laukaR*, see HEIZMANN, "Die Formelwörter der Goldbrakteaten", pp. 550-555.

[22] See I. REICHBORN-KJENNERUD, *Vår gamle trolldomsmedisin* 2 (Oslo, 1933: *Norske Videnskaps-Akademi i Oslo: II. Hist.-filos. Klasse: Skrifter* 2), p. 23; J. DE VRIES, *Altgermanische Religionsgeschichte*, 2 vols. (Berlin, 1956: *Grundriß der Germanischen Philologie* 12), 2, p. 41; M. OLSEN, *Norges innskrifter med de yngre runer* 2 (Oslo, 1951), pp. 660-663; KRAUSE, "Untersuchungen zu den Runennamen, I", pp. 60-63; KJ, pp. 246-247.

Fig. 1   Års II bracteate with the one-word formula **laukaʀ** (Picture credit: IK 8).

(horse-healing) suggests itself. Additionally, plants of the genus *allium* were used to treat all sorts of wounds, swellings and inflammations, both in animals and humans.[23]

The word **laukaʀ** occurs in isolation some seven to eight times, for example on the Års II bracteate (IK 8; see Fig. 1 and Table 1). Several other charm words such as **lina** ('flax, linen') and possibly **salu** ('seaweed, samphire?') belong to the lexical field of healing plants and medicinal herbs or the products thereof (see below).[24]

A salient example in the older runic corpus is **laþu** (from PGmc **laþō*, extended form *laþōdu*) (meaning 'personal invitation, citation, summons (to numinous powers'), possibly also 'intimate gift' and 'invitational tablet'), as invitations were sent on invitational tablets; compare ON *lǫð* ('bidding, invitation'), MHG *lade* ('board').[25] The word is etymologically related to German *Einladung*; cf. also Gothic *laþōn* (weak vb. 'invite'), *laþōns* ('invitation, call') and *laþa-leikō* (adv. 'willingly, gladly', which renders Greek ἥδιστα).[26] The form **laþu** occurs in isolation on the Højstrup C-type bracteate IK 83 and in

---

[23] Cf. *supra*, n. 22; see also W. HEIZMANN, "Bildformel und Formelwort: Zu den *laukaʀ*-Inschriften auf Goldbrakteaten der Völkwerwanderungszeit", in: *Föredrag vid Riksantikvarieämbetets och Vitterhetsakademiens symposium 8-11 Sept. 1985* (Stockholm, 1987: *Kungl. Vitterhets Historie och Antikvitets Akademien: Konferenser* 15), pp. 145-153; ID., "Die Formelwörter der Goldbrakteaten", p. 548; ID., "Lein(en) und Lauch in der Inschrift von Fløksand und im *Vǫlsa þáttr*", in: *Germanische Religionsgeschichte: Quellen und Quellenprobleme*, ed. H. BECK, D. ELLMERS, and K. SCHIER (Berlin and New York, 1992: *Ergänzungs-Bände zum Reallexikon der Germanischen Altertumskunde* 5), pp. 365-395.

[24] For a summary of competing theories, see BECK and HAUCK, "Zur philologischen und historischen Auswertung", p. 59.

[25] On the runic attestations of *laþu*, see HEIZMANN, "Die Formelwörter der Goldbrakteaten", pp. 544-550.

[26] See J. DE VRIES, *Altnordisches etymologisches Wörterbuch*, 2nd edn. (Leiden, 1962), henceforth AEW, at p. 373a, under *lǫð*; W.P. LEHMANN, *A Gothic Etymological Dictionary* (Leiden, 1986), henceforth GED, at p. 227b, under L.16. *laþon*.

Fig. 2   Sjælland II bracteate with the inscription **hariuha haitika : farauisa : gibu auja** (Picture credit: IK 98).

several formulaic contexts, sometimes in conjunction with **alu**; see the two bracteates IK 58 and IK 149, under combined formulas and twin formulas.

Alternatively, the one-word formula **laþu** may be interpreted as a finite verb ('I summon, invite'), parallelling the verbal interpretation of **alu** ('I provide strength', or 'I nurture, make prosper') (see below). The Trollhättan bracteate from Västergötland (IK 189) has the fixed phrase **tawo laþodu** ('I prepare an invocation / summons', i.e. 'I invite [a god or a helping spirit]' in order to cure an animal or a human being).[27] Two further, less certain instances are **wraitalaþo** (possibly meaning 'I wrote an invitation', or 'the act of writing (an) invitation / summons') on two Trollhättan bracteates (IK 638 and IK 639), and **tawolaþoþm** (...), *tawō laþō þm* (...) (unless the word separation *tawō laþōþ* is to be preferred) ('I prepare an invitation, *þīstilaR mīstilaR?* (...)') on the Halskov-Overdrev-C bracteate IK 70. However, these bracteate inscriptions must be interpreted with utter caution and they raise several as yet unanswered questions with regard to word division, grammatical categories and endings.[28]

The one-word formula **auja** occurs in several contexts, for example on the Sjælland bracteate II-C IK 98, where it is stated that 'I [viz. the bracteate amulet?] give good fortune': *gibu auja* (IK 98; see Fig. 2).[29] The complete inscription runs as follows: **hariuha haitika : farauisa : gibu auja** ("Hariūha I am called, the travel-wise [or, the one who knows dangerous things], I give good

---

[27] See O. GRØNVIK, "Runebrakteater fra folkevandringstida med lesbare og tydbare urnordiske ord", *Arkiv för nordisk filologi* 120 (2005), pp. 5-22, at p. 14; DÜWEL, "Runenkenntnis als Oberschichtenmerkmal", p. 276; cf. also S.E. FLOWERS, *Runes and Magic: Magical Formulaic Elements in the Older Runic Tradition* (Bastrop, 2014; originally PhD thesis, University of Texas), p. 180; and S. POULSEN, "ᛖᚲ [...] **wraitalaþo**: The Proto-Norse strong preterite 1SG ending in light of the Trollhättan II bracteate", *NOWELE* 73 (2020), pp. 22-45.

[28] For a concise report, see DÜWEL, "Runenkenntnis als Oberschichtenmerkmal", pp. 275-276, with reference to S. NOWAK, *Schrift auf den Goldbrakteaten: Untersuchungen zu den Formen der Schriftzeichen und zu den formalen und inhaltlichen Aspekten der Inschriften* (PhD thesis, University of Göttingen, 2003), p. 241.

[29] For a complete list of runic attestations, see HEIZMANN, "Die Formelwörter der Goldbrakteaten", pp. 578-581.

luck!"); compare the presentation of the Skodborg bracteate below (IK 161; see Fig. 6). While its etymology is disputed, Early Runic *auja* is clearly reflected in Old Norse *ey* ('luck, well-being'; in *Landnámabók*) and in the Old Norse prefix *Ey-* which occurs in dithematic names, e.g. *Eyjólfr*, *Eyvindr*, *Eysteinn*; compare also Gothic *awi-liudōn* (weak vb. 'thank') and *awi-liuþ(s)* ('(expression of) thanks').[30]

Another possible one-word formula is *salu*, which is only attested twice, viz. **salu-salu** on the Lellinge bracteate-B IK 105 and in (deliberately?) rearranged or muddled order on the Kongsvad Å bracteate: **foslau** (IK 101). Krause suggests that this sequence is to be interpreted as **f-o**, the initial and the final rune of the older *fuþark*, plus **salu** by way of an anagram which is scrambled or consciously rearranged. However, as W. Heizmann notes, the complete bracteate rune rows of Grumpan IK 260 Vadstena IK 377,1 end with **d**, not **o**.[31] In my view, this indicates the influence of the Greek and Roman alphabet (see the Conclusion below).

But what does this one-word formula *salu* mean? At least three solutions have been offered: (1) there may be a connection with Latin *salus* ('well-being, health'), hence the common notion of a healing word much as *laukaR*; (2) it may have the meaning 'a giving over, offering, sacrifice' (cf. ON *sala* f. ('sale, selling'), OE *salu ~ sala* ('idem'), OHG *sala* ('transfer, delivery, transmission')) in the sense of a divine gift or sacrifice to a god, e.g. Baldr (cf. Gothic *saljan* ('sacrifice'), OE *sellan* ('idem'), ON *selja* ('hand over, offer'));[32] or (3) it may refer to a therapeutic herb, used like *laukaR*, for magical protection, viz. a species of seaweed, samphire (cf. ON *sǫl*).[33] The third interpretation places **salu** in the group of healing plants and herbs together with *līna* and *laukaR*; see the twin formulas.

---

[30] See AEW, p. 106b, under *ey* 2 and *ey* 4; GED, pp. 52b-53a, under A240. *awi-liuþ*.

[31] See HEIZMANN, "Die Formelwörter der Goldbrakteaten", p. 588 with note 286, cf. also N.L. WICKER and H. WILLIAMS, "Bracteates and runes", *Futhark* 3 (2012), pp. 151-213, at p. 197.

[32] See Th. VON GRIENBERGER, Review of S. BUGGE and M. OLSEN, *Norges Indskrifter med de ældre Runer* 1-2, *Göttingische Gelehrte Anzeigen* 168.1 (1906), pp. 89-163, at pp. 138-141; accepted by E.H. ANTONSEN, *A Concise Grammar of the Older Runic Inscriptions* (Tübingen, 1975: *Sprachstrukturen: Reihe A: Historische Sprachstrukturen* 3), p. 71; cf. also K. DÜWEL, *Von Göttern, Helden und Gelehrten: Ausgewählte Scandinavica minora*, ed. R. NEDOMA (Vienna, 2020), pp. 32 and 33-34.

[33] See LUNDEBY, "Urnordisk **salu**", pp. 33-40; AEW, p. 578, under *sǫl*; cf. *supra*, pp. **193-194**, with n. 20.

Fig. 3 Tjurkö-II bracteate with the iconography of a horse and rider plus a swastika and the formulaic word **ota** (Picture credit: IK 185).

Still another one-word formula is **ota**, which occurs by itself on four C-type gold bracteates: IK 55 Fjärestad-C, IK 185 Tjurkö II-C and two finds fromGadegård, Bornholm.[34] The spelling **ota** probably reflects a sixth-century transitional form of PGmc *ōhtan ('terror'; cf. classical Old Norse ótti m., oblique singular ótta ('fear, dread')).[35] Given that this etymology is correct, the one-word formula is apotropaic: "frightening off adversaries or maleficent influences in a manner similar to the way the medieval magical sign called the ægishiálmr ('helm (covering) of terror, awe'; cf. Reginsmál 14ff.; Fáfnismál 17, 44, etc. (...))".[36] As stated in the prose passage of Reginsmál, "hann átti ægishiálm er ǫll kvikvindi hrœdduz við" ("he had an helm of awe which frightened all beings").[37]

The aforementioned runestone from Elgesem, KJ 57, features the isolated charm word **alu** (see below Fig. 4), as do at least five bracteates from the sixth or seventh centuries; see IK 44 Djupbrunns I, IK 78 Slangerup (Hjørlunde Mark), IK 97 Kläggeröd, all of which are C-type bracteates, plus one A-type and one B-type bracteate, i.e. IK 24 Bjørnerud and IK 74 Heide respectively.[38] In addition, there are several possible misspellings or disguised or botched

---

[34] On the runic attestations of **ota**, see HEIZMANN, "Die Formelwörter der Goldbrakteaten", pp. 574-577.

[35] See K. DÜWEL, Runenkunde, 4th edn. (Stuttgart and Weimar, 2008), p. 175; cf. also FLOWERS, Runes and Magic, p. 175.

[36] See FLOWERS, Runes and Magic, p. 175, with a general reference to N. LINDQVIST, En islandsk Svartkonstbok från 1500-talet (Galdrabók) (Uppsala, 1921).

[37] See Edda: Die Lieder des Codex Regius nebst verwandten Denkmälern, I, ed. H. KUHN, 5th edn. (Heidelberg, 1983: Germanische Bibliothek: Reihe 4), p. 176.

[38] On the complete list of twenty-nine objects containing alu, see HØST, Von Göttern, Helden und Gelehrten, p. 297; cf. also W. KRAUSE, Die Sprache der urnordischen Runeninschriften (Heidelberg, 1971: Germanische Bibliothek: Reihe 3), henceforth SuR, here at p. 152; L. IMER, Jernalderens runeindskrifter i Norden [II.] Katalog (Copenhagen, 2015: Aarbøger for Nordisk Oldkyndighed og Historie 2014): pp. 18 (Bjørnerud, Vestfold, Norway), 49 (Djupbrunns I, Gotland, Sweden), 148 (Kläggeröd, Skåne, Sweden), 250 (Slangerup, Sjælland, Denmark), and 114 (Heide, Schleswig-Holstein, Germany).

forms of the word, such as on the C-type bracteate IK 199 from Denmark, which has **tlu** for *alu*?

Outside Scandinavia **alu** appears in England on the runic urns of Loveden Hill and Spong Hill and in southern Germany on the bracteate from Hüfingen.[39] Hence the total amount of *alu*-inscriptions has reached the number of thirty, including a recent Danish find on a drinking-vessel from Uglvig (near Esbjerg in Sønderjylland).[40]

Early Runic *alu* is probably an independent lexeme in the runic lexicon with the meaning 'good fortune, prosperity, success'. Makaev compares the typological use of **alu** in the runic corpus with the use of the formula ἀγαθὴ τύχη ('happiness, good fortune') in Greek votive inscriptions.[41]

The one-word formula **alu** also occurs in combination with other formulaic words, e.g.: IK 26 Börringe bracteate **tanulu al[u] laukaʀ**, where *Tanulu* is probably a woman's name derived with an *l*-suffix (meaning 'tempter, enchantress', or 'little enticing things'?);[42] IK 166 Skrydstrup bracteate **laukaʀ ‖ alu** *laukaR alu*; and IK 149 Skåne bracteate **laþulaukaʀ.gakaʀalu** *laþu laukaR, ga(u)kaR alu* (cf. also twin formulas and combined formulas). The apotropaic charm word *alu* can formally be identified with Old Norse *ǫl* n. ('beer'; cf. also *ǫlðr* n. 'intoxicating drink, beer'; pl. 'ale-drinking, carousal' < **aluþra*), Old English *ealu*, oblique case *ealoð* (Mod.E 'ale') and Dutch *aal*, which is why Zimmermann highlights the drinking ceremony in the ruler's hall as the word's frame of reference.[43]

---

[39] See DÜWEL, *Von Göttern, Helden und Gelehrten*, p. 297, W. HEIZMANN, "Die Hüfinger Kleinbrakteaten und die völkerwanderungszeitlichen Goldbrakteaten des Norden", in: *Alemannien und der Norden*, ed. H.-P. NAUMANN (Berlin and New York, 2003: *Ergänzungs-Bände zum Reallexikon der Germanischen Altertumskunde* 43), pp. 371-385, and DÜWEL, NEDOMA and OEHRL, *Die südgermanischen Runeninschriften*, pp. 291-296.

[40] See <https://natmus.dk/nyhed/enestaaende-fund-runer-er-dukket-op-paa-et-lerkar/> (date of access: 24.02.2021).

[41] See E.A. MAKAEV, *The Language of the Older Runic Inscriptions: A Linguistic and Historical-Philological Analysis*, trans. J. Meredig (Stockholm, 1996: *Kungl. Vitterhets Historie och Antikvitets Akademiens Handlingar: Filol.-filos. serien* 21), p. 101, with reference to W. LARFELD, *Griechische Epigraphik*, 3rd edn. (Munich, 1914), pp. 306-307.

[42] See SuR, p. 47; L. PETERSON, *Lexikon över urnordiska personnamn* (Uppsala, 2004), p. 16, under **tanulu**.

[43] See U. ZIMMERMANN, "Bier, Runen und Macht: Ein Formelwort im Kontext", *Futhark* 5 (2014), pp. 45-64; for critical comment, however, see HEIZMANN, "Die Formelwörter der Goldbrakteaten", pp. 533-544.

But **alu** has also been interpreted as a finite verb meaning 'I give strength, nurture', which fits well into the context of amulets, but less so that of weapons and stone monuments (including gravestones, urns and slabs). Its wide range of uses on bracteates, runestones, and other objects suggests a contrastive polysemy charged with positive and negative connotations comparable to Latin *sacer* ('blessed / accursed') and Greek ἀπά ('prayer / curse').[44] This suggestion is based on E. Rooth, who connected the difficult word with the verbs Early Runic **alan* and Old Norse and Old Swedish *ala* ('grow, thrive; nurture, nourish, bring up (children)'), hence the meaning of **alu** ('I thrive, prosper, or nurture'). Compare further the nouns ON *alað* (n. 'nourishment'), *eldi* (n. 'procreation; offspring' < **aliþija-*) and *ǫld* (f. 'age, lifetime (of a generation); mankind, human world').[45]

The common denominator is probably that **alu** establishes a direct relation to human and non-human powers of different kinds. Its function is apotropaic. This might be the reason why it occurs in dithematic names and hypocoristics such as Early Runic *Alu-gōd* (Værløse clasp, KJ 11) and *Alukō*, which is probably a hypocoristic form with the *kōn*-suffix (Førde stone, KJ 49). It is noteworthy that the related Old Norse compound *ǫlrúnar* ('ale runes?'; or, 'a type of protective runes / taboo runes?'), mentioned in *Sigrdrífumál* 7 (and again in stanza 19), is not completely understood.[46]

Ǫlrúnar scaltu kunna, ef þú vill, annars qvæn
 vélit þic í trygð, ef þú trúir;
á horni scal þær rísta oc á handar baki
 oc merkia á nagli Nauð.

---

[44] See Th.L. MARKEY and B. MEES, "Early Nordic *alu* and **al-* 'to nourish'", *Journal of Indo-European Studies* 42.1-2 (2014), pp. 1-17, at p. 9.

[45] See E. ROOTH, *Altgermanische Wortstudien* (Halle an der Saale, 1926), pp. 9-10; cf. also L. ELMEVIK, "De urnordiska runinskrifternas **alu**", in: *Runor och namn: Hyllingsskrift till Lena Peterson den 27 januari 1999*, ed. L. ELMEVIK and S. STRANDBERG (Uppsala, 1999: *Namn och samhälle* 10), pp. 21-28, at pp. 25 and 28: Elmevik suggests a compromise solution for the etymology of ON *ǫl* n. 'the beverage that "grows", "swells", but also possibly "the nourishing, strength-giving beverage"'; cf. also IMER, *Jernalderens runeindskrifter i Norden* [I], p. 108.

[46] See in particular S. FEIST, "Runen und Zauberwesen im germanischen Altertum", *Arkiv för nordisk filologi* 35 (1919), pp. 243-287, at pp. 280-281; SuR, p. 145; cf. also K. VON SEE *et al.*, *Kommentar zu den Liedern der Edda*, 5, *Heldenlieder* (Heidelberg, 2006), pp. 558-560; AEW, p. 7b, under *alu*; NOWAK, *Schrift auf den Goldbrakteaten*, pp. 208-225; ELMEVIK, "De urnordiska runinskrifternas **alu**", pp. 21-28; DÜWEL, *Von Göttern, Helden und Gelehrten*, pp. 297-298.

> Ale-runes must you know if you do not want another's wife
> to beguile your trust, if you trust her;
> on a horn they should be cut and on the back of the hand,
> and mark your nail with *Nauð* ('need').[47]

E. Polomé interprets *ǫlrúnar* as "runes intended to protect by means of a magic charm which absorbs the damaging effect of a poisonous drink" ("*runes destinées à protéger d'un charme magique celui qui boit contre l'effet pernicieux d'un breuvage frelaté*").[48] The prose passage *Frá dauða Sinfiǫtla* ("The death of Sinfiotli") relates that Sigurd's half-brother Sinfiotli has been killed by just such a poisoned horn.[49]

In any case, Early Runic **alu** goes back to PGmc **aluþ-*, a neuter consonantal stem, which may be connected with sorcery and ecstasy in a magic-religious context; E. Polomé compares Hittite *alwanza* ('enchant') and *alwanzatar* ('enchantment, magic power' < **alwanza-* 'bewitched, enchanted', '*frappé d'un charme*'), as well as Greek ἀλύω ('I am frantic, outside myself') and ἀλύσσω ('I am excited, ecstatic').[50] On these grounds, W. Betz suggests that *alu* is a cognate of Tocharian *ale* ('flat hand, palm') and that it directly replaces the protective-apotropaic gesture of the man with spread open hands on the Upplandic Krogsta stone KJ 100.[51] Elmer Antonsen, building on Polomé's approach, conjoins the two etymologies of **aluþ*, i.e. 'ale' versus 'magic charm' to mean "[a beverage] which induces the ecstatic state", or straightforwardly "beverage of libation, endowed with special powers through ritual".[52] Similar

---

[47] See *Edda*, ed. KUHN, p. 191; trans. C. LARRINGTON, *The Poetic Edda*, revised edn. (Oxford, 2014), p. 163 with n. 7 (p. 304; my italics; M.S.).

[48] See E. POLOMÉ, "Notes sur le vocabulaire religieux du germanique 1. Runique *alu*", *La Nouvelle Clio* 6 (1954), pp. 40-55, at p. 55.

[49] See *Edda*, ed. KUHN, p. 162; trans. LARRINGTON, *The Poetic Edda*, p. 138.

[50] See SuR, p. 145 and FLOWERS, *Runes and Magic*, p. 170, both with reference to POLOMÉ, "Notes sur le vocabulaire religieux du germanique", pp. 45-50. For a critical review, see ELMEVIK, "De urnordiska runinskrifternas **alu**", p. 23. Cf. also B. MEES, *The English Language before England: An Epigraphic Account* (New York and London, 2023), pp. 188-189.

[51] W. BETZ, "Zum germanischen etymologischen Wörterbuch", in: *Festgabe für L.L. Hammerich* (Copenhagen, 1962), p. 11; cf. also HEIZMANN, "Die Formelwörter der Goldbrakteaten", pp. 542-543, on the notion of "*apotropäische Konnotation*".

[52] See E.C. POLOMÉ, "Beer, runes, and magic", *Journal of Indo-European Studies* 24 (1996), pp. 99-105; E.H. ANTONSEN, *Runes and Germanic Linguistics* (Berlin and New York, 2002: Trends in Linguistics: Studies and Monographs 140), pp. 198-199, cf. HEIZMANN, "Die Formelwörter der Goldbrakteaten", p. 541 with n. 54; cf. also G.R. MURPHY, "*Mid alofatun*: Secular beer, sacred ale", in: *Interdigitations: Essays for Irmengard Rauch*, ed. G.F. CARR, W. HARBERT, and L. ZHANG (New York, 1999), pp. 183-188.

cultural practices are found elsewhere, e.g. the use of peyote in some Native American rituals.

In his socio-cultural approach, Anders Andrén put forward a "political interpretation of the bracteates", claiming that the runic charm words **laþu – alu – laukaʀ** are patterned on the Latin triad *dominus – pius – felix*, which means *Dominus noster, pius N.N.* [the name of the emperor], *felix Augustus*.[53] Andrén argues for a transformation from Latin to Early Nordic and Old Norse, with concomitant changes in the levels of meaning:

> *Dominus* is a general word for a person with power, while *laþu* refers to the act – the invitation – which manifests the power. *Felix* signifies abstractly a desirable quality or condition, while *laukaR* refers to the object – the leek – which promotes felicity. Finally *pius* indicates correct behaviour towards gods and men, and this concept has been translated with *ale*, the medium used to express *pietas*.[54]

Despite the widespread use of this Latin formula on Roman coins and medallions in the 300s and 400s, there are no good grounds on which to assume that the Latin triad was rehearsed by Early Nordic and Old Norse traditions (compare Table 1). Indeed, this assumption seems very far-fetched, and the only inscription which combines the three one-word formulas is IK 149 (see the discussion of tandem and combined formulas). On the whole, this triple equation between Latin and Early Runic does not stand up to close scrutiny and may be said to be superficial at best; see Table 1:

Table 1: Distribution of the formulaic words **alu, laþu,** and **laukaʀ** on gold bracteates.[55]

IK 149	Skåne (I)-B		laþu	laukaʀ	gakaʀ	alu
IK 58	Fyn (I)-C	horaʀ	laþu		aadraaaliuu	alu
IK 42	Darum I-B	frohila	laþu			

---

[53] See A. ANDRÉN, "Guld och makt – en tolkning av de skandinaviska guldbrakteaternas funktion", in: *Samfundsorganisation og regional variation: Norden i romersk jernalder og folkevandringstid*, ed. C. FABECH and J. RINGTVED (Århus, 1991: Jysk Arkaologisk Selskabs Skrifter 27), pp. 245-265, at pp. 250-253; for a critical review, see IMER, *Jernalderens runeindskrifter i Norden* [I], p. 108.

[54] See ANDRÉN, "Guld och makt", p. 256.

[55] This list has been adapted and modified from ANDRÉN, "Guld och makt", Fig. 6, on p. 251; cf. also HEIZMANN, "Bildformel und Formelwort", pp. 149-151.

IK 163	Skonager IV-C	**niuwila**	**la(þ)u**			
IK 83	Højstrup-C		**laþu**			
IK 26	Börringe-C	**tanulu**		**laukaʀ**		**alu̯**
IK 166	Skrydstrup-B			**laukaʀ**		**alu**
IK 8	Års (II)-C			**laukaʀ**		
IK 298	Lynge-Gyde-C			**lakʀ**		
IK 229	Denmark (I)-C			**lakʀ**		
IK 267	Hammenhög-C			**lakʀ**		
IK 301	Maglemose (II)-C			**lakʀ**		
IK 330	Sjælland			**lakʀ**		
IK 43	Darum V-C	**niujil**				**alu**
IK 135	Ølst-C	**hagalu**				
IK 24	Bjørnerud-A					**alu**
IK 44	Djupbrunns I-C					**alu**
IK 74	Heide-B					**alu**
IK 97	Kläggeröd-C					**alu**

The fact that the one-word formulas *alu*, *laþu*, and *laukaR* feature both separately and in various combinations on the bracteates dated to the sixth and seventh centuries and on runestones of the older period provides a key to their functional interpretation in terms of formulaic charm words.[56]

Another one-word formula is Early Runic **ehwaR* (> ON *iór*; m. 'horse, stallion'), which appears on no fewer than fifteen bracteates (cf. Latin *equus* and OInd. *aśvaḥ*). Düwel emphasises that this and other lexemes for 'horse' in Old Germanic pertain to the everyday lexicon rather than the sacred vocabu-

[56] See HEIZMANN, "Die Formelwörter der Goldbrakteaten", pp. 533-544 (on **alu**), 544-550 (on **laþu**), and 550-573 (on **laukaʀ**); cf. also GRØNVIK, "Runebrakteater fra folkevandringstida", pp. 5-22, and IMER, *Jernalderens runeindskrifter i Norden* [I], pp. 99-113.

Fig. 4   The runestone from Elgesem featuring the one-word formula **alu**. Photo: Julius Magnus Petersen, National Museum of Denmark.

lary.[57] As *ehwaR* is the name of the *e*-rune ᛖ, it is eminently possible that **e** represents this one-word formula in a maximally shortened form. However, reading these inscriptions is problematic in many instances, as the majority of the bracteate smiths were not good spellers, to say the least. Among the various attested forms is **eh͡e** (on the Åsum bracteate IK 11) from Early Runic **ehwē*, which presumably means '(dedication) to the horse', dative sg. of the noun **ehwaR* (m. 'horse, stallion'), hence a dedication formula.

This formulaic word occurs both in isolation and in various runic contexts, often in disguised or misspelled forms, e.g. **eh͡wu**) on the Skåne IV C-type bracteate IK 352, unless this represents a vocative or a feminine noun ('mare').[58] The horse plays a central role in Germanic healing rituals and fertility cults, and it forms part of the Odin cult; Adam of Bremen records in his description of the sacrificial feast in Uppsala that horses were sacrificed along with men and dogs.[59] A case in point is the testimony of the runic inscription from Stentoften (in

---

[57] See DÜWEL, *Von Göttern, Helden und Gelehrten*, pp. 31-32.

[58] See SuR, p. 161; J. MCKINNELL and R. SIMEK, *Runes, Magic and Religion: A Sourcebook* (Wien, 2004: *Studia Medievalia Septentrionalia* 10), p. 82; HEIZMANN, "Die Formelwörter der Goldbrakteaten", pp. 582-587. On the possibility of a feminine *wō*-stem Early Runic *ehwū*, see ANTONSEN, *A Concise Grammar*, p. 60.

[59] For standard references, see R. SIMEK, *Dictionary of Northern Mythology*, trans. A. HALL (Woodbridge, 1993), pp. 157-158; on Snorri's famous account of the horse sacrifice, see DÜWEL, *Von Göttern, Helden und Gelehrten*, p. 92, with n. 120.

Fig. 5 Lellinge bracteate with the reduplication formula **salu-salu** and a swastika (picture credit: IK 105).

Santesson's interpretation of 1989).[60] This runic inscription indicates that horses were sacrificed in Blekinge as well. Medieval pictographic stones from Gotland also testify to the central status of the horse in cultic tradition – compare the Roes stone (KJ 102).[61]

Equine iconography is widely represented on C-type bracteates – compare IK 8 Års 2, IK 98 Sjælland II, IK 185 Tjurkö II, and IK 377 Vadstena (see Figs. 1-3 and 7) – and it forms an integral part of several runestones from the older period, e.g. KJ 99 Möjbro, KJ 101 Eggja and KJ 102 Roes. Heizmann notes that the aforementioned one-word formula *laþu* refers to the invocation or "summons of helping spirits in animal form which are intended to support the healing process of Balder's foal" (*"Zitation tiergestaltiger Hilfsgeister, die beim Heilungsprozeß des Balder-Fohlens mitwirken sollen"*).[62] Another possible equine formula is represented by the palindrome **sueus** on the Kylver stone KJ 1 on Gotland, which possibly contains the Old Gutnish word *eus* ('stallion') together with a tree-like symbol (probably representing the world tree) and the complete older *fuþark*.

Runic Formula Type 2: The Reduplication Formula

Reduplication, the repetition of charm words, is a case of the extension of the minimal one-word formula. In several instances, charm words or ritual words are reinforced by iteration, hence the double word formula IK 105 Lel-

---

[60] See SUNDQVIST, "Contributions of the oldest runic inscriptions", pp. 134-136 and M. SCHULTE, "Die Blekinger Runeninschriften als Status- und Machtembleme – Ein kulturhistorischer Syntheseversuch", in: *Archäologie und Runen*, ed. GRIMM and PESCH, pp. 175-194, at pp. 183-189, both of whom refer to L. SANTESSON, "En blekingsk blotinskrift: En nytolkning av inledningsraderna på Stentoften-stenen", *Fornvännen* 84 (1989), pp. 221-229.

[61] See S. LINDQVIST, *Gotlands Bildsteine*, 2 vols. (Stockholm, 1941-1942), 2, p. 51. On the horse and the fertility cult in Germanic, see F. STRÖM, *Diser, Nornor, Valkyrjor: Fruktbarhetskult och Sakralt Kungadöme i Norden* (Stockholm, 1954: *Kungl. Vitterhets Historie- och Antikvitets-Akademiens handlingar: Filol.-filos. serien* 1), pp. 22-31.

[62] See HEIZMANN, "Die Formelwörter der Goldbrakteaten", p. 548; cf. also ID., "Bildformel und Formelwort", pp. 147-149.

Fig. 6   Skodborg B-bractate with the inscription **auja alawin auja alawin auja alawin j** (= ᛃ) **alawid** (picture credit: IK 161).

linge Kohave-B **salu-salu** (see Fig. 5) and IK 377 Vadstena-C **ṭuwa-tuwa**, followed by a complete *fuþark* inscription of twenty-four runic characters: **fuþarkgw : hnijïbʀs : tbemlŋod:**.

Lundeby and Williams identify **tuwa-tuwa** as a protective formula akin to the *līna laukaR* formula.[63]

Another prominent example is the tripled **auja** on the bracteate from Skodborg-B (IK 161; see Fig. 6), which is usually rendered as 'luck, well-being' (G *Glück*).[64] The triple charm word **auja** is probably coupled with a triple vocative, and therefore not a straightforward example of the reduplication formula: "*auja, Alawin! – auja, Alawin! – auja, Alawin!*" ("Hail, Alwin! Hail, Alwin! Hail, Alwin!"). The Early Runic nominative would be *AlawiniR*, possibly an Odinic name.[65] What follows is a **j**-rune which is conveniently interpreted as an ideographic rune ᛃ **jāra* (meaning 'good year', 'good harvest') in a parallel fashion to the Stentoften stone KJ 96, and a cognate personal name *Alawid*, probably again in the vocative.[66] The inscrip-tion is commonly interpreted as an invocation of *auja* ('good fortune') and of *jāra* ('good harvest') for the two men named Alwin and Alwid, or for Alwin alone.[67] As N. Wicker and H. Williams state, "[t]he concept of 'luck' was after all tremendously important in ancient times, and so were the crops".[68]

---

[63]   See LUNDEBY and WILLIAMS, "Om Vadstenabrakteatens **tuwa**", pp. 21-22.

[64]   See AEW, p. 19 and 106, under *auja* and *ey*, respectively.

[65]   See WICKER and WILLIAMS, "Bracteates and runes", pp. 202-203.

[66]   On the **j**-rune, see E. SALBERGER, "An ideographic rune on the Skodborg bracteate", *Acta Philologica Scandinavica* 24 (1961), pp. 18-32. Cf. also P. STILES, "On the interpretation of older runic **swestaʀ** on the Opedal stone", *NOWELE* 3 (1984), pp. 3-48, especially pp. 29-30: he takes **j** as representing the conjunction *ja* 'and', hence the sequence of vocatives, **alawin ja alawid**, '*Alawin* and *Alawid*!'

[67]   See SuR, p. 163; cf. also FLOWERS, *Runes and Magic*, p. 175.

[68]   WICKER and WILLIAMS, "Bracteates and runes", p. 203.

The type of iteration addressed here – viz. morphological doubling, or more precisely iconic (full) reduplication – fulfils several functions in different languages, not least attenuation and / or conversely reinforcement, i.e. intensification with verbs, nouns and other word classes.[69]

An important principle in historical linguistics is the 'uniformitarian principle' stating that the forces and principles at work in older languages are of the same kind and order of magnitude as those which operate in living languages which are far better documented than Early Runic.[70] In this case, it can be assumed that reduplication had the same kinds of functions in Early Runic that it has in modern languages.

Reduplication tends to convey emotional attitudes towards the item in question and reinforces the underlying expression in one way or another: Lat. *quisquis* ('whoever (that may be)'), Mod.G *Eff-Eff* ('something known by heart'; e.g. *etwas aus dem Eff-Eff können*), and Mod.E 'goody-goodies' ('people who are self-righteously or cloyingly good'), 'like-like' ('to have romantic feelings for someone').[71] One major function of reduplication (in this case iconic, full reduplication) is to express the plural, e.g. Warlpiri *kurdu-kurdu* ('children'), *kamina-kamina* ('girls'), with the base-words: *kurdu* 'child' and *kamina* 'girl' respectively.[72] Cross-linguistically, several other functions can be identified rather clearly in different word classes:

1. Continuatives and iteratives
2. Augmentatives
3. Multiplicatives and distributives
4. Diminutives
5. Approximatives.[73]

---

[69] See C. RUBINO, "Reduplication: Form, function and distribution", in: *Studies on Reduplication*, ed. B. HURCH (Berlin and New York, 2005: *Empirical Approaches to Language Typology* 28), pp. 11-30, at p. 19.

[70] On the background of the 'Uniformitarian principle', see W. LABOV, *Sociolinguistic Patterns* (Philadelphia, 1972: *Conduct and Communication* 4), p. 275.

[71] See A. MARANTZ, "Re reduplication", *Linguistic Inquiry* 13.3 (1982), pp. 435-482; C. WILTSHIRE and A. MARANTZ, "Reduplication", in: *Morphologie / Morphology. Ein internationales Handbuch zur Flexion und Wortbildung*, 1, ed. G. BOOIJ et al. (Berlin, 2000: *Handbücher zur Sprach- und Kommunikationswissenschaft*, 17.1), pp. 557-567.

[72] See WILTSHIRE and MARANTZ, "Reduplication", p. 557.

[73] See W. ABRAHAM, "Intensity and diminution triggered by reduplicating morphology: Janus-faced iconicity", in: *Studies on Reduplication*, ed. B. HURCH (Berlin and New York, 2005: *Empirical Approaches to Language Typology* 28), pp. 547-568, at pp. 550-551.

Towards a Typology of Runic Formulas 211

Fig. 7   Vadstena bracteate with the reduplication formula **tuwa-tuwa** followed by the complete rune-row of the older fuþark (picture credit: IK 377,1).

In Construction Morphology, reduplication, or morphological doubling, is identified as a prototypical example of a construction with a holistic property, which means that the resulting form as a whole consisting of *two* identical constituents expresses only *one* modified meaning.[74] Various languages provide instances of noun reduplication (i.e. iconic reduplication) that carry the meaning of intensity and emphasis, or, more precisely, the state of being a 'real' *x* (a 'prototypical', or 'really good' type of *x*), for instance Spanish *café café* ('real(-ly good) coffee'), *lana lana* ('real(-ly good) wool'), English 'salad-salad' ('real(-ly good) salad'), Dutch *vakantie-vakantie* ('a real(-ly good) holiday') and Dutch *leuk-leuk* (emphatic) ('nice-nice; very nice indeed!').[75] Intensification is also evident in Hebrew *gever* ('man'), *gever gever* ('manly man, man among men').[76] The lexical-semantic contribution by means of reduplication can be accommodated in the following schema, based on Construction Grammar:[77]

The reduplication formula
[NOUN$_i$ – NOUN$_i$]$_j$ ↔ [prototypical, excellent interpretation of NOUN$_i$]$_j$

The iterated sequences *salu-salu*, *tuwa-tuwa*, and *auja-auja-auja* lend themselves to an interpretation in terms of ritual charm words with a positive load,

---

[74] See G. Booij, "Construction morphology", in: *The Cambridge Handbook of Morphology*, ed. A. Hippisley and G. Stump (Cambridge, 2016), pp. 424-448, at p. 428.

[75] For further English, Dutch and Spanish examples, see Booij, "Construction morphology", p. 428, with reference to J. Ghomeshi *et al.*, "Contrastive focus reduplication in English (The salad-salad paper)", *Natural Language and Linguistic Theory* 22 (2004), pp. 307-357 and E. Felíu Arquiola, "Las reduplicaciones léxicas nominales en Español actual", *Verba* 38 (2011), pp. 95-126.

[76] I owe this example to Marc Pierce, University of Texas, in an email dated 10 February 2021.

[77] Based on Felíu Arquiola, "Las reduplicaciones léxicas nominales", p. 117.

possibly in the original context of ritual sacrifice. In light of an Odinic interpretation, the blessing emanates from the bracteate god Odin, or an Odinic priest, and takes effect in rituals of healing and regeneration.[78] Thus, comparing Vedic *dúvas* ('worship, ritual gift, oblation'; MW, p. 488c), Grønvik suggested a translation of **ṭuwa-tuwa** as 'sacrifice-sacrifice', or 'offering-offering', which makes sense in regard to the reduplication formula: 'a proper worship', i.e. a well accomplished and well executed sacrifice.[79] As noted above, Lundeby and Williams connect *tuwa* with ON *tó* ('raw wool'), and thus class it as a parallel to the *līna laukaR* formula in that it refers to healing plants and textiles. However, Erik Moltke argues for an apotropaic function which does not preclude Grønvik's aforementioned interpretation from a historical point of view: Moltke suggests that the sequence **salu-salu** (as well as **ṭuwa-tuwa**) is "doubtless to be interpreted as a doubled protective word",[80] hence a functional charm word, which might stem from an original ritualistic context. It is thus possible to argue that these two words, *salu* and *tuwa*, have lost their original meanings, which were established in the context of ritual and sacrifice; cf. OInd. *dúvas* (only nom.pl. 'offering, oblation') in the ritual literature of the *Rig-Veda*. Thus, it seems safe to state that these bracteates tend to carry a formulaic (probably originally divine) utterance in addition to the magic power of their iconography; compare the semantics of the *rūnō raginakundō* formula below.

Runic Formula Type 3: The Twin Formula

The twin formula, also known as the 'pair formula' or, more technically, the 'binomial', is a neat combination of two words, which are conventionally linked by a conjunction (e.g. Mod.E 'bread and butter') or by a preposition (e.g. Mod.E 'rags to riches'), and often coupled with alliteration; the elements of a twin formula can be (near-)synonymous, antonymous or complementary.[81]

---

[78] On *auja*, see HEIZMANN, "Die Formelwörter der Goldbrakteaten", p. 581.

[79] See O. GRØNVIK, "Runeinnskriften på gullhornet fra Gallehus", *Maal og Minne* 1999, pp. 1-18; for critical discussion, see BECK and HAUCK, "Zur philologischen und historischen Auswertung", p. 59.

[80] See E. MOLTKE, *Runes and their Origin: Denmark and Elsewhere*, trans. P.G. FOOTE (Copenhagen, 1985), p. 112.

[81] See BUSSMANN, *Routledge Dictionary*, p. 501a, under 'twin formula'; moreover M.R.V. SOUTHERN, "Formulaic binomials, morphosymbolism, and Behaghel's Law: The grammatical status of expressive iconicity", *American Journal of Germanic Linguistics & Literatures* 12.2 (2000), pp. 251-279. It is noteworthy that Bussmann's definition of the twin formula includes the

Juxtaposition may occur without a conjunction, e.g. Early Runic *līna laukaR* ('flax / linen and leek'). This is the asyndetic subtype of the twin formula where words are joined without the use of a conjunction or preposition.

The asyndetic formula is encountered in the older runic corpus, whereas the syndetic twin formula is common in Old Norse, e.g. (*alt*) *lopt ok lǫgr* ('(all) air and sea'; Skírnismál 6,5, cf. Helgakviða Hundingsbana I, 21,3-4); *geð ok gaman* ('lust and sexual enjoyment / pleasure'; Hávamál 99,5, 161,3, Hárbarðsljóð 18,12); *rǫ́ð (ǫll) ok regin* ('the ruling divine powers'; Hákonarmál 18), or (*hefir þú*) *erindi sem erfiði* ('Is (the result of your) errand / mission (i.e. its success) equal to the trouble?'; Þrymskviða 10,1-2).[82] Among the non-alliterative twin formulas is *ár ok friðr* ('(good) year and peace'); Snorri Sturluson, among others, uses the phrase *blóta til árs ok friðar* ('to sacrifice for peace and prosperity').[83]

Twin formulas are fixed lexical entities which may preserve opaque words, e.g. Mod.G *mit Kind und Kegel* ('with bag and baggage'; literally 'with child and illegitimate children'). A case in point is the aforementioned poetic formula ON *rǫ́ð ok regin* which is usually rendered as 'the ruling Gods or Powers' (cf. G *Räte und Mächte*). As Düwel stresses, the term *ráð*, pl. *rǫ́ð* n. (lit. 'decision, decree; advice, counsel') does not fit into the nomenclature of the Nordic gods: "Whatever the final decision, *ráð* cannot be included in a corpus of Nordic names of gods" ("*Wie immer man sich entscheidet,* ráð *kann nicht in ein Corpus der nordischen Götterbezeichnungen aufgenommen werden*").[84]

All of these twin formulas, whether alliterative or non-alliterative, obey Behaghel's Fourth Law, viz. the law of increasing parts (G *Gesetz der wachsenden Glieder*).[85] Among Behaghel's five laws or general forces of word order rules is the tendency within a phrasal unit (or formula) for shorter terms to come before longer ones; he stipulates "that among (...) phrasal constituents, whenever possible, the shorter precedes, the longer follows" ("*daß von (...) Gliedern, soweit möglich, das kürzere vorausgeht, das längere nachsteht*").[86] Indeed, there is a tendency rather than a law within a phrasal unit – already

---

pairing of identical elements, which I identify as the 'Reduplication formula' in my typology; see above p. **207**.

[82] On the *rǫ́ð ok regin* formula, see DÜWEL, *Von Göttern, Helden und Gelehrten*, pp. 98-101, 106-111.

[83] On the *ár ok friðr* formula, see particularly K. DÜWEL, *Das Opferfest von Lade und die Geschichte vom Völsi: Quellenkritische Untersuchungen zur germanischen Religionsgeschichte* (Habilitation thesis, Göttingen, 1971), pp. 66-69, and *passim*.

[84] DÜWEL, *Von Göttern, Helden und Gelehrten*, p. 100.

[85] See particularly SOUTHERN, "Formulaic binomials", pp. 263-267.

[86] O. BEHAGHEL, *Deutsche Syntax*, IV: *Wortstellung* (Heidelberg, 1932), pp. 4-7, esp. p. 6.

apparent in classical Antiquity – to proceed from shorter to longer constituents, and not vice versa. Southern postulates that "the more fixed [or, as I would add, formulaic] the phrase, the more the effects of Behaghel's Fourth Law (BL) are likely to be observed. (...) Fixed idioms display this particularly well".[87] As Southern argues, the dynamics behind this law is a tendency towards increasing weight, which is certainly valid for the formula:

> Fixed phrases, like other specifically oral modes of expression (such as proverbs and nursery rhymes), tend to be faithful guardians of a language's underlying phrasal architecture; and BL's rightward contour matrix (semantic or syntactical, phonological or prosodic) maps above all the poetics of the comfortably familiar phrase.[88]

As mentioned, word pairs are very often alliterative, hence twin formulas play a major role in metrical texts, in particular in the Germanic long-line, cf. the aforementioned example of the syndetic Old Norse *iǫrð / upphiminn* formula:

iǫrð fannz æva | né upphiminn.[89]

While the one-word formula (as defined above) is restricted to the written runic medium, twin formulas have a much wider diffusion than this; see the following attestations of the *iǫrð / upphiminn* formula in the literary languages of the Northwest Germanic branch.

Table 2: *Diffusion of the* iǫrð / upphiminn *formula in Old Germanic*[90]

eorðan ic bidde / and **upheofon** (Old English charm)
eorðan eallgrene / ond **upheofon** (*Andreas* 798)
eorþan mid hire beorgum / ond **upheofon** torhtne mid his tunglum (*Christ* 967-968)
ero ni uuas / noh **ufhimil** (*Wessobrunner Prayer*)

[87] See SOUTHERN, "Formulaic binomials", p. 263.
[88] See SOUTHERN, *ibid.*
[89] *Vǫlospá* 3,5-6.
[90] The twin formula is identified in bold face. For further detail, see K. DÜWEL, *Runenkunde*, pp. 137-138; L. LÖNNROTH, "*Iǫrð fannz æva né upphiminn*: A formula analysis", in: *Specvlvm Norrœnvm: Norse Studies in Memory of Gabriel Turville-Petre*, ed. U. DRONKE *et al.* (Odense, 1981), pp. 310-327 (reprinted with a postscript in ID., *The Academy of Odin: Selected Papers on Old Norse Literature* (Odense, 2011), pp. 219-241); cf. also SCHULTE, "Memory culture in the Viking Age", pp. 61-65, with further references.

thit uueroldriki, **ertha** */ endi* **upphimil** *(Heliand* 2885-2886)

iǫrð fannz œval né **upphiminn** *(Vǫlospá* 3:5-6)

hvaðan **iǫrð** *um kom / eða* **upphiminn** */ fyrst, inn fróði iǫtunn (Vafþrúðnismál* 20:4-6)

er eigi veit / **iarðar** *hvergi / né* **upphimins**: *áss er stolinn hamri (Þrymskviða* 2:5-7)

iǫrð dúsaði / ok **upphiminn** *(Oddrúnargrátr* 17:5-6)

iǫrð bið ek varða / oc **upphimin** (Ribe rune stick)

iǫrð s[k]al rifna ok **upphiminn** (Skarpåker rune stone; Sö 154)

Awareness of formulaic expressions in the last two centuries has spawned indepth research on twin formulas in Old Germanic, in particular in poetry and legal texts. Among the pioneering works are Moritz Heyne's *Formulae alliterantes* of 1864 and Richard Meyer's *Die altgermanische Poesie nach ihren formelhaften Elementen beschrieben* ('Old Germanic poetry described according to its formulaic elements'). This type of formula plays a key role in Germanic poetry, as it is instrumental in different metrical structures, not least *fornyrðislag* and *ljóðaháttr* in the Eddic lays.[91]

But let us return to the runic formula. In the corpus two asyndetic twin formulas are in evidence: **linalaukaʀ** *līna laukaR* ('linen / flax (and) leek') on the Fløksand bone scraper KJ 37 (cf. the set phrase Mod.G *Lein(en) und Lauch)*[92] and **laþulaukaʀ** *laþu laukaR* ('summons / invitation (and) leek') on the Skåne bracteate IK 149 (see below Fig. 8). Both runic variants display typical features of the twin formula: first, alliteration, and secondly, the law of increasing parts, viz. Behaghel's Fourth Law (see above).

Moreover, it is not ruled out that the runic twin formula in fact is a dvandva compound since the neuter nouns *līna* and *laþu* can be interpreted as proterothemes of the two compounds *līna-laukaR* and *laþu-laukaR*, displaying stemforms. However, this does not invalidate the present analysis.

The fixed status of the twin formula *līna laukaR* is further corroborated by two facts. First, the name of the *l*-rune in the so-called *Hrabanic* rune-rows, which are preserved in the tenth/eleventh-century *Codex Ratisbonensis*, is *līna* and not *laukaR*.[93] This demonstrates that *laukaR* was closely associated in runic

---

[91] For discussion, see M. SCHULTE, "Early Scandinavian legal texts – Evidence of preliterary metrical composition?", NOWELE 62-63 (2011), pp. 1-21, especially pp. 8-10.

[92] See M. OLSEN and H. SCHETELIG, "En indskrift med ældre runer fra Fløksand i Nordhordaland", *Bergens Museums Aarbog* 7 (1909), pp. 18-23.

[93] See KRAUSE, "Untersuchungen zu den Runennamen, I", pp. 62-63 (reprinted in ID.,

traditions with *līna*, and vice versa. Secondly, Old Norse-Old Icelandic tradi-tions clearly indicate the status of a twin formula in this case. The fourth verse of *Vǫlsa þáttr*, preserved in the fourteenth-century *Flateyarbók*, has strong sexual and magical connotations and supports the notion of a fertility formula in the Old Norse context.[94] Despite claims of high age, however, the stanza as such displays word forms that do not seem to be much older than the manuscript, in particular the personal name *Mǫrnir* and the *ija*-formation *blœti* (n. 'offering') derived from the base word *blót* ('idem').[95]

Fig. 8   Skåne I bractate with the twin formula **laþulaukaʀ** and the charm word **alu** (picture credit: IK 149,1).

Aukinn ertu, Vǫlsi,   ok upp tekinn,
líni gœddr,   en laukum studdr.
Þiggi Mǫrnir   þetta blœti!
En þú, bóndi sjálfr,   ber þú at þér Vǫlsa!

You have grown large, Vǫlsi, and stand upright / have been elevated,
enriched with flax / linen, and strengthened by leek.
May Mǫrnir receive this offering!
And you, farmer yourself, carry / take on Vǫlsi!

Schriften zur Runologie und Sprachwissenschaft, pp. 221-222). In line with this approach, cf. HEIZMANN, "Die Formelwörter der Goldbrakteaten", pp. 555-556.

[94] A. HEUSLER and W. RANISCH, *Eddica minora: Dichtungen eddischer Art aus den Fornaldarsǫgur und anderen Prosawerken* (Dortmund, 1903), p. 124 (my translation, M.S.). For elaboration, see SuR, p. 112; STRÖM, *Diser, Nornor, Valkyrjor*, pp. 22-23; HEIZMANN, "Lein(en) und Lauch", pp. 376-380, ID., "Die Formelwörter der Goldbrakteaten', pp. 558-573, DÜWEL, *Runenkunde*, p. 30; MCKINNELL and SIMEK, *Runes, Magic, and Religion*, pp. 98-99.

[95] See I. BECK, *Studien zur Erscheinungsform des heidnischen Opfers nach altnordischen Quellen* (PhD thesis, Munich, 1967), p. 103; G. SOMMER, *Abstrakta in der altisländischen Familiensaga* (PhD thesis, Göttingen, 1964), p. 40, and DÜWEL, *Von Göttern, Helden und Gelehrten*, pp. 23 and 28 with nn. 5-7.

Runic Formula Type 4: Alliterative Non-twin Formulas

Further alliterative formulas remain to be addressed among the asyndetic formulas. As mentioned, asyndetic twin formulas include the Early Runic *līna laukaR* formula which is lacking any connector or conjunction. A large group of asyndetic formulas consists of word pairs of different word classes, e.g. a noun plus an adjective. Consider the following integration of the alliterative formula *rúnar reginkunnar* in the Eddic poem *Hávamál* 80,1-3, which produces a regular *ljóðaháttr* half-stanza with three lifts.[96]

>   *Þat er þá reynt,   at þú at rúnum spyrr,*
>   *inom reginkunnom.*

>   That is now proved, what you asked of the runes,
>   of divine origin.

The *rūnō raginaku(n)dō* formula (meaning 'runes godsent') makes its appearance in the older runic corpus prior to 550/600 AD, viz. on the Noleby stone, and it is rehearsed on the Sparlösa stone from Västergötland (Vg 119) around 800 AD.[97]

>   **runofahiraginakudo**[98]
>   *rūnō fāhi raginakundō*
>   "I paint a rune, one descending from the gods".

>   [...] **rAþ | runaRþaRRakixukutu** [...][99]
>   [...] *rāþ rūnaR þāR raginukundu* [...]
>   "[...] interpret (these) runes, those descending from the gods!"

Edith Marold rightly notes that Noleby displays a perfect Germanic long-line with two lifts connecting the two half-lines via alliteration.[100] At this point, my

---

[96] See *Edda*, ed. KUHN, p. 29; trans. LARRINGTON, *The Poetic Edda*, p. 23. For metrical assessment, see, e.g. NAUMANN, *Metrische Runeninschriften*, p. 45.

[97] For dating, see IK, p. 151, cf. moreover DÜWEL, *Von Göttern, Helden und Gelehrten*, p. 110; IMER, *Jernalderens runeindskrifter i Norden* [II], p. 191.

[98] Noleby stone, KJ 67.

[99] Sparlösa stone, Vg 119.

[100] See MAROLD, "Vers oder nicht Vers?", p. 83 and 101, with reference to H. KLINGENBERG, *Runenschrift – Schriftdenken – Runeninschriften* (Heidelberg, 1973: Germanische Biblio-

earlier negative statement that "the claim of higher metrical organization [in the Noleby inscription – M.S.] seems unwarranted, since the formula is *not* integrated into a larger metrical matrix beyond the half-line" needs to be corrected.[101] It seems therefore vital to state that this pattern with two lifts forms a perfectly regular long-line, which can be scanned as an A1/A1 type according to the metrical scheme established by Eduard Sievers (1893); note that ***L*** (= lift) denotes a fully stressed alliterative lift, in contradistinction to *X*, which is a less prominent (non-alliterative) stressed syllable, and *D* (= dip) is an unstressed syllable.[102] Furthermore, *ragina-* achieves its lift (***L***) by metrical resolution.

rūnō fāhi | *raginakundō*
L-D X-D | ***L*-*D*** *X-D*

In his revision of oral formulaic theory, Paul Acker highlights this type of formula as the 'slot filler' formula, with a range of subgroups.[103] By way of conclusion, it seems safe to say that the alliterative formula, including the twin formula and other alliterative couplets, is the glue of Old Germanic poetry, not least the Germanic long-line and the Eddic *fornyrðislag* and *ljóðaháttr* metre. As mentioned, its range is much wider than that of the runic formula proper.

Runic Formula Type 5: Tandem and Combined Formulas

If a runic formula features two or more elements without being a twin formula in the strict sense, it is a tandem or combined formula. This type of formula allows for a looser connexion between its elements than the twin formula. The tandem and combined formulas, as I define them here, lack metrical coherence and their sequential order is reversible and not fixed, e.g. *laukaR alu* or *alu laukaR* (IK 26 versus IK 166; see below). Most importantly, the diagnostic features of alliteration and Behaghel's Law (viz. irreversible word order),

---

thek: Reihe 3), p. 127; O. GRØNVIK, *Fra Ågedal til Setre: Sentrale runeinnskrifter fra det 6. århundre* (Oslo, 1987), p. 105.

[101] See SCHULTE, "Early Scandinavian legal texts", p. 10, with reference to H.P. NAUMANN, "Zum Stabreim in Runeninschriften", *Jahrbuch für Internationale Germanistik* 42 (2010), pp. 143-166, at p. 150.

[102] See MAROLD, "Vers oder nicht Vers", p. 83, with recourse to E. SIEVERS, *Altgermanische Metrik* (Halle a.d. Saale, 1893).

[103] See P. ACKER, *Revising Oral Theory: Formulaic Composition in Old English and Old Icelandic Verse* (New York and London, 1998), *passim*; cf. also SCHULTE, "Early Scandinavian legal texts", pp. 1-21, for the wide range of twin formulas, in legal texts among others.

which are prerequisites of twin formulas such as *līna laukaR* and *laþu laukaR*, are absent in the type of tandem and combined formulas (see above on the twin formulas).

The combination of different one-word formulas can be interpreted in terms of entrenchment, reinforcing the semantics of each of its single elements (compare the discussion of the reduplication formula).

For instance, when appearing in tandem, the one-word formulas *alu* (a word of blessing and / or protection) and *laukaR* (a typical healing word) reinforce each other's semantics. A case in point is the tandem formula **lauka͡R ǁ alu** on the Skrydstrup bracteate (IK 166), which combines the healing word *laukaR* and the apotropaic charm word *alu*. Extended collocations with the one-word formulas *alu* and *laukaR* are found on the Börringe bracteate IK 26 **tanulu alu laukaR** and on the Skåne bracteate IK 149 **laþulauka͡R.ga͡kaRalu** (see Fig. 8).[104] It is noteworthy that **ga͡kaR** may be interpreted as *gaukaR* (m. 'cuckoo'; ON *gaukr*, Norw. *gauk*), a Germanic symbol of spring, renewal, and fertility.[105] The same collocation of **alu** together with **laþu** occurs on the Fyn I bracteate IK 58, here in combination with an appellative or a man's name **horaR** (cf. Gothic *hōrs*, ON *hórr* m., both meaning 'male adulterer, seducer', but also Latvian *kãrs* ('longing, lustful'), OIr. *carae* ('friend'), Latin *cārus* ('beloved, dear') plus a non-lexical sequence **aaḍraaaliuu̯**.[106]

In several inscribed amulets, the one-word formula is combined with personal names, where different syntactic relationships between these elements are involved. It suffices to mention the following examples: IK 42 Darum-I bracteate-B **frohila laþu** ('Frōhila, invitation / summons!' (or possibly, 'Frōhila, I [viz. the textual amulet] invite / summon [viz. a god for N.N.]!'; IK 43 Darum-V bracteate-C **niujil[a] alu** 'Niujil(a), hail / protection!' (or possibly,

---

[104] See H. BECK, "Zur Götter-Anrufung nach altnordischen Quellen (in Sonderheit der Brakteaten)", in: *Kontinuität und Brüche in der Religionsgeschichte: Festschrift für Anders Hultgård zu seinem 65. Geburtstag am 23.12.2001*, ed. M. STAUSBERG (Berlin and New York, 2001: *Ergänzungs-Bände zum Reallexikon der Germanischen Altertumskunde* 31), pp. 57-75, at p. 64; GRØNVIK, "Runebrakteater fra folkevandringstida", p. 10; cf. also POLOMÉ, "Notes sur le vocabulaire religieux du germanique", pp. 46-48.

[105] Cf. H. BIEDERMANN, *Symbolleksikon*, trans. F.B. LARSEN (Oslo, 1992), pp. 132-133, under *gjøk*.

[106] See in particular WICKER and WILLIAMS, "Bracteates and runes", pp. 198-202, with reference to E.H. ANTONSEN, "The graphemic system of the Germanic *fuþark*", in: *Linguistic Method: Essays in Honor of Herbert Penzl*, ed. I. RAUCH and G.F. CARR (The Hague and New York, 1979: *Janua linguarum: Series maior* 79), pp. 287-297, at p. 295.

Fig. 9 Darum I bracteate featuring the inscription **frohila laþu** (picture credit: IK 42).

'Niujil(a), I [viz. the inscribed amulet] protect [you]'); similarly IK 26 Börringe - bracteate-C **tanulu : al[u] laukaR** ('Tanulu [a woman's name], hail, health / healing!' or possibly, 'Tanulu, I protect [you], health / healing!'). Also compare the aforementioned blessing on the Skodborg bracteate: **auja alawin** [...] ('Hail, Alawin!'; see Fig. 6 above).

The abovementioned fertility and healing formula **lina laukaR** on the Fløksand bone scraper KJ 37 is followed by an **f**-rune ᚠ which may stand for its actual rune-name in the older fuþark, **fehu* ('(movable) property, wealth'); compare the triple **f**-rune ᚠᚠᚠ on the Gummarp stone KJ 95 designating 'property and wealth'. The system of ideographic runes (*Begriffsrunen*), is fairly well attested in the group of transitional inscriptions of the 600s, in particular on the Stentoften stone KJ 96, where ideographic ᛃ in its archaic form stands for Early Runic **jāra* (< PGmc **jēra-*; n. '(good) year', i.e. 'prosperous year, good harvest').[107] Another possible example with a combined formula – here as the expression of a curse – is found on the stone fragment from Kinneve (KJ 52) which bears the following fragmentary inscription: ///**siR alu h**, i.e. the ending of a personal name plus the charm word *alu* plus the *h*-rune which may stand for its rune-name **hagala* (n. 'hail, destruction').

Further combinations of different formulas are in evidence, e.g. one-word formulas and *fuþark* inscriptions, whether complete or incomplete, as in the disguised and shortened formulas.

---

[107] See SCHULTE, "Die Blekinger Inschriften als Status- und Machtembleme", p. 186, with reference to K. DÜWEL, "Begriffsrunen", in: *Reallexikon der Germanischen Altertumskunde* 2, 2nd edn., ed. H. BECK, D. GEUENICH, and H. STEUER (Berlin, 1976), pp. 150-153, at p. 151; cf. also K. DÜWEL, "Zeichenkonzeption im germanischen Altertum", in: *Semiotik / Semiotics*, ed. R. POSNER *et al.* (Berlin, 1997), pp. 803-822, at p. 805.

Runic Formula Type 6: Riddle-like, Disguised and Shortened Formulas

Many Viking-age runic inscriptions consist solely of a variant of the exhortation *ráð rúnar*, or *ráð rétt rúnar*.[108] The imperative of the verb *ráða* occurs almost entirely in the sense of 'read!' or, more specifically, 'interpret, decipher, guess!' (cf. G *er-raten*), as in the climax of *Buslubœn* in *Bósa saga*.[109] For instance, the Gol stave church has the following variant of the *ráð rúnar* formula: **raþ rett runar þesar**, *ráð rétt rúnar þessar* ('Guess / get these runes right!'). The *ráð rúnar* formula, just like the *thistle-mistle* formula, can be shortened to the extreme. This is probably the case with the Hoppestad church (N 408) **rrar**: This sequence may stand for **raþ ret rúnar**, *ráð rétt rúnar*.[110] This perhaps illustrates a form of minimalism, showing that the formula may have been so common in certain circles that it only needed three or four initials in order to be activated.

This modus operandi applies to the bracteate inscriptions as well: a shortened formula with few graphemes may hint at its 'full form' (*Vollform*), e.g. **lakʀ, IkaʀR, lauʀ, luʀ, Iʀ** and even **l** may all stand for **laukaʀ**; see, for example, Denmark I in Fig. 10.[111] Needless to say, this graphic minimalism is supported by the acrophonic principle and the system of the rune-names, e.g. **f** stands for **fehu* and **l** for **laguʀ* or *laukaʀ* (on one occasion, **l** stands for its twin *līna* in the tenth/eleventh-century *Codex Ratisbonensis*); see above on the ideographic runes. In a similar vein, **lþu** on the Skonager-IV C-type bracteate IK 163 may very well represent *laþu*, as Krause assumes.[112] The inscription reads **niuwila lþu**; this is probably a personal name combined with the one-word formula *laþu*, meaning 'invitation / summons', or in a verbal interpretation 'I invite / call upon (a god or helping spirit)'.

---

[108] For discussion, see J. NORDBY, "*Ráð þat*, if you can!", *Futhark* 3 (2012), pp. 81-88; ID., "DR 415 Berlin: Yet another *ráð þat* inscription?", *Futhark* 5 (2014), pp. 189-193, cf. also N. DVERSTORP, *Ráð rúnar: En undersökning av verbet* ráða *och hur det används i runinskrifter* (unpublished thesis, Växjö, 2000).

[109] See SCHULTE, "*Tistel-mistel*-formelen", pp. 98-102.

[110] Cf. T. SPURKLAND, *Norwegian Runes and Runic Inscriptions*, trans. B. VAN DER HOEK (Woodbridge, 2005), p. 180.

[111] See *supra*, n. 3; cf. moreover SuR, p. 175; BECK and HAUCK, "Zur philologischen und historischen Auswertung", p. 60; DÜWEL, *Runenkunde*, p. 53. For methodological criticism, however, see IMER, *Jernalderens runeindskrifter i Norden* [I], pp. 108-109.

[112] See SuR, p. 163.

Fig. 10 Danmark I bracteate displaying the shortened word formula **lkaʀ** for *laukaR* (Picture credit: IK 229).

The question remains as to whether such shortenings are 'botched attempts' to copy the formula in question, or deliberate short forms which disguise the proper formula in order to delude evil spirits, much as is the case with anagrams and palindromes. Readers, not least evil spirits, are captivated by palindromes which – in spite of their brevity – result in a maze of endless loops, e.g. the palindrome **sueus** on the Kylver stone.[113] Therefore, the question can be restated as follows: are we dealing with simple error or with *arcanisation*, i.e. the deliberate covering up of meaning in the context of magic?[114] As a matter of fact, the second possibility may be valid in several cases that could involve a graphological minimalism, since the notion of a *fixed graphic formula* renders "the marking of every distinctive feature unnecessary".[115]

The inversion of letters in written formulas is likewise common, whether they are muddled or rearranged according to certain principles. A case in point is the extremely short and mighty one-word formula *alu* which appears as **aul**, **lua** or even **tua**. This phenomenon is well known from classical Antiquity.[116] To mention just one runic example which depends on the chosen interpretation: Krause argued that in the aforementioned inscription on the three double-bracteates from Kongsvad Å-Å (IK 101), **foslau** contains a minimal *fuþark* inscription (with its first and last rune **f-o**) followed by a disguised rendering of the

---

[113] See L. BLAU, *Das altjüdische Zauberwesen* (Straßburg, 1898), p. 147.
[114] On different techniques of 'arcanisation' with the older *fuþark*, see K. DÜWEL, "Magische Runenzeichen und magische Runeninschriften", in: *Runor och ABC: Elva föreläsningar från ett symposium i Stockholm våren 1995*, ed. S. NYSTRÖM (Stockholm, 1997: *Runica et mediævalia: Opuscula* 4), pp. 13-37, at pp. 34-35; ID., *Runenkunde*, p. 52. For critical comment, see K. LÜTHI, "South Germanic runic inscriptions", in: *Runes and their Secrets: Studies in Runology*, ed. M. STOKLUND *et al.* (Copenhagen, 2006), pp. 169-182, at pp. 177-178.
[115] See NORDBY, "*Råð þat*, if you can!", p. 86.
[116] Cf. A. DIETERICH, "ABC-Denkmäler", *Rheinisches Museum für Philologie*, N.F. 56 (1901), pp. 77-105, at pp. 99-100.

charm word *salu*.[117] Given the validity of this approach, it is noteworthy that this minimal formula **f-o** yields a lexical pair: the initial **f**-rune (**fehu*), which denotes 'livestock, (movable) property', and the final **o**-rune (**ōþalan*), which stands for 'inherited property' (Norw. *odal*), complement each other. This all-encompassing formula parallels the use of the Roman letters *A* and *O*, surely a loan from the Greek *alpha* and *omega*, which likewise symbolises completeness, structure and order.[118] The *fuþark* order **f-o** on the two bracteates – as compared to the order **f-d** on the Kylver stone – is likely to be influenced by the Greek and Roman alphabets.[119]

As outlined in the introduction, *fuþark* inscriptions as such are excluded from this study, but the minimal formula is not. The powerful formula *alpha et omega* finds its direct expression in at least three passages of the *Book of Revelation*, i.e. *The Revelation of St. John the Divine* (my emphasis – M.S.).

*Ego sum **alpha et omega**, principium et finis, dicit Dominus Deus, qui est et qui erat et qui venturus est, omnipotens (Apocalypse* 1:8);

*Factum est: ego sum **alpha et omega**, initium et finis. Ego sitienti dabo de fonte aquae vitae gratis (Apocalypse* 21:6);

*Ego sum **alpha et omega**, primus et novissimus, principium et finis (Apocalypse* 22:13).

If this approach is valid, which I think it is, runic inscriptions such as the Kongsvad bracteate exemplify two major strategies for writing the runic formula: abbreviation and distortion. The condensation of runic formulas via shortening and the reordering of runic sequences together express the potential of the written runic formula. This sets it clearly off from related phenomena, not least the Eddic type of formula and the literary poetic formula as such.[120] However, it is a difficult task for the modern interpreter to distinguish between botched attempts by illiterate carvers and the deliberate use of the techniques outlined above.

---

[117] See KJ, p. 258; moreover K. DÜWEL in IK 1, p. 180; BECK and HAUCK, "Zur philologischen und historischen Auswertung", p. 60.

[118] On the use of the *alpha et omega* formula, see F. DORNSEIFF, *Das Alphabet in Mystik und Magie* (Berlin, 1925), pp. 122-125.

[119] On the assumption of classical impact, see DÜWEL and HEIZMANN, "Das ältere Fuþark", p. 8; HEIZMANN, "Die Formelwörter der Goldbrakteaten", p. 588 with note 286.

[120] See *supra*, n. 4.

By Way of Conclusion

The question arises as to what the achievement of this study is. The present paper aims at a systematic description and typology of the *runic formula*, based on linguistic and metrical criteria. It offers a systematic classification and definition of six types of runic formulas in relation to each other: 1. one-word formulas (charm words); 2. reduplication formulas; 3. twin formulas; 4. alliterative non-twin formulas; 5. tandem and combined formulas; and 6. disguised and shortened formulas.

But what assures the formulaic status of the different formulas thus identified? A straightforward answer is that these formulas consist of similar building blocks, viz. one-word formulas, and that they obey further principles and laws. The criteria of *formulaicity* applied in this typology include frequency, lexical semantics and etymology, the fixedness of serial strings (i.e. Behaghel's Law), metricality and alliteration, and different degrees of condensation of the runic formula. All these criteria taken together shape a straightforward linguistic approach to the formula in the older runic corpus.

One major conclusion that emerges from this analysis is that runic formulas depend on the oral and written medium at the same time. The runic formula is a *hybrid* which obeys the laws of epigraphy and phonology, most importantly Behaghel's Law and the laws of alliteration; compare the overlap between the runic formula and the Eddic formula, e.g. *rūnō raginakundō*. One general problem, however, regards the status of certainty and reliability of runic interpretations. Few interpretations of bracteate inscriptions can be accepted without demur; compare the discussion of the sequence **foslau** on the Kongsvad bracteate IK 101 (see above). However, we depend on this type of runic evidence unless we abandon its significance altogether.

The approach taken in this study sheds new light on the runic formula and its potential, both in terms of magic and in a plain usage-based approach, as outlined in the Introduction. In fact, the distinction between the 'runic sacred lexicon' in the sphere of cult, religion and magic on the one hand and the 'profane lexicon' of everyday life on the other may be said to be artificial at best, as it is made by modern humans.[121] The term *alu* for instance is used both as a profane and a sacred word, and the equine terminology on the whole is not exclusively sacred or ritualistic in spite of the ample archeological evidence of the horse sacrifice in ancient Germanic societies. After all, the notion of ele-

---

[121] See, e.g. MAKAEV, *Language of the Oldest Runic Inscriptions*, pp. 101: "word[s] of the runic sacred lexicon".

vated stylistic features of the 'runic sacred lexicon' (G *Sakralwörter*), put forward by several scholars, has a Romantic touch and is slightly misleading. In ancient times, including the Middle Ages and certainly in the earlier periods, the world of magic belonged to everyday life as did the bracteate amulets. It therefore follows that the formulas discussed here are both sacred and profane.

Revisiting Formula and Mythic Patterns and the Interplay between the *Poetic Edda* and *Vǫlsunga Saga*

SCOTT A. MELLOR

Background to Oral-Formulaic Theory, Oral Voice, and the Icelandic Tradition

As the student of oral-formulaic theory knows, it has been almost one hundred years since Milman Parry began his investigation on formula and orality in the *Iliad* and *Odyssey* that led him to the then-living South Slavic material. He began by looking at noun-epithets,[1] then enjambement[2] and finally oral verse-making and formula.[3] Moving from the very spe-

---

[1] M. PARRY, *L'épithète traditionnelle dans Homère* (Paris, 1928), English trans. in: ID., *The Making of Homeric Verse: The Collected Papers of Milman Parry*, ed. A. PARRY (Oxford, 1971), pp. 1-190; ID., "Studies in the epic technique of oral verse-making: I, Homer and Homeric style", *Harvard Studies in Classical Philology* 41 (1930), pp. 73-147; reprinted in: ID., *The Making of Homeric Verse*, ed. A. PARRY, pp. 266-324.
[2] M. PARRY, "The distinctive character of enjambement in Homeric verse" *Transactions of the American Philological Association* 60 (1929), pp. 200-220, reprinted in: ID., *The Making of Homeric Verse*, ed. A. PARRY, pp. 251-265.
[3] M. PARRY, "Studies on the epic technique of oral verse-making, II: Homeric language as the language of an oral poetry", *Harvard Studies in Classical Philology* 43 (1932), pp. 1-50, reprinted in: ID., *The Making of Homeric Verse*, ed. A. PARRY, pp. 325-364; ID., "The traditional

---

New Light on Formulas in Oral Poetry and Prose, ed. Daniel SÄVBORG and Bernt Ø. THORVALDSEN, *Utrecht Studies in Medieval Literacy*, 57 (Turnhout: Brepols, 2023), pp. 227-258.

BREPOLS 🕮 PUBLISHERS   DOI <10.1484/M.USML-EB.5.133554>

cific noun-epithets to a more general formulaic structure of the traditional heroic song, Parry eventually defined the formula "as a group of words which is regularly employed under the same conditions to express a given essential idea".[4] At the time, suggesting the orality of these two works of classical 'literature' amounted to a stoning offense and arguments ensued over issues of enjambement,[5] poem length and more.[6] Parry was hampered by the perceived value, or lack thereof, of so-called low culture, or oral traditions. Realising also that he had to find an analogous poetic tradition still extent brought him to the South Slavic poets for comparison.[7]

After Parry's untimely death in 1935, his work was continued and expanded by his student Albert B. Lord. Though there were some publications in the interim, the 25-year gap between Parry's work and Lord's seminal text, *The Singer of Tales*[8] can be explained in part by a world war and the technological challenges of recording the South Slavic poets. Imagine in the 1930s and '40s recording the poet's song, which can go on for hours, with an Edison machine that records some 5-10 minutes at a time. Scholars today see Lord's work as the cornerstone to the Oral-Formulaic Theory and, perhaps, a move to some aspects of performance theory, as Lord concentrated on the then-living tradition of the oral poet and his heroic song and combined it with a comparison of the dead, ancient Greek tradition. Unlike many of the nineteenth-century predecessors of folklore collection, Lord gave context to the South Slavic poet, something which remains elusive for us, who study the distant past, and expanded his view of formulaic from simply formula, which he modified only slightly to "a group of words which is regularly employed under the same metrical conditions to express a given essential idea",[9] to include larger chunks of the narrative, the

---

metaphor in Homer (TM)", *Classical Philology* 28 (1933), pp. 30-43, reprinted in: ID., *The Making of Homeric Verse*, ed. A. PARRY, pp. 365-375; ID., "Whole formulaic verse in Greek and Southslavic heroic song", *Transactions of the American Philological Association* 64 (1933), pp. 179-197, reprinted in: ID., *The Making of Homeric Verse*, ed. A. PARRY, pp. 391-403.

[4] PARRY, "Studies in the epic technique of oral verse-mking, I", in: ID, *The Making of Homeric Verse*, p. 272.

[5] See, e.g. D.L. CLAYMAN and T. VAN NORTWICH, "Enjambement in Greek hexameter poetry", *Transactions of the American Philological Association* 107 (1977), pp. 85-92, and H.R. BARNES, "Enjambement and oral comporition", *Transacrions of the American Philological Association* 109 (1979), pp. 1-10.

[6] M. ARSCHMANN, "The concept of the formula as an impediment to our understanding of medieval oral poetry", *Medievalia et Humanistica* 8 (1977), pp. 63-76.

[7] PARRY, "Whole formulaic verse in Geek and Douthslavic heroic song".

[8] A.B. LORD, *The Singer of Tales* (Cambridge MA, 1960).

[9] LORD, *The Singer of Tales*, p. 30.

theme and mythic patterns, which are expanded and clarified in later works.[10] However, those of us who work with now dead oral traditions, using only texts for our small keyhole glimpses into those traditions, are left with only the original analogies to work with, which is, of course, problematic to say the least. The insistence that there was a strong divide between written and oral, found among places in Lord's own book in chapters five, "Song of Songs", and six, "Writing and Oral tradition", as well as in subsequent works, might at first seem to leave us out in the cold, but Lord himself continued to work with the Greek material and traditional heroic song from other cultures as well.[11] Some scholars, like Francis Magoun, working at the same institution as Lord, looked at Parry and Lord's preliminary work and had knowledge of the observations and theory that was to come and were able to look, already before the publication of *The Singer of Tales*, at formula in medieval texts, in Magoun's case *Beowulf*, with limited success.[12] Further, the immediate scholarly reaction to Lord's work in the realm of ancient, written texts can arguably be seen as dividing into two groups: an embracing of the theory and its application to medieval and classical texts and a negative reaction, critical to the foundation of the oral-formulaic theory and its relationship to written texts. Furthermore, some scholars sought to redefine the formula to suit the needs of the various traditions, while others sought to apply it as it was.[13]

In *The Singer of Tales*, Lord looked at the dichotomy between written and oral traditions. For medievalists, there was a dilemma. Though the study of oral narrative had begun with ancient written texts, by the 1960s much of Lord's work centred around the living tradition in South Slavic. To be sure, there is a difference between the study of a living tradition and attempts to look at the written remnant of traditional oral poetry, or prose, in written texts. One issue

---

[10] A.B. LORD, "Beowulf and Odysseus", in: ID., *Epic Singers and Oral Tradition*, pp. 133-139; ID., "The traditional song", in: *Oral Literature and the Formula*, ed. B.A. STOLZ and R.S. SHANNON (Ann Arbor, 1976), pp. 1-15 (followed by a 'Response' by G.F. ELSE (pp. 17-190 and 'Discussion' (pp. 20-29); ID., *The Singer Resumes the Tale* (Ithaca, 1995).

[11] A.B. LORD, "Homer's originality: Oral dictated texts", in: *Epic Singers and Oral Tradition*, ed. LORD, pp. 38-48; ID., *The Singer of Tales*; ID., "Beowulf and Odysseus"; ID., "The influence of a fixed text", in: *To Honor Roman Jakobson: Essays on the Occasion of His Seventieth Birthday, 11 October 1966* (The Hague, 1967), 2, pp. 1199-1206, reprinted in: LORD, *Epic Singers and Oral Tradition*, pp. 170-185; ID., "The traditional song".

[12] F.P. MAGOUN, "The oral-formulaic character of Anglo-Saxon poetry", *Speculum* 42 (1953), pp. 446-467.

[13] D.K. FRY, "Old English formulas and systems", *English Studies* 48.3 (1967), pp. 193-204; J.W. BRIGHT, *Bright's Old English Grammar and Reader*, ed. F.G. CASSIDY and R.N. RINGLER (Chicago, 1971); ARSCHMANN, "The concept of the formula"; J. HARRIS, "Eddic poetry", in: *Old Norse-Icelandic Literature*, ed. C. GLOVER and J. LINDOW (Ithaca, 1985), pp. 68-156.

is that the texts are frozen at that point and not allowed to organically change with the culture that tells it; another is the lack of corpus from which to draw. How many repetitions are needed to declare a line or half line a formula or formulaic? Medievalists also worked through the analogy of the South Slavic living tradition, and that effort brought with it the criticism of the comparison: we were working with written documents to illuminate a dead oral tradition. Though contemporary descriptions of composition found within medieval Icelandic literature can be tantalisingly close to shedding light on the structure, strategies, and methods of poetry in Iceland, they often lead to more questions than answers. One of my favourites is found in *Thorgils Saga ok Hafliða*, the report of the wedding at Reykhólar in 1119, which reads:

> *Hrólfr af Skálmarnesi sagði sögu frá Hröngviði víkingi ok frá Óláfi Liðsmannakonungi, ok haugbroti Þráins berserks, ok Hrómundi Gripssyni, ok margar vísur meðr. En þessari sögu var skemt Sverri konungi; ok kallaði hann slíkar lygi-sögur skemtilegastar. Ok þó kunnu menn at telja ættir sínar til Hrómundar Gripssonar. Þessa sögu hafði sjálfr saman setta. Ingimundr prestr sagði sögu Orms Barreyjarskálds, ok vísur margar; ok flokk góðan við enda sögunnar, er Ingimungr hafði ortan. Ok hafa Því margir fróðir menn þessa sögu fyrir satt.*[14]

> Hrólfr from Skálmarnes told a saga about Hröngvið the Viking and about Óláf, the Liðsmen's king, and about the barrow theft of Þráin the berserk, and about Hrómund Grípsson, with many strophes included. And this saga delighted King Sverr; and he said such lying stories (*lygisögur*) were most enjoyable of all. And nevertheless, many men were able to trace their lineage to Hrómundr Gripsson. This saga he himself had put together. Ingimund the priest told the Saga of Orm the Skáld of Barra, with many verses and, at the end of the saga, a good *flokkr* [a poetic form] which Ingimund had composed. And many wise men believe this saga to be true.

Points of interest in the passage are the inclusion of both prose and poetic forms in the storytelling, which is seen in the texts from the time, and that Hrólfr is both retelling poetry which was composed by someone else as well as composing poetry of his own on the spot. Of lesser interest to this discussion, though nevertheless interesting, is the relationship to truth: they are called lying stories, yet men trace genealogies from them. In this passage, I cannot help but to be reminded of Parry's own observations in 1933:

---

[14] *Sturlunga Saga*, ed. G. VIGFUSSON (Oxford, 1878), pp. 19-20.

Revisiting Formula and Mythic Patterns 231

> In the summer of 1933 I met in Gatsko, in Hertsegovinna, Mitcho Savitch, a man then eighty-two years old. He had never learned to write. He dictated to me a number of poems which told of the uprising against the Turks in 1876, in which he took part, and he also dictated to me the story of his life. It began: 'I was twenty-two years old when I took part in my first battle at Ravno above Gatsko ...' The account goes on in a prose which keeps falling into verse ...[15]

The similarity in the descriptions is salient, especially in the patterns to the storytelling and the oral nature of the narrative. The teller is described as unable to write nevertheless, there is a written culture around the storyteller, comparable to the case of twelfth- and thirteenth-century Iceland.

The strict distinction between oral and written was largely emphasised in early days. Walter Ong tried to bridge the gap with his work *Orality and Literacy*,[16] presenting a provocative discussion of the different mindsets between oral and literate people and cultures. One thing to note in the case of medieval Iceland, however, is that the aforementioned written and oral cultures existed at the same time, again in comparison to the South Slavic tradition of 1933. Ong advocated the position, which Lord had proposed previously, that people organise their thoughts differently in oral and literate cultures, and that one is not compatible with the other. There is an immediacy in oral traditional co-composition. However, Ong also described an oral *residue* found in the ancient texts. We can then extrapolate that the narrative tradition found in medieval Iceland employed several strategies when moving from an oral to a written tradition and composing their traditional narratives in this new medium. Around the same time as Walter Ong, Carol Clover had already suggested that the authors of prose Icelandic sagas had borrowed strategies from classical texts, the Christian tradition of Saints' lives and medieval romances from the continent when writing their stories.[17] But what of the Icelandic traditional narrative style, both prose and poetic, necessarily oral in nature, coming as it did from a pre-literate tradition? How much of the oral tradition could still be found in this now written material, both for the poetic, which always seemed to find stronger argument for oral, and in the prose material, an arguably even more elusive medium for traditional oral material? When all is said and done,

---

[15] PARRY, "Whole formulaic verse in Greek and Southslavic heroic song", in: ID., *The Collected Papers of Milman Parray*, ed. A. PARRY, pp. 389-390.

[16] W.J. ONG, *Orality and Literacy: The Technologizing of the Word* (London and New York, 1982 *New Accents*).

[17] C.J. CLOVER, *The Medieval Saga* (Ithaca, 1982).

the aural nature of the sagas has been commented on by too many scholars to enumerate here.

There were several relevant works on Old Norse, or Old Icelandic, as well as other Old Germanic language material written by a handful of scholars through the 1980s. The early works were dominated by the pursuit of formula within these written poetic texts. As mentioned, Magoun had made his attempt to find the formula and formulaic lines and half lines in *Beowulf*. A more comprehensive study of the oral in Old English poetry would be conducted by Donald Fry a decade later.[18] Another noteworthy inclusion to the discussion was that of Edward Haymes, who worked with the Germanic *Heldenlied*,[19] also looking for formula in Old Germanic poetry. Closer to home was Joseph Harris' contributions "Eddic poetry as oral poetry"[20] and "Eddic poetry"[21] and Lars Lönnroth, who touches on Eddic poetry as oral poetry in his book *Den dubbla scenen: Muntlig diktning från Eddan till ABBA*.[22] Lönnroth also focussed on the audience and audience feedback, or lack thereof, in a written text and the problematics of orality within a written text. The value of using an oral-formulaic method on a written text in the Icelandic context was beginning to be called into question, since it was viewed as being too different from the South Slavic and Ancient Greek material and there was no good modern analogy. I remember attending a conference where a scholar claimed that one could not even prove there was a pre-literate oral tradition – countered by Lönnroth, by the way. Whereas it is strictly speaking true that we cannot prove the existence of a pre-literate oral tradition, one had to wonder if this scholar was suggesting that narrative only came into being with the written text? Gísli Sigurðsson suggested that not to work in the direction of an existing oral tradition was to miss an opportunity, to quote his article "Classification of Eddic heroic poetry":

> Before we go any further, we have to make a decision that cannot be based on any scientific evidence. We have to answer the question whether we should apply

---

[18] FRY, "Old English formulas and systems"; D,K, FRY, "Old English formulaic themes and type-scenes", *Neophilologus* 52 (1968), pp. 48-53.

[19] E.R. HAYMES, "Oral poetry and the Germanic *Heldenlied*", *Rice University Studies* 62 (1979), pp. 47-54.

[20] J. HARRIS, "Eddic poetry as oral poetry: The evidence of parallel passages in the Helgi poems for questions of composition and performance", in: *Edda: A Collection of Essays*, ed. R.J. GLENDENNING et al. (Winnipeg, 1983: *University of Manitoba Icelandic Studies* 4), pp. 210-242.

[21] HARRIS, "Eddic poetry".

[22] L. LÖNNROTH, *Den dubbla scenen: Muntlig diktning från Eddan til ABBA* (Lund, 1978); ID., "*Iorð fannz æva né upphiminn*: A formula analysis", in: *Speculum Noroerum: Norse Studies in Memory of Gabriel Turville-Petre*, ed. U. DRONKE et al.(Odense, 1981), pp. 310-327.

Lord's model to Eddic poetry. If we say "no", we have to argue for very special circumstances in Iceland and Scandinavia which can hardly be parallelled elsewhere and ignore all the advances made in the field of oral research in the last decades. If we say "yes", we can profit from all the research which we would otherwise have to ignore.[23]

By the mid 1990s, scholars were looking beyond strictly finding formulae. In 1958, Robert Kellogg wrote *A Concordance to Eddic Poetry* with an eye to using this database to look at the Eddic poetry and oral formula; by 1991 an article of his focussed on evaluating the oral vs. literate strategies found in the manuscript. In his article "Literacy and orality in the Poetic Edda",[24] Kellogg synthesises Lord and Ong to suggest there are different *voices* found in the prose text and discussed the compiler's relationship to the text. Kellogg writes:

> the Compiler does occasionally reveal, like Snorri, a consciousness of the discontinuity between the worlds of the ancient story and the present more rational, scholarly, literary time. He does this primarily by referring to "heathen times" or "antiquity" (the word *forneskja* in Icelandic) and to "old stories" (*fornar sögur*).[25]

Identifying different *voices* within a text is still an intriguing idea, especially as he suggests a relationship between the old and new media, as well as the discourse of prose and poetry and whether the written text falls back, at least in part, on a traditional, oral system, and, furthermore, that the compiler may be aware of this. My own contribution, written at the end of the 1990s, took this position of oral *voice* and oral system as a point of departure and was an attempt to rethink the language of the bard, looking not just for oral formula but also attempting to look at the syntax of poetry through regularly used syntactic and semantic strings in place of formula and themes,[26] influenced by a short comment made in an Old English reader by Fredric Cassidy and Richard Ringler,[27] to which I will return below. At roughly the same time as my work, Paul

---

[23] G. SIGURDSSON, "On the classification of Eddic heroic poetry in view of the oral theory", in: *Poetry in the Scandinavian Middle Ages: Atti del 12° Congresso internazionale di studi sull'alto medioevo – The Seventh International Saga Conference, Spoleto, 4-10 September 1988* (Spoleto, 1990), pp. 245-255, at p. 246.

[24] Robert KELLOGG, "Literacy and orality in the poetic Edda", in: *Vox intexta*, ed. A.N. DOANE and C.B. PASTERNACK (Madison, 1991), pp. 89-101.

[25] KELLOGG, "Literacy and orality in the poetic Edda", p. 93.

[26] S.A. MELLOR, *Analyzing Ten Poems from* The Poetic Edda (New York, 2008).

[27] *Bright's Old English Grammar and Reader*, ed. CASSIDY and RINGLER , p. 270; P. ACKER, *Revising Oral Theory: Formulaic Composition in Old English and Old Icelandic Verse* (New York, 1998).

Acker was writing his work on both Old English and Old Icelandic verse,[28] which evaluated and also went further than strict formula. Since my dissertation was finished and deposited in early March of 1999, and his had come out only a few months earlier, I was unaware of it and it remains a glaring omission in my own book, made all the more salient since it took nine years from deposit to publication, though we come to things from slightly different angles, as he coins the term *syndetic formulas* but still looks at systems in the poetics. Reconciling these two analyses would seem to be a relatively easy thing to do and a worthy endeavour which I will begin to do below.

In this context, I would be remiss if I did not mention John Miles Foley who made significant contributions to oral-formulaic theory from the 1980s until his death in 2012, especially in his work comparing the Old English tradition with Serbian poetry[29] and in his work moving towards an oral *voice* within medieval text.[30] By 2004, with the publication of his book *Writing the Oral Tradition*, Mark C. Amodio tried to take on this notion of oral vs. written in a transitional literate culture, looking more at the culture rather than just at the text. His work looked predominately at medieval Old English tradition, and I believe that there are parallels with Old Icelandic, both having strong vernacular traditions in writing that drew upon traditional narrative culture with tremendous interplay between the oral, aural, and written. Amodio writes:

> Medieval textual communities were not (...) composed of only those with enough literate skills to be able to encode and decode written texts but include a wide range of people, from the illiterate to the fully literate. What was required for a textual community "was simply a text, an interpreter, and a public. The text did not have to be written; oral record, memory, and repeated performance sufficed. Nor did the public have to be fully lettered. Often, in fact, only the *interpres* had a direct contact with literate culture, and, like the twelfth-century heretic Peter Waldo, memorised and communicated his gospel by word of mouth". Through their situation in these textual communities, non-literates were exposed to the text underlying the oral (readerly) performance they attended as well as to the world of textual culture and to its modes of constituting and authenticating meaning.[31]

---

[28] ACKER, *Revising Oral Theory*.

[29] J.M. FOLEY, "Literary art and oral tradition in Old English and Serbian poetry", *Anglo-Saxon England* 12 (1983), pp. 183-214.

[30] J.M. FOLEY, "Orality, textuality, and interpretation", in: *Vox Intexta*, ed. DOANE and PASTERNACK, pp. 34-45.

[31] M.C. AMODIO, *Writing the Oral Tradition: Oral Poetics and Literate Culture in Medieval*

Amodio engages Brian Stock in his thoughts on the same topic from two decades earlier regarding societies that had an oral base and were now working within a written tradition.[32] After all, as Amodio writes, "[w]hether the oral poet is one who (re)composes in performance, recites verbatim from memory, or reads aloud from a written text, the poem, and the tradition body forth upon his voice".[33] I still maintain that this is a reasonable place of departure for looking at the Old Icelandic material, especially the poetic material, but perhaps also valuable for the analysis of prose saga narratives in terms of narrative strategies. One conclusion that can be drawn from the oeuvre of oral-formulaic scholarship in the medieval Germanic traditions is that the emphasis of oral-formulaic theory has, until recently, predominantly been on the poetic tradition, since it has an arguably more marked language system, but there was a prose oral tradition as well, and there may well be interplay between poetic and prose narrative strategies when the traditional, oral narratives were initially written down. The question remains, however: can the multiple narrative strategies of the written texts be untangled so as to identify when traditional, oral strategies are being employed in either the poetics or prose or both?

This background on oral-formulaic scholarship leads us to the conference at Tartu in the winter of 2019 entitled "The formula in oral poetry and prose: New approaches, models and interpretations", where a paper was delivered on which this article is based, and where scholars interested in various aspects of oral-formulaic theory gathered to consider the question of new approaches, models, and interpretations, including the formulaic system(s) found in poetics and prose and their relationship to traditional, oral, heroic narrative. Though the emphasis has often been on the formula in traditional, oral poetry, indeed this conference demonstrated some interesting developments on ongoing formula study for poetry and prose. It was claimed by Albert B. Lord through his direct investigations of the Serbo-Croatian material that poetic narrative is said to be traditional when it consists of three elements key to the oral-formulaic theory: 'formula', as mentioned above, but also the 'theme' and 'narrative patterns'. Since this article must be limited due to restrictions of space, I will briefly touch upon progress and considerations on the issue of formula in Eddic scholarship and then focus on some considerations of 'narrative patterns', and the

---

England (Notre Dame, 2004), p. 20, referring to B. STOCK, *Listening for the Text: On the Uses of the Past* (Philadelphia, 1990), p. 37.

[32] STOCK, *Listening for the Text*, p. 37.
[33] AMODIO, *Writing the Oral Tradition*, p. 22.

interplay of both in the heroic poetry of the Edda and the *Vǫlsunga Saga*, and on how mythic pattens may well find themselves more lasting in narratives that transition from oral to written media, a topic as yet underdeveloped in scholarship. I must regrettably leave more of that topic for a later time.

Formula and the Formulaic System in the Poetic Edda

One of the questions begged by the discussion of orality and Old Icelandic poetry is whether Eddic material in any way represents an earlier oral tradition. Though there are some commonalities with what Lord observed, the scholarship to date seems to indicate that formulaic systems are culture and poetic system specific. Much of the extant Eddic poetry is found in the manuscript *Codex Regius 2365 4°* from c. 1270, which, because of scribal errors, is believed to be a copy from an earlier manuscript[34] or a compilation of earlier written works,[35] possibly from the end of the twelfth century.[36] Generally, the earliest antecedents of the didactic, religious, and narrative poems found in *Codex Regius 2365 4°* are considered to have been oral, since they concern or take place in pre-literate Scandinavia. These poems may well represent the writing down of an earlier, now lost oral tradition. Since the 1970s, this issue was debated by scholars like Andreas Heusler, Edward R. Haymes, Hans Kuhn, Robert Kellogg, Anatoly Liberman, and Lars Lönnroth among others. Medieval Icelanders employed the strategies of an oral system, at least in part, when writing down their traditional poetry at the dawn of writing in Iceland; I am not including runic writing here. As discussed above, several scholars have looked at fixed and near-fixed formula in the poetic systems found in old English, Old Norse / Icelandic, and some of the other Old Germanic languages. Robert Kellogg in his doctoral dissertation in 1958 created a concordance of the *Poetic Edda* with the context of each word.[37] This was useful, but by no means a complete analysis. He did, however, offer some commentary as to the formulaic nature of Old Norse alliterative poetry in his book *The Nature of Narrative*, co-authored with Robert Scholes, in which he states his belief that Eddic poetry is analogous to South Slavic poetry, but in his own work he does not go much

---

[34] P. Hallberg, *The Icelandic Saga*, trans. P. Schach (Lincoln, 1962).
[35] G. Lindblad, "Studier i Codex Regius av äldra Eddan" (Lund, 1954); id., "Poetiska Eddans fornhistoria och skrivskicket i Codex Regius", *Arkiv för Nordisk Filologi* 95 (1980), pp. 142-167.
[36] J. de Vries, *Altnordische Literaturgeschichte* (Berlin, 1967), p. 479.
[37] R. Kellogg, *A Concordance of Eddic Poetry* (PhD thesis, Harvard, 1958).

further than that.[38] Lars Lönnroth admits that the analysis made by Kellogg was useful in describing the language of the Edda, but maintains that the manner in which the Eddic poems were composed is not analogous.[39] Lönnroth and others doubt that the poems were improvised, drawing an analogy with skaldic poetry. Joseph Harris[40] and Gísli Sigurðsson[41] believe that the poetry, though not necessarily totally analogous to South Slavic, nevertheless derives ultimately from an oral tradition and it is at least useful to apply Lord's theory. My own supposition[42] is that Eddic poetry is not similar to continental or Roman poetic forms, so what else would medieval Icelanders have fallen back on when writing their traditional stories down but their own oral poetic system? And though there are differences among the Germanic poetic systems, not the least of which is the Icelandic stanzaic structure versus Old English stichic, the similarities point to a divergent oral tradition. The development of the various poetic systems is well beyond the purview of this work, but will be a worthy study for the future, and it is possible that a thorough application of oral theory might be a good beginning. Though marked, poetic language is a language; therefore, it might be advantageous to analyse the structure as language.

In 1998, Paul Acker published his book *Revising Oral Theory*, where he looked at the formula in linguistic, syntactic terms, and not just as strictly speaking formula, but as formulaic systems.[43] He coined the word 'syndetic' formula, borrowing the term from rhetorical analyses, where he recognised the simultaneous fixed and unfixed, or flexible, nature of some formula, both in Old English and Old Icelandic. If *duguþe ond geogoþe* can be seen as a fixed formula, occurring twice in the poem *Beowulf*, then *duguþe ond iogoþe* can be seen as part of the same syndetic formula, and why not *hord ond rice*, or even *lif of lice*, all of which have the same syntactic structure.[44] In my work,[45] I also discussed the syntactic structure of the formulaic system in Icelandic poetry to

---

[38] R. KELLOGG and R. SCHOLES, *The Nature of Narrative* (Oxford, 1966).
[39] LÖNNROTH, "*Iorð fannz æva né upphiminn*".
[40] HARRIS, "Eddic poetry as oral poetry"; ID., "Eddic poetry".
[41] G. SIGURÐSSON, "Ástir og útsaumur: Umhverfi og kvenleg einkenni hetjukvæda Eddu", *Skírnir* 160 (1986), pp. 126-152; ID., "Eddukvæði", in: *Íslensk Þjódmenning VI*, ed. F.F. JÓHANSSON (Reykjavík, 1989), pp. 293-314; ID., "On the classification of Eddic heroic poetry"; ID., "Another audience – another saga: How can we best explain different accounts in *Vatndæla saga* and *Finnboga saga ramma* of the same events?", in: *Text und Zeittiefe*, ed. H.L.C. TRISTRAM (Tübingen, 1993), pp. 359-375.
[42] MELLOR, *Analyzing Ten Poems from* The Poetic Edda.
[43] ACKER, *Revising Oral Theory*.
[44] ACKER, *Revising Oral Theory*, p. 14.
[45] MELLOR, *Analyzing Ten Poems from* The Poetic Edda.

derive a way to ascertain what might be part of an earlier oral poetic language from a linguistic perspective. Poetry is a marked language, a language with its own syntactic and semantic structures. Syntactic structures may be discernable that point to the previous, traditional oral strategies of composition on which these written poems are based. Like Acker, I sought to show that Eddic poetry was formulaic through its structures and as flexible as any language needs to be to convey an array of ideas, but through the marked language of poetics. Though not included in his analysis, Acker would certainly call the line *Oc hann þat orða allz fyrst um qvað*, found three times in *Þrymsqviða*, a syndetic formula, and *oc hon þat orða allz fyrst um qvað*, found in the poems *Brot af Sigurðarqviðo* and *Oddrúnargrátr* as part of that same syndetic formula. In my analysis, the half-lines *Oc hann þat orða* and *oc hon þat orða* can be seen as part of the same *string*, defined as "groups of grammatical units, or structures, regularly employed to fill a metrical line",[46] and include the half line "*er hann fimm sono*" also found in *Brot af Sigurðarqviðo* which has a similar syntax and is found in the first half line of a full line. These *strings* can be used together with formula as Lord defines them to aid our understanding of the strategies the poet employs to construct the poem.

In his analysis of the poem *Alvísmál*, Acker looked at the flexible patterning found in the poem.[47] In the lines below, the poet needs to alliterate between the two half-lines. Acker shows the ingenuity of the poet by demonstrating two strategies to accomplish the same goal while varying the lines. When employing the word *goðom* [gods], the poet alliterates the items, what Acker calls the concept-word or *heiti*, with each other. However, in order to vary the poem, the poet sometimes employs a synonym, *ásom* [Æsir], in which cases the *heiti* alliterate with it. I have rearranged Acker's examples here:

Alv12: *Himinn heitir með mǫnnom enn hlýrnir með goðom,*
It is called heaven among men, but heaven among the gods

Alv14: *Máni heitir með mǫnnom enn mylinn með goðom,*
It is called fire among men, but moon among the gods

Alv16: *Sól heitir með mǫnnom enn sunna með goðom,*
It is called ale among men, but sun among the gods

---

[46] MELLOR, *Analyzing Ten Poems from* The Poetic Edda, p. 69.
[47] ACKER, *Revising Oral Theory*, pp. 64-66.

Alv10: *Iorð heitir með mǫnnom enn með ásom fold,*
Earth it is called among men, but among Æsir earth

Alv26: *Eldr heitir með mǫnnom enn með ásom funi,*
Fire it is called among men, but among Æsir flame

Alv34 *Ǫl heitir með mǫnnom enn með ásom biórr,*
Ale it is called among men, but among Æsir beer

Acker writes,

> [t]he first whole line in each of Alvíss's answer-stanzas, then, is constructed with strict economy, further, the second half-line in these stanzas gives evidence that at least one formulaic poet consciously employed two slot-filler systems related to each other by inversion.[48]

He concludes that here we have an opportunity to see the strategies of the poet including the degree of variation in constructing the poem. We also have an opportunity to see the skill the poet has in the poetic language.

For my own analysis of the Poetic Edda, I drew upon ten of the poems.[49] There are no instances of a similar strategy being employed in these ten poems; however, the string *enn* + prepositional phrase without *heiti* is employed often and is largely found in the first half line. There is only one instance with *með* found in my data sample but several with other prepositions:

Helgaqviða Hundinsbana I:

> 17 *enn með baugbrota biór at drecca.*
> But with ring-breakers to drink beer

Vǫlundarqviða:

> 25 *Enn ór augomiarcnasteina*
> But from their eyes gems

> 35 *enn ór augom iarcnasteina*
> But from their eyes gems

---

[48] ACKER, *Revising Oral Theory*, p. 65.
[49] MELLOR, *Analyzing Ten Poems from* The Poetic Edda.

25 *enn ór tönnom tveggia þeir*
    But from the teeth of the two

36 *Enn ór tönnum tveggia þeira*
    But from the teeth of the two

Oddrúnargrátr:

28 *enn í ormgarð annan lögðo.*
    but in the serpent's home another they put.

Helgaqviða Hundinsbana I:

43 *enn í annat sinn Imðar dóttir,*
    But another time Inth's daughter,

Þrymsqviða:

16 *enn á briósti breiða steina,*
    and on (his) breast board gems

19 *enn á briósti breiða steina,*
    and on (his) breast board gems,

Vǫlundarqviða:

11 *enn á fótom fiotur um spenntan.*
    but on (his) feet fetters bound.

Helgaqviða Hundinsbana I:

15 *enn af þeim liómom leiptrir qvómo;*
    but from them light the flashes came;

15 *Enn af geirom geislar stóðo.*
    But from (the) spears the sparks stood.

17 *Enn af hesti Högna dóttir*
    But from (her) horse Hǫgni's daughter

Helgaqviða Hundinsbana II:

> 27 *enn at Hlébiorgom Hrollaugs synir;*
> but at Hlébiorg Hrollaug's sons;

> 27 *Enn at Styrkleifom Starcaðr konungr,*
> But at Styrkleifar Starcaðr king,

Guðrúnarhvǫt

> 15 Enn um Svanhildi sáto þýiar,
> But around Svanhildr maidens sat,

Helgaqviða Hundinsbana II:

> 51 *dauðir dólgar, mær, enn um daga liósa'.*
> ghosts of the dead, maid, but when day's light'.

*Oddrúnargrát*r:

> 12 *Man ec, hvat þú mæltir enn um aptan,*
> I remember, what you said, but in the evening,

Note that there are only two that occur in the second half-line. Both instances when the *enn* + prep. phrase is found in the second half line, have other unusual syntactic qualities, including a final verb in one case and a syntactically complicated first half-line in the second. Acker's example includes a noun, *heiti*, and one might conclude that, whereas *enn* + prep. is employed by the traditional poet in the first half-line, the inclusion of a *heiti* moves that half-line to the second half line, similar to the inclusion of a verb final, which in Acker's examples are not expressed but implied, e.g. *enn hlýrnir með goðom* heitir ('but heaven among the gods *it is called*'). If other instances are found, it would be interesting to note whether this hypothesis holds.

Another example of how the syntax and *strings* can help analyse the strategies of the traditional poet can be found by analysing the poem *Grípisspá*, which I evaluated in my monograph.[50] Several scholars have suggested that this is a young poem, perhaps composed by the compiler at the time the poems were written down. One of the most interesting series of repetitions in *Codex Regius 2365 4°* is found in section G. The *segðu* ('tell me') series is the largest single group of variable repetitions.

---

[50] MELLOR, *Analyzing Ten Poems from* The Poetic Edda.

Group 1

HH2:1	*Segðu Hæmingi, at Helgi man,*
Vm:11, 13, 15, 17	*Segðu mér, Gagnráðr, allz þú á gólfi vill*
Fm:12	*Segðu mér, Fáfnir, allz þic fróðan qveða*
Alv: 9, 11, 13, 15, 17, 19, 21, 23, 25, 27, 29, 31, 33	*Segðu mér þat, Alvíss – öll of röc fíra*
Fm:14	*Segðu mér þat, Fáfnir, allz þic fróðan qveða*
Rm:19	*Segðu mér þat, Hnicarr, allz þú hvárttveggia veizt,*
Skm:40	*Segðu mér þat Scírnir, áðr þú verpir söðli af mar*
Rm:3	*Segðu þat, Andvari, ef þú eiga vill*
Ls:1	*Segðu þat, Eldir, svá at þú einugi*
Skm:3	*Segðu þat, Freyr, fólcvaldi goða,*
Skm:11	*Segðu þat, hirðir, er þú á haugi sitr*

Group 2

Vm:20, 22	*Segðu þat iþ eina / annat, ef þitt œði dugir*
Vm:24	*Segðu þat iþ þriðia, allz þic svinnan qveða*
Vm:26, 28	*Segðu þat iþ fiórða / fimta, allz þic fróðan qveða*
Vm:30, 32	*Segðu þat iþ sétta / siaunda, allz þic svinnan qveða*
Vm:34	*Segðu þat iþ átta, allz þic fróðan qveða*
Vm:36	*Segðu þat iþ níunda, allz þic svinnan qveða*
Vm:38	*Segðu þat iþ tíunda, allz þú tíva röc*

Vm:40	*Segðu þat iþ ellipta, hvar ýtar túnom í*
Vm:42	*Segðu þat iþ tólfta, hví þú tíva röc*
HH:34	*Segðu þat í aptan, er svínom gefr*
Hrbl:8	*segðu til nafns þíns, ef þú vill*
Þrk:10	*segðu á lopti löng tíðindi!*
HHv:27	*segðu gørr grami*

Group 3

Grp:6	*Segðu mér, ef þú veizt, móðurbróðir:*
Grp:8	*Segðu, gegn konungr, gerr, enn ec spyria*
Grp:10	*Segðu, ítr konungr, ættingi, mér,*
Grp:30	*segðu, Grípis, þat, ef þú siá þicciz;*

Group 4

Grp:38	*atalt með öllo enn segðu Grípir!'*
Grp:42	*mærr, með mönnom mér segðu, Grípir! –,*
Grp:44	*mægð með mönnom mér segðu, Grípir!*
Grp:48	*oc á siálfa sic? segðu, Grípir, þat!'*
Grp:50	*eggiar rioða? enn segðu, Grípir!'*

The *segðu* phrases occur in several poems and they occur as half-line repetitions in the first half-line in all poems but one, to which I will return. It is a variable repetition, though there are poems that employ it as a fixed verbatim repetition together with its alliterating second half line, for example "*Segðu mér, Gagnráðr, allz þú á gólfi vill*" ("Tell me, Gagnráðr, if you on the floor will"), from *Vafþrúðnismál* found four times and alliterating *Gagnráðr* with *gólfi*, and "*Segðu mér þat, Alvíss – öll of röc fíra*" ("Tell me it, Alvíss – (who know) all wisdom of men") used in *Alvíssmál* thirteen times and alliterating *Alvíss* with *öll*. Several instances of a variable repetition found in *Vafþrúðnismál* give us insight as to the use of the formula and how that usage can deviate from the norm. There are seven full line examples where the variable is the number and the alliterating word. We could write the *string*: "*Segðu þat iþ* n, *allz þic a qveða*" ("Tell it the *n*, if you *a* are called") where *n* is the number and *a* is the alliterated word. Both *fiórða* ('fourth') and *fimta* ('fifth') alliterate with *fróðan* ('wise') and *sétta* ('sixth') and *siaunda* ('seventh') alliterate with *svinnan* ('wise'). Comparable to Acker's *heiti* sequence involving *með goðom* ('with the gods') where the *heiti* alliterates, these examples alliterate with the number word. These four examples represent the most regular variations of this formula. The examples of *þriðia* ('third') and *níunda* ('ninth') do not alliterate the ordinal number with the second half line. These two examples alliterate *svinnan* in the second half line with *segðu* to employ the already used *allz þic svinnan qveða* for continuity of phrase. As the examples are expanded to include the *eina* ('first') *annat* ('second'), *tíunda* ('tenth'), *ellipta* ('eleven'), and *tólfta* ('twelve') a similar process continues. For first and second, "*Segðu þat iþ eina / annat, ef þitt œði dugir*" ("Tell it the *first / second*, if your wisdom suffices"), both ordinal numbers alliterate with *œði* ('wisdom'), and for "*Segðu þat iþ ellipta, hvar ýtar túnom í*" ("Tell it the eleventh, where men in dwelling"), it is again the ordinal number that alliterates this time with with *ýtar* ('men'). Ten and twelve, "*Segðu þat iþ* n*, allz / hvi þú tíva röc*" ("Tell it the *n*, if / why you (know) wisdom of the gods"), also alliterate the ordinal number, this time with *tíva*. Only eighth, "*Segðu þat iþ átta, allz þic fróðan qveða*" ("Tell it the eight, if you wise are called"), does not follow this schema. Either the poet is alliterating *átta* ('eighth') with *allz* ('if'), or *þat* ('it') with *þic* ('you'), neither of which seems likely, or the poet is abandoning alliteration altogether in favour of the established formulaic phrases, which strikes me as a more oral / aural strategy than a visual one. Though it must be acknowledged that some of these lines are abbreviated in the manuscript and might result from the scribe, I doubt these observations are solely a result of scribal economy and more likely represent a traditional use of formula. Furthermore, this analysis is corroborated by Acker's observations and gives insight into the poetic system.

  Consistently, *Segðu* ('tell') is the stable part of the repetition. The unmarked *string* is "*Segðu mér þat*" ("Tell me it"), but there is naturally variation as we saw above. Many times, the pattern concludes with a vocative, shown in the first grouping, which is most often the alliterating element in the half-line – again, comparable to Acker's *heiti* sequence. In the second grouping above, rather than a vocative, there is more information included, e.g. "*Segðu þat iþ þriðia*" ("tell it a third one") (Vm:24) or "*segðu á lopti*" ("tell in the air") (Þrk:10). In these cases, the alliteration is most often with the new information. Note that *segðu gørr grami* is a short line in *ljóðaháttr* and so there is only internal alliteration. In *Grípisspá*, however, a variant pattern emerges. The poet of *Grípisspá* does not conform to the usual *string*, though in the first four iterations the phrase does appear in the first half line, as is seen in group 3. However, the alliteration pattern, and even the *string*, is not what is found in other poems. In "*Segðu mér, ef þú veizt*, móðurbróðir" ("tell me, if you know motherbrother") the poet does not alliterate with *veizt* ('know') as might be expected, but rather with *mér* ('me'). In "*Segðu, ítr konungr, ættingi, mér*" ("Tell, excellent king, kinsman, me"), the poet changes the 'string' by putting *mér* ('me') at the end of the second half line. And in "*segðu, Grípis, þat, ef þú siá þicciz*" ("Tell, Gripir, it, if you see can") the poet departs again from the pattern by not alliterating with *Grípis*, but with *segðu* ('tell') and changing the *string* by placing *þat* at the end of the half line. The final five occurrences are not found in the first half-line at all but are in the second, a variation that only occurs in *Grípisspá*. Though the usage is arguably formulaic, this poet varies the formula in a way that is much more in line with a more visual, perhaps literary, strategy for composition rather than what has been proposed as a traditional oral *string*. It is further evidence for what several scholars have said, that the poem *Grípisspá* is younger, perhaps composed at the time of compilation and that the poet is not working within the oral tradition but in an emerging written one.

Acker claimed some twenty years ago, that "... we may observe that for Eddic poetry, oral-formulaic theory has made a fitful progress"; yet this line of analysis may have stalled in recent years. This line of inquiry has not exhausted itself and there is still more to glean from the Eddic poems regarding their relationship to a previous oral tradition.

Mythic Patterns in Heroic Eddic Poetry and the Interplay with Vǫlsunga Saga

In the 1970s and 1980s, students at Harvard University, who took Albert B. Lord's Humanities 9 course, were sometimes asked to find mythic patterns in contemporary literature and film. That similar narrative patterns, for example *absence – devastation – return*, can be found in narratives from the South Slavic epic of *Marko Kralavić* and in the three thousand year old Greek poem *The*

Iliad, as well as in Tolkien's *The Lord of the Rings* trilogy, James Bond novels, or even films like *Star Wars: New Hope*, indicates that these patterns may represent a fairly stable narrative structure that, to some extent, transcends poetry and poetic systems, cultures, time, mode, and media, and offers insights into narrative strategies that singers, compilers and authors employ even when changing media, like from oral to written.

In 1978, Albert B. Lord wrote an article, "Interlocking mythic patterns in *Beowulf*", in which he identifies narrative patterns found in traditional storytelling. In this article, he finds "... two narrative patterns that are found fairly widely disseminated in epic or story tradition".[51] Lord compares these two narrative patterns in *Beowulf*, the *Odyssey,* and *Gilgamesh*, demonstrating that they are found in multiple cultures and times and, I argue, are more likely to be preserved through changes in media, for example from traditional oral poetic narrative to a written prose variant, than oral poetic formulae. In one of his narrative patterns, Lord observes that the *absence – devastation – return* is marked by a preceding quarrel, which often motivates the absence. In this article, Lord states:

> Readers of the *Iliad* will recognise, of course, that this is the often-remarked pattern of the main part of the poem with (1) the withdrawal of Achilles from battle because of his quarrel with Agamemnon, (2) the ensuing difficulties of the Achaeans and death of Patroclus, which motivates (3) the return of Achilles to the battle and the victory of the Archaens that follows.[52]

Lord then proceeds to demonstrate how this pattern is found in the *Odyssey* and *Beowulf*. This pattern and, to some extent, the preceding quarrel can also be seen in the heroic *Vǫlsungr* cycle, found in both a poetic version in the Poetic Edda and a prose one in *Vǫlsunga Saga*.

In the medieval Germanic world, there is a multi-generational heroic narrative which comprises the stories of three generations of heroes: Vǫlsungr, Sigmundr, and Sigurðr, and which includes the aftermath of the death of Sigurðr. The poems of another hero, *Helgi*, are often associated with this heroic cycle, and can be included to increase data. The narrative, termed here the *Vǫlsungr* cycle, can be found in several sources and analogues. The primary poetic variant of the *Vǫlsungr* cycle is found in the medieval Icelandic collection of the *Poetic Edda*. It mostly is comprised of the Helgi and Sigurðr narratives with the

---

[51] A.B. LORD, "Interlocking mythic patterns in *Beowulf*", in: *Epic Singers and Oral Tradition*, pp. 140-146, p. 140.

[52] LORD, "Interlocking mythic patterns in *Beowulf*", p. 140.

aftermath, and only briefly mentions Vǫlsungr and Sigmundr. The earliest extant manuscript, *Codex Regius* 2365 4°, contains 45 leaves, or 90 pages of text, and is approximately five inches wide by seven inches tall written in a Gothic hand on vellum using ink. There is a lacuna following leaf 32, which some scholars, among them Peter Hallberg[53] and Gustaf Lindblad,[54] take to be a missing gathering of eight leaves. The missing text is in the middle of one of the poems for the lead hero, Sigurðr, the poem called *Brot af Sigurðarqviðo* (*Fragment of the lay of Siguðr*). *Codex Regius* 2365 4° has been edited by modern editors to consist of 29 poems, eighteen of which are the heroic poems associated with the *Vǫlsungr* cycle, and two short prose works. The earliest antecedents of most of these didactic, religious, and narrative poems in *Codex Regius 2365 4°* are considered to have been oral (see above). The narrative action takes place during the Germanic Migration Period, typically dated from the late fourth through sixth centuries CE, in the pre-literate Germanic world in Northern Europe. Within the structure of the text, there are prose descriptions; two are longer and thus are traditionally considered separately.

A prose variant of the *Vǫlsungr* cycle can be found in the *Vǫlsunga Saga*, also from medieval Iceland, which is found in *Codex Regius 1824b 4°*. This extant manuscript dates from about 1400, though is believed to have been compiled no later than sometime between 1260 and 1270,[55] around the same time as the earliest extant *Poetic Edda* manuscript. This text is primarily prose with a few poems embedded in the text, some of which are taken from the *Poetic Edda*. The narrative begins before the birth of Vǫlsungr and includes some of his tale as well as the story of Sigmundr and Sigurðr and the aftermath of the latter's death. There are also visual forms of some elements of the heroic cycle, some of which predate the written copies; I refer here to the eleventh century Ramsund rock in modern day Sweden, the thirteenth-century Hylestad portal and the ninth-century Oseberg ship in modern day Norway, and the tenth-century Andreas cross on the Isle of Man, to name but a few, which suggests the narrative's wide Germanic appeal over the medieval period. Narrative examples outside Iceland are also to be found, for example textual references found in the Old English poems *Beowulf* and *Deor*. And perhaps of greater interest generally, a more complete narrative variant of the story is found in Middle High German in the *Nibelungenlied*, with some thirty-seven copies, several from as

---

[53] P. HALLBERG, *The Icelandic Saga*, trans. P. SCHACH.
[54] LINDBLAD, "Studier i Codex Regius av äldra Eddan"; ID., "Poetiska Eddans fornhistoria och skrivskicket i Codex Regius".
[55] *The Saga of the Volsungs*, ed. and trans. R.G. FINCH (London, 1965), pp. IX-XIII.

early as the thirteenth century, around the same time as the Icelandic copies, and I might also mention here the Icelandic texts, *Þiðreks saga* from the fourteenth century and, of course, Snorri Sturluson's *Prose Edda*, assumed to have been written around 1220, where parts of this tale are mentioned several times and it is briefly told.

Vǫlsunga Saga is categorised by scholars as one of the *fornaldarsögur* ('legendary sagas'). As I noted in my earlier monograph,[56] medieval Icelandic *fornaldarsögur* remain relatively under-investigated when compared with *Íslendingasögur* ('family sagas'), another medieval Icelandic saga form, which are largely written before *fornaldarsögur* and deal with the settlement of Iceland and the conversion to Christianity. In comparing the two genres, *Íslendingasögur* are considered more realistic and have frequently been used in discussions concerning life in medieval Iceland, if not aiding in depictions of life at the time of the events, at least at the time they were written down. The *fornaldarsögur* narratives may be based on historic events and personages; however, they take place over a wide time span and geographical area, and the historical figures, if we can call them that, lived over several hundred years and many could not possibly have known each other. As with other European heroic epic traditions, the narratives are more concerned with the heroic deeds, possibly the ethics of leadership and the hero, and are less concerned about, or at least seem sceptical of, the historical veracity of the narrative and the inclusion of dragons and other mythical elements. The *Vǫlsunga Saga* is arguably the most famous example of the *fornaldarsögur*, shown by its many analogues. It relies on narrative mythic patterns and themes, if not oral formulae, and may help us understand the formulaic, perhaps even the oral-formulaic, nature of narrative that changed media: from a now lost assumed oral narrative by way of one written down in poetic form to this written prose version.

Few attempts have been made to apply Lord's narrative patterns to Eddic poetry or *Vǫlsunga Saga*. In 2001, I looked at these patterns in two prose works that were purported to have come to us through a poetic form: the nineteenth-century Armenian narrative *The Daredevils of Sassoon* and the *Vǫlsunga Saga*.[57] Robert Kellogg wrote,

> [t]he Parry / Lord model was developed to describe orally composed epic poetry, and the eddic lays are too short and episodic to be called epic. But from the work

---

[56] MELLOR, *Analyzing Ten Poems from* The Poetic Edda.
[57] MELLOR, *Analyzing Ten Poems from* The Poetic Edda.

of Parry and Lord the possibility has arisen of considering the relationship between epic and eddic poetry in a new way.[58]

Analysing the narrative patterns found in *Vǫlsunga Saga* and *Vǫlsung Cycle*, however, may shed some light on the narrative strategies that continued to be employed even after the move from oral to written narrative. *Vǫlsunga Saga* will be the primary text in this section, given the lacuna in the *Poetic Edda*, though both are consulted, and some comparisons will be made. The analysis in this section will show that several narrative patterns found in the saga and the poems are consistent with general patterning found in other epics, and some observations regarding the interplay between the prose and poetic variants will be made.

As Lord stated in his article "Interlocking mythic patterns in *Beowulf*", there is a mythic pattern sequence *absence – devastation – return*, where the absence of the hero leads to devastation of the family and / or the country, which is corrected with the return of either him or his surrogate:

> (1) A powerful figure is not present or, for various reasons, is powerless in a situation of danger to his people. (2) During the period of his absence, or inability or unwillingness to act effectively, things go badly for those around him, and many of his friends are killed. Finally, (3) the powerful figure returns or his power is restored, whereupon he puts things to right again. The first element in the pattern is sometimes preceded by a quarrel, which motivates either the absence of the powerful figure or his loss of power.[59]

In the article, Lord follows this mythic pattern in *Gilgamesh*, the *Odyssey*, and *Beowulf*. After the death of Enkidu, Gilgamesh wanders in search of everlasting life. His absence leaves no king in Uruk, and though this does not seem to cause great devastation in Uruk, there is rejoicing upon his return. In the *Odyssey*, Odysseus has been away at the Trojan war. On his way home he has many adventures. Upon his return he finds that suitors for his wife have beset his home. Order is restored when Odysseus kills the suitors, reclaiming his home and wife, and his true identity has been recognised. When the suitors' relatives wish to avenge their deaths, disaster is averted by the intervention of the gods. In *Beowulf*, the absence of an effectual king leads to the slaughter wrought by Grendel. Only with the return of an effectual hero, Beowulf, is order restored.

---

[58] KELLOGG, "Literacy and orality in the poetic Edda", p. 99.
[59] LORD, "Interlocking mythic patterns in *Beowulf*", p. 140.

The pattern can also be recognised in *Vǫlsunga Saga* which is also marked by a preceding quarrel. A one-eyed man, whom the audience knows to be Óðinn, thrusts a sword into a tree growing in the middle of the hall and states "*Sá er þessu sverði bregðr ór stokkinum, þá skal sá þat þiggja at mér at gjǫf ...*" ("The man to pull out this sword from the trunk shall receive it from me as a gift ...").[60] Sigmundr successfully pulls the sword from the trunk. Siggeirr, who has just married Sigmundr's sister, Signý, wants it for himself. When Sigmundr refuses to give it to him, Siggeirr leaves angry and lures Sigmundr and his father Vǫlsungr to an ambush where Vǫlsungr is killed: the loss of the powerful figure. Things continue to go badly for Sigmundr, who loses all his brothers, and he spend a considerable amount of time hiding and plotting revenge. Initially, for Sigmundr, the new generation of leader, things go badly, including loss of those around him, and he is unable to act effectively without a companion. Sigmundr eventually accomplishes his revenge with the help of his sister. In disguise, she sleeps with him and gives birth to his companion, Sinfjǫtli, whereupon they kill Siggeirr. Sigmundr returns to his home kingdom to reclaim his crown. The death of the father, Vǫlsungr, leads to devastation and loss of the kingdom, which is only restored by the return of the new generation hero, Sigmundr, who avenges his father's death. It should be noted that none of this episode is found in the *Poetic Edda*. Siggeirr is barely mentioned, just once when Guðmundr says to Sinfjǫtli "*Stiúpr vartu Siggeirs*" ("You were Siggeirr's stepson") and it is implied that this is an insult. We can only imagine what narrative variant was available to the author of *Vǫlsunga Saga*. Even in Snorri's *Prose Edda*, Siggeirr is mentioned only once and is simply said to have been related to Vǫlsungr by marriage.

Similarly, the pattern occurs for the next generation. Sigmundr is invited to a feast at king Eymili's hall. King Lyngvi is also there. They are introduced to king Eymili's daughter, Hjǫrðís. Both men are interested in her. Eventually, King Lyngvi tells Hjǫrðís that she must choose between them, and she chooses Sigmundr. Lyngvi leaves angry. Sigmundr and Lyngvi then meet on the battlefield, and Sigmundr falls after a man with one eye, again Óðinn, breaks in half the sword he received from Óðinn. Hjǫrðís, pregnant with Sigurðr, now goes into exile and has her son. Only after Sigurðr has avenged his father's death by killing King Lyngvi, can he reclaim the throne and restore order to the kingdom. The text reads: "*Ferr Sigurðr nú heim með fǫgrum sigri ok miklu fé ok ágæti er hann hafði fengit í þessi ferð. Váru nú veizlur gervar í mót honum heima í ríkinu*" ("So Sigurðr set out for home. A splendid victory was his, and

---

[60] *The Saga of the Volsungs*, ed. and trans. FINCH, pp. 4-5.

also much wealth and renown which he had won on the expedition. Back in his own country a festive welcome was prepared for him").[61] Part of this episode has a parallel in the *Poetic Edda* in the poem *Reginsmál*. Though Sigmundr and Lyngvi's conflict for Hjǫrdís' hand is not directly mentioned, the conflict is implied. The poem reads:

Nú er blóðugr örn bitrom hiorvi
bana Sigmundar á baki ristinn;
öngr er fremri, sá er fold ryði,
hilmis arfi, oc Hugin gladdi[62]

Now the blood eagle is, with a biting sword,
carved on the back of the bane of Sigmundr;
few are worthier, he who reddened the earth
the heir of the king, and gladdened Huginn.

In both the prose and the poetry, the narrative says that King Hjálprekr gives Sigurðr manned ships, though in the *Poetic Edda* this is in prose and not part of the poetics. In both the prose and poetics, the subsequent section describes the chance meeting of Sigurðr and Hnikarr, who is really Óðinn in disguise. Here, the *Vǫlsunga Saga* prose author incorporates a piece of the poetics directly from the *Poetic Edda* into his prose text:

Hnicar héto mic, þá er Hugin gladdi
Vǫlsungr ungi oc vegit hafði.
Nú máttu kalla karl af bergi,
Feng eða Fiolni; far vill ec þiggia[63]

Hnikar they called me
when Hugin I gladdened,
vanquished and slew,
O Volsung youth!
The man from the cliff
call by the name
of Feng or Fjolnir
I would fare hence with you[64]

---

[61] *The Saga of the Volsungs*, ed. and trans. FINCH, pp. 30-31.
[62] *Edda: Die Lieder des Codex Regius nebst verwandten Denkmälern*, ed. H. KUHN, 2 vols. (Heidelberg, 1983), p. 179.
[63] *Edda: Die Lieder des Codex Regius nebst verwandten Denkmälern*, ed. H. KUHN, p. 178.
[64] *The Saga of the Volsungs*, ed. and trans. FINCH, p. 29.

This inclusion of a direct piece of poetry suggests that the author of *Vǫlsunga Saga* had access to either the written text or the oral poem (likely the former), and we see an interplay between the poetic and prose form in the retelling of the narrative in this new, prose writing medium. Both texts go on to report that Sigurðr meets and kills Lyngvi, *Vǫlsunga Saga* in prose and the *Poetic Edda* in a combination of prose and poetry.

In a third instance of the pattern found in *Vǫlsunga Saga*, after Sigurðr has killed the dragon he is told about a shield maiden asleep on the mountain. Sigurðr follows the advice of the birds and finds Brynhildr. He eventually leaves her and through Grímhildr's trickery marries her daughter, Guðrúnn, and Brynhildr is tricked into marrying Gunnarr. One day at the river Rhine, a quarrel between Guðrún and Brynhildr breaks out over the rank and standing, and the deception is revealed. The text reads:

> Guðrún svarar með reiði, "Þá værir ef þú þegðir en lastaðir mann minn. Er þat allra manna mál at engi hafi slíkr komit í verǫldina fyrrir hversvetna sakir, ok eigi samir þér vel at lasta hann, því at hann er þinn frumverr, ok drap hann Fáfni ok reið vafrlogan, er þú hugðir Gunnar konung, ok hann lá hjá þér ok tók af hendi þér hringinn Andvaranaut, ok máttu nú hér hann kenna".
>
> Brynhildr sér nú þenna hring ok kennir. Þá fǫlnar hon, sem hon dauð væri. Brynhildr fór heim ok mælti ekki orð um kveldir.

"You'd be wiser to hold your peace", answered Gudrun angrily, "than to speak slightingly of my husband. Everyone says that no man born into this world is in any way like him. And it is not fitting for you to speak slightingly of him, for he is your lover, and he killed Fafnir and rode through the leaping flames when you thought it was King Gunnar, and he slept with you and took from your arm the ring Andvaranaut, and here – now you can see for yourself!"

Brynhild then saw the ring and recognised it. Then she turned deathly pale. Brynhild went back and did not utter a word that evening.[65]

When she finds out she has been deceived, Brynhildr successfully plots the death of Sigurðr, just as with Siggeirr who plotted and caused the death of Vǫl sungr and Lyngvi with Sigmundr. However, here the pattern is broken because there is no subsequent return with the next generation of heroes avenging the death and restoring order when the hero returns to the kingdom. In fact, it might be argued at this point order is not restored, certainly not with the return of the hero.

---

[65] *The Saga of the Volsungs*, ed. and trans. FINCH, pp. 50-51.

The pattern is found in the poetic variant as well. In *Fáfnismál* (*The Lay of Fafnir*) from the *Poetic Edda*, after he has eaten of Fáfnir's heart, Sigurðr learns of the shield-maiden from a pair of Odinnic birds and seeks her out. However, Brynhildr from *Vǫlsunga Saga* is called Sidrdrífa in this and the subsequent poem, *Sigrdrífomál*. She awakens to meet Sigurðr and gives him some wisdom fit for a hero. The story continues in the poem *Brot af Sigurðar qviðo* (*Fragment of the Lay of Sigurðr*), which is noa fragment due to the lacuna. When the text continues, Sidrdrífa is called Brynhildr and already wants Sigurðr dead for reasons that are unclear until a later poem, *Sigurðarqviða scamma* (*The Short Lay of Sigurðr*), which explains that Gunnarr wanted to marry Brynhildr, but she was tricked into thinking Sigurðr was Gunnarr. When she discovers the deception, she plots the death of Sigurðr. This variation in names has an echo in the three *Helgi* poems from the *Poetic Edda* and gives us some small insight into the variants of these narratives. In the poems *Helgaqviða Hundingsbana in fyrri* (*The First Lay of Helgi Hunding's Bane*), *Helgaqviða Hiǫrvarðzsonar* (*The Lay of Helgi Hiǫrvarð's Son*) and *Helgiqviða Hundingsbana ǫnnor* (*The Second Lay of Helgi Hunding's Bane*), the compiler of the *Poetic Edda* has felt compelled to explain to the reader that in these three stories the names of the main characters are sometimes different due to the old belief in reincarnation: "*Þat var trúa í fornescio, at menn væri endrbornir, enn þat er nú kǫlluð kerlingavilla*" ("It was true in olden times, that men would be born again, but that is now called an old wives' tale").[66] A folklorist understands the idea of variant, but it seems as though the compiler of the *Poetic Edda* feels a need to reconcile the differences in narrative, suggesting variations in narratives not uncommon in oral traditions.

From the examples given above in Lord's original analysis, only the *Odyssey* ends with the restoration of the hero and an end to all conflict at the hands of the gods. The narrative ends happily with a truce between all warring factions and Odysseus' death is not mentioned. *Gilgamesh* ends with the death of Gilgamesh, presumably of old age. Though the king has died, we are told: " ... do not be sad at heart, do not be grieved or oppressed".[67] This ending is also meant to be uplifting and optimistic about the future. The Germanic tradition seems not to share an optimistic view of the future. *Beowulf* ends with the death of Beowulf who, though old, dies in glory fighting a dragon which he also kills.

---

[66] *Edda: Die Lieder des Codex Regius nebst verwandten Denkmälern*, ed. KUHN, p. 161; trans. mine.
[67] P. SCHACH, "Some thoughts on Völuspa", in: *Edda: A Collection of Essays*, ed. GLENDENNING *et al.*, pp. 86-116, at p. 116.

However, Beowulf's death and pessimism for the future undermines any happy ending to the story. He sees the end of the Geats through conflicts of revenge and the encroaching Swedes. The end of the *Vǫlsungr Cycle*, both poetic and prose, is also tragic. After Sigurdr is killed, Guðrún, his wife, marries Atli, which results in the death of her brother Gunnarr. In turn she avenges his death by killing her own husband. In the end, all are dead, and Guðrún is left to wander in misery.

In a second mythic pattern presented in Lord's article, the hero overcomes a man-eating male monster and then he must overcome a female monster or a divine temptress. This pattern is often accompanied by the death of a companion ultimately followed by a quest to the other world. Lord maintains that *Gilgamesh* represents an ancient example of this pattern. Gilgamesh and his companion Enkidu kill a man-eating monster, Humbaba. A further offence is committed when Gilgamesh insults and rejects Ishtar, Queen of heaven, who is seen in this pattern as a divine temptress attempting to seduce Gilgamesh. After a third offence, the killing of the bull of heaven, the gods kill Enkidu. Gilgamesh, now confronted with the reality of death, goes on a quest for immortality ending in a journey to the underworld and the home of Utnapishtim, made immortal by the gods for having saved humanity from the deluge. Gilgamesh eventually returns home to rule his people without having acquired immortality but having gained an understanding of the meaning of life. Lord suggests a motif in such heroic narrative, namely that before a hero such as Gilgamesh can go into the underworld, a companion, in this case Enkidu, must die as a blood sacrifice to open the way to the underworld. This mythic pattern is also found in the *Odyssey* as Lord points out. Odysseus does not kill, but rather blinds the man-eating monster Polyphemus, who is also the son of Poseidon. The enchantress, Circe, is the divine temptress who tries to capture Odysseus, with whom she has fallen in love, just as Ishtar in *Gilgamesh*. Later, a companion, Elpinor, falls off the roof of Circe's palace and dies. Although a seemingly meaningless event, Lord points to this death as necessary to the motif, to open the way to the underworld into which Odysseus goes to consult with his dead friend Agamemnon among others. In Lord's final example, *Beowulf*, Beowulf kills Grendel, another man-eating monster. Beowulf must then overcome a female monster, Grendel's mother, who is a female monster that needs to be overcome rather than a divine temptress. Grendel's mother has killed Æshere, a beloved chancellor to Hrothgar, thereby opening the way to the underworld for Beowulf. This death of a near companion to Hrothgar and not Beowulf may further show a structural relationship between Hrothgar and Beowulf, namely that they represent the idea of a hero at different effectual moments. However, Lord points out that Æshere's death does not occur in the expected place. Structurally, Æshere's death opens the way for Beowulf to go into the other world to fight Grendel's mother and eventually defeat her. This wrong sequence may be something significant to the Germanic variation of storytelling, as it occurs in much the same way in the *Vǫlsungr Cycle*.

In the *Vǫlsunga Saga*, the pattern observed by Lord in his article happens twice, and on one of these two occasions, the pattern is also found in the poetic material of the *Poetic Edda*. In a lesser example of the pattern found in *Vǫlsunga Saga*, Sinfjǫtli, Sigmundr's son, is also his companion. They spar with each other in much the same way as Enkidu and Gilgamesh. Together they kill Siggeirr avenging Vǫlsungr's death, Sigmundr's father, and Sinfjǫtli's grandfather. While Siggeirr is not a man-eating monster, he does kill King Vǫlsungr, causing devastation to the Vǫlsungr family and, therefore, fills that role in the pattern. Later, Sinfjǫtli woos a woman who is also being courted by the brother of Borghildr, Sigmund's wife. Borghildr is the queen and so, though not divine nor really a monster, fulfils the role in the pattern by setting up a conflict with the main hero, Sigmundr. Borghildr attempts three times to kill Sinfjǫtli by poisoning his beer, and on the third attempt is successful. Sinfjǫtli's death is the blood sacrifice. Sigmundr, distraught by Sinfjǫtli's death, goes on a quest to a fjord, carrying Sinfjǫtli's body which is taken by Óðinn to the underworld. It is not clear that Sigmundr defeats Borghildr, but the texts states that "*Ok eptir þat snýr Sigmundr heim, rekr nú í brott drottningina, ok litlu síðar dó hon*" ("After this Sigmund returned home and he now banished the queen, who soon afterwards died").[68] The pattern in this episode follows what Lord sees as the sequence in *Beowulf*: killing the man-eating monster, the insult to the female monster, followed by the death of the companion, and then the overcoming the female monster. The pattern that Lord observed in other texts has here changed slightly, away from divine beings and monsters towards everyday people.

A second example of this pattern is found in both *Vǫlsunga Saga* and the *Poetic Edda*, in the poems *Fáfnismál*, *Sigrdrífomál*, and *Brot af Sigurðarqviðo*. With divine advice from the god Óðinn, Sigurðr succeeds in killing a man-eating monster, the dragon Fáfnir. Strictly speaking, the poem *Fáfnismál* does not say that Sigurðr was aided by Óðinn, just that Sigurðr pierced Fáfnir's heart when passing over the pit, and even this is in prose and not in the poem. That it was Óðinn comes from the prose narrative in *Vǫlsunga Saga*. Both prose and poems claim that, after killing the dragon, Reginn, Sigurðr's foster father and

---

[68] *The Saga of the Volsungs*, ed. and trans. FINCH, p. 19.

Fáfnir's brother, wants to eat the dragon's heart and asks Sigurðr to roast it. The poem *Fáfnismál* reads:

27. "*Sittu nú, Sigurðr, enn ec mun sofa ganga, oc halt Fáfnis hiarta við funa! eiscǫld ec vil etinn láta eptir þenna dreyra drycc*".[69]

    "Sit now, Sigurðr, and I will go to sleep,
    and roast Fáfnir's heart in the fire!
    the heart I want to eat
    since I have drunk of the blood".

When Sigurðr tastes it, he discovers he can understand the birds who tell him that Reginn is plotting to kill him, and Sigurðr kills him first. Reginn is Sigurðr's companion. Though the actual killing of Reginn is in prose, the proceeding stanza from the poem makes it clear:

39. "*Verðra svá ríc scöp, at Reginn scyli mitt banorð bera; þvíat þeir báðir brœðr scolo brálliga fara til Heliar heðan*".[70]

    "It will not be such a rich fate, that Reginn should
    tell my death-tale;
    for they, both brothers, will soon
    go to Hel hence".

It is an odd twist to the element 'death of a companion' that Sigurðr kills his own companion in this sequence. However, just as in the other examples, the killing of Reginn is the blood sacrifice that opens the way for Sigurðr to reach Sigrdrífa / Brynhildr, surrounded by a ring of fire in the other world. Sigrdrífa, so called in the poems *Fáfnismál* and *Sigrdrífomál* but Brynhildr in *Brot af Sigurðarqviðo* and in the saga, fills the role of divine temptress. Unlike *Gilgamesh* and the *Odyssey*, the death of the companion and overcoming the divine temptress / monster are out of sequence, just as in *Beowulf*. Furthermore, unlike Ishtar in *Gilgamesh*, Circe in *Odysseus*, and Grendel's mother in *Beowulf*, in the end Brynhildr will destroy Sigurðr and there will be no subsequent generation to return order to the Vǫlsung family.

---

[69] *Edda: Die Lieder des Codex Regius nebst verwandten Denkmälern*, ed. KUHN, p. 185.
[70] *Edda: Die Lieder des Codex Regius nebst verwandten Denkmälern*, ed. KUHN, p. 187.

There are other narrative patterns Lord observed that might be explored in future scholarship and, perhaps, other patterns not yet discussed, waiting to be discovered. Nevertheless, the evidence above seems to indicate that the medieval Norse narrative tradition has pattern similarities with narrative traditions elsewhere in the world. Lord's observations and narrative patterns and this analysis put the Norse narrative tradition in a broader context and allow scholars to explore aspects of the formulaic nature of narrative beyond just formula. Furthermore, there is every indication that the author of the *Vǫlsunga Saga* falls back on a mythic pattern tradition when writing prose for narrative structure, though he might also use other narrative structures, especially those employed in the *Íslendingasögur,* as well. I am thinking of Theodore M. Anderson's conflict structure,[71] which seems to be a component of the structure at the end of the saga – but that is outside the purview of this article.

Conclusion

Stories have the power to organise and unite people. The narratives a people tell give us insight into their cultural values and ethics, what they find entertaining, and their emotional responses to a series of events. By analysing their stories, we hope to gain insight into their culture, including their narrative structures and compositional strategies. What are culturally specific components of a story and what aspects of storytelling do cultures have in common? In his scholarly oeuvre, Albert B. Lord saw types of patterning in South Slavic epic and compared them to ancient texts from the past, identifying formulae, themes, and narrative patterning. Arguably, formulae, those patterns of language used to tell the story, are the most culturally specific, since they are created in a culture's marked poetic language. There are narrative patterns that are culturally specific, however, as are some narrative patterns: *absence – devastation – return*; or overcoming a man-eating male monster and then a female monster or a divine temptress accompanied by the death of a companion and followed by a quest to the other world as has been demonstrated by Lord and the argument and observations above, are productive elements of patterning in storytelling that go beyond culture, time, and mode. Albert B. Lord's analysis and method from the South Slavic material continues to be a productive approach, even when trying to understand the now dead oral tradition that pre-

---

[71] T.M. ANDERSSON, *The Problem of Icelandic Saga Origins: A Historical Survey* (New Haven, 1964), p. 5.

dates the *Poetic Edda*. The medieval storytellers' approaches to heroic composition can help to illuminate the transition from oral to written traditions. Lord's ideas are a useful starting point for the investigation of the composition of the medieval Icelandic poetic system and strategies, the *fornaldarsögur*, and the interplay between the two. The Icelanders borrowed from written styles from outside their culture, from saints' lives and classical literature, but they also used their own earlier oral tradition as they were creating new composition styles. Part of these new narrative styles were based on an oral tradition and in many examples retained some of the narrative and aural patterning, despite changing to a new medium.

Same Meaning, Different Words: Retelling as a Mode of Transmission in Old Norse-Icelandic *Konungasögur* Tradition[*]

DARIA GLEBOVA

Introduction

In the last forty years saga scholarship has acknowledged the fluid nature of medieval Icelandic manuscript transmission: more and more sagas are seen as living, evolving narratives and not as fixed texts.[1] One of the outcomes of this turn has been the change in the attitude towards variation in textual criticism: similarly to variants in oral transmission, written variants started to be seen as equally important, be they found in a saga extant in several distinct

---

[*] This publication was prepared within the framework of the Academic Fund Program at the HSE University in 2021-2022 (grant № 21-04-066).

[1] The overview of the existing works in this vein can be found in S. ÓSKARSDÓTTIR, "Expanding horizons: Recent trends in old norse-icelandic manuscript studies", *New Medieval Literatures* 14 (2012), pp. 203-233, and in the essay collections *Creating the Medieval Saga: Versions, Variability and Editorial Interpretations of Old Norse Saga Literature*, ed. E. LEITHBRIDGE and J. QUINN (Odense, 2010), and *New Studies in the Manuscript Tradition of 'Njáls Saga': The Historia Mutila of 'Njála'*, ed. E. LEITHBRIDGE, and S. ÓSKARSDÓTTIR (Kalamazoo, 2018).

New Light on Formulas in Oral Poetry and Prose, ed. Daniel SÄVBORG and Bernt Ø. THORVALDSEN, *Utrecht Studies in Medieval Literacy*, 57 (Turnhout: Brepols, 2023), pp. 259-285.

versions or in a large number of copies varying at the micro-level.[2] From a tool for establishing the relationship between the manuscripts or finding a version closer to the oral original[3] the study of variation has become a way to meet the people behind the textual transmission: a particular scribe, a reader, a text version compiler, a modern editor, etc. However, as there is no general classification of the variation types within saga manuscript traditions (medieval as well as post-medieval), the course of written transmission is still not clear. To which extent a saga text could be reworked? To what influences the form of variation was subjected? And how did the 'genre' of the text affect the form and the amount of variation?

---

[2] On the equality of oral variants see A. LORD, *Singer of Tales*, 2nd. edn, ed. S.A. MITCHELL and G. NAGY (Cambridge MA, 2000), p. 100, and see also the discussion in G. NAGY, *Poetry as Performance: Homer and Beyond* (Cambridge, 1996), pp. 9-10. For the discussion of the influence of orality studies on text perception in the saga scholarship, see P. HERMANN, "Methodological challenges to the study of Old Norse myths: The orality and literacy debate reframed", in: *Old Norse Mythology – Comparative Perspectives*, ed. P. Hermann et al. (Cambridge MA, 2017), <http://nrs.harvard.edu/urn-3:hul.ebook:CHS_HermannP_etal_eds.Old_Norse_Mythology.2017> (accessed 24.12.2020). An example of the approach can be found in E. LETHBRIDGE, "Gísla Saga Súrssonar: Textual variation, editorial constructions and critical interpretations", in *Creating the Medieval Saga*, ed. LETHBRIDGE and QUINN, pp. 123-152, where the versions of *Gísla saga Súrssonar* are analysed as equally significant as an original text, as well as its secondary revisions. For the analysis of one of the redactions of *Ljósvetninga saga* as an independent, self-sufficient work, see: Y. TIROSH, *On the Receiving End: The Role of Scholarship, Memory, and Genre in Constructing 'Ljósvetninga saga'* (PhD Thesis, University of Iceland, 2019). A discussion of micro-variation in the manuscript tradition of *Njáls saga* can be found in S. ÓSKARSDÓTTIR and E. LEITHBRIDGE, "Whose Njála? Njáls saga editions and textual variance in the oldest manuscripts", in: *New Studies in the Manuscript Tradition of 'Njáls saga'*, ed. LEITHBRIDGE and ÓSKARSDÓTTIR, pp. 1-27, at p. 10. Much has been done in the field of the transmission of *fornaldarsögur* and *riddarasögur*, see, e.g. K. SEIDEL, *Textvarianz und Textstabilität: Studien zur Transmission der Ívens saga, Erex saga und Parcevals saga* (Tübingen, 2014); P. LAVENDER, *Whatever Happened to 'Illuga Saga Gríðfóstra'?: Origin, Transmission and Reception of a Fornaldarsaga* (PhD thesis, University of Copenhagen, 2014); K. KAPITAN, *Studies in the Transmission History of* Hrómundar saga Greipssonar (PhD Thesis, University of Copenhagen, 2018).

[3] For the discussion of the changes in the philological disposition towards variation, see M. DRISCOLL, "The words on the page: Thoughts on philology, old and new", in: *Creating the Medieval Saga*, ed. LEITHBRIDGE and QUINN, pp. 87-104. An overview of the works concerned with oral / written variation in the *Íslendigasögur* can be found in Th.M. Andersson, *The Problem of Icelandic Saga Origins: A Historical Survey*, (New Haven and London, 1964: *Yale Germanic Studies* 1), pp. 129-182. The idea of distinguishing saga variation by type, oral or written, was first suggested by Knut Liestøl, who believed that oral variation differs from scribal variation by special features; see K. Liestøl, *The Origins of the Icelandic Family Sagas*, trans. A.G. JAYNE (Oslo, 1930), p. 37.

Although most often the semantic, narrative changes are studied, the very form of variation can be illuminating. The existing research shows that the amount of variation could depend on the scribe's skill or professional identity. For an academic scribe in seventeenth- or eighteenth-century Scandinavia, the best copy was a copy without variation. This can be seen, for example, from the professional evolution of Ásgeir Jónsson, who started from creating variants and then moved to making the least a number of variations possible.[4] This view on copying ideals is not limited to post-Reformation times: close copies occur in the medieval period as well. For instance, among the three hands that were copying *Eriks saga rauða* in *Hauksbók*, one hand always compressed and reworked the text, while the other two kept very closely to the exemplar; it was suggested that the creative scribe was Haukr himself and the other two were his secretaries.[5] Thus, both in medieval and post-medieval times there were scribes who would strive to copy the saga text with the least variation possible and those who had a different, more creative relationship with the transmitted text.

Apart from scribal identity and stylistic preferences, the relationship between the scribe and the text could be influenced by the scribe's perception of the discourse to which the copied text belonged. For example, in different medieval traditions the tendency for high amount of variation during the transmission has been marked as a special feature of 'functional literature' such as medical or law texts, lexicons or legendary hagiography, apocryphal literature, etc. These texts were for 'use' in contrast to the texts that had to be 'preserved' (like Plato and Aristotle in the book culture of Byzantium).[6] Within the saga corpus, the idea of 'use' is the most evident in the tradition of codices associated with *konungasögur*. Since the compilers were using the existing written sources to

---

[4] See the example in the study of post-medieval Kringla copies made by Ásgeir Jónsson in J.-G. JØRGENSEN, *Det tapte håndskriftet Kringla* (Oslo, 1999), p. 231.

[5] S.B.F. JANSSON, *Sagorna om Vinland: Handskrifterna titl Erik den rödes saga*, 1 (Lund, 1944), pp. 228-258; D. SÄVBORG, "Blockbildningen i Codex Upsaliensis: En ny metod att lösa frågan om Snorra Eddas ursprungsversion", in: *Maal og minne* 104.1 (2012), pp. 12-86, at pp. 22-28; ID., "Snorra Edda and the Uppsala Edda", in: *Snorri Sturluson – Historiker, Dichter, Politiker*, ed. H. BECK *et al.* (Berlin and Boston, 2013), pp. 247-266, at pp. 252-255.

[6] For an example of Byzantine apocryphal literature transmission as functional literature, see J. BAUN, *Tales from Another Byzantium: Celestial Journey and Local Community in the Medieval Greek Apocrypha* (Cambridge, 2007), p. 35, with bibliography in n. 3. The transmission of texts for specialists such as law texts, lexicons, and legendary hagiography has been the focus of *Überlieferungsgeschichte*; see: W. WILLIAMS-KRAPP, "Die Überlieferungsgeschichtliche Methode: Rückblick und Ausblick", in *Internationales Archiv für Sozialgeschichte der deutschen Literatur* 25.2 (2000), pp. 4-8. On East Slavonic chronicles as functional literature, see: V.M. ZHIVOV, *The History of the Language of Russian Written Legacy*, 2 vols. (Moscow, 2017), p. 217 (in Russian).

create a new historical narrative, the narratives relevant to the history of the Norwegian kings can be seen as 'functional literature' as described above.[7]

This chapter will focus exclusively on one form of variation that appears in the *konungasögur* tradition: a close 'retelling', when almost all of the details of the source text are preserved but in a different wording. To describe how this form functioned, I will discuss two examples of saga reuse from different periods of the *konungasögur* tradition – a skáld saga *Bjarnar saga hítdœlakappa* in the compilation based on the *Separate saga of St. Óláfr*, *Bæjarbók á Rauðasandi* (c. 1370-1390), and *Ágrip af nóregs konungasögum* in *Heimskringla* (c. 1220-1230). Although both types of sources and the works using them differ significantly, I will show that both compilers were copying their sources in a similar way, supposedly shaped by the textual environment of historiographical discourse.

1. Bjarnar saga hítdœlakappa in Bæjarbók á Rauðasandi (AM 73 b fol.)[8]

Bjarnar saga hítdœlakappa tells the story of the difficult relationship between two Icelandic poets, Bjǫrn Arngeirsson and Þórðr Kolbeinsson. The existing scholarship distinguishes two separate traditions of *Bjarnar saga hítdœlakappa* preservation. One of them is the long saga tradition: here, the conflict between Þórðr and Bjǫrn over a woman, Oddný Þorkelsdóttir, first evolves in the Norwegian setting and then rekindles in Iceland culminating in Bjǫrn's death. This version survive only in post-medieval paper manuscripts, all of which stem from the MS AM 551 d α, 4to (c. 1600-1650;[9] henceforth

---

[7] Th.M. ANDERSSON, "Kings' Sagas (*Konungasögur*)", in: *Old Norse-Icelandic Literature: A Critical Guide*, ed. C.J. CLOVER and J. LINDOW (Ithaca NY, and London, 1985), p. 197. Several studies have shown that the compilers of the *konungasögur* codices often had a specific narrative strategy; see the study of *Morkinskinna* in Á. JAKOBSSON. *A Sense of Belonging: Morkinskinna and Icelandic Identity, c. 1220*, trans. F. HEINEMANN (Odense, 2014) and, on *Flatejárbók*, E.-A. ROWE, *The Development of Flateyjarbók: Iceland and the Norwegian Dynastic Crisis of 1389* (Odense, 2005). In both cases the narrative strategy manifested itself mainly in the general composition of the codex, i.e. the choice of *þættir* and their order.

[8] Manuscripts are referred to by 'AM', indicating the collection of Arní Magnússon (1663-1730), now divided between Copenhagen (Den Arnamagnæanske Samling) and Reykjavík (Stofnun Árna Magnússonar í íslenskum fræðum). Of the manuscripts from this collection mentioned in this article, AM 162, 488, and 551 are to be found in Reykjavík; the others in Copenhagen.

[9] J. LEC. SIMON, *A Critical Edition of Bjarnar saga Hítdœlakappa* (PhD thesis, University

551). This manuscript has lost the opening chapters and has an irretrievable lacuna in the middle.[10]

Another tradition focuses only on the Norwegian events of the saga and is found in the expanded compilations based on the *Separate saga of St. Óláfr*. Two manifestations of this tradition are known: first, a short anecdote found in *Tómasskinna* (GKS 1008 fol., *c.* 1400),[11] relating how Bjǫrn unexpectedly obtained St. Óláfr's garters; secondly, the story of the conflict between Bjǫrn and Þórðr until Bjǫrn's return to Iceland, preserved in *Bæjarbók á Rauðasandi* (AM 73 b fol.; *c.* 1370-1390)[12] and its paper copies. Thus, *Bæjarbók* corresponds to the first part of the saga in *551* (until ch. 10 in the edition in volume 3 of *Íslenzk fornrit*). The following discussion will address the *Bæjarbók* version of *Bjarnar saga*.

The *Bæjarbók*'s version is so close to the one in *551*, that from Árni Magnússon's times it was used to reconstruct the lost beginning of the saga tradition stemming from *551*. Still, views on the relationship between the versions have been subject to change. The most cautious evaluation was suggested by R.C. Boer, who just stated that the *Bæjarbók*'s version is different in wording and sometimes makes the text longer or shorter.[13] The next generations of scholars concentrated mostly on the beginning of the *Bæjarbók*'s version, suggesting that it is an adaptation to the needs of *Óláfs saga helga* or a summary of the original beginning.[14] The differences between the versions were commented upon mainly by J. LeC. Simon, who argued – without providing a close analysis of the expansions though – that *Bæjarbók*'s version expands the text every

of London, 1966), 1, p. 44; *Katalog over Den Arnamagnæanske Håndskriftsamling*, ed. K. KÅLUND (Copenhagen,1888-1894), 1, p. 691.

[10] The most detailed study of relationship between the *Bjarnar saga* manuscripts is available in SIMON, *A Critical Edition*, 1; for overviews of *Bjarnar saga* preservation, see: R.C. BOER, "Einleitung", in: *Bjarnar saga Hítdælakappa*, ed. R.-C. BOER (Halle, 1893) and S. NORDAL, "Formáli", in: *Bjarnar saga Hítdælakappa*, ed. S. NORDAL and G. JÓNSSON (Reykjavík, 1938: *Íslenz Fornrit* 3), pp. 111-211 (henceforth: *ÍF* 3). The only medieval witness of *Bjarnar saga* is a short fragment from the fourteenth century, AM 162 F, fol., that does not include the part of the saga that this chapter is focused on, and therefore is not discussed here.

[11] *Katalog over de oldnorsk-islandske håndskrifter i det store kongelige bibliotek og i universitetsbiblioteket (udenfor den Arnamagnæanske samling) samt den Arnamagnæanske samlings tilvækst 1894-99*, ed. K. KÅLUND (Copenhagen, 1900), p. 18.

[12] S. KARLSSON, *Sagas of Icelandic Bishops: Fragments of Eight Manuscripts* (Copenhagen, 1967), p. 21. Kålund's date is *c.* 1400 (KÅLUND, *Katalog over Den Arnamagnæanske Håndskriftsamling*, p. 49).

[13] BOER, *Bjarnar saga*, p. X.

[14] SIMON, *A Critical Edition*, 1, p. 26; A. FINLAY, "Introduction", in: *The Saga of Bjorn, Champion of the Men of Hitardale*, trans. A. FINLAY (Enfield Lock, 2000), p. XLVII.

time it comes to the episodes with king Óláfr.[15] Overall, the general view is that the *Bæjarbók*'s version is a reworking of *Bjarnar saga* for the sake of its inclusion in *Separate saga of St. Óláfr*. The question is how this reworking has been done.

Method

To see the differences between the versions, one needs to compare them on the parallel fragment (ch. 5,5-10 according to *ÍF* 3 edition). In this procedure I have been following Simon's work on the *Bjarnar saga* manuscript tradition, which improved Boer's stemma by taking more manuscripts into account.[16] First, since *Bæjarbók* was lost in the Copenhagen fire of 1795, its text is used according to its later paper copies, AM 71 fol. (*71*) and AM 73 a fol. (*73 a*). Secondly, the long saga version is used according to *551*, as all of the manuscripts of this group are thought to be copies from it.[17] To check the readings of *551* I have used AM 488 4to (*488*).[18] As the main goal of this study is to look at the difference between the versions as represented in *Bæjarbók* and in *551*, I have been interested only in the examples such as AB ≠ CD, i.e. manuscripts of one group sharing the same reading against the shared reading of another group. To prepare the data for analysis I have used two following rules: the reading is marked by a footnote but not analysed as variation 1) if the reading is different between the manuscripts, representing the version (e.g. AB≠C≠D), or 2) if the reading is different between the manuscripts of one version but is shared by at least one manuscript from another version (eg. AC≠B). I did not include orthographical data in the analysis[19] or inversion of words if all of the morphological and lexical forms remained unchanged. These heuristics allowed me to see all those cases when *71/73 a* ≠ *551/488*. These data became the main material for the analysis of variation between the *Bjarnar saga* versions.

---

[15] SIMON, *A Critical Edition*, 1, pp. 26-27.

[16] See the expanded genealogical tree in SIMON, *A Critical Edition*, 1, p. 148.

[17] Here Simon's results are different from Boer's, who believed that Rask 28 was an independent copy of the *551* exemplar (BOER, *Bjarnar saga*, pp. VIII, XIV).

[18] According to Simon, *488* is a very close copy of *551* made by Ásgeir Jónsson around 1689 before he got access to *Bæjarbók* or *73 a* (SIMON, *A Critical Edition*, 1, p. 52). There are cases, however, when the readings of *488* are the same as *71/73 a*, so it can be useful for variation control.

[19] In this experiment, the so-called Norwegianisms are not counted as variation as well.

Variation between the versions

First of all, a note must be made on the length of the compared texts. Quite often the versions of a medieval text relate to one another as an extended to an abridged one. Although *Bæjarbók*'s version does not include any events after Bjǫrn's return to Iceland, the parallel fragment is by no means significantly extended or shortened: *Bæjarbók*'s version (henceforth: *O*) is around **3050** words (3050 in *71*, 3064 in *73 a*), the *551* version (henceforth: *A*) is around **2955** (2955 in *551*, 2923 in *488*). If one looks at the amount of words by shorter chunks of the fragment (for example, the chapters in *ÍF 3*), one will see that most of the chapters are almost the same in length, except for ch. 9, where the difference is more than 100 words. See the figures below (Table 1):[20]

Table 1

Ch. in *ÍF 3*	O	A
5	238	226
6	254	266
7	1065	1029
8	452	448
9	722	593
10	331	389

This close similarity in length does not mean full similarity in meaning. First of all, both versions include information that cannot be found in the alternative one. For example, *A* version often has more details about the people travelling with Þórðr or Bjǫrn (the *A* version additions are in italics; here and further on the original orthography is preserved in the quotations from the manuscripts; the expanded abbreviations are marked by '( )'; the ends of the line are marked by '|'; the translation is made as close to the original as possible):

---

[20] The counting is done on the prepared text of *O* and *A*, i.e. in cases when, e.g. 71/73a/488 ≠ 551, the reading of *A* version was not marked as a variation. The difference between the text in the manuscripts and the prepared text is around 10-20 words. This preparation should be seen as an instrument and not as a critical edition of any version of the two, as its main purpose lies in finding solid examples of *71/73 a* ≠ *551/488* correspondence.

Þa vorú þeir med Þorði synir | Eyðs Þorkiell og Þorgrimúr. Þar fór og Kalfúr illwiti
then were [there] with Þórðr Eið's sons, Þorkell and Þorgrimr. There went also Kálfr íllviti (*551*, 2r; *488*, 13v);

Þorðr hafði litið ſkıp, *nockrir vikver | ſkir menn vorú a ſkipi með honúm,* nær xxx *| manna vorú allz a ſkıpinú*
Þórðr had [a] small ship, *several men from Vik were on [the] ship with him,* around thirty men *were altogether at the ship*'(*551*, 2r; *488*, 13v);

Þeir Þorðúr geingú *nú |* á batin(n), og *súo henir výkverſkú men(n), og vılldú þ(eir) til| Eıgna sin(n)a*
Þórðr and his men went *now* in the boat and *so [did] the Vik men, and wanted they to [get to] their possessions* (*551*, 3v; *488*, 15v);

Nú koma þeir ä kon(un)gz fúnd, og *lie | tú effter men(n) syna fleſta og súo fie og ſkip. Þeir* komú ...
Now come they to meet the king and *left behind many of their men, and money, and [the] ship. They* came ... (*551*, 3v; *488*, 15v-16r);

Þeir Biorn | geingú xij. saman í hollina, þa er k(onu)ngúr sat yfer dryck | iú, *en fimm tyger man(n)a vorú epter við ſkip.* Bıorn *gıeck | fyrer k(onu)ng og* kúaddi han(n) vel
Bjǫrn and his men went twelve together in the hall, then when [the] king was sitting at drinking, *but five tens of men were behind at [the] ship.* Bjǫrn *went before the king and* greeted him well' (*551*, 3v; *488*, 16r)).

On the other hand, *O* version additions are often connected to the main character's characteristics, for instance there are several appraisals of Bjǫrn and specifications of his relationship with king Óláfr:

og Rææýndiſt han(n) hin(n) beſte | drengr í óllúm Raúnúm
and he proved himself [to be] the best fellow in [the] whole realm' (*71*, 70r; *73 a*, 87r);

Óláfúr k(onung)r gaf *Býrne ſkýckiú göða og miog* van | daða, og hiet h(onu)m *fúllkómlega* sin(n)e vinattú, og kallaðe han(n) | vera Róſkan(n) dreng. *Segiſt og súa at Biörn hafe gorðſt | hyrðmaðúr hins heilaga Oläfs k(onu)ngs.*
King Óláfr gave Bjǫrn a mantle *good and very* elaborate and promised him *perfectly* his friendship and called him a brave man. *It is said also that Bjǫrn has been made a retainer of St. Óláfr, [the] king*' (*71*, 70v; *73 a*, 87v).

Consequently, the relationship between the versions cannot be described simply in terms of extension or abridgment.

To start with a more nuanced description, one should note the frequent morphological, lexical, and syntactical variation that is found throughout the compared fragments. The distribution of the variation can be illustrated by the table below – the variation is a little bit lower in chs. 5 and 6 and then stays around 40-50 % (Table 2).[21]

Table 2

Ch. in *ÍF* 3	O	A
	No. of words involved in variation / No. of words in the fragment	
5	74/238 (31%)	64/226 (28%)
6	59/254 (23%)	74/266 (28%)
7	463/1065 (43%)	420/1029 (41%)
8	212/452 (47%)	207/448 (46%)
9	381/722 (53%)	257/593 (43%)

This variation can be partly explained by differences in the narrative strategies of *O* and *A*, for instance in the characterisation of Þórðr and Bjǫrn. Although the characters are already close to black and white in *A*,[22] the *O* version separates them even further. This distinction manifests itself in *O* not only in the additional appraisals of Bjǫrn but also in a specific attitude towards Þórðr. Although *O* never slides into any humiliating comments about Þórðr, there are some hints in the narrative that allow the audience to see his pitifulness. For instance, when the protagonists meet at the Brenneyjar, in *O* Þórðr acknowledges his complete capitulation to Bjǫrn:

O: hitt man Räð, sagðe Biórn at þú ser dre | pin(n), og lúke ſúa um med ockúr. þ(ér) múnút nú þi (sic!) räða, ſag | ðe Þórðúr
"it would be better", said Bjǫrn, "for you to be killed and, *thus*, it would be finished between us". *"It is you choice now"*, said Þórðr (71, 68v; 73 a, 85v.).

---

[21] The division of the fragments is made according to the chapters in *ÍF* 3 for the convenience of reference; however, the chapter division in the manuscripts is different, which means that any other kind of division could work as well.

[22] FINLAY, *Introduction*, p. XI.

In this way, in *O* it is specifically stressed that Þórðr is in a weaker position – which makes Bjǫrn's decision to spare Þórðr's life even more virtuous than it is in the more neutral *A*.[23]

These small details accompany the striking imbalance in Þórðr's and Bjǫrn's first conversation with king Óláfr: while in *A* Þórðr is able to talk to Óláfr directly, in *O* this ability is restricted to Bjǫrn. This feature can be seen in two examples. The first one is found in ch. 7 (*ÍF* 3, p. 126): Þórðr seeks Óláfr's help to get inheritance from his deceased uncle in Denmark (see Table 3). Here is the sequence of events in *A*: after Þórðr's arrival, I) he tells the king about his matter; II-III) his friend and relative, Þorkell Eyjólfsson, persuades the king to help Þórðr; IV) the king agrees to help and issues a letter to his friends in Denmark. In *O* the sequence of events and Þórðr's position change considerably as Þórðr is well received *because* II) Þorkell Eyjólfsson has already introduced Þórðr's matter to the king; I) they talk *together* about the matter again; IV-III) they ask the king to issue a letter to his friends in Denmark. Therefore, in *O* Þórðr completely depends upon Þorkell Eyjólfsson, while in *A* he is allowed to present his case on his own. See Table 3, where the additions are marked in *italics*, inversion is <u>underlined by one line</u>, and synonymous wording is **in bold**. (The same system is used further down; in addition, entirely different information will be <u>underlined by two lines</u>.)

Table 3

O: <u>var h(onum) þar</u> ₁**allvel** fagnat, (II) *þvíat* þ(ar) var þá *fyrir* Þorkell *Eyjúlfſſon*, og túlkaðe vel ₂**mál Þórðar**, (I) ₃ ſögðu ₄þ(eir) k(onu)ge ₅**málavöxtu** á, um ferð ₆**hanns**, *og beidde at* (IV) ₇**k(onu)ngrin(n)** ₈ ſkyllde ſkrifa með h(onum) til vina inna í Danmörk, (III) at hann ₉**næðe** ₁₀**arfinum**. *Konungrinn gørir svá.* (71, 67v)	A: <u>Honum var þar</u> ₁**vel** fagnad. (I) ₃**segir** ₄**han(n)** ko(nu)ngi ₅**vauxtú** á um ferð ₆**sỹna**. (II) Þorkell var þá þar og túlkaði vel ₂**málið** *við konung*, (III) að han(n) ₉**fengi** ₁₀**fie sitt**. (IV) ₇**K(onungr)** ₈**liet giora honum Brieff** til vina sinna í Danmörk *ok setti fyrir sitt insigli*. (551, 2r)

The same pattern continues when Bjǫrn first meets the king (ch. 8, *ÍF* 3, pp. 130-131; Table 4). In general, in *A* this meeting is described similar to the

---

[23] See also the discussion of the Bjǫrn's figure in the *konungasögur* version of the saga in S.-E. GRØNLIE, *The Saint and the Saga Hero Hagiography and Early Icelandic Literature* (Cambridge, 2017), pp. 243-246.

aforementioned meeting between the king and Þórðr: there are 1) *greetings* (Þórðr is well received / Bjǫrn greets the king), then 2) *the first address to the king by the unknown Icelander* (Þórðr describes his affair to the king (Table 3, I) / Bjǫrn names himself to the king), 3) *the second introduction by someone close to Óláfr who knows the unknown Icelander well* (Þorkell Eyjólfsson discusses Þórðr's matter (Table 3, II-III) / Þórðr identifies Bjǫrn as his abuser) and, finally, 4) *the result of this introduction* (Óláfr helps Þórðr with his business (Table 3, IV) / Óláfr orders to put Bjǫrn in irons). In *O* this pattern is changed: if in *A* the king turns to Þórðr, thus making him a mediator between him and a new Icelander, in *O* Óláfr continues talking to Bjǫrn:

Table 4, *A*: "*K(onu)ngúr seigir: Er eý(gi) þetta sokú dólgr| þin(n) Þorðúr*"
"the king said: 'Isn't it your enemy, Þórðr?'"

Table 4, *O*: "'*Ertú ſókúdölgúr þorðar*', sagðe k(onung)r"
"'Aren't you the enemy of Þórðr?' said the king".

Hence, in both examples in *O* Þórðr is positioned further from Óláfr than he is in *A*: in *O* Þórðr cannot address the king without any preparatory mediation and he cannot be an introducing mediator himself. On the contrary, Bjǫrn is immediately allowed a direct conversation with Óláfr and he does not need a mediator to be introduced to the king. It may be supposed that the position close to the saintly king significantly adds to the character description and functions as a mark of approval: the character who is morally judged by the narrator cannot get too close to the holiness of the saint. The *A* version, on the other hand, is more neutral in its representation of the characters as both Þórðr and Bjǫrn communicate with Óláfr directly.

Table 4

| O: Epter ₁**fund þ(eira) Biarnar og Þorðar**, atti Biórn ſtefnu við ₂**lið** ſ**itt**, og ₃**sagðe**ſt vilia ₄**fin(n)a** Oläf k(onung), og ₅**koma af ser Reiðe han(n)s fyrer fiär upptóku þe**ſſ**a.** Aúðún kuaðz[1] vilia\| fýlgia h(onu)m ₆**þúiat h(onu)m liekú L(an)dmún(ir) at** ſ**taðfe**ſ**ta**ſ**t í Nor(e-gi).\|

₇**fara þ(eir) nú** ä k(onun)gs fúnd, og komú ₈**þar iij nättum** ſ**iðar** en\| þ(ei)r Þorður, þ(ei)r biórn g(en)gu[2] tölf ſaman í hóllina *f(yrir) k(onu)ng\|in(n)*, þä er han(n) ſat[3] yfer ₉**drýkkiúborðúm, (1) kvadde Biórn\| ₁₀k(onu)ngin(n) ₁₁sœmeliga,**

(2) ₁₂**k(onu)ngrin(n)** ₁₃ ſ**púrðe** hver han(n) ₁₄**være,** en hann\| seger til sin, (3) ₁₅**ertú** ſókúdölgúr ₁₆**þorðar** ₁₇**sagðe** k(onung)r. ₁₈**Biórn** ₁₉**kúeð**ſ**t\|** vÿſt ₂₀**han(n)** v(era), (4) ₂₁**þú ert diarfúr maðúr** ₂₂ ſ**(egir)** k(onungr), ₂₁**er þú fer** (sic!) ä min(n)\| **fúnd og han(n)s**, *og tande men(n) úpp* **og taki þä og seti** *þä í*\| Jarn. | A: Eptir ₁**þetta** ätti Biorn ſteffnu við ₂**Auðun fielaga sin(n).** Og ₃**kuað**ſ**t** vilia ₄**fara til fundar við** Olaff k(onung), og ₅**vil eg e(igi) Reyði han(n)s yffer mier fyrer kaup man(n)a Rän.** Áuðún kúa\|ðſſt vilia fylgia honúm, ₆**og lietú heim að Landinú við Nor\|eg** *sem Biorn of Í*ſ*land.*

Nú ₇**koma** þeir ä kon(un)gz fúnd, og lie-\|*tú effter men(n) syna fle*ſ*ta og súo fie og* ſ*kip. Þeir* komú[4] þrem\| Nottúm syðar ₈**á kon(un)gs fúnd** en(n) þeir Þorðr. Þeir Biorn\| geingú xij. saman í hollina, þa er k(onu)ngúr sat yfer ₉**dryck\|iú,** *en fimm tyger man(n)a vorú epter við* ſ*kip.* Biorn *gieck\| fyrer k(onu)ng og* **(1)** kúaddi ₁₀**han(n)** ₁₁**vel.**
(2) ₁₂**K(onu)ngúr** ₁₃**spyr** hver[5] han(n) ₁₄**sie\|** han(n) seigir til sÿn.
(3) **K(onu)ngúr** ₁₇**seigir** ₁₅**Er eý(gi) þetta** sokú dólgr\| ₁₆**þin(n) Þorðúr.** *En(n)* ₁₈**han(n)** ₁₉**kúaz** výſt ₂₀**þan(n)** vera.
(4) **Ko(nu)ngúr** ₂₂**kúad\|** ₂₁**han(n) diarffan man(n) vera,** er han(n) Þorði á hanz fúnd ad\| fara, og bað þa taka og setia í Jarn[6]. |

[1] kuaðz] 73/551/488, 17 kúeðſt.
[2] g(en)gu] 73 a/551/488; 71 gänga.
[3] han(n) ſat] 71; þ(ei)r ſaatu 73a; k(onu)ngúr sat 551/488. There is no unity in the variants, so I do not include the example in the analysis.
[4] komu] 71/71 a/551; 488 koma.
[5] hver] 71/73/488; 551 húor.
[6] srtia í Jarn] 551; 488 í Jarn ſetia.

The variation between *O* and *A*, however, is not limited to 'ideological' narrative changes. Even in the quoted examples the variants are dispersed all over the fragment and often are not connected to the characterisation of the protagonists. For instance, Table 4 displays several contextual lexical synonyms,[24] morphological synonyms,[25] and even rhetorical synonymous constructions[26] that do not depend, grammatically or syntactically, on changes 15-18, i.e. Þórðr's role as a mediator. Some of the synonymous variants are explained by local surroundings, e.g. cases 8 and 10: in *A* the first "*á konungs fund*" is followed by a comment about Bjǫrn's people, so the repetition in 8 works as a linking device used to come back to the main strand of the narrative; in *O*, on the contrary, this comment is cut out and the narrator uses only anaphoric "*þar*". And yet the general amount of synonymous changes that can be explained most probably only by scribal preference is impressive.

Similarly, in Table 3 the main content change occurs in positions 3, 4, and 6: due to the rearrangement of the sequence of events, Þórðr speaks to the king together with Þorkell instead of speaking alone.[27] The rearrangement also influences the syntactic construction in phrase IV, where the independent clause in *A* becomes a reported clause with a subjunctive in *O*.[28] Once again, however, a number of variants cannot be explained by the narrative change, see for example the amount of contextual synonyms.[29] Thus, all narrative discrepancies introduced in *O* are complemented by an abundance of independent synonymous variants. It is also remarkable that all these variants stay in the same positions: in Table 3 they keep the positions within each clause even after the shift in clause order (Table 3, I: 3-6; II: 2; III: 9-10; IV: 7-8), while in Table 4 the order of variants is changed only in cases of the speech introduction, e.g. 17,

---

[24] See subindex, 1: *fund þ(eira) Biarnar og Þorðar* ("meeting their, Bjǫrn and Þórðr") / *þetta* ("this"); 2: *lið ſitt* ("people his") / *Auðun fielaga sin(n)* ("Auðun, partner his"); 3: *sagðeſt* / *kuaðſt* (= "said" 3sg.pret.mid.voice); 4: *fin(n)a* Oläf k(onung) ("meet Óláf konung") / *fara til fundar við* Olaff k(onung) ("go to the meeting with Óláf konung"); 7: *fara* ("go") / *koma* ("come"); 8: *þar* ("there") / *á konungs fund* ("to the meeting with the king"); 9: *yfir drikkjuborðum* ("at the drinking table'") / *yfir drikkju* ("at the drinking"), 11: *sæmiliga* ("honourably") / *vel* ("well").

[25] 13: *spurði* (3sg.pret.) / *spyrr* (3sg.pres.); 14: *væri* (3sg.pret.subj.) / *sé* (3sg.pres.subj.); 19: *kveðsk* (3sg.pres.mid.voice) / *kvaðsk* (3sg.pret.mid.voice).

[26] 5: indirect speech in *O* / direct speech in *A*; 21: direct speech in *O* / indirect speech in *A*.

[27] A: ₃**segir** ₄**han(n)** ... um ferð ₆**sỹna** ("says ₃sg.pres. he... about journey his pos.pron.") / O: ₃ ſögðu ₄**þ(eir)** ... um ferð ₆**hanns** ("said 3pl.pret. they ... about journey his pers.pron.").

[28] A: ₇**K(onungr)** ₈**liet giora honum Brieff** "King granted ₃sg.pret.ind. [to] make him [a] letter"/ O: *og beidde at* ₇**k(onu)ngrin(n)** ₈ **ſkyllde ſkrifa með h(onum)** "and asked that the king should 3sg.pret.subj. write with him [a letter]".

[29] 1: *allvel* ('all well') / *vel* ('well'); 2: *mál Þórðar* ('business of Þórðr gen.sg.') / *málið* ('business def.art.' (= business defined)'); 5: *málavöxtu* ('state of the case') / *vöxtu* ('the circumstance of a case'); 9-10: *næði arfinum* ('obtain ₃sg.pret. inheritance def.art.') / *fengi fé sitt* ('get ₃sg.pret. money his posess.pron.' = 'gain property defined').

22. In this way both versions preserve the majority of the details, even though in a different, synonymous wording.

A similar pattern of variation has been described by Daniel Sävborg in his analysis of *Eriks saga rauða* in *Hauksbók*.[30] In that case, however, the rewriting was accompanied by significant compression of the copied text, and thus could be explained by the compiler's goal to use shorter and more compact phrasing.[31] The case of *Bjarnar saga* is different, as there is no pattern of abridgment or expansion: both versions are using sometimes longer and sometimes shorter wording. Alternatively to *Hauksbók*, in *Bœjarbók*'s version of the saga the variants can be partly explained by the new character representation, i.e. it is a change in the narrative strategy that triggers variation. Still, the question is why there are so many cases of synonymous variation that is not connected to necessary narrative changes, i.e. these variants are non-functional from a narrative point of view.

It seems unlikely that this form, reminiscent of a close retelling, comes from differences in the oral versions of the saga: the parallel fragment contains cases when phrases are longer than six words or even several clauses are left intact.[32] A remarkable feature is that not only they are intact, but they are also thematically noteworthy. For example, such a case is found in the last part of the anecdote about Bjǫrn receiving St. Óláfr's garters in ch. 9 (Table 5). An almost identical fragment concerned with the whereabouts of Bjǫrn's body and the relics (2) is boxed in between two fragments with a denser variation (1 and 3). One could suggest that the person who copied this fragment had a different copying style: in this way, the change in copying modes would be similar to the *Hauksbók* situation discussed above. Alternatively, the short length of the fragment and its specific content might also indicate that the *Bœjarbók* compiler *did not want* to change anything in this particular fragment as it was agreeable with their own view on the matter.

---

[30] SÄVBORG, "Snorra Edda and the Uppsala Edda".
[31] SÄVBORG, "Snorra Edda and the Uppsala Edda", p. 255.
[32] See the discussion of the length of the word-for-word correspondence between the versions in Scandinavian fairytales and in the *Íslendingasögur* in H. MAGERØY, "Eventyrvariantar og sagaversjonar", in: *Einarsbók: Afmæliskveðja til Einars Ól. Sveinssonar*, ed. B. GUÐNASON, H. HALLDÓRSSON, and J. KRISTJÁNSSON (Reykjavík, 1969), pp. 233-254, at p. 248. A similar – although broader – attitude has been articulated by Theodore M. Andersson: "We are now more likely to believe that two passages of nearly identical content sharing several significant words must be scribally linked" (ANDERSSON, *Kings' Sagas*, p. 211).

Table 5

	O (71, 70 v)	A (551, 5r)
1	og varð Býrne e(igi) at húgat ₁**fýrre** en(n) menn| vorú klædder at ₂**han(n)** hafðe ₃**Ræmú k(onu)ngs úm föt ser**, *geck| han(n) þá þegar til k(onu)ngs* og sagðe h(onu)m ₄til þeſſarar vanhýggiú| ₅**k(onu)ng(r)in(n) mællte, lätúm vera kýrtt** *Biörn*, **þviat ſea er at| óngu verre, er þú hefer ätt**, Biórn hafðe ₆**ræmúna k(onu)ngs| naút jafnan(n) siðan** úm föt ₇**ser** meðan han(n) lifðe, 37/60 (61 %)	Og varð Byrni eý(gi) athúgad ₁**fyrr** en(n) men(n) vorú klæddir| að ₂**Biorn** hafði ₃ ſ**kiptt vm reymarnar við kong(sic!)**, og sagði| honúm *þegar* til vanhyggjú ₄**sin(n)ar**, *en(n)* ₅**kongúr(sic!)** ſ**kipaði| kyrtt vera, og kúað þá eý(gi) verre er han(n) hafði**. Bıorn| hafði ₆**ávallt** þeſſa **Reým** vm fót ₇**sin(n)** *á* meðan han(n) lif|ði. 27/50 (54 %)
2	og með| hen(n)e var han(n) niðúr gra-fin(n) og ₁**lóngúm tima** siðar, *þä er*| bein han(n)s vorú úpp tekin(n) og færð til an(n)arar kirkiú, þä var| ú ſama Ræma ofúin(n) úm ₂**legg** ₃**Biarnar**, en(n) allt var an(n)|at fúit og er þat nú meſsúfatalýnde i Górdúm ä Akraneſe.| 5/46 (11 %)	Og med hen(n)i var han(n) niðúr gra-fin(n). Og ₁**þa myklú**| sýðar er bein hans vorú upptekin(n) og færð til an(n)arar| kyrkiú, þa var sú *hin* sama Ræma ófúin(n), vm ₂**föt|legg** ₃**Biorns**, en(n) alltt var ánnad füid, og er þad Nú| Meſſú fata Lindi í Gordúm á Akranesi. 5/47 (10 %)
3	₁Sva er sagt ₂at ij. vetúr ₃**være** biórn ₄**með Olafe k(onu)nge** *í goðre| virðin-gú*. Óláfúr k(onung)r gaf *Býrne* ſkýckiú *göða og miog* van|daða, og hiet h(onu)m *fúllkómlega* sin(n)e vinattú, og kallaðe han(n)| vera ₅**Róſkan(n) dreng**. *Segiſt og súa at Biörn hafe gorðſt| hy|rðmaðúr hins heilaga Oläfs k(onu)ngs.* 32/47 (68 %)	₁Og nú ₂vm| vetúrin(n) eptter ₃**var** Bıorn ₄**í Noregi**, *og gaff Olafúr kon-g(ur) (sic!)*||/5v/ ſkıckıú vandaða, og hiet honúm sın(n)e vinattú og kallaði| han(n) vera vaſkan(n) man(n) og ₅**gó-ðan(n) dreing**| 7/29 (24 %)

A similar example is present in the final dialogue between Þórðr and Odd-ný, when Oddný accuses Þórðr of being full of lies and deceit (Table 6). Unlike many previous fragments, here the amount of variation is quite low; it mostly contains morphological changes[33] or additions of individual words, except for one syntactical change.[34] From the point of view of narrative strategy discussed above this rejection of the rewriting technique is not surprising – Oddný's accusation adds to Þórðr's infamous portrayal and thus does not contradict the general characterisation strategy in *Bæjarbók*.

Table 6

O: Nær getr þú *þúi*, ʃ(egir). hon. ₁**fregit**∥ /71r/ hefer ek ₂**þaú** tïðinði ₃**at ʃkip er komit i Hrútafióröð**, og er þar| ä Biörn sä er þú sagðer andaðan, Þorðúr mællti, <u>vera|</u> mä at þ(ér) þý-ke(sic!) þat tiðinði, vïʃt erú þat tiðinde ₄ ʃ**agðe** hon| og <u>veit eg nú en gíórr</u> hverʃú eg em gefinn. Eg húgða þig| vera ₅**Ró kan(n)** dreng, en þú ert fúllúr af lýge og laú úng, þat| er mællt ₆ ʃ**agðe** Þorðúr at yferbœtúr see til alls *lagðar*. mig| grúnar *þat* s(egir): hon at ealfúr múne han(n) hafa ₇ ʃ**kipat** ser *laú|nin(n)* og bœtúrnar, Þorðúr mællte haf þat fýrer att sem| þer sýniʃt,	A: Nær gietúr þú| seigir hún. ₁**friett** hefi eg ₂**það** *er mier þykıa(sic!)* tyðinði, *mi|er er sogð* ₃ ʃ**kipkoma í hrúta fyrði**, og er þar á Biorn sá er þú| sagðer ándadan. Þorðúr mællti. *Það* <u>má vera</u> *seiger h(an)n|* að þier þýki(sic!) það tyðindi, Vyʃt erú það Tyðinði ₄**seígir** hún| Og en(n) gior veýt eg nú seigir hún(sic!) húorʃú eg er giefın(n), Eg| húgða þig vera ₅**goðan** dreing, en(n) þú ert fúllúr aff| Lygi o(g) Laúʃúng. Það er mælltt ₆**seıgir** Þ(ór)ðúr, að yfferbœtúr| sie til allz. Mıg grúnar, seigir hún, ad sıalfúr múni hann| hafa ₇ ʃ**kapaðar** sıer Bœtúrnar, haff *þú* það fyrer satt em| þier syneʃt seıgir han(n).
19/101 (20%)	21/106 (21%)

Consequently, it can be argued that the compiler of the *O* version alternated between two different copying strategies: the 'retelling' mode (with much synonymous variation) and the close copying technique. The semantic salience of the closely copied fragments points to the hypothesis that the choice of copying strategy depended on the scribe's interpretation of the text. In the last part of this section, I will try to show what this interpretation consisted of.

To pinpoint the narrative strategy of the *Bæjarbók* compiler, we should recount the main features of this version discussed so far: 1) the opening chapters with the prehistory of Bjǫrn and Þórðr's relationship has been briefly sum-

---

[33] 6-7: ʃ**agðe** ₃ₛg.pret. / **seıgir** ₃ₛg.pres.

[34] 1-3, O: ₁**fregit** hefer (sic!) ek ₂**þaú** tïðinði ₃**at ʃkip er komit i Hrútafióröð** ('I have learned_fregna.3sg.pret.part. those_posess.pron.f.acc.sg. news that a ship has come in Hrútafjórðr_acc.sg.') / A: ₁**friett** hefi eg ₂**það** *er mier þykıa (sic!) tyðinði, mi\|er er sogð* ₃ ʃ**kipkoma í hrúta fyrði** ('I have learned_fretta.3sg.pret.part. this_dem.pron.n.acc.sg. *that seems to me* news, *I was told* [about] the arrival of a ship in Hrútafjórðr_dat.sg.').

marised in the first chapter; 2) *Bæjarbók* has more appraisals of Bjǫrn and more details demeaning Þórðr, and this strategy is followed both in the highly varied and closely copied fragments; 3) the final conversation between Þórðr and Óddný, where she accuses Þórðr of lying, is copied closely too. This last detail is particularly noteworthy, as it is not connected directly to Bjǫrn, the protagonist of the saga, and St. Óláfr, the protagonist of the compilation. As the compiler explicitly stated at the beginning of the *þáttr* that they left out everything that is not connected to *Óláfs saga helga,* it is reasonable to think that they should have cut Þórðr and Óddný's dialogue as an unnecessary detail. However, the compiler decides to leave this fragment, almost without variation. Why?

In my opinion, the answer to this question can be found at the very beginning of the *Bjarnar saga* fragment in *Bæjarbók,* where Þórðr is described as very conscious of his reputation: "*Hann var skáld mikit ok **helt sér mjǫk fram til virðingar***";[35] if the beginning was summarised and this detail was still preserved in the text, then it was important for the compiler. This opening description and the final conversation with Óddný form a circular structure, where a man who is very careful about his reputation loses it right in front of his wife. Such conceptual details, both at the beginning and at the end of the saga, create a special accent on Þórðr's image and consequently invite the reader to reassess Þórðr's role in the *þáttr*.

So far, *Bjarnar saga* in *Bæjarbók*'s version of the *Separate saga of St. Olaf* has been seen as a story of the right relationship of the sinner, Bjǫrn, to the saint, Óláfr, because the figure of Bjǫrn becomes even more pious when it is juxtaposed with other *þættir* included in *Bæjarbók*.[36] While most of them follow the canonical list of *þættir* usually included in the *Separate saga of St. Olaf,* there are two texts that are included in *Bæjarbók* only: one of them is *Bjarnar saga,* in its longer version, with the conflict between Bjǫrn and Þórðr; the other is a fragment from *Laxdæla saga,* narrating the story how Þorkell Eyjólfsson met with Óláfr and how he tried to build a church in Iceland of the same height as the one built by Óláfr.[37] Thus, unlike Bjǫrn, who listens to Óláfr and changes his ways of life, Þorkell does not follow the king's advice, persists

---

[35] *ÍF* 3, p. 111. "He was a considerable poet, and did much to maintain his own reputation", translation in: *The Saga of Bjorn,* ed. FINLAY, p. 1.

[36] GRØNLIE, *The Saint and the Saga Hero,* p. 244.

[37] This corresponds to ch. 74-76 in the editions; cf. *Laxdæla saga,* ed. E.Ól. SVEINSSON (Reykjavík, 1934: *Íslenzk Fornrit* 5), pp. 215-224 (henceforth *ÍF* 5). There are, in addition, several fragments from *Fóstbræðra saga,* but it appears also in *Flateyjarbók,* similarly based on the *Separate saga of St. Olaf.*

in his plans, and dies in the storm, losing all the timber for the church.[38] In this perspective, the main reason to include *Bjarnar saga* in the same codex with the fragment from *Laxdæla saga* is to make a special contrast between the described Icelanders.

However, Þórðr's figure in this story seems to be no less important than Bjǫrn's – not only due to the accent on Þórðr at the beginning and end of the *þáttr*, but also as he is closely connected to Þorkell Eyjólfsson. Firstly, those two characters are associated: not only the *þáttr* starts with the figure of Þorkell Eyjólfsson and then proceeds to Þórðr – they are also friends and kin[39]. Moreover, they share the same characteristic of being conscious of their reputation: Þorkell is described earlier in *Laxdæla saga* with a similar formula as Þórðr: "*Þorkell Eyjólfsson gerðisk höfðingi mikill.* **Helt hann sér mjǫk til vinsælda ok virðingar**".[40]

According to ONP,[41] the characteristic *halda sér til virðingar* is rarely used – much more often, characters care for someone else's reputation and not their own (cf. in the same *Laxdæla saga*: "*Faðir hans* **hélt honum mjǫk til virðingar**"[42]). The cases of *halda sér til virðingar* are not so widespread and they also have one thing in common. The character who is described in this way is either not able to hold his reputation, or even perishes: Þórðr's secret comes out and destroys his relationship with Óddný, and Þorkell Eyjólfsson destroys his relationship with Óláfr and then dies in the storm. Another character described in this way, Bjǫrn Sæmundarson, in *Sturlunga saga*,[43] steps forward to handle the lawsuit against Sturla Þórðarson and not only fails but does not even show up when the case is being discussed. The similarity of all three contexts allows one to see *halda sér til virðingar* as a formula[44]. Considering the semantic aura of *halda sér til virðingar,* and the beginning of *Bjarnar saga* in *Bæjarbók* with Þorkell Eyjólfsson and Þórðr, it is possible to argue that the *þættir* made from *Bjarnar saga* and *Laxdæla saga* could be brought together. These are stories about two powerful men who worry too much about their reputations, which becomes their undoing as Þórðr loses his wife's respect and Þorkell loses not

---

[38] GRØNLIE, *The Saint and the Saga Hero*, p. 244.
[39] Þorkell is Þórðr's *vinr* (*ÍF* 3, p. 126) and *frændi* (*ÍF* 3, p. 209).
[40] Ch. 70; *ÍF* 5, p. 204.
[41] *Old Norse Prose Dictionary*, at <https://onp.ku.dk> (accessed 18.06.2023).
[42] Ch. 24; *ÍF* 5, p. 68.
[43] "*Biorn [Sæmundar] son bio þa i Gunnars-hollte,* **hann hellt ser mest til mannvirðingar** *þeira bre ðra*", in: *Sturlunga saga*, ed. K. KÅLUND, 2 vols. (Copenhagen, 1906-1911), 1, p. 426.
[44] As described in D. SÄVBORG, "The formula in Icelandic saga prose", *Saga-Book* 42 (2018), pp. 51-86.

only Óláfr's good faith but also his life. This interpretation explains the interest of *Bæjarbók*'s compiler in the last dialogue between Þórðr and Óddný and their reluctance to change or cut it (Table 6), even though it is not connected to the story of Bjǫrn and Óláfr. This dialogue becomes the moral of Þórðr's story anticipated from his very first description.

The interest in stories of overbearing men who get punished for their wrong choices seems to come from the *Separate saga of St. Olaf* itself. The story of Þorkell is inserted right after the story of Asbjǫrn selsbani, a Norwegian noble man who was behaving as a *konungr* in pagan Hálogaland — he was providing a public feast three times per year. He killed king Óláfr's retainer but was allowed to stay alive on condition that he agreed to serve in Óláfr's guard[45]. Unfortunately, Asbjǫrn was ill advised by his fellow Hálogaland chieftain and he never joined the guard; in this way, he wronged the king twice and was killed later. Asbjǫrn's story is that of a powerful man who did not listen to Óláfr and paid the price with his head, similar to the story of Þorkell[46] – both of them thought too much of themselves and both died. The story in *Bjarnar saga* is different from this group as Þórðr does not do anything wrong in front of Óláfr (although later, in the longer version of the saga, he kills his retainer Bjǫrn) and, most importantly, according to the saga he does not die. However, the story of Þórðr most probably has been seen as similar to Þorkell's story because it shares the same set of motifs: 1) it is a story of a famous and powerful Icelander who 2) tries to gain more power, either taking something from Óláfr or receiving his help,[47] and 3) at the end his sins are made visible due to the interaction with Óláfr and he gets punished. As *Bæjarbók* is coming from the same region as *Bjarnar saga* and *Laxdœla saga*,[48] I believe that *Bjarnar saga* and the

---

[45] Corresponding to ch. 117-120 in *Óláfs saga helga* in *Heimskringla*. *Bjarnar saga* is inserted after the fragment about the jarls of Orkney (after ch. 103 according to *Óláfs saga helga* in *Heimskringla*). For the edition of the *Separate Saga of St. Olaf*, see *Den store saga om Olav den Heilige: efter pergament håndskrift i Kungiliga Biblioteket i Stockholm nr. 2 4to med varianter fra andre håndskrifter*, ed. O.A. JOHNSSON and J. HELGASON, 2 vols. (Oslo, 1941).

[46] In a way, it is also the story of Þorgeirr, one of the protagonists of *Fóstbrœðra saga*, that is inserted in *Bæjarbók* right after the fragment from *Laxdœla saga* – Þorgeirr decides to leave Óláfr against his advice.

[47] Asbjǫrn wants to continue giving public feasts and needs to import barley from Óláfr's territories; Þorkell needs Óláfr's timber to build the church that would be higher that the king's; Þórðr receives Óláfr's help to get the money from his deceased relative — potentially it will help him to become more prominent in Iceland (although this motivation is never stated explicitly).

[48] Most of the events in *Laxdœla saga* occur in the Helgafell region and *Bæjarbók* has also been traced back to Helgafell scriptorium (S. DRECHSLER, *Illuminated Manuscript Production in Medieval Iceland: Literary and Artistic Activities of the Monastery at Helgafell in the Fourteenth Century* (Turnhout, 2021), pp. 27, 44, 146-147); *Bjarnar saga* also takes place close to

story of Þorkell Eyjólffsson have been included in *Bæjarbók* as examples from the local tradition, answering the thematic thread that already existed in Óláfs saga. Hence, the focus on the overbearing men interacting with Óláfr created a specific copying situation, where the compiler kept the fragments they needed intact and worked more creatively on the parts of the text that could be, in their opinion, refined. This creative editing process led not only to cuts, additions, and changes, important for the narrative strategy, but also to the general retelling mode that I have tried to describe above.

To understand this form better, let us consider one more example from the *konungasögur* tradition.

2. Ágrip af nóregskonungasögum *and* Heimskringla

Heimskingla is known to have been drawing information from several contemporary written histories of the Norwegian kings; among them was one of the so-called Norwegian synopses, *Ágrip af nóregskonungasögum*.[49] I will focus on the story preceding the death of jarl Hákon Sigurðsson – one of the episodes in which *Heimskringla* relates to *Ágrip* very closely.[50] To see how the story from *Ágrip* is used in *Heimskringla*, I have compared the only existing manuscript of *Ágrip* with the text of *Heimskringla* according to the *Kringla* copies provided in Finnur Jónsson's edition (AM 35 fol., AM 36 fol., AM 63 fol.).[51] As my analysis is based on the critical editions and their apparatus, it should be approached with caution; however, it can be seen as a useful model to be verified in future work.

Helgafell region.

[49] The overview of the *Heimskringla* sources can be found in G. Storm, *Snorri Sturlassöns historieskrivning: En kritisk undersøgelse*. (Copenhagen, 1873); B. AÐALBJARNARSON, "Formáli", in: *Heimskringla*, ed. B. AÐALBJARNARSON, 3 vols. (Reykjavík, 1941) (*Íslenzk Fornrit* 36-38); D. WHALEY, *Heimskringla: An Introduction* (London, 1991), pp. 63-74. For the discussion of *Ágrip*'s preservation see M.-J. DRISCOLL, "Introduction", in: *Ágrip af Nóregskonungasögum: A Twelfth-Century Synoptic History of the Kings of Norway*, ed. and trans. M.-J. DRISCOLL, 2nd edn. (London, 2008), pp. IX-XXV.

[50] I have discussed this case in comparison to Old East Slavonic *Primary Chronicle* in a recent article; see: D. GLEBOVA "Retelling as the historian's art: Approaching the forms of transmission in historical writing of Old Rus' and Scandinavia", *Slavianovedenie* 4 (2020), pp. 30-49 (in Russian).

[51] Snorri Sturluson. *Heimskringla: Nóregs konunga sǫgur*, ed. F. JÓNSSON, 3 vols. (Copenhagen, 1893-1901), 1 (henceforth: Hkr.); see the discussion of the manuscripts and their usage in the edition *ibid.*, pp. II-LIV, and also JØRGENSEN, *Det tapte håndskriftet Kringla*, pp. 9-90. *Ágrip* is taken according to *Ágrip af Nóregskonungasögum*. For the edition, see n. 49.

Similar to the case of the *Bjarnar saga* versions, there is a significant difference in the narrative strategy in Hákon's story in *Ágrip* and in *Heimskringla*. In both works the story begins with the jarl wishing to meet Guðrún Lundasól from Gaulardal – in the general storyline this episode acts as a motivation for Hákon's confrontation with people of Gaulardal, which leads to his decision to leave his retinue and hide alone with his slave Karkr, thus giving the latter a possibility to kill Hákon during his sleep. However, in each version this meeting with Guðrún functions in different ways (see Table 7). In *Ágrip* it illustrates Hákon's resentful, unethical character: the jarl seeks Guðrun's audience *til ósæmðar* ('for shameful reasons'), and Guðrún fights for her honour by summoning the neighbourhood ready to help her. In this way jarl Hákon at first deals only with a woman and his ignoble desires but then *suddenly* opposes the whole region of Norway – for this he is brutally punished by an ignominious death. The narrator of *Heimskringla* downgrades Guðrún's role in the resistance to the jarl and gives the leading role to her husband, Ormr: Hákon sends people to take his wife and now it is Ormr who summons the people to stand against the jarl (*Ágrip*: "þá hafði *hón* svá liði safnat at" ("then *she* has summoned the people") / *Heimskringla*: "þá váru komnir *til Orms* margir menn ór bygðinni, er *hann* hafði orð sent" ("then had come many men *to Ormr* from the neighbourhood to whom *he* had sent a word")). With this change, in *Heimskringla* Hákon confronts the people of Gaulardal from the very beginning; his desire to get Guðrún works as a manifestation of power, even if he is unsuccessful, rather than as an illustration of his moral qualities as it does in *Ágrip*.

Table 7

#	Ágrip, Ch. 13, p. 22	Hkr., Kap. 48, p. 348
1	*En hann fýsti eitthvert sinni til* konu ₁**þeirar** er Guðrún ₂hét Lundasól. *Hón bjó á Lundum í Gauladali,*	*Hákon jarl var á veizlu í Gaulardal at Meðalhúsum, en skip hans lágu út við Viggju. Ormr lyrgja er maðr nefndr, ríkr bóndi, hann bjó á Búnesi, hann átti* konu, ₁**þá** er Guðrún ₂er nefnd,[1] *dóttir Bergþórs af Lundum*; *hon var kǫlluð* Lundasól, *hon var kvenna fríðust.*

II	₁*ok* ₂**gerði hann** *af Meðalhúsum* **þræla sína at** ₃**taka hana ok flytja sér** *til ósœmðar.* En ₄**meðan þrælarnir mǫtuðusk,** þá <u>hafði hón svá liði safnat at</u> þá ₅**var eigi kostr at** ₆**flytja hana,** *ok* ₇**sendi hón þá orð** *Hákoni* jarli at hón mundi eigi ₈**á hans fund soekja,** nema hann sendi *konu þá er hann hafði er* ₉**Þóra hét á Remoli.** *En eftir þau orð sækir hann upp í Gauladal með ǫllu liði sínu.*	₁₂**Jarl sendi þræla sína** *til Orms þeirra ørenda,* at ₃**hafa Guðrúnu,** *konu Orms,* ₃**til jarls.** *Þrælar báru upp ørendi sín; Ormr bað þá fyrst fara til náttverðar,* en ₄**áðr þrælar hǫfðu matazk,** þá <u>váru komnir til Orms margir menn ór bygðinni, er hann hafði orð sent. Lét Ormr</u> þá ₅**engan kost,** at ₆**Guðrún fœri með þrælunum.** ₇**Guðrún mælti, bað þræla svá segja** jarli, at hon myndi eigi ₈**til hans koma,** nema hann sendi *eptir henni* ₉**Þóru af Rimul;** *hon var húsfreyja rík ok ein af unnostum jarls. Þrælarnir segja, at þeir skulu þar svá koma ǫðru sinni, at bóndi ok húsfreyja munu þessa iðrast skambragðs, ok heitast þrælarnir mjǫk ok fara brott síðan.*
III	En <u>Halldórr á Skerðingssteðju</u> ₁**skar upp** ǫr ₂**allt at dalinum, ok** ₃**sótti alla vega flokkr á mót hónum.**	En <u>Ormr</u> ₁**lét fara** *herǫr* ₂**fjögurra vegna um bygðina,** ok ₃**lét þat boði fylgja, at allir skyldu með vápnum fara at Hákoni jarli** *ok drepa hann, ok sendi til Halldórs á Skerðingssteðju, en Halldórr lét þegar fara herör.*

¹ et nefnd] het F/ J1 (Hkr., p. 348).

According to Gustav Storm and Bjarni Aðalbjarnason, the figure of Ormr, unknown to the compiler of *Ágrip*, comes to the *Heimskringla* narrator from *Óláfs saga Odds*,[52] just as the mentioning of Brynjólfr's story and some other details.[53] Thus, *Óláfs saga Odds* provided new information that allowed the *Heimskringla* narrator to rethink the story of Hákon's downfall. Again the change in the narrative strategy is accompanied by a huge amount of synonymous variation not directly connected to the introduction of Ormr (see Table 7). Some of the variants correspond to the narrator's choice of syntax, such as period structuring (e.g. to connect the sentences with *ok* ('and') or to start paratactically from the subject; see II, 1: ₁*ok* gerði hann ('and made he') / ₁Jarl

---

[52] *Óláfs saga Odds*, ed. in: *Færeyinga saga – Óláfs saga Odds*, ed. Ó. HALLDÓRSSON (Reykjavík, 2006: *Íslenzsk Fornrit* 15), pp. 276.
[53] For a discussion of *Óláfs saga Odds* in relation to *Ágrip*, see: STORM, *Snorri Sturlassöns historieskrivning*, pp. 141-142, and B. AÐALBJARNARSON, *Formáli*, pp. CXIV-CXVI.

sendi ('Jarl sent')).[54] Other variants are contextual synonyms possibly manifesting the new narrator's preference of wording.[55] The sequence of variants remains unchanged and is very dense.

A similar correspondence between *Ágrip* and *Heimskringla* continues in the description of Karkr's dreams (Table 8). The majority of variants are morphological or lexical synonyms positioned in close proximity to each other (from 0 to 3 words between the variant readings) and thus forming variant sequences. Although not formulaic *per se*, these sequences are reminiscent of lexico-grammatical stable structure that is natural for formulaic language,[56] e.g.:

Table 8 (I) en þeir $_7$**fluttusk** í helli $_8$**einn** er $_9$**enn** $_{10}$**heitir** Jarlshellir *í Gauladali* / en þeir $_7$**fóru** í helli $_8$**þann,** er $_9$**síðan** $_{10}$**er kallaðr** Jarlshellir = en þeir ('and they') + $_7$verb for movement + í helli ('in cave') + $_8$pronoun connected to 'helli' + er ('that') + $_9$time adverb + $_{10}$naming construction.

Table 8 (II) $_{13}$*En* $_{14}$**jarlinn** $_{15}$**skilði** $_{16}$**í því kominn** $_{17}$**endadag** $_{18}$**sinn** / $_{13\ 14}$**hann** $_{15}$**grunaði** $_{16}$**at slíkt mundi vera fyrir** $_{17}$**skamlífi** $_{18}$**hans** = $_{13}$variant for periodic structure (beginning with 'enn' or with the subject) + $_{14}$anaphoric indication for jarl (with def.art / pers. pron.) + $_{15}$ verb for 'understand, think' + $_{16}$ construction for 'in this way comes' (with participle / with subjunctive + infinitive) + $_{17}$ noun for 'the end of life' + $_{18}$ pronoun signifying subject (possessive / personal in gen.sg.)

---

[54] For a discussion of periodic structure in Old Norse-Icelandic sagas, see: A.-C. BOUMAN, *Observations on Syntax and Style of Some Icelandic Sagas, with Special Reference to the Relation Between Viga-glums Saga and Reykdœla Saga* (Reykjavik and Copenhagen, 1956); Y.K. KUZMENKO, "Some syntactic and stylistic peculiarities of period in Old Icelandic prose", in: *Works on the Historical Syntax of Germanic Languages* (Leningrad, 1991) (in Russian).

[55] II, 2: **gerði** þræla sína ('made his servants go') / **sendi** þræla sína ('sent his servants'); 3: **taka hana ok flytja sér** ('to take her and bring to him') / **hafa Guðrúnu,** konu Orms, **til jarls** ('take Gudrun, Orms wife, to jarl'); 4: **meðan þrælarnir mǫtuðusk** ('while the servants were eating') / **áðr þrælar hǫfðu matazk** ('before the servants had eaten'), etc.

[56] See SÄVBORG, "The formula in Icelandic saga prose".

Table 8

#	Ágrip, Ch. 13, p. 22	Hkr., Kap. 48, p. 350
I	₁En ₂hann ok þræll hans ₃Karkr riðu vakar nekkurar ok ₄drekkðu þar hesti ₅hans ok létu eftir ₆skikkju hans *ok svá sverð á ísinum*, en þeir ₇fluttusk í helli ₈einn er ₉enn ₁₀heitir Jarlshellir *í Gauladali*. Ok sofnaði þar þrællinn, *ok lét illa*, ₁₁ok sagði síðan, er ₁₂hann vaknaði, at maðr svartr ok illiligr fór hjá hellinum, ok ₁₃óttaðisk hann at hann mundi inn ganga, ₁₄ok sagði hónum at Ulli var ₁₅drepinn.	*Fór* ₂jarl[1] ₁þá ok þræll hans *með honum*, ₃er Karkr er nefndr. Íss var á Gaul, ok ₄hratt *jarl* þar ₄í hesti ₅sínum, ok *þar* lét hann eptir ₆mǫttul sinn, en þeir ₇fóru í helli ₈þann, er ₉síðan ₁₀er kallaðr Jarlshellir. Þá[2] sofnuðu þeir; *en* er ₁₂Karkr vaknaði, ₁₁þá segir hann draum sinn, at maðr svartr ok illiligr fór hjá hellinum, ok ₁₃hræddisk hann *þat*, at hann myndi inn ganga, ₁₄en *sá maðr* sagði honum, at Ulli var ₁₅dauðr.
II	₁*En* ₂jarlinn ₃svaraði at *þá* myndi vera drepinn ₄sunr hans, *ok svá varð ok*. ₅Sofnar ₆þrællinn ₇í annat sinni, ok lætr ₈eigi betr en fyrr, ₉sagði síðan at inn ₁₀sami maðr ₁₁hafði þá ₁₁farit ofan aftr, ok bað segja ₁₂jarlinum at þá váru lokin sund ǫll. ₁₃*En* ₁₄jarlinn ₁₅skilði ₁₆í því kominn endadag sinn, *ok fluttisk til Remols til konu þeirar er Þóra hét, er var friðla hans*,	₁₂Jarl ₃segir, at ₄Erlendr[3] mundi drepinn. ₅*Enn* sofnar ₆Þormóðr Karkr[4] ₇öðru sinni ok lætr ₈illa í svefni[5], *en er hann vaknar*, ₉segir hann draum sinn, at *hann sá* þá inn ₁₀sama mann ₁₁fara ofan aptr ok bað *þá* segja ₁₂jarli, at þá váru lokin sund ǫll. *Karkr segir jarli drauminn;* ₁₃ ₁₄hann ₁₅grunaði, at slíkt myndi vera fyrir skamlífi hans. *Síðan stóð hann upp, ok gengu þeir á bœinn Rimul; þá sendi jarl Kark á fund Þóru, ok bað hana koma leyniliga til sín.*

[1] jarl] hann AM 45 fol. (henceforth: F) (Hkr., p. 350).
[2] þá] F (Hkr., p. 350).
[3] Erlendr] s. hans AM 37 fol. (henceforth: J1) (Hkr., p. 350).
[4] Þormóðr Karkr] þrællinn J1 (Hkr., p. 350).
[5] í svefni] sem fyrr J1 (Hkr., p. 350).

Hákon's death episode in *Heimskingla* is much shorter than the fragment of *Bjarnar saga* discussed above. Only one place here shows a more or less long identical sequence of words (see the description of the first Karkr's dream in Table 8 (I, 11-15)), so it is impossible to speak about switching between the copying modes. However, *Heimskringla* contains a number of fragments, including parts of the Snjófrið episode (see a fragment in Table 9, II), which are transmitted from *Ágrip* almost word-for-word. The existence of such close copied fragments presents a conundrum similar to the one already discussed: either a part of the Snjófrið episode was copied by a different hand or the *Heimskringla* compiler switched between modes of copying. Anyway, it is important to note that Hákon's death episode was hugely influenced by another source while the Snjófrið episode is known only from *Ágrip* (and this might have been the case in the thirteenth century as well). One of the possible conjectures is that the example of *Heimskringla* shows how different the goals of the compiler could be: with Snjófrið they aimed to preserve the text as it was not found anywhere else, while with Hákon's story they wanted to improve it.

Table 9

	Ágrip, Ch. 4-5, p. 6	Hkr., Kap. 24, p. 134
I	Ok hann festi ok fekk ok unni svá með œrslum, at ríki sitt ok allt þat er **hans tígn** byrjaði þá **fyrlét** hann ok sat **hjá** henni *nótt ok dag náliga, meðan þau lifðu bæði, ok* .iij. vetr *síðan hón var dauð*.	en konungr festi *Snæfriði* ok fekk, ok unni svá með œrslum, at ríki sitt ok alt þat, er **honum** byrjaði, þá **fyrir lét** hann. *Þau áttu iiii. sonu, einn var Sigurðr hrísi, Hálfdan háleggr, Guðrøðr ljómi, Rǫgnvaldr réttilbeini. Síðan dó Snæfriðr, en litr hennar skipaðisk á engan veg, var hon þá jamrjóð, sem þá, er hon var kvik.* Konungr sat æ **yfir** henni *ok hugði, at hon myndi lifna. Fór svá fram iii. vetr, at*
II	Syrgði hann hana dauða, en landslýðr allr syrgði hann villtan. En þessa villu at lægja kom til læknanar Þorleif<r> spaki, er með viti lægði þá villu *ok* með eftirmæli með þessum hætti: 'Eigi er, konungr, kynligt, attu munir svá fríða konu ok kynstóra, ok tígnir hana á dúni ok á guðvefi sem hón bað þik. En tígn þín er þó minni en hœfir – ok hennar – í því at hón liggr of lengi í sama fatnaði. Er mykłu sannligra at hón sé hrœrð.	hann syrgði hana dauða, en allr landzlýðr syrgði hann viltan; en þessa villu at lægja kom til læknar[1] Þorleifr spaki, er með viti lægði þá villu *fyrst* með eptirmæli með þessum hætti: eigi er, konungr, kynligt, at þú munir svá fríða konu ok kynstóra ok tígnir hana á dúni ok á guðvefi, sem hon bað þik, en tígn þín er þó minni, en hœfir, ok hennar í því, at hon liggr ofrlengi í sama fatnaði, *ok* er miklu sannara[2], at hon sé hrœrð, *ok sé skipt undir henni klæðum.*

[1] læknar] læknanar J1 (Hkr., p. 134).
[2] sannara] sannligra F/J1 (Hkr., p. 134).

Conclusions

The close analysis of variation between the versions of *Bjarnar saga hítdælakappa* shows that, while they are very similar in length, they do have much micro-variation between them. Although some of this depends on the change in the characterisation of the protagonists, Þórðr and Bjǫrn, most of the variant readings are synonymous and dispersed in a dense and more or less random way, i.e. this variation is non-functional from a point of view of narrative strategy. This type of correspondance between the versions, which I have called a 'retelling', is sometimes interrupted by the blocks of text that in both versions are very similar and that are also in accordance with the narrative strategy of *Bæjarbók*: for example, while the scene of Oddný's disappointment in Þórðr follows the general line of Þórðr's characterisation in *Bæjarbók* as a proud Icelander who is punished, information about the relics agrees with the strategy of St. Óláfr's holy story that *Bæjarbók* is based on. These two observations give an opportunity to argue that the scribe who copied *Bjarnar saga* in *Bæjarbók* could switch between the two modes of copying: the text was copied closely when it agreed with the scribe's view, and it was copied in the mode of 'retelling' when there was something in conflict with the scribe's general perception of the story.

The very form of the retelling poses many questions, as it is not clear why synonymous variation invades the text far beyond the narrative changes. The example from *Ágrip* within *Heimskringla* helps to understand this form better. When the compiler of *Heimskingla* looks for the sources on the early history of Norwegian kings, he turns to *Ágrip*. However, the scribe already knows *Óláfs saga Odds* that provides them with new information and changes their interpretation of the story – the focus moves from Guðrún to Ormr, her husband, and with him to the *bóndar* of Gaulardal in general. This new perception of the narrative does not allow the scribe to copy the text word-for-word from *Ágrip*, as was supposedly done with the Snjófrið episode, and thus they turn to the retelling mode: it is not enough to just add the name of Guðrún's husband or to change the name of the character who sends the signal arrow, the words between and around the narrative changes are also substituted by their synonymous morphological, lexical, or syntactical equivalents. The crossroads between at least two different sources creates a specific linguistic situation that forms a very particular language practice – a copying of the text by retelling it. A similar linguistic situation can be reconstructed for *Bjarnar saga* in *Bæjar-*

bók, as the narrative strategy of the codex influences the copying mode of the saga text.

The language practice behind the retelling stays, however, the most intriguing part, as it cannot be explained only by ideological narrative changes or by consistent usage of any particular style. The problem is that this small and random micro-variation does not come from the scribes' general interpretation of the text or their pragmatic decision to compress or expand the source or make it more or less archaic. Rather, it is a manifestation of individual scribal preferences that emerge due to the very necessity to change the narrative. Here the form of variation discussed in the chapter becomes especially significant, as the sequences of synonyms are a feature quite common in oral composition and formulaic language. As a means of opening the discussion, it might be suggested that in a situation when the scribes were dealing with texts that they perceived as historiography, the source text worked as a borderline just the same as the tradition did for the singers of oral poetry. Although the necessity to change the narrative made them freer in expressing their language preferences, they were also constrained by the source text and the environment of historiography and, thus, could not move further than synonymy would allow them to go. Thus, the retelling can be seen as a form of scribal improvisation within the given textual structure. The question remains whether there is a correlation between the existing genre distinction and the type of variation in the medieval Old Norse-Icelandic saga manuscript tradition.

Depicting Violence in *Íslendingasögur*: A Formula on the Verge of Legal Tradition

EUGENIA KRISTINA VOROBEVA

The ongoing debate about the nature of formulaic language has long focused on its oral origins, bringing forth the 'oral' part of the oral-formulaic theory. However, lately, scholars tend to turn more and more attention to the second part of the compound, allowing for various degrees of orality, aurality, and literacy. Whether formulaic expressions come from oral composition or shared cultural literary tradition (or both), they play an important role in the literary works we know, surviving exclusively in a manuscript form – as a written text.[1] Recent studies in Old English suggest that shared formulaic sequences and parallels might as well have been part of a literate booklore tradition and may even have originated from works composed in Latin.[2] The formulaic theory focuses primarily on verse form which follows metrical struc-

---

[1] For a concise discussion of the saga-origins see J.L. BYOCK, "Saga form, oral prehistory, and the Icelandic social context', *New Literary History* 16.1 (1984), pp. 153-173.

[2] See A. ORCHARD, "Old English and Anglo-Latin: The odd couple", in: *A Companion to British Literature Part I: Medieval Literature 700-1450*, ed. R. DEMARIA, H. CHANG, and S. ZACHER (Malden, MA, and Oxford, 2014), pp. 273-292. For a comprehensive and helpful overview of a formulaic theory, see A. POWELL, *Verbal Parallels in Andreas and its Relationship to Beowulf and Cynewulf* (PhD thesis, University of Cambridge, 2002), pp. 17-49.

New Light on Formulas in Oral Poetry and Prose, ed. Daniel SÄVBORG and Bernt Ø. THORVALDSEN, *Utrecht Studies in Medieval Literacy*, 57 (Turnhout: Brepols, 2023), pp. 287-302.

BREPOLS PUBLISHERS   DOI <10.1484/M.USML-EB.5.133556>

ture and it thus requires specific fillers attuned to rules and conventions of both metre and, as is the case with Germanic languages, alliterative patterns. Hence the iconic definition suggested by Milman Parry, which has already turned into a fossilised formula itself.[3] However, as time progressed, the study of formulas has been expanded to their role and function in prose and has developed into a more comprehensive system of formula-theme-motif.[4]

Formulas, Violence, and the Family Sagas

The idea of formulas resonates with the family saga genre and its narrative style, keen to implement literary conventions, stock scenes, characters, and widely known imagery.[5] The sagas are often seen as constructed according to particular patterns and following certain narrative scripts.[6] Therefore, the saga narrative can be seen as based on a "formula for a story pattern" and characterised by formulaic syntax – notions usually applied to the structure of poetic texts and exclusively legendary sagas.[7] Although many scholars have addressed formulas in their research of the *Íslendingasögur*, until Daniel Sävborg's article

---

[3] "The formula in the Homeric poems may be defined as a *group of words which is regularly employed under the same metrical conditions to express a given essential idea*" (M. PARRY, "Studies in the epic technique of oral verse-making, I, Homer and Homeric style", *Harvard Studies in Classical Philology* 41 (1930), pp. 73-148, at p. 80).

[4] See, e.g. D. FRY, "Old English formulaic themes and type-scenes", *Neophilologus* 52 (1968), pp. 48-54. On Fry's modification of a formulaic system, see also POWELL, *Verbal Parallels*, p. 29.

[5] C.J. CLOVER, "Icelandic family sagas", in: *Old Norse-Icelandic Literature: A Critical Guide*, ed. C.J. CLOVER and J. LINDOW (Ithaca, 1985), pp. 239-315, at p. 288. See Lars Lönnroth's discussion of formula and how it might evolve into a theme and a motif in L. LÖNNROTH, *Njáls Saga: A Critical Introduction* (Berkeley, 1976).

[6] Th.M. ANDERSSON, *The Icelandic Family Saga: An Analytic Reading* (Cambridge, MA, 1967); J.L. BYOCK, *Feud in the Icelandic Saga* (Los Angeles and London, 1983). For a comprehensive overview of the structuralist approach, see L. LÖNNROTH, "Structuralist approaches to saga literature", in: *Learning and Understanding in the Old Norse World: Essays in Honour of Margaret Clunies Ross*, ed. J. QUINN, K. HESLOP, and T. WILLS (Turnhout, 2007), pp. 63-73.

[7] M. FOX, *Following the Formula in Beowulf, Örvar-Odds Saga, and Tolkien* (Cham, 2020), p. IV. Fox gives a useful summary of formula-related scholarship in the field of the Old English literature and argues for "the broad applicability of the term formula for the compositional process" (p. IX): "That formula is in fact very complicated, for it begins with a formula for a story-pattern, and that formula has various smaller levels of formula embedded within it" (p. IV). Also, for the similar approach to the Old Norse material, see S.A. MELLOR, "Revisiting the formula and mythic patterns and the interplay between *the Poetic Edda* and *Vǫlsunga saga*", in this volume, pp. 221-251.

on formulas in the *Íslendingasögur* there was no comprehensive "description of formulas in saga prose", nor was their "role as a central stylistic feature" sufficiently clarified.[8]

As formulas "arouse the expectation of the audience",[9] it can be hardly surprising that feuding – an element central to the plot – relies heavily not only on stock scenes and motifs but also on formulaic lexical framing. It is well attested that such formulas as *venja kvámur sínar* ('to be wont to visit'), *vera í blári kápu* ('to wear a black cape') or even Grettir's 'no reaction' formula introduce a conflict and are "charged with connotations of violence".[10] However, owing perhaps to the "fusion of letters and axes",[11] the sagas of the Icelanders display various lexical means and formulas used not only to imply the possibility of violence in the future but also to describe confrontations and infliction of wounds *per se*. These expressions often comply with alliterative patterns, thus making the sequence at once more rhythmic, self-contained, and, as a result, more memorable or recognisable: a feature also ascribed to a medieval Icelandic law code.[12] Considering that medieval Icelandic society experienced "quite a long period of not even mere interplay, but the very merging of culture and tradition with the law",[13] it is not surprising that the violence-related language shares with the law codes more than just a penchant for alliteration.

Legalism and Formulaic Syntax in the Sagas

Many attack scenes in the sagas are constructed after the pattern encountered in the law-code *Grágás,* extant in two manuscripts dated from around 1260 and 1280, or rather in its section on homicide – *vígslóði*.[14] An attack is

---

[8] D. SÄVBORG, "The formula in Icelandic Saga Prose", *Saga-Book* 42 (2018), pp. 51-86, at p. 51.

[9] *Ibid.*, p. 81.

[10] SÄVBORG, 'The formula in Icelandic saga prose', p. 66; S. RANKOVIĆ, "The exquisite tempers of Grettir the Strong", *Scandinavian Studies* 89 (2017), pp. 375-412, at pp. 385-394.

[11] W.I. MILLER, *Bloodtaking and Peacemaking: Feud, Law, and Society in Saga Iceland* (Chicago, 1997), p. 36.

[12] For the discussion of alliteration, orality and formulas in *Grágás,* see M.P. MCGLYNN, "Orality in the Old Icelandic Grágás – Legal formulae in the assembly procedures section", *Neophilologus* 93 (2009), pp. 521-536.

[13] M. KOSZOWSKI, 'Medieval Iceland: The influence of culture and tradition on law", *Scandinavian Studies* 86.3 (2014), pp. 333-351, at p. 335.

[14] *Laws of Early Iceland: Gragas, the Codex Regius of Gragas, with Material from Other Manuscripts*, ed. A. DENNIS, P.G. FOOTE, and R. PERKINS, 1 (Winnipeg, 2006), p. 13.

considered a basic opening act of a transgression and is usually denoted as *hlaup, ahlaup,* or *frumhlaup.* While the law code features the descriptive noun, the sagas prefer the verb (*hlaupa*): it depicts an action performed by saga characters in legalistic terms and also describes movement, often accompanied by a preposition often accompanying the verb. Such an opening of the scene – starting with *hlaupa* – usually introduces a wider confrontation which is sometimes similarly described by the verbs used in *Grágás* to talk about the actions constituting an attack and calling for an outlawry. Their number is limited to nine situations, five of which are punished by 'minor outlawry' – *fiorbaugs garðr* (unless there are such aggravating circumstances as major or mortal wounds), while the other four ensue *scog gangr,* or 'major outlawry'. These are expressed by the following verbs: 1) *höggva* ('to cut'), *leggja* ('to thrust'), *skjóta* ('to shoot'), *verpa* ('to throw'), and *drepa* ('to strike'); and 2) *fella* ('to fell'), *ruska* ('to shake'), *ræna* ('to wrest'), and *kyrkja* ('to strangle').[15] The second group is not very frequent in the sagas. However, the first five verbs often describe a violent transgression and, as mentioned above, are introduced by the verb *hlaupa*. Quite frequently in the *Íslendingasögur* these verbs are complemented in a sentence with weapons used and bodily parts involved in the attack. The following passage from *Ljósvetninga saga,* for instance, illustrates this pattern: "*Síðan* hljóp *hann fram með brugðit sverð, ok* hjó *þegar til Guðmundar, en hann hopaði undan*" ("Then he dashed forward with a raised sword and immediately dealt a blow to Gudmundr, but he backed down").[16] Or, yet another comprehensive example, this time from *Valla-Ljóts saga*: "*Hann sprettr upp ok* hleypr *at honum ok* hjó *hann* banahǫgg" ("He sprung up and attacked him and dealt him a death-blow").[17] In these examples, *hlaupa* is followed by the verb from the list above – *höggva,* which in the latter case is a part of an alliterative formulaic sequence *höggva banahögg* ('to deal a death-blow') appearing in multiple sagas. Moreover, in both instances, *hlaupa* itself becomes a part of an alliterative pattern: *hljóp – hjó – hopaði* and *hann – hleypr – hánum – höggr – hann – banahögg,* respectively.

Found in *Grágás* and employed in the saga narrative, this sequence of verbs turns the scene into a formulaic and somewhat legalistic account of a

---

[15] *Grágás: Islændernes Lovbog i Fristatens Tid, udgivet efter det Kongelige Bibliotheks Haandskrift,* ed. V. FINSEN, 1-2 (Odense, 1974; originally Copenhagen, 1852), pp. 144-145.

[16] The text of the saga is cited from *Ljósvetninga saga,* in: *Ljósvetninga saga,* ed. Björn SIGFÚSSON (Reykjavík, 1940: *Íslenzk Fornrit* 10), pp. 3-147, at p. 52. All translations throughout the article are my own, unless otherwise stated.

[17] The text of the saga is cited from *Valla-Ljóts saga,* in: *Eyrfirðinga sögur,* ed. Jonas KRISTJANSSON (Reykjavík, 1956: *Íslenzk Fornrit* 9), p. 235.

transgression: the narrative description follows the lexical and syntactical order found in the law code, thus composing the prepared legal case. Such narrative arrangement of an attack automatically introduces the deed into the legal sphere.

Wounds as Embodied Violence

Injuries, wounds, and the punishment following their infliction are rather meticulously described in *Grágás*. The law code goes into detail and elaborates on what is to be considered an injury, or more specifically, a blow or a wound; it goes so far as to differentiate between various degrees, each of which is concisely outlined and accompanied by a commentary. There were distinguished minor (*minna sár*) and major wounds (*meira sár*).[18] The latter is encountered in the text of *Grágás* to refer to serious wounds which could lead to one's death and apparently encompassed such categories as *heilundar, holundar, oc mergundar sár* ('internal, brain, or marrow wound'). These terms were not, however, used in the family sagas.[19] Instead, a collocation *mikit sár* ('big wound') was a general, albeit in no case unique, way of describing any serious injury in the sagas of the Icelanders. It could be easily juxtaposed with the legal category of *meira sár* ('major wound'), as *meira* is the comparative degree of an adjective *mikill*.[20] *Áverki* ('injury') is another term present in both saga and legal traditions: in the latter it denotes any physical damage to one's body, be

---

[18] *Grágás*, ed. FINSEN, p.153. Cf. *Norges Gamle Love Indtil 1387*, ed. R. KEYSER and P.A. MUNCH (Christiania, 1847), 2, p.117: "*skolu þeir hafa auerka bot eptir uirðingu. huart sem auerki er meiri eða minni*" ("they shall have compensation for the injury according to its value, whether it be a major or minor injury).

[19] See, however, an example of its use in legendary sagas. *Hervarar saga ok Heiðreks* manifests the following use of these categories: "*En ekki var þat kvikt, hvárki menn né kvikendi, er lifa mætti til annars dag, ef sár fekk af honum, hvárt sem* var meira eða minna [emphasis mine – E.V.]" ["And there was no living thing, neither man nor creature, that could live another day, if they got a wound by him [viz. by Tyrfing the sword – E.V.], whether it be a major or minor [wound]"] – *Hervarar saga ok Heiðreks*, ed. G. TURVILLE-PETRE (London, 1956; reprinted Exeter, 2014), p.1. The legendary sagas obviously do not function according to Icelandic legalities. The example is even more curious as it describes the effect produced by the magic sword Tyrfing, causing death to anybody it hits, regardless of the seriousness of the injury – therefore, an elaboration that both major (which is to be expected) and minor (*sic!*) wounds inflicted by this sword seems superfluous, as all its wounds were considered lethal.

[20] 'meiri', in: R. CLEASBY, Guðbrandur VIGFÚSSON, and W.A. CRAIGIE, *An Icelandic-English Dictionary* (Oxford, 1957), s.v.

it a wound or a blow.[21] In the family sagas, though, it might be used interchangeably with *sár* when collocated with an adjective *mikill* – *mikill áverki* ('big injury') – and referred likewise to wounds which belonged to the category of serious injuries. Following Hannah Burrows' argument and terminology, it might be assumed that these collocations can be seen as "legalities" constituting a "saga law" which functions within the logics of individual sagas and differs from the "reality of *Grágás*".[22] Therefore in the saga reality both *mikit sár* and *mikill áverki* might be seen as a case of the so-called legal formulas, even though they do not follow the law code verbatim.[23] For this reason they will be further referred to as 'legalistic' formulas hereafter.

Addressing inflicted wounds and injuries was an important part of both the law code and the saga narrative, where they acted as embodied violence, a kind of 'currency' in a feud: in the sagas of Icelanders "the tallying of injuries and wounds" played a significant role within the legal tradition and was used for "exacting appropriate compensation from the opposing party".[24] Moreover, as one passage from *Njáls saga* clearly shows, demonstration of the injuries inflicted by perpetrators served as a testimony of transgression: "*(...) fóru [þeir] þegar á fund hans ok sǫgðu honum hrakning sína ok sýndu honum sár sín*" ("they came to him and told about their maltreatment and showed him their wounds").[25]

---

[21] *Grágás*, ed. FINSEN, pp. 149-150.

[22] H. BURROWS, "Cold cases: Law and legal detail in the *Íslendingasögur*", *Parergon*, 26.1 (2009), pp. 35-56, at p. 36.

[23] LÖNNROTH, *Njáls saga*, p. 45. Sävborg has regarded them as "quotations within the sagas rather than precisely saga formulas proper". However, it might be argued in this case that these formulas are the ones belonging to the 'saga law' and cannot be seen as quotations in the strict sense (SÄVBORG, "The Formula in Icelandic saga prose", p. 56). See also an article by Helgi Skúli Kjartansson, who considers it unlikely that "verbal fidelity" was valued too highly at any stage of the *Grágás* transmission (Helgi Skúli KJARTANSSON, "Law recital according to Old Icelandic law: Written evidence of oral transmission?", in: *Á austrvega: Saga and East Scandinavia*: *Preprint Papers of the 14th International Saga Conference, Uppsala, Sweden, August 9-15*, 1, ed. A. NEY, H. WILLIAMS, and F. CHARPENTIER LJUNGQVIST (Gävle, 2009), pp. 373-378, at p. 374).

[24] Haki ANTONSSON, *Damnation and Salvation in Old Norse Literature* (Cambridge, 2018), p. 109. For a more detailed analysis of the tallying mechanism in *Eyrbyggja saga* see E. VOROBEVA, "Balancing of wounds and injuries in *Eyrbyggja Saga* and the poetics of saga narrative", in: *Problemy istorii i kultury srednevekovogo obschestva. Materialy XXXVIII vserossijskoy nauchnoy konferentsii studentov, aspirantov i molodyh uchenyh 'Kurbatovskiye Chtenija'* [Problems of History and Culture of Medieval Society. Materials of XXXVIII All-Russian Medievalist Conference *'Kurbatovskiye Chtenija'*] (Saint Petersburg, 2018), pp. 120-125.

[25] The text of the saga is quoted after *Brennu-Njáls saga*, ed. Einar Ól. SVEINSSONN (Reykjavík, 1954: *Íslenzk Fornrit* 12), p. 222.

Formula Stating a Serious Injury

However, the intersection of the saga language used to talk about injuries and the law code could have been even more complicated and allusive. *Ok var þat*, and its variations, is a rather common construction used in various saga genres for making a factual statement. As a formula of introduction, either opening or closing a narrative period, it might be considered a typical boundary-marking formula.[26] It could have introduced miscellaneous information relating, for example, to the financial situation, time, relationship, size of one's house, the scale of the battle, or, a matter of particular interest to this article, an outcome of a transgression. The last instance usually concludes descriptive confrontation scenes and serves as a switch from a 'telling' to a 'showing' type of narration:[27] it states the result of an assault, commenting either on wounds (*ok var þat X sár*) or character's condition in general. For example, it might point out a character's inability to fight after being badly injured – *ok varð hann þegar óvígr* ('and immediately he became unfit for fighting').[28]

Therefore, it can be established that the basic productive formula *ok var þat X* ('and that was X') – with its variations *var-varð*, optional conjunction, occasional negation, and differing grammatical gender of a demonstrative pronoun – might have been used to state, among many other things, the outcome of a confrontation.[29] However, for this particular kind of situations a more specific formula can be derived from the basic unit which could be written down as *ok*

---

[26] SÄVBORG, "The formula in Icelandic saga prose", p. 61. On period in the saga prose, see I. KUZMENKO, "Nekotoriye sintaktiko-stilisticheskiye osobennosti perioda v drevneislandskoy proze", in: *Ocherki po istoricheskomu sintaksisu germanskih yazikov* ["Some syntactic and stylistic peculiarities of period in Old Icelandic prose", in: *Notes on Historical Syntaxis of Germanic languages*] (Leningrad, 1991), pp. 140-151.

[27] On differentiation between 'descriptive' and 'dramatic' scenes, see H. BURROWS, "Some *þing* to talk about: Assemblies in the *Íslendingasögur*", *Northern Studies*, 47 (2015), pp. 47-75, at pp. 52-53. On switching between 'telling' and 'showing' narration, see, quoted in Burrows, C.J. CLOVER, "Scene in saga composition", *Arkiv för nordisk filologi* 89 (1974), pp. 57-83, at p. 59.

[28] *Eyrbyggja saga*, in: *Eyrbyggja saga*, ed. Einar Ól. SVEINSSON and Matthías ÞÓRÐARSON (Reykjavík, 1935: *Íslenzk Fornrit* 4), chs. 44-46. Cf. also *Laxdæla saga*, in: *Laxdæla saga*, ed. Einar Ó. SVEINSSON (Reykjavík, 1934: *Íslenzk Fornrit* 5), ch. 55.

[29] Andrew Pawley defines productive formula as a "construction type that is partly lexically specified and so can generate a number of formulaic expressions that belong to the same family" (A. PAWLEY, "Grammarians' languages versus humanists' languages and the place of speech act formulas in models of linguistic competence", in: *Formulaic Language*, 1, *Distribution and Historical Change*, ed. R. CORRIGAN, E.A. MORAVCSIK, H. OUALI, and K.M. WHEATLEY (Amsterdam, 2009), pp. 3-26, p. 6; quoted after SÄVBORG, "The formula in Icelandic saga prose", p. 69).

var þat mikit sár / mikill áverki ('and that was a big wound'). Following Sävborg's case study it might be argued, though, that the derivative formula is in fact *ok var þat X sár*, where an adjective modifies a stable element *sár*, or its substitute of equal value *áverki*, and is an optional element.[30] However, as mentioned above, *mikit sár* and *mikill áverki* function as legalistic formulas on their own and are infused with very specific meaning. Therefore, it is to be assumed that these collocations fall under the semantic constraint and any modification is to be seen either as a conscious distortion or as an implementation of a basic formula '*ok var þat*'.

Ok Var Þat: *Another Legalistic Formula*

Affinity to the law code often shows in the saga's use of vocabulary, including formulaic expressions and their position within the text. The position and the meaning of the formulaic unit together constitute a narrative device and "may be employed as a 'conscious semantic and narratological tool'" in the same way as legalities or poetry are.[31] The sequence *ok var / varð þat mikit sár* ('that was a big wound') functions as such a tool and occurs throughout many sagas of the Icelanders, as well as of other saga genres. This chapter, however, will focus exclusively on its manifestations in some of the *Íslendingasögur*.[32] When found there, this sequence draws on the perception of wounds, injuries, and killings as tangible violence calling for an appropriate punishment. This impression is intensified by the position of this formulaic sequence in the saga texts, as it concludes an account containing a description of a confrontation and featuring a perpetrator, a weapon, and damaged body-parts:

> *Þorleifr tók spjót, er stóð í durunum, ok lagði til Þórðar blígs, ok kom lagit í skjǫldinn ok renndi af skildinum í ǫxlina,* ok var þat mikit sár [emphasis mine – E.V.].[33]

---

[30] SÄVBORG, "The formula in Icelandic saga prose", pp. 68-81.
[31] BURROWS, 'Cold cases', p. 37. (she quotes G. NORDAL, "Why Skaldic verse? Fashion and cultural politics in thirteenth-century Iceland", in: *Sagas and Societies: International Conference at Borgarnes, Iceland, 5-9 September 2002*, ed. T. JONUKS, Aksel KRISTINSSON, and S. WÜRTH (Tübingen, 2004), pp. 1-10.)
[32] A comprehensive cross-generic analysis would require a corpus-study involving proper search tools, which need yet to be developed.
[33] The text of the saga is quoted from *Eyrbyggja saga*, ed. Einar Ól. SVEINSSON and Matthías ÞÓRÐARSON, p. 121.

Þorleifr took a spear which stood by the door and thrusted it at Þórðr blígs. The thrust came at the shield, but glanced off the shield into the shoulder, *and that was a big wound.*

As formulaic *ok var / varð þat* introduces a legalistic term into the narrative, it is no longer a mere marker of period ending but also a legalistic formula serving as a testimony to perpetrated violence. Altogether it puts the audience face to face with legalities of the saga, which are not obligatory for the narrative construction but "may be drawn upon for a variety of purposes" in the *Íslendingasögur*,[34] and – when in a feud situation – affects significantly its perception of the story told.

The legalistic character of this formula is intensified by its aural proximity and its syntactic structure similar to the type of parataxis *ok varðar þat* ('and that was deemed') found in *Grágás*: and constituting a legal formulaic statement of punishment. It is likewise present in a treatment of the homicide section, *vígslóði*, which deals with physical violence: *"ok varðar þat fior baugs garð"* ("and that is deemed a lesser outlawry") and *"ok varðar þat scog gang"* ("and that is deemed a full outlawry"). In many *Íslendingasögur* these formulas follow after the description of transgressions and conclude a legal provision by prescribing a particular type of punishment.[35]

The relative homophony of these two kinds of formulaic parataxis, especially that of the verb, further intensifies semantic similarity between the two and creates an allusion based on intertextuality. The sagas feature either *vera* ('to be') or *verða* ('to become') in their indicative preterite form of third-person singular: *var* and *varð*. In the law code, however, *varðar* – though aurally reminiscent of the saga formulas – is in the present tense and is derived from the verb *varða* used as a legal term to declare a punishment fit for the crime.[36] The distinction between all three is all the more relative for, as an easily recognis-

---

[34] BURROWS, "Cold cases", p. 37

[35] Cf. For instance *Grágás*, ed. FINSEN, p. 148: "Þat er mælt. ef *maðr* lygz sare á. eða særir sik sjalfr eþa ræðr aNan maN til. at særa sik hvatki er honom gengr til þess **oc varðar þat fiorbaugs Garð** [highlight in bold is my own – *E.V.*]" ("It is prescribed that if a man falsely says he has a wound, or wounds himself or gets another man to wound him, whatever his reason, **the penalty is lesser outlawry**" (*Laws of Early Iceland*, 1, p.141)). Or, *Grágás*, ed. FINSEN, p.145: "Þat er oc mælt. ef *maðr* særir maN **at þat varðar scog Gang**. [...] Ef *maðr* vøgr maN. **oc varðar þat scog Gang**" ("It is also prescribed that if a man wounds someone **the penalty is outlawry**. [...] If a man kills someone, **the penalty is outlawry**" (*Laws of Early Iceland*, 1, pp.139-140)).

[36] See 'varða', in: *An Icelandic-English Dictionary*; also '²varða vb.', in: *Ordbog over det norrøne prosasprog – ONP: A Dictionary of Old Norse Prose* <https://onp.ku.dk/onp/onp.php?o84395>, s.v. (accessed 28 February 2021).

able verbal sequence, they were frequently abbreviated to just 'v' in the manuscripts.[37] Therefore, as the *ok var / varð þat mikit sár* formula is both aurally and syntactically reminiscent of expressions used in medieval Icelandic legal discourse, there might be a (un-)conscious attempt to "imitate the recital word for word",[38] or even convergence between the two modes of language. The conjecture is all the more convincing as in "Commonwealth-period Iceland there was doubtless much confusion as to what exactly was and was not law", attested both by the law code attempts to introduce a hierarchy of legal authority and by the saga evidence.[39]

As befits formulas, *ok var / varð þat mikit sár* marks the narrative discourse and "arouses our expectations of the following story and creates a framework for its understanding".[40] What might be called a legalistic formula functions as a meta-commentary by the narrator, who acts as a coroner or a forensic examiner and infuses the narrative with expectations of proceedings.[41] Indeed, thus marked wounds frequently evoke a legalistic discourse and become a subject of a lawsuit as they require monetary compensation or might take part in a reckoning only to be counterbalanced by other damage done. Alternatively, the saga narrative might contain an explicit statement that no compensation was received, which in fact highlights an expectation of it and the oddity of a current situation.

It might be argued that this introduction of the injuries does not differ much from the more well-researched introduction of the characters: it is likewise rooted in the textual referentiality.[42] However, here this referentiality has more to it and reflects the nature of the legal system itself: by inviting "the audience

---

[37] This can be seen, e.g. in the quotation from Vilhjálmur Finsen's edition of *Grágás*, which indicates all the editorial expansions.

[38] Helgi Skúli KJARTANSSON, "Law recital", p. 374. Supposedly, attempts to imitate the law recital might have been made both in the sagas of the Icelanders, which can be regarded together with Burrows's idea of legalities, and in the law code, which preserves many formulas indicative of spoken language.

[39] BURROWS, "Cold cases", p. 41.

[40] SÄVBORG, "The formula in Icelandic saga prose", p. 57.

[41] Most of the time, the issue would be resolved without addressing it at the thing; it would be resolved outside it. For a concise summary, see Th.M. ANDERSON and W.I. MILLER, *Law and Literature in Medieval Iceland: Ljósvetninga Saga and Valla-Ljóts Saga* (Stanford, 1989), pp. 22-31. Alternatively, W.I. MILLER, "Avoiding legal judgment: The submission of disputes to arbitration in medieval Iceland", *American Journal of Legal History* 28.2 (1984), pp. 95-134, at pp. 97, 101. Miller reintroduces the point made by Andreas Heusler (A. HEUSLER, *Das Strafrecht der Isländersagas* (Leipzig, 1911)) that in medieval Iceland vengeance, arbitrated settlement, and legal action existed simultaneously as socially acceptable dispute-processing modes.

[42] SÄVBORG, "The formula in Icelandic saga prose", p.61.

to compare this case with all others in the same tradition and to interpret it in the light of all the others" it follows the principle of the law, the interpretation of which was guided by culture and tradition.[43] Moreover, its legalistic formulaic nature aligns *ok var / varð þat mikit sár* with both publishing of wounds and law recital: it signposts the fact for the saga audience which takes on the role of witnesses and therefore makes it a legal and, assuming the sagas were intended to be read aloud, orally articulated fact.[44] It may be even assumed that once being spoken it acquired its binding force – not unlike the laws which had to be recited every three years to be valid.[45]

Formula and Its Distortion as Narrative Device

The formula 'and that was a big wound' was apparently well-known and widely recognised, which allowed for a certain degree of creativity in its implementation, thus turning it into an artistic narrative tool. For instance, confused with legal subtext, it could be contrasted with the context to emphasise a character's predicament, or even posturing. Thus, *ok var þat mikit sár* is sometimes applied to the saga protagonists' wounds or injuries, even after they were outlawed and therefore deprived of any legal rights, pushed outside the scope of the law altogether: "*Bǫrkr skýtr eptir honum spjóti, ok kom í kálfann á honum ok skar út ór, ok varð þat mikit sár*" (emphasis mine – *E.V.*) ("Bǫrkr shot with a spear after him, and it came to his calf and jutted out of it, and that was a big wound").[46] It is tantalising to suggest that this stylistic device might have been used to show the narrator's disagreement with the verdict and to highlight the dramatic nature of the situation expressed in one's inevitable inaction and inability to get any compensation for injuries one had to suffer.

---

[43] SÄVBORG, "The formula in Icelandic saga prose", p. 61; KOSZOWSKI, "Medieval Iceland: The influence of culture and tradition on law", p. 339.
[44] Helgi Skúli KJARTANSSON, "Law recital according to Old Icelandic law", p. 377.
[45] *Ibid.*, pp. 373-374.
[46] The text of the saga is quoted from *Gísla saga Súrssonar*, in: *Vestfirðinga sögur*, ÍF 6, ed. Björn K. ÞÓRÓLFSSON and Guðni JÓNSSON (Reykjavík, 1943: *Íslenzk Fornrit* 6), pp. 3-118, at p. 88. Similar examples can be found in multiple sagas, but especially prominent are the outlaw sagas. Both *Grettis saga* and *Gísla saga* use this formula and contain numerous examples of its application to the outlawed protagonists. On the implications of outlawry see E.R. BARRACLOUGH, "Inside outlawry in *Grettis saga Ásmundarsonar* and *Gísla saga Súrssonar*: Landscape in the uutlaw sagas", *Scandinavian Studies* 82.4 (2010), pp. 365-388, at pp. 366-368; or, on outlawry in general, E.M. WALGENBACH, *Outlawry as Secular Excommunication in Medieval Iceland, 1150-1350* (PhD thesis, Yale University: ProQuest Dissertation, 2016).

In some cases it could be modified to take part in a wordplay or an allusion to engage the saga audience. Saturated with legal detail and characterised by law "inextricably interwoven through the narrative and the plot", *Eyrbyggja saga* provides a vivid example of this literary technique in the following passage:[47]

Steinþórr bað Snorra þá rétta fram hǫndina, ok svá gerði hann. Þá reiddi Steinþórr upp sverðit ok hjó á hǫnd Snorra goða, ok varð þar við brestr mikill [emphasis mine – E.V.]; *kom hǫggit í stallahringinn ok tók hann mjǫk svá í sundr, en Snorri varð eigi sárr.*[48]

Steinþórr then asked Snorri to stretch out his hand, and he did so. When Steinþórr drew the sword and struck at Snorri goði's hand, and that came to be *with a big crash*; the stroke fell on the temple-ring and it split nearly asunder, but Snorri was not hurt.

This manifestation of the formula appears in its usual place in the sentence: it follows the description of a blow and states its outcome, which is characterised rather by noise than by an injury. The collocation 'big crash' (*brestr mikill*) fills the exact slot usually designated for a 'big wound': however different its meaning, it is still evocative of *mikit sár*. Consequently, except for adding a necessary preposition *við*, the formulaic sequence preserves its structure without any major distortions. One can easily imagine the suspense building, the rising tension among the audience, as the narrative of the saga progressed through the usual sequence: from drawing a sword to hitting a hand and then going on to the anticipated statement starting with "*ok varð þar*". Can one perhaps also imagine multiple sighs of relief to follow?[49]

Presumably, the reference to the discussed legalistic formula is so obvious that it presupposes a particular outcome, i.e. a wound. As it is not the case, the

---

[47] BURROWS, "Cold cases", p. 43-44.
[48] *Eyrbyggja saga*, ed. Einar Ól. SVEINSSON and Matthías ÞÓRDARSON, p. 123.
[49] Note that this appears to resonate with Greenfield's definition of the "originality in the handling of conventional formulas" as "the degree of tension achieved between the inherited body of meanings in which a particular formula participates and the specific meaning of that formula in its individual context". Alternatively, with Fry, who claimed that "the tradition enables poets to manipulate audiences' expectations by adapting the conventions to their own purposes, and 'play[ing] against their audiences' memory of poetry" (D. FRY, "The memory of Cædmon", in: *Oral Traditional Literature: A Festschrift for Albert Bates Lord*, ed. J.M. FOLEY (Columbus, OH, 1981), pp. 282-293, at p.282; S.B. GREENFIELD, "The formulaic expression of the theme of 'exile' in Anglo-Saxon Poetry", *Speculum* 30 (1955), pp. 200-206, at p. 205; quoted after POWELL, *Verbal Parallels*, pp. 31-32).

situation requires further elaboration. The period is therefore expanded by adding that it is the temple-ring that got damaged but not Snorri. It is explicitly emphasised in the text that he "was not wounded" ("*varð eigi sárr*") – a specification intended to prevent any automatic derivation of injuries from an otherwise well-known formula. At the same time, as its structure is uncorrupted, it still functions as a trigger for legalistic connotations and, as such, re-introduces Steinþórr's action not as a mere assault but as a more serious transgression. Moreover, though factually it is just a kind of blow which, according to *Grágás*, is not enough to initiate a law-suit and can be vindicated only during a short time after its infliction;[50] both semantically and lexically it is shaped into a misdeed equal to a serious wound, to be compensated and dealt accordingly at the tallying. Although the conflict to which this incident belongs is resolved outside the *þing*, its settlement still takes place in a setting closely associated with legal practices.[51] However, it is still difficult not to think of comic relief as Snorri displays gullibility and stretches his hand only to be hit and lose his ring to damage. Therefore, Burrow's suggestion that *Eyrbyggja saga* parodies the saga style by citing legalities might resonate with this passage as it "subverts expectations of the traditional motif" by distorting the formula to achieve a somehat humorous effect.[52]

A similar (and a slightly controversial) example of switching a wound with something else might be provided by *Ljósvetninga saga*. *Vǫðu-Brands þáttr* features two confrontation scenes, which constitute the repetitive pattern, and twice the description of Brandr's transgression is concluded with the formulaic expression. In both cases, however, the formula indicates the size of the crowd present rather than the size of the wound:

> *En um morgininn, er menn váru komnir í sæti sín, gekk Brandr fyrir Hárek, keyrði øxi í hǫfuð honum ok vá hann. Nú spruttu upp hvárratveggju þeira menn, ok varð þar þrǫng mikil.*[53]

And in the morning when men had come to their seats Brandr went to Hárek and plunged an axe in his head and killed him. Now both sides spring up and there was a big crowd.

---

[50] *Grágás*, ed. FINSEN, p. 147.
[51] See *supra*, n. 42; see also BURROWS, "Some *þing* to talk about".
[52] BURROWS, "Cold cases", p. 52.
[53] *Ljósvetninga saga*, ed. Björn SIGFÚSSON, p. 128.

And: "*Ok at skilnaði þeira veitti Brandr honum mikinn áverka. Þar var þrǫng mikil, ok var þar kominn Ófeigr ór Skǫrðum*" ("And at their parting Brand inflicted a big injury on him. There was a big crowd, and Ófeigr came from Skǫrð"). While the first instance preserves the familiar descriptive sequence and follows a 'participants – weapon – location on the body' model, this second occurrence is less vivid as the scene takes place at the public games where the participants do not wield any weapons. However, the scene still mirrors the above-cited example, which follows the general pattern of the *þáttr*.[54] The kind of substitution found in the first passage is probably due to the immediately stated death of the opponent, which makes any remarks on the size of a wound unnecessary. Still, as these transgressions happen in explicitly public spaces and in the presence of multiple witnesses, the crowd becomes an important juristic fact.

Another creative use of this formula might be seen in altering, or even degrading, the seriousness of the wound featured turning it into litotes which is favoured by the saga style. This alteration was often done by substituting the usual modifier *mikill* ('big') with a different adjective so as to augment the expressive potential of the formula. *Ljósvetninga saga* provides a vivid example of reducing a wound to its lesser analogue:

> *Síðan snýr hann at með húskarla fjóra ok setr øxarhamar í hǫfuð Odda,* ok var þat svǫðusár í enninu, ok blæddi mikit [emphasis mine – E.V.]. *Þá spratt hann upp ok mælti: "Búinn em ek at berjask".*[55]

Then he turns back with four followers and sets his axe-hammer at Oddi's head, and that was a superficial wound on the forehead and [it] bled a lot. Then Oddi jumped up and said, "I am ready to fight".

As in the previously mentioned case of *brestr mikill*, this one also requires further commentary on the situation: it is revealed that the wound, albeit superficial, led to extensive bleeding. Furthermore, a Björn hasty remark from Oddi, who declares his readiness to fight, seems to play along with the narrative frame: despite much blood, the wound is not serious and has no risk of incapacitating Oddi.[56] Complemented with Oddi's reaction, it creates a comic effect: as

---

[54] For a more detailed discussion of the *Vǫðu-Brands þáttr*'s narrative structure, see E.K. VOROBEVA, 'Violence "in the flesh" and in the narrative: On poetics of the *Islendingasögur*", *Casus: The Individual and Unique in History* 15 (2020), pp. 292-310, at pp. 304-306.

[55] *Ljósvetninga saga*, ed. Björn SIGFÚSSON, p. 80.

[56] Compare with *Laxdæla saga,* ed. Einar Ól. SVEINSSON, p. 192, where a similar wound

Depicting Violence in Íslendingasögur

if Oddi attempts to contradict a possible narrative unfurling around his headwound; moreover, it resonates with the hurly-burly of the confrontation itself. Similar to the example above from *Eyrbyggja saga*, it is tempting to suggest here a certain mockery of the saga style, so prone to citing legalities, thus adding yet another saga to the list of *Njáls saga, Eyrbyggja saga*, and *Laxdæla saga*.

Overall, it is highly probable that an almost forensic description of a wound – containing a detailed account of by whom, where, and by what weapon it was inflicted – triggered the use of this formulaic sequence in order to state its outcome. For instance,

> *[...] en Már Hallvarðsson gekk næst Snorra, ok lagði Svartr atgeirinum til hans, ok kom lagit á herðarblaðit ok renndi út undir hǫndina ok skar þar út, ok varð þat eigi mikit sár.*[57]

> And Már Hallvarðsson walked close to Snorri, and Svart thrust his halberd into him, and the thrust came to the shoulder and sliced across the arm, and that did not come to be a big wound.

Or,

> *Þorkell er þá kominn mjǫk svá at honum ok hǫggr til hans; hǫggit kom á hǫndina fyrir ofan úlflið, ok var þat ekki mikit sár.*[58]

> Then Þorkell comes rather close to him and strikes him; the stroke came at his arm just above a wrist, and that was not a big wound.

(*í enninu*) is listed as a serious injury: "*[...]; lagit kom í stálhúfu Þorsteins svarta, svá at í enninu nam staðar; var þat mjǫk mikill áverki*" ("blow came to the steel cap of Þorstein svarta so that there was a dent on the forehead; that was a very big wound"). But also, earlier in the same saga p. 98: "*Þórðr vildi upp spretta, er hann fékk áverkann, ok varð þat ekki, því at hann mæddi blóðrás*" ("Þórðr wanted to jump up when he got an injury, but it would not be because he was lost much blood"). Oddi's ability to jump up promptly defines, therefore, the bleeding from his wound as not dangerous to his life and counteracts an almost formulaic evocation of *mikit* (here used adverbially in dative singular) to define *blæddi*, prompting the audience not to confuse Oddi's injury with a dangerous wound which comes to mind due to formulaic frame.

[57] *Eyrbyggja saga*, ed. Einar Ól. SVEINSSON and Matthías ÞÓRÐARSON, p. 66.

[58] The text of the saga is quoted from *Laxdæla saga*, ed. Einar Ól. SVEINSSON, p. 173. The saga features at least four other cases of the formula featuring both *áverki* and *sár* without negation; see p.169 and p.192.

Therefore, after such passages related to slight wounds, it is not uncommon to see the formula interspersed with negation which might be seen either as a widely used stylistic device, litotes, or as a means to downgrade and neutralise the legal connotations.

Conclusions

As saga style is characterised by the ample use of both formulaic language and legalities, it is not surprising that the sagas of the Icelanders contain formulas which can be called 'legalistic formulas' since they are not strictly legal but still reflect perceptions of a legalistic discourse found in the sagas. At the same time, they show close affinity to the language used in the medieval law code *Grágás* and, therefore, bear easily recognisable intertextual connotations. This article explored the idea of legalistic formulas using examples of such formulaic expressions as *mikit sár / mikill áverki* and *ok var / varð þat mikit sár*. They allowed the narrator to infuse the narrative with additional meanings and turn a factual description of any wound into a legal case, thus prompting the audience to form their expectations of an appropriate vindication – either to prove them right or to raise their awareness of ensuing injustice. The legalistic nature of these formulas also allowed for a degree of creativity induced by either the narrative surroundings or the conscious distortion of the formula. Thus, it could be a poetic device, an artistic tool, which, when paired with a plot, was capable of highlighting or even creating a specific mood or a theme within the narrative.

Formulaic Word-Play in the Poems of the *Anglo-Saxon Chronicle*

INNA MATYUSHINA

According to the Parry-Lord theory, formulas are viewed as solely utilitarian elements, necessary for extempore composition during performance but lacking an aesthetic function.[1] The presupposition of the formulaic theory is that a poet capable of writing has no need for formulas, since their use would consciously limit his creative individuality.[2] In applying the key concepts of the formulaic theory to the study of Old English poetry, Francis P. Magoun proposed that the formulaic style is characteristic of oral (as opposed to written) poetry, acknowledging that in a written text a poet could quote himself or other poets in order to achieve a rhetorical or literary effect.[3]

The key principles of oral formulaic theory determined the main directions of scholarly criticism: the denial of an artistic role in the formulaic style and its

---

[1] M. PARRY, "Studies in the epic technique of oral verse-making, I: Homer and the Homeric style", *Harvard Studies in Classical Philology* 41 (1930), pp. 73-138, at p. 125; A.B. Lord, *The Singer of Tales* (Cambridge MA, 1960), pp. 65-66.
[2] PARRY, 'Studies in the epic technique of oral verse-making, I', p. 144.
[3] F.P. MAGOUN, "Oral-formulaic character of Anglo-Saxon narrative poetry", in: *Essential Articles for the Study of Old English Poetry*, ed. J.B. BESSINGER and S.J. KAHRL (Hamden, 1968), pp. 319-351.

New Light on Formulas in Oral Poetry and Prose, ed. Daniel SÄVBORG and Bernt Ø. THORVALDSEN, Utrecht Studies in Medieval Literacy, 57 (Turnhout: Brepols, 2023), pp. 303-325.

BREPOLS PUBLISHERS   DOI <10.1484/M.USML-EB.5.133557>

inherence in the oral tradition. The orality of Old English epic was questioned by Arthur Brodeur, who saw in the creator of *Beowulf* a learned poet acquainted with the Old and New Testament and patristic literature, as well as capable of making original stylistic and semantic contributions to the poetic tradition.[4] Other opponents of the oral formulaic theory considered that the presence of the formulaic style could not be viewed as an argument in favour of the oral origin of Old English poetry.[5] Formulaic style ceased to be regarded as an inherent feature of oral poetry after the stylistic studies of translated Old English texts by Larry Benson.[6] The analysis of phraseology in the Old English *Metres of Boethius* (based on the translations of *De consolatione philosophiae*) and *The Phoenix* (the first part of which is a translation of the Latin poem *De Ave Phoenice*, ascribed to Lactantius), revealed the presence of the formulaic style (preserved as a relic of the oral-poetic tradition) in written poetry.[7]

The second concept of the oral-formulaic theory which rejected the aesthetic value of formulas was refuted by Stanley Greenfield, who was the first to note that the use of the formulaic style in a poetic text does not preclude artistic excellence in its creator[8] and showed that in Old English poetry formulas possess an aesthetic value.[9] The majority of scholars who shared Greenfield's views on the aesthetic value of the formulaic style devoted their works to the study of *Beowulf*.[10]

---

[4] A.G. BRODEUR, *The Art of Beowulf* (Berkeley, 1959), pp. 4-6.

[5] R.D. STEVICK, "The oral-formulaic analysis of Old English verse", in: *Essential Articles for the Study of Old English Poetry*. ed. BESSINGER and KAHRL, pp. 393-403; A. RENOIR, "Oral-formulaic context: Implications for the comparative criticism of mediaeval texts", in: *Oral Traditional Literature: A Festschrift for Albert Bates Lord*, ed. J.M. FOLEY (Columbus, OH, 1981), pp. 416-439; ID., "Repetition, oral-formulaic style, and affective impact in mediaeval poetry: A tentative illustration", in: *Comparative Research on Oral Traditions: A Memorial for Milman Parry*, ed. J.M. FOLEY (Columbus, OH, 1987), pp. 533-548; H.L. ROGERS, "The crypto-psychological character of the oral formula", *English Studies* 47 (1966), pp. 89-102.

[6] L. BENSON, "The literary character of Anglo-Saxon formulaic poetry", *Publications of the Modern Language Association* 81 (1966), pp. 334-341.

[7] BENSON, "The literary character of Anglo-Saxon formulaic poetry".

[8] S.B. GREENFIELD, "Grendel's approach to Heorot: Syntax and poetry", in: *Old English Poetry: Fifteen Essays*. ed. R.P. CREED (Providence, 1967), pp. 275-284, at pp. 283-284; ID., *The Interpretation of Old English Poems* (London, 1972), pp. 31-36. The importance of Greenfield's study for the development of the formulaic theory was appraised by Alexandra Hennessey Olssen: "Stanley B. Greenfield was one of the first Anglo-Saxonists to call attention to the fact that formularity is compatible with artistry and that Anglo-Saxonists needed to pay close attention to the artistry of the texts rather than merely listing formulaic devices" (A.H. OLSEN, "Oral-formulaic research in Old English Studies: Part II", *Oral Tradition*, 3 (1988), pp. 138-190, at p. 146).

[9] GREENFIELD, *The Interpretation of Old English Poems*, p. 36.

[10] The works by Eric Stanley (E.G. STANLEY, *Continuations and Beginnings: Studies in Old*

Commenting on the oral-formulaic theory, Victor Zhirmunsky accounted for the use of the formulaic style in Old English poems by the peculiarities of archaic poetic art, in which the typical and the traditional prevailed over the individual.[11] Comparing the style of *Beowulf* with the literary poems associated with the name of Cynewulf, Zhirmunsky pointed out that the creator of the latter "applied traditional forms and formulas to new Christian themes, having mastered the art of oral heroic epic".[12] According to Zhirmunsky, formulas could be retained in literary poetry as stylistic features whose use was governed by the strict canons of epic verse. As was pointed out by Mikhail Steblin-Kamenskii, a particular type of poetic art requiring the use of the formulaic style "could have been preserved in medieval written literature, in which authorship was manifested not in oral performance but in writing".[13]

Accounting for the use of the formulaic style in the poems of the *Poetic Edda* by its origin in oral poetry, Eleazar Meletinsky attached special importance to the connection of particular formulas (e.g. a bid for a hearing or sitting on a mound) with magic and ritual.[14] However, according to Meletinsky, in the Eddic lays the magical function of formulaic repetitions is weakened in comparison with their ornamental or stylistic functions, which consist in organising

---

English Literature (London, 1966), pp. 104-140), John Niles (J. NILES, "Formula and formulaic system in *Beowulf*", in: *Oral Traditional Literature: A Festschrift for Albert Bates Lord*, ed. FOLEY, pp. 394-415), Calvin Kendall (C.B. KENDALL, *The Metrical Grammar of Beowulf* (Cambridge, 1991)) and Andy Orchard (A. ORCHARD, *A Critical Companion to Beowulf* (Cambridge, 2003), pp. 85-91) study the use of artistic devices in *Beowulf*, *The Dream of the Rood*, *Judith*, *The Meters of Boethius*, and the 'Riddles' of the *Exeter Book*. Geoffrey Russom combined the views on the aesthetic function of the formulaic style and on the oral origin of Beowulf (G. RUSSOM, "Aesthetic criteria in Old English heroic style", in: *On the Aesthetics of Beowulf and Other Old English Poems*, ed. J.H. HILL (Toronto and Buffalo, 2010), pp. 64-80).

[11] V.M. ZHIRMUNSKIY, *Sravnitel'noe literaturovedenie: Vostok i Zapad* [Comparative Literary Studies: The East and the West] (Leningrad, 1979), p. 169. Similar views have been expressed in several studies of formulaic style, e.g. by Jeffrey Alan Mazo, who called the poet of *Beowulf* "a master of traditional art" (J.A. MAZO, "Compound diction and traditional style in *Beowulf* and *Genesis A*", *Oral Tradition* 6.1 (1991), pp. 79-92, at p. 82).

[12] V.M. ZHIRMUNSKIY, "Srednevekovye literatury kak predmet sravnitel'nogo literaturovedeniya" [Medieval literature as an object of comparative literary criticism], *Izvestiya AN SSSR: Otdelenie literatury i yazyka* 10.3 (Moscow, 1971), pp. 185-197, at p. 185. The use of heathen formulas in Christian poetry has been analysed in: MAGOUN, "Oral-formulaic character of Anglo-Saxon narrative poetry".

[13] M.I. STEBLIN-KAMENSKII, *Istoricheskaya poetika* [Historical Poetics] (Leningrad, 1978), p. 149.

[14] E.M. MELETINSKIY, *Edda i rannie formy eposa* [*Edda* and the Earliest Forms of Epic] (Moscow, 1968), pp. 87, 94.

units of verse.[15] Thus, although Meletinsky's primary interest lies in connecting the origins of Eddic poetry with folklore, he does not deny the stylistic (i.e. aesthetic) function of formulaic style.

The aesthetic function of formulaic style in Eddic poetry, which was observed by Eleazar Meletinsky,[16] was studied in great detail by Elena Gurevich, who rationalised the lack of scholarly attention to formulaic style. She pointed out that the oral formulaic theory does not lead to the study of formulas as such, because the oral or literary nature of a text is established mostly by quantitative data, signalling the presence or absence of a given number of formulaic phrases.[17] Viewing Eddic lays as traditional canonical art not restricted to the preliterate epoch, Elena Gurevich demonstrated that the employment of various structural and semantic types of formula signifies their use as an aesthetic compositional device.[18]

A paradox, inherent in the formulaic theory, between formulaic style and its aesthetic impact, was analysed by Olga Smirnitskaya, who pointed out that scholars adhering to its main postulates have to look for the means of artistic impact of medieval poetry not on the level of formulas or words but on the level of plot organisation or composition.[19] Olga Smirnitskaya found limitations in formulaic theory in its tenets that the unity of verse and language within formulas is regarded as a technical means of enabling an epic poet to produce poetic texts *ex tempore*.[20] She pointed out that, if formulaic style had been a technical tool for facilitating extemporaneous oral improvisation, it would have become completely automatised in form, incompatible with the nature of art itself, and would have therefore not survived the transition onto parchment.[21] Following Olga Smirnitskaya's approach to formulaic style, it is possible to view formulas both as stable collocations of epic speech (units of traditional phraseology, *loci communes*, repetitions) and as metrical and linguistic units, comprising structural characteristics of the poetic language.[22]

---

[15] MELETINSKIY, *Edda*, p. 21.
[16] MELETINSKIY, *Edda*, pp. 20-21.
[17] E.A. GUREVICH, "Parnaya formula v eddicheskoy poezii (Opyt analiza)" [Binary formula in Eddic poetry: An attempt at analysis], in: *Khudozhestvennyy yazyk srednevekov'ya* (Moscow, 1982), pp. 61-82, at p. 61.
[18] GUREVICH, "Parnaya formula", p. 82.
[19] O. SMIRNITSKAYA, *Stikh i yazyk drevnegermanskoy poezii* [The Verse and Language of Old Germanic Poetry] (Moscow, 1994), p. 237.
[20] SMIRNITSKAYA, *Stikh i yazyk*, p. 5.
[21] SMIRNITSKAYA, *Stikh i yazyk*, p. 226.
[22] SMIRNITSKAYA, *Stikh i yazyk*, pp. 211-213.

* * *

Although formulas in Eddic lays[23] and Old English poetry[24] have become objects of minute analysis, the formulaic style of texts belonging to the written tradition has attracted considerably less attention.[25] Formulas have been analysed in sagas[26] and in Middle English poems of the twelfth and thirteenth centuries[27] but not in the poems of the *Anglo-Saxon Chronicle*, which undoubtedly belong to the tradition of literature rather than of oral performance.[28] An analysis of these poems, which (unlike other Old English texts) can be dated,[29] shows that the use of formulaic style does not impose limitations on the artistic individuality of their creator. The aim of the present article is to demonstrate that in the poems of the *Anglo-Saxon Chronicle* formulas not only become a character-

---

[23] MELETINSKIY, *Edda*, pp. 20-21; GUREVICH, "Parnaya formula", pp. 61-82; SMIRNITSKAYA, *Stikh i yazyk*, pp. 207-218; L. LÖNNROTH, "*Iǫrd fannz æva né upphiminn*: A formula analysis", *Speculum Norroenum: Norse Studies in Memory of Gabriel Turville-Petre*, ed. U. DRONKE, G.P. HELGADÓTTIR, G.W.WEBER, and H. BEKKER-NIELSEN (Odense, 1981), pp. 310-327; S.A. MELLOR, *Analyzing Ten Poems from the* Poetic Edda: *Oral Formula and Mythic Patterns* (Lewiston, 2008), pp. 69-112, 169-287.

[24] SMIRNITSKAYA, *Stikh i yazyk*, pp. 231-238; S.B. GREENFIELD, "The formulaic expression of the theme of exile in Anglo-Saxon poetry", in: *Essential Articles for the Study of Old English Poetry*, ed. BESSINGER and KAHRL, pp. 352-362; STANLEY, *Continuations and Beginnings*, pp. 104-140; NILES, "Formula and formulaic system in *Beowulf*; ORCHARD, *A Critical Companion to Beowulf*, pp. 85-91; RUSSOM, "Aesthetic criteria in Old English heroic style".

[25] For the study of works analysing formulaic style see: SMIRNITSKAYA, *Stikh i yazyk*, pp. 171-232: J.M. FOLEY, *Oral-Formulaic Theory and Research: An Introduction and Annotated Bibliography* (New York, 1985), pp. 41-47; A.H. OLSEN, "Oral-formulaic research in Old English studies, Part I", *Oral Tradition* 1 (1986), pp. 548-606; EAD., "Oral-formulaic research in Old English studies, Part II"; P. ACKER, *Revisiting Oral Theory: Formulaic Composition in Old English and Old Icelandic Verse* (London, 1998), pp. 85-110; ORCHARD, *A Critical Companion to Beowulf*, pp. 85-86; B.Ø. THORVALDSEN, *Svá er sagt i fornum vísindum: Tekstualiseringen av de mytologiske eddadikt* (Bergen, 2006), pp. 19-34, FROG, "*Alvíssmál* and orality I: Formula, alliteration and categories of mythic being", *Arkiv för nordisk filologi* 126 (2011), pp. 17-71, at pp. 19-28.

[26] D. SÄVBORG, "The formula in Icelandic saga prose", *Saga-Book of the Viking Society for Northern Research* (2018), pp. 51-86.

[27] M.C. AMODIO, *Writing the Oral Tradition: Oral Poetics and Literate Culture in Medieval England* (Notre Dame, 2004).

[28] The only exception might be *The Rime of King William*, where the composition, organisation, semantics, and style could bear similarities with contemporary folklore (I. MATYUSHINA "Vilhelm Zavoevatel v Anglosaksonskoy Chronike: ot koronazii do konchiny" [William the Conqueror in the *Anglo-Saxon Chronicle*: From coronation to death], *Arbor Mundi: Vestnik RGGU: Seriya "Literaturovedenie: Y azykoznanie: Kul'turologiya"* (Moscow, 2021), pp. 86-115).

[29] The only *Chronicle* poem ('The Death of Edgar') referred to in Marc Amodio's book is interpreted within the framework of intertextuality (AMODIO, *Writing the Oral Tradition*, p. 58).

istic feature of the style, performing a compositional or stylistic function, but also take part in formulaic word-play used for specific artistic purposes.[30]

In the most famous *Chronicle* poem, the *Battle of Brunanburh*, comprising the annal for 937 (in MSS A, B, C, D),[31] seventy-two formulas occur in a hundred and forty-eight lines (49%) and thus are used more frequently than in most other Old English poems, including *Beowulf*, in which one formula occurs in approximately thirteen lines.[32] Implementing the methodology of Donald Fry, who stated that the definition of a formula should be widened to include compound words,[33] it is possible to calculate an increase in the number of formulas in the *Battle of Brunanburh* to eighty-four (57%). It can be suggested that the formulaic style of the *Battle of Brunanburh* is endowed with a specific function which is most probably connected with expressing eulogising intent. As was pointed out by Janet Thormann, "the traditional heroic language in itself ... enacts a political claim by representing the contemporary event as the re-enactment of the values and achievements of the past".[34] Formulaic language, traditionally associated with heroic poetry, is used in the *Battle of Brunanburh* as an ideal means of praising the victory of two illustrious leaders: Æthelstan, King of Wessex, and his brother Edmund. The significance of the event, which ensured that nearly the whole of England, including the Danelaw, came under the rule of Wessex, accounts for why the poem on the *Battle of Brunanburh* was included into four manuscripts of the *Chronicle* (the Parker, Worcester, and both Abingdon manuscripts).

---

[30] Cf. a study of the functions of formulaic style in the *Anglo-Saxon Chronicle* poems (I. MATYUSHINA, "Funkzii formulnogo stilya v poemah Anglosaksonskoy Chroniki" [The functions of formulaic style in the *Anglo-Saxon Chronicle* poems], *Studia Litterarum* 4 (2019), pp. 62-87).

[31] The texts are edited in *The Anglo-Saxon Chronicle: A Collaborative Edition* (Cambridge, 1983), 3, ed. J. BATELY (MS A); 4, ed. S. TAYLOR (MS B); 5, ed. K. O'BRIEN O'KEEFE (MS C); and 6, ed. G.P. CUBBIN (MS D).

[32] As pointed out by John Niles, 33 of the first 50 short lines of *Beowulf* take part in formulaic systems employed in the poem, but only one line in six (17%) contains formulas reproduced unchanged in the rest of the poetic corpus (NILES, "Formula and formulaic system in *Beowulf*", p. 409). According to Whitney F. Bolton, *Beowulf* contains 248 formulas in 3182 lines (12.8), *Genesis A*: 167 formulas in 2319 lines (13.9), *Andreas*: 146 formulas in 1722 lines (11.8), Christ: 129 formulas in 1664 (12.9), *Guthlac*: 128 formulas in 1379 lines (10.8), *Christ and Satan*: 99 formulas in 729 lines (7.4), *Phoenix*: 70 formulas in 677 lines (9.7), *Seafarer*: 13 formulas in 124 lines (9.5) (W.F. BOLTON, "A poetic formula in '*Beowulf*' and seven other Old English poems: A computer study', *Computers and the Humanities* 19 (1985), pp. 167-173).

[33] D.K. FRY, "Old English formulas and systems", *English Studies* 48 (1967), pp. 193-204.

[34] J. THORMANN, "The *Battle of Brunanburh* and the matter of history", *Mediaevalia* 17 (1994), pp. 5-13, at pp. 8-9.

It is harder to understand why another poem about Æthelstan's brother Edmund, which is traditionally called by editors *The Redemption of the Five Boroughs*, is also included into the same four manuscripts of the *Chronicle* (MSS A, B, C, D for the year 942). The poem is dedicated to the victory of King Edmund over the Five Boroughs (Leicester, Nottingham, Derby, Lincoln and Stamford), omitting to mention that in order to regain these lands, he first had to lose them.[35] The role of this poem in the *Chronicle* remains unclear, as it narrates the victory of the king who merely managed to regain space he had lost, thus unwittingly attracting attention to his prior defeat.

It is symptomatic that in the poem *On the Redemption of the Five Boroughs* formulaic phraseology is used less sparingly than in the *Battle of Brunanburh* (10 formulas in 13 long lines, or 26 half-lines). The formulaic style contributes to the depiction of Edmund as an active hero: a "defender of warriors" ("*wiggendra hleo*"[36]), "protector of kinsmen" ("*mæcgea mundbora*"), an "accomplisher of deeds" ("*dædfruma*"), whereas the Danes are presented as passive subjects, bound by the fetters of heathendom. As pointed out by Jayne Carroll, the poem "makes full use of conventional heroic vocabulary", as three formulas employed in connection with Edmund also occur in *Beowulf*: *mundbora, dyre dædfruma,* and *wiggendra hleo*.[37] The formulaic denotations of the ruler that were used in the *Chronicle* poem, reproduce models which were productive in skaldic poetry: the model underlying the formula 'the ruler of the Angles', *Engla þeoden*, follows the model widespread in skaldic panegyrics (cf. "*Hǫrða konungr*" ("the King of the Hǫrðar"), i.e. people of Hordaland, in Einarr Helgason skálaglamm's *Vellekla*;[38] "*Jóta gramr*" ("the prince of the Jótar"), "*Hǫrða dróttinn*" ("the ruler of the Hǫrðar"), and in the drápa for Magnus

---

[35] Sources preserve little information about king Edmund, and scholars usually dismiss him, expressing opinions like: "Athelstan was succeeded by his brother Edmund, and he by his brother Eadred; both were conscientious monarchs about whom comparatively little is known; neither lived long" (Ch. BROOKE, *The Saxon and Norman Kings* (Glasgow, 1979), p. 125).

[36] Texts of the *Chronicle* poems are quoted from: *The Anglo-Saxon Minor Poems: The Anglo-Saxon Poetic Records: A Collective Edition*, ed. G.Ph. KRAPP and E. VAN KIRK DOBBIE, 6 vols. (New York, 1931-1953), 6 (1942).

[37] *Beowulf*, ed. in: *The Anglo-Saxon Poetic Records*, 4, pp. 3-98, lines 1480 and 2779, 2090, and 429, 899, 1972, 2337 respectively. J. CARROLL, "When were the Vikings in England? Viking wars and the *Anglo-Saxon Chronicle*", in: *Beowulf and Other Stories: A New Introduction to Old English, Old Icelandic and Anglo-Norman Literatures*, ed. R. NORTH and J. ALLARD, 2nd edn. (London, 2014), pp. 329-378, at p. 364.

[38] "Einarr skálaglamm Helgason, *Vellekla* 12", ed. E. MAROLD, in: *Poetry from the Kings' Sagas*, 1, *From Mythical Times to c. 1035*, ed. D. WHALEY (Turnhout, 2012: *Skaldic Poetry of the Scandinavian Middle Ages* 1 – henceforth SkP I), pp. 283-329, at p. 298.

the Good *Hrynhenda* by Arnórr Þórðarson jarlaskáld).[39] The formulas 'protector of warriors', *wiggendra hleo*, and 'guardian of kinsmen', *mæcgea mundbora* (both are used of Edmund), can be compared with the skaldic denotations of the king as 'the guardian, protector of people' (cf. *folk vǫrðr* in Einarr Skúlason's fragment)[40] or as 'the guardian, protector of land' (cf. *grundar vǫrðr* in *Gráfeldardrápa*, a memorial poem on Harald the Greyhide by Glúmr Geirason).[41] The effect of accumulating formulaic denotations of the ruler in the poem *On the Redemption of the Five Boroughs* is to focus the attention of a contemporary audience on what he has achieved: honorific titles indicate that the king has successfully protected the space he is responsible for.[42]

The formulaic denotation of the ruler as *dyre dædfruma*, 'dear accomplisher of deeds', brings to mind the Old Norse kenning with a similar first component: "*frumsmiðr bragar*", "the first smith of poetry", denoting Bragi, the first poet and the god of poetry in *Snorra Edda*. The Old English poem referring to the ruler as "dear accomplisher of deeds" can also be compared to skaldic poems in its use of the epithet 'dear', which occurs in numerous skaldic panegyrics: "*alldýr konungr*", "very dear king" (Hallfreðr vandræðaskáld 'Erfidrápa Óláfs Tryggvasonar', *Óláfs saga Tryggvasonar*, 107), "*jǫfur dýrr*",[43] "dear prince" (Eyvindr skáldaspillir *Haralds saga Gráfeldar 1*). The Old English poem, referring to the ruler with the formula 'dear accomplisher of deeds', is similar to skaldic poems in its use of the base word meaning 'accomplisher' (*viðr*, 'the one who accomplishes'). Words with identical semantics (*vinnanda, fremjanda*) are used as part of kennings of man in *Snorra Edda*: "*Svá, at kalla hann vinnanda eða fremjanda fara sinna eða athafnar, víga eða sæfara eða veiða*,[44] "Thus, by calling him the accomplisher or the performer of his journeys or conduct, of battles or sea-voyages or hunting". Like the king in the poem *On*

---

[39] "Arnórr jarlaskáld Þórðarson, *Hrynhenda, Magnússdrápa* 3", ed. D. WHALEY, in: *Poetry from the Kings' Sagas*, 2, *From c. 1035 to c. 1300*, ed. K.E. GADE (Turnhout, 2009: *Skaldic Poetry of the Scandinavian Middle Ages* 2 – henceforth SkP II), pp. 183-206, at pp. 185-186.

[40] "Einarr Skúlason, Fragments 2", ed. K.E. GADE, in: *Poetry from Treatises on Poetics*, ed. K.E. GADE and E. MAROLD (Turnhout, 2017: *Skaldic Poetry of the Scandinavian Middle Ages* 3 – henceforth SkP III), pp. 151-168, at p. 153.

[41] A. FINLAY, Introduction to: "Glúmr Geirason, *Gráfeldardrápa*", ed. A. FINLAY, in: *Poetry from the Kings' Sagas* 1, ed. WHALEY, pp. 245-266, at p. 245.

[42] For the study of parallels between skaldic *erfidrápa* and the poem *On the Redemption of the Five Boroughs*, cf. I. MATYUSHINA, "Skaldic panegyric and the *Anglo-Saxon Chronicle* poem on the Redemption of the Five Boroughs", *International Journal of Language and Linguistics* 7.3 (2020), pp. 13-23.

[43] SkP I, p. 229.

[44] The text of *Skáldskaparmál* is quoted from: *Snorri Sturluson, Edda: Skáldskaparmál: Introduction: Text and Notes*, ed. A. FAULKES (London, 1998), p. 40.

Formulaic Word-Play in the Poems of the Anglo-Saxon Chronicle

the Redemption of the Five Boroughs, who has accomplished the acquisition of space, the ruler of skaldic panegyrics is shown as an active character, performing deeds, protecting lands, and winning battles.

As in the Old English poem, in skaldic poetry we find formulaic designations of the ruler in terms of dynasty. The denotation of Edmund as "Edward's son (or heir)", "*Afera Eadweardes*", in the poem *On the Redemption of the Five Boroughs*, finds parallels in skaldic panegyrics: in the denotation of Glumr Geirason as "Geiri's heir", "*arfvǫrðr Geiri*" (B, I, 541, 11),[45] used in *Íslendingadrápa* by Haukr Valdísarson; of Canute as "Svein's son", "*Sveins sonr*", used in *Róðudrápa* by Þórðr Sjáreksson;[46] and in the denotation "Tryggvi's son", "*Tryggva sonr*", in the *Erfidrápa Óláfs Tryggvasonar* by Hallfreðr vandræðaskáld.[47] Like skalds, who varied kennings according to established models inherited from Old Norse poetry, the creator of the Old English poem constructs his formulaic designations of the ruler in accordance with the canons of poetic phraseology, which he had inherited from the tradition of alliterative verse.

In the poem *On the Redemption of the Five Boroughs*, variations in formulaic denotations of the ruler, indicating his accomplishments and defining his status through the space he had regained, take the place of the narrative development of a poetic theme. Like a skaldic vísa, with its communicative deficiency caused by its hypertrophic form, the Old English poem contains only an announcement of the heroic deed and its evaluation. As in skaldic vísas, which do not narrate events in linear succession but rather register actions, the subject of the Anglo-Saxon poem is a statement of fact, not a narration of the redemption of the boroughs or of the courage of the hero (as in other *Chronicle* poems). All of these are implied symptomatically by mentioning the accomplished deeds of King Edmund (he conquered Mercia, he freed the Danes). The absence of linear narration in the poem is manifested in the scarcity of finite verbal forms, two of which (*geode*, 'went', and *alysde*, 'set free') refer to King

---

[45] The new edition of *Íslendingadrápa by Haukr Valdísarson* is unavailable. I have used the text from the old edition in *Den norsk-islandske skjaldedigtning*, B, *Rettet tekst*, ed. F. JÓNSSON (Copenhagen, 1912; reprinted 1973), p. 541. I have followed the usual convention of quoting this edition. The letter B refers to the normalised version (*Rettet tekst*), rather than to the text according to manuscripts; the Roman numeral I refers to the volume; the number 541 refers to the page number; and 11 refers to the stanza of the poem, i.e. of *Íslendingadrápa*.

[46] "Þórðr Særeksson (Sjáreksson), *Róðudrápa*", ed. K.E. GADE, in: *Poetry from the Kings' Sagas 1: From Mythical Times to c. 1035*, ed. WHALEY, pp. 236-243, at p. 243.

[47] "Hallfreðr vandræðaskáld Óttarsson, *Erfidrápa Óláfs Tryggvasonar* 13", ed. K. HESLOP, in: *Poetry from the Kings' Sagas 1: From Mythical Times to c. 1035*, ed. WHALEY, pp. 403-440, at p. 419.

Edmund. As in skaldic verse, verbs in the poem are so colourless and lacking in information,[48] that they are close to functional verbs. They focus attention not on a narrative sequence in time but on the other dimension: space, acquired and protected. Verbal forms (*geode, scadeþ, gebegde*) occupy the fourth (and least important) position in the line, and only one is put in the position of key alliteration (*alysde*), when the verb becomes the thematic centre of the whole poem. On the contrary, compound words (*mundbora, dædfruma, brimstream, hæfteclommum, weorþscipe*), proper names (*Eadmund, Eadweardes*), toponyms (*Myrce, Dor, Hwitanwyllesgeat, Humbra, Ligoraceaster, Lincylene, Snotingaham, Deoraby*) and ethnonyms (*Engla, Dæne, Norðmannum*) are always marked by alliteration, creating double alliterative patterns in four lines composed of formulas (*mæcgea mundbora, dyre dædfruma, brada brimstream, afera Eadweardes*). A binary formula with compound words (*Ligoraceaster and Lincylene*), containing crossed alliteration, underlines the importance of the spatial extent of the realm Edmund managed to redeem.

An epic formula *lange þrage* (employed in *Beowulf, Genesis A*, and in the poem *On the Redemption of the Five Boroughs*, in which it is stated that the Northmen, i.e. Óláfr Guðfriðarson, subjected the Danes to heathendom for "a long time") can be interpreted as an example of wordplay, since it contradicts historical reality: according to the chronology of Simeon of Durham, Olaf could not have ruled the Five Boroughs for more than two years. In all three texts the formula *lange þrage* appears in the context of heathendom. In the *Chronicle* poem it is employed in the context of fighting against the heathens (*hæþena*), the Northmen (*Norðmenn*) who invaded England together with Olaf Guðfriðarson and are distinguished from the Danes, the second or third generation of the Vikings who settled in the British Isles and adopted Christianity.[49]

Formulaic wordplay in the *Chronicle* poem establishes an association between the Northmen (because of whom the Danes were "forced by necessity", *nyde gebegde,* to heathendom in the poem *On the Redemption of the Five Boroughs*), and their ruler Óláfr Guðfriðarson (Anlaf, who "forced by necessity", *nede gebeded*, had to escape from the Battle of Brunanburh). It is possible that the creator of the poem *On the Redemption of the Five Boroughs* consciously

---

[48] L. HOLLANDER, "The role of verb in Skaldic poetry", *Acta Philologica Scandinavica* 20 (1949), pp. 267-276.

[49] As pointed out by Jayne Carroll, the poem contains a distinction "between the newly arrived heathen Norsemen and the Danes of the Danelaw" who "are depicted as assimilated members of the Christian kingdom of England and, in fact, function metonymically for eastern Mercia's Anglo-Danish population as a whole" (CARROLL, "When were the Vikings in England?", p. 336).

follows the model of the *Battle of Brunanburh*, using the same alliterative pattern as the latter: "*þær geflemed wearð // Norðmanna bregu, / nede gebeded, // to lides stefne / litle weorode*" ("There the ruler of the Northmen, compelled by necessity, was put to flight, to ship's prow, with a small troop").[50] The ruler of the Northmen, whose flight is described in the quoted lines by the creator of the *Battle of Brunanburh*, is Óláfr Guðfriðarson, who could not possess the Five Boroughs for long (*lange þrage*). The use of the same formula, *nede gebeded*, in relation to Anlaf (Óláfr) in the *Battle of Brunanburh* and *nyde gebegde* in connection with the Danes, subjected to oppression by the Northmen in the poem *On the Redemption of the Five Boroughs,* could have created the effect of an ironic denigration of King Edmund's enemy, Óláfr Guðfriðarson, and was probably appreciated by a contemporary audience. It is possible to suggest that in the poem *On the Redemption of the Five Boroughs*, formulaic wordplay containing inherent allusions to skaldic poetry, pointed out in connection with the denotations of the ruler, has the function of underlining the victorious superiority of the Wessex ruler over his Old Norse adversaries, to whom he first lost land and then regained it.

* * *

The opposite extreme in the use of formulas in the *Chronicle* poems can be found in *The Death of Alfred Æþeling* (MSS C, D) which is included in the annals for 1042. The poem is composed in rhymed verse (rhyme being a rare and usually ornamental device in alliterative poetry, in which the organising principle of metrical composition is alliteration) and contains only four formulas in 38 lines: *leofan Gode*, 'beloved God'; *bliðe mid Criste*, 'blissfully with Christ'; *seo saul is mid Criste*, 'his soul is with Christ'; *frið namon*, 'made peace'. The first three formulas belong to the domain of Christian poetry, whereas the last one, *frið namon*, has parallels in heroic verse. The formula *frið namon* is included in the lines summarising the main theme of the poem on the death of Alfred, devoted to the most brutal crime, unrivalled since the time of the Viking invasion (the blinding and the death of a young heir to the throne and his companions): "*Ne wearð dreorlicre dæd / gedon on þison earde, // syþþan Dene common / and her frið namon*" ("There has not been a worse deed committed on this earth, since the Danes came and made peace here"). These lines invert a hyperbolic formula *Ne wearð + syþþan*, which occurs in the *Bat-*

---

[50] *The Battle of Brunanburh*, line 33.

tle of Brunanburh ("*Ne wearð wæl mare // on þys iglande / æfre gyta // folces gefylled / beforan þyssum // swurdes ecgum ... siððan eastan hider // Engle and Sexe / upp becomon*" – "Never before in this island was there a greater slaughter of people killed by the edges of swords ... since the Angles and Saxons came here from the east"), and evokes associations with the formulaic style of panegyric poetry, in which the glory of a battle is correlated with another great event: the coming of the Anglo-Saxons to the British Isles.

The same formula (*ne wearð* + *syþþan*) is used in the rhythmical annals of MS E for 978, in which the assassination of Edward the Martyr, King Æthelred's half-brother, is described as the worst deed performed for (or by) the Angles: "*Ne wearð Angelcynne nan wærsa dæd gedon, þonne þeos wæs syððon hi ærest / Bryton land sohton*" ("No worse deed was done for (or by) the race of the Angles than this, since they first sought out the land of Britain"). However, in the poem on the death of Alfred the chronology is established not by the beginning of British history, the Great Migration, but by the Viking invasion, which, as was thought by Wulfstan, was imposed on the inhabitants of the British Isles as punishment for their sins. The assassination of Alfred is considered by the creator of the poem as the worst crime committed since Canute and his descendants took the throne. The implicit associations with the traditional chronological frames set in other *Chronicle* annals (for 937, 978) make the audience realise the scope and effect of the Viking invasion: in the poem on the death of Alfred, the Danes take the place of the Angles and the Saxons, both as the invaders of Britain and as the rulers who replaced the Wessex heir, cruelly slaughtered by his own noblemen. The creator of the poem holds those in power responsible not only for the Danish invasion, but also for the assassination of Alfred: he implicitly accuses Godwine, whose betrayal is presented as in effect treason.[51]

In the expressive exclamation that no worse crime was committed since the Danes came to the British Isles, the creator of the poem uses the ambivalent formula *frið niman*, 'take peace', which is also employed in the *Battle of Maldon*. In the latter it occurs in a highly significant context: the speech of the Viking messenger, in which he ostensibly proposes peace but in fact threatens

---

[51] Th.A. BREDEHOFT, *Textual Histories: Readings in the Anglo-Saxon Chronicle* (Toronto, 2001), pp. 110-111. As pointed out by Thomas Bredehoft, "the shift in the specifics of the historical comparison (from the worst deed done since the English came, to the worst since the Danes came) serves to identify the English treachery as worse than any perpetrated by the Danes" (Th.A. BREDEHOFT, "History and memory in the *Anglo-Saxon Chronicle*", in: *Readings in Medieval Texts: Interpreting Old and Middle English Literature*. ed. D.F. JOHNSON and E. TREHARNE (Oxford, 2005), p. 117).

Formulaic Word-Play in the Poems of the Anglo-Saxon Chronicle 315

war. The Viking offers the Anglo-Saxons a chance to avoid battle if they "give ransom with good will and accept peace from us" (*"syllan ... feoh wið freode and niman frið æt us"*[52]), and promises that the Vikings will then "leave by sea and remain at peace with them" (*"on flot feran and eow friþes healdan"*[53]). It is not unlikely that the formula *frið niman* in the poem on the death of Alfred preserves the negative associations arising from the context of the hostile speech of the Viking messenger, which causes justified anger among the Anglo-Saxon troops and leads to their death in a bloody battle. Moreover the meaning of the verb *niman*, 'to take away or remove something from somebody' (cf. *"gif mec deaþ nimeþ"* – "if death takes me"; *"gif mec hild nime"* – "if battle takes me"; *"leton weg niman ... frætwa hyrde"* – "allowed the waves to take the guardian of treasures"[54]) facilitates a new interpretation of the lines about the coming of the Danes: it could mean not only 'make peace' (as rendered in scholarly editions and translations of the *Chronicle*) but have a simultaneously opposite meaning, 'take away peace' ("There has not been a worse deed committed on this earth, since the Danes came and took peace from us"). It is possible to suggest that the formulaic play in the poem on the death of Alfred, based on the use of formulas *ne wearð* + *syþþan* and *frið niman*, implies that the murder of the Wessex heir was regarded by contemporaries as a crime caused by the coming of the Danes, who brought war rather than peace to the British Isles. The use of formulaic style in the poem on Alfred's death is not only highly artistic, but also functions as a means of conveying meanings which could not be expressed explicitly by the creator of the poem but had to be deliberately concealed.

* * *

The use of formulaic style in the poem on the death of Alfred's brother, King Edward the Confessor (preserved in the annals of MSS C and D for 1065 but describing events of 1066), has, as far as is known, not been studied in detail, although every line of the poem includes formulas which have parallels in the main corpus of Old English poetry.[55] Formulas present in the poem are

---

[52] *The Battle of Maldon*, ed. in: *The Anglo-Saxon Poetic Records*, 6, pp. 7-16, ll. 38-39.
[53] *Ibid.*, l. 41.
[54] *Beowulf*, lines 447, 452, and 3132 respectively.
[55] An exhaustive list of formulaic phrases with their parallels can be found in the appendix to the article by Katherine O'Brien O'Keefe (K. O'BRIEN O'KEEFE, "Deaths and transformations: Thinking through the 'end' of Old English verse", in: *New Directions in Oral Theory*, ed. M.A.

either reproduced or varied in other Old English poems, or possess "potential reproducibility",[56] which becomes a crucial consideration bearing in mind the fragmentary nature of the extant texts. Half of the formulas are reproduced in the poetic corpus unaltered, while the other half shows insignificant variation in one of the components: e.g. the noun in the formula noun + participle II (in the formula *lande bereafod* constituting a formulaic system with phrases *since bereafod, ealdre bereafod, golde bereafod, blæde bereafod, dome bereafod* ('deprived of land' or 'deprived of treasures, life, gold, power, fame') or the noun in the formula adjective + noun (in the formula *cræftig ræda* constituting a formulaic system with phrases *wordes cræftig, niða cræftig, leoþa cræftig* ('crafty in advice, speech, song'); or in the formula *freolic wealdend* comprising a formulaic system with the phrase *freolic frumbearn* ('famous lord' or 'famous leader'). Verbs in the formulaic systems employed in the poem are not subject to substitution, only their grammatical form can be varied: e.g. plural (*welan brytnodan*, they 'dispersed treasures') or singular (*weolan brytnode*, he 'dispersed treasures'). The formulaic style of the poem on the death of Edward the Confessor can be called exhaustive, since in no other poem, including *Beowulf* and the *Battle of Brunanburh*, do formulas occur so frequently.[57]

The composition of the poem about King Edward is based on formulas, since they are endowed with special functions that allow them to convey veiled implications: the formula *wis, welþungen* ('wise, well-famed') is used to characterise Beowulf,[58] and the same formula is applied to the king in the poem on King Edward, who is called "much famed" ("*wel geþungen*"[59]); in *Beowulf* the hero is denoted with the help of the formula 'a man endowed with great virtues' (*guma cystum god*[60]); correspondingly, in the poem on King Edward the hero is described in the same formula as "the king endowed with great virtues" ("*kyningc kystum god*"[61]). Traditional formulas have the function of establishing associative links with the canons of heroic poetry in order to recreate key motifs (such as fame, wisdom, merit, generosity), characterising the hero of the poem, King Edward the Confessor. Formulas are designed to convey the image

---

AMODIO (Tempe, AZ, 2005), pp. 173-178).
[56] SMIRNITSKAYA, *Stikh i yazyk*, p. 213.
[57] Katherine O'Brien O'Keefe lists parallels between every formula used in each half-line of the *Chronicle* poem on the 'Death of Edward' and other Old English poems (O'BRIEN O'KEEFE, "Deaths and transformations", pp. 173-178).
[58] *Beowulf*, line 1927.
[59] *The Death of Edward*, line 9A.
[60] *Beowulf*, lines 1486 and 2543.
[61] *The Death of Edward*, line 23a.

of a hero, evoking well-known associations; therefore their main function can be called associative.

The traditional motif of royal glory is revealed in the poem about King Edward with the help of a formulaic list of peoples inhabiting the country which is ruled by him. A list of the peoples ("*Walum and Scottum and Bryttum eac ... Englum and Sexum*"[62] – "The Welsh and the Scots and the Britons also ... the Angles and the Saxons") reminds the audience of the *þulur* from *Widsith* which enumerate all the peoples known to the Anglo-Saxons: "*Ætla weold Hunum, / Eormanric Gotum, // Becca Baningum, / Burgendum Gifica. // Casere weold Creacum / ond Celic Finnum*"[63] (*Widsith*, lines19-21). The analogy with the formulaic list of peoples in *Widsith* enables the creator of the poem to establish an associative connection with King Edward's boundless possessions and emphasises his main feature as a ruler: he succeeded in uniting all the peoples who inhabited his country.

The formulaic list of the peoples subjected to King Edward could have been intended to contrast with his loneliness in youth, when he was "deprived of lands" ("*lande bereafod*"[64]) and had to "live along the paths of exile far on earth" ("*wunode wræclastum wide geond eorðan*"[65]). As has been shown by Stanley Greenfield, formulas consisting of 'a noun in the genitive case + a participle of the verb *bereafian*' occur not only in *Beowulf* (cf. *since bereafod, ealdre bereafod, golde bereafod*[66]) but also in Christian poems[67] (*dome bereafod*;[68] *blæde bereafod*[69]). Greenfield called formulas similar to those quoted above 'deprivative', because verbs used in them convey the semantics of deprivation:[70] *benæman* (*wuldre benæmed*, 'deprived of glory'[71]); *bedreosan* (*eorlum bedroren*, 'deprived of earls'[72]); *bescierian* (*eðle bescierede* – 'deprived of patrimony';[73] *wuldres bescierede* – 'deprived of glory'[74]); *bedælan* (*dreame be-*

---

[62] *Ibid.*, lines 9b-11b.
[63] *Widsith*, ed. in: *The Anglo-Saxon Poetic Records*, 3, pp. 149-153, lines 19-21.
[64] *Ibid.*, line 16.
[65] *Ibid.*, line 17.
[66] *Beowulf*, lines 2746, 2825, and 3018 respectively.
[67] GREENFIELD, "The formulaic expression of the theme of exile in Anglo-Saxon poetry", p. 355.
[68] *Christ III*, ed. in: *The Anglo-Saxon Poetic Records*, 3, pp. 27-49, line 168.
[69] *Genesis*, ed. in: *The Anglo-Saxon Poetic Records*, 1, pp. 3-87, line 859.
[70] Stanley Greenfield lists synonymous formulas in relation to the object to which they refer, in order to show the richness of the imagery of exile (GREENFIELD, *ibid.*).
[71] *Christ and Satan*, ed. in: *The Anglo-Saxon Poetic Records*, 1, pp. 135-158, line 120.
[72] *Genesis*, line 2099.
[73] *Christ III*, line 32.
[74] *Christ and Satan*, line 342.

dæled – 'deprived of joy';[75] *cnosle bedæled* – 'deprived of kin';[76] *dreamum bedælde* – 'deprived of joys';[77] *hroðra bedæled* – 'deprived of peace';[78] *duguðum bedæled* – 'deprived of warriors';[79] *eallum bedæled, duguðum and dreamum* – 'deprived of all, warriors and joys';[80] *goda bedæled* – 'deprived of grace';[81] and in the Old English elegies: *winemægum bidroren* – 'deprived of dear relatives';[82] *eðle bedæled* – 'deprived of land'.[83]

Deprivative formulas constitute a formulaic system with verbs synonymous with the verb *bereafian*, 'deprive' and are used in the *Chronicle* poems to create images associated with the theme of exile. Thus in the poem on the death of King Edgar[84] the formulaic style is used to reveal the theme of exile in connection with the Northumbrian ruler Oslac:

> *And þa wearð eac adræfed / deormod hæleð, // Oslac, of earde / ofer yða gewealc, // ofer ganotes bæð, / gamolfeax hæleð, // wis and wordsnotor, / ofer wætera geðring, // ofer hwæles eðel, / hama bereafod*
>
> And then also the brave-spirited warrior Oslac was driven from the land, over the rolling waves, over the gannet's bath, grey-haired warrior, wise and eloquent, over the commotion of waves, over the whales' domain, deprived of homes.

Oslac being 'deprived of homes' (*hama bereafod*[85]) or King Edward being 'deprived of lands' (*lande bereafod*[86]) inevitably evoke associations with elegiac exiles, because the motifs of deprivation and loss, central to the theme of exile, are traditionally associated with elegiac imagery. The use of the formula, containing the verb 'to deprive' (*bereafian*), could have enabled the creator of the poem on the death of King Edward to establish associations with the entire formulaic system, emphasising the key motif of a hero deprived not only of material wealth (land, treasures and gold), but also of spiritual goods (joy, consolation and comfort).

---

[75] *Beowulf*, line 1275.
[76] *Widsith*, line 52.
[77] *Christ and satan*, line 343.
[78] Cynewulf, *Juliana*, ed. in: *The Anglo-Saxon Poetic Records*, 3, pp. 113-133, line 390.
[79] *Genesis*, line 930; *Christ and satan*, line 121.
[80] *Christ III*, lines 1407-1408.
[81] *Christ and satan*, line 185.
[82] *Seafarer*, ed. in: *The Anglo-Saxon Poetic Records*, 3, pp. 143-147, line 16.
[83] *Wanderer*, ed. in: *The Anglo-Saxon Poetic Records*, 3, pp. 134-137, line 20.
[84] MSS D and E, *sub anno* 975.
[85] *Ibid.*, line 7.
[86] *Ibid.*, line 16.

The second key formula in the *Chronicle* poem, which refers to the creation of the image of King Edward, doomed in his youth "to live on the roads of exile" ("*wunode wræclastum*"), is found mainly in elegies.[87] With the help of this formula, Edward is likened to the exiled heroes of the Old English elegies *The Wanderer* and *The Seafarer*, whose heroes are also forced to roam the roads of exile (*wadan wræclastas*):

Oft him anhaga / are gebideð, // metudes miltse, / þeah þe he modcearig // geond lagulade / longe sceolde // hreran mid hondum / hrimcealde sæ // wadan wræclastas[88]

Often the lone-dweller waits for grace, mercy of the Lord. Although he, sorrowful in heart, must long row by hands along the waterways, (along) the ice-cold sea, tread the paths of exile;

hu ic earmcearig   iscealdne sæ // winter wunade / wræccan lastum, // winemægum bidroren, / bihongen hrimgicelum; hægl scurum fleag[89]

how I, sorrowful in misery, on the ice-cold sea lived the whole winter on the paths of exile, bereft of friendly kinsmen, hung about with icicles; hail flew in showers.

The description of exile with its deprivation and suffering is the key theme of the Anglo-Saxon elegies, and Edward's grievous fate in his youth is close to that of an elegiac hero. Like the hero of *The Seafarer*, King Edward was destined to wander along the roads of exile, "to seek the land of a foreign people" (*elþeodigra eard gesece*[90]), associated in the poem with adversity, dangers, separation, and loss. The *Chronicle* poem endows the image of Edward with associations with the exiles of the Anglo-Saxon elegies, depicted as sad in spirit, deprived of friends, suffering from loneliness and yearning for their native land.

---

[87] Katherine O'Brien O'Keefe points out that King Edward "treads the paths of exile (much like the Wanderer), but he does so with patience ('a bliðemod') in the twenty-eight years of his absence" (O'BRIEN O'KEEFE, "Deaths and transformations", p. 170), whereas Catherine Clarke interprets the exile imagery in the poem in terms of "the traditional Christian understanding of earthly life as a period of exile from God" and draws parallels with Hebrews 11:13-16 (C.A.M. CLARKE, *Writing Power in Anglo-Saxon England: Texts, Hierarchies, Economies* (Woodbridge, 2012: Anglo-Saxon Studies), p. 64).
[88] *Wanderer*, lines 1-5.
[89] *Seafarer*, lines 15-21.
[90] *Ibid.*, line 38.

The depiction of King Edward as an exile evokes associations not only with Old English elegies, but also with Christian epic, in which the motif of exile is widely used.[91] In the poem *Christ and satan*, for example, the torments of hell include "wandering along the paths of exile" (*wadan wræclastas*[92]); the hero of *Daniel* warns Nebuchadnezzar that "the Lord will cut him off from the kingdom and send him into exile, devoid of friends" (*Metod ðec aceorfeþ of cyningdome, ðec wineleasne on wræc sendeð*[93]); in *Genesis A*, Adam and Eve are doomed for their disobedience to exile (*þu scealt oðerne / eðel secean, // wynleasran wic, / and on wræc hweorfan // nacod niedwædla* – "you must look for another homeland, a dwelling more deprived of joy, go into exile from Paradise, naked wretch"[94]); Cain who killed his brother has to "retire into exile" (*on wræc hweorfan*[95]) "far from his father's house" (*fædergeardum feor*[96]). Associations with the key formulas of Christian epic enable the creator of the poem on the death of King Edward to use the formulaic style in order to show the universality of human suffering after the Fall and to depict the hardships of life as an inevitable evil awaiting the human race in the earthly vale.

Formulas responsible for the key theme of exile in Old English Christian, heroic, and elegiac poetry usually have strictly defined semantics. As pointed out by Stanley Greenfield, formulas are used to indicate the 'status' of an exile (e.g. *nacod niedwædla*, "naked wretch" in *Genesis*[97]), his 'deprivation' (*lande bereafod*, "deprived of land", in the poem on the death of King Edward[98]), his 'state of mind' (*modcearig*, "sorrowful of mind";[99] *earmcearig*, "sorrowful in misery", *The Seafarer*[100]), or his "movement into exile" (*wunode wræclastum*).[101] The motif of movement is usually conveyed in Old English poetry with more detail than other motifs concerning the theme of exile, and can include factors such as distance from homeland or endurance of the suffering found in

---

[91] Renée Trilling interprets a parallel with Biblical heroes, "in whom the Anglo-Saxons saw literary models for their own identity, as a nostalgic gesture towards the ancient Anglo-Saxon past" (R.R. TRILLING, *The Aesthetics of Nostalgia: Historical Representation in Old English Verse* (Toronto, 2009), p. 210).

[92] *Christ and satan*, line 120a.

[93] *Daniel*, ed. in: *The Anglo-Saxon Poetic Records*, 1, pp. 111-132, line 568.

[94] *Genesis*, lines 927-929.

[95] *Ibid.*, line 1014b.

[96] *Ibid.*, line 1053a.

[97] *Ibid.*, line 929.

[98] Line 16.

[99] *Ibid.*, line 5.

[100] *Seafarer*, line 15.

[101] GREENFIELD, "The formulaic expression of the theme of exile", pp. 354-356.

isolation.[102] Thus Oslac, mentioned in the *Chronicle* poem on the death of King Edgar, is destined to make his way along the "heaving of waves" ("*ofer yða gewealc*"), along the "land of whales" ("*ofer hwæles eðel*"); the same formulas *yþa gewealc* ('rolling of waves') and *hwæles eþel* ('the whales' estate') are twice mentioned in *The Seafarer* 8, 60.[103] Fourfold repetition of the prepositional adverb *ofer*, 'along, through', preceding the four formulas denoting the sea (*ofer yða gewealc, ofer ganotes bæð, ofer wætera geðring, ofer hwæles eðel*, 'along the rolling of waves', 'along the waters of the cormorant', 'along the battle of waters', 'over the land of whales'), emphasises the motif of the hero's movement along the stormy waves that carry him far from home, from family, from friends, from native land. The use of the formulaic style in the poem on the death of King Edward is fully consistent with the canonical treatment of the theme of exile in Old English poetry. Two formulas briefly summarise the key motifs of this theme: deprivation (*lande bereafod* – 'deprived of lands'[104]) and movement (*wunode wræclastum wide geond eorðan* – 'lived on the roads of exile far on earth'[105]), containing all the associations necessary to create an archetypal image of an exile.

After his exile, Edward finds his homeland and, like the leader of a *comitatus*, defends his land, country, and people (*eðel bewerode, // land and leode,*[106]). The formula *land and leode* is also found in the Christian poem *Andreas*;[107] moreover, as in the poem on the death of King Edward the Confessor (He on worulda her wunode þrage on kyneþrymme – "Here in the world he lived up to a time in royal glory"[108]) it occurs in the immediate vicinity of the deprivative formula synonymous to "*lande bereafod*" (*rices berædde*), "deprived of land (country)" and of the compound word *cyneþrym*, 'royal glory':

> *Hafast nu þe anum / eall getihhad // land ond leode, / swa dyde lareow þin. // Cyneþrym ahof, / þam wæs Crist nama, // ofer middangeard, / þynden hit meahte swa. // Þone Herodes ealdre besnyðede, // forcom æt campe / cyning Iudea, //* rices berædde, */ ond hine rode befealg,*

---

[102] *Ibid.*, p. 356.
[103] *Poem on the death of King Edgar*, lines 8, 60. Cf. GREENFIELD, "The formulaic expression of the theme of exile", p. 356.
[104] *Poem on the death of King Edgar*, line 16.
[105] *Ibid.*, line 17.
[106] *Poem on the death of King Edward*, lines 24b-25.
[107] *Andreas*, ed. in: *The Anglo-Saxon Poetic Records*, 2, pp. 3-51, line 1321a.
[108] *Poem on the death of King Edward the Confessor*, lines 4-5.

Now you took it all on yourself, land and people, as your Master did. He was exalted by his royal glory, for his name was Jesus, in the middle world, while he could do it. Herod took his life, the king of the Jews defeated him in battle, deprived him of his kingdom and nailed him to the cross.[109]

Two formulaic and one verbal coincidence might not be enough to conclude that the Old English poem about St. Andrew was chosen as a model by the creator of the *Chronicle* poem on the death of King Edward the Confessor. However, it can be assumed that the compiler of the *Chronicle* sought to endow the image of his hero with associations with the glorified saint. It is plausible that the poem on the death of King Edward was composed in the context of his emerging cult, as Edward was canonised less than a hundred years after his death (in February 1161).

It is possible to make another suggestion concerning the function of formulas in the poem on the death of King Edward: the formulas in the poem are not only endowed with associative functions, they are also deliberately cultivated as a stylistic device for the sake of creating poetic word-play. The creator of the poem, probably intentionally, does not give the exact date of King Edward's death, but says only that it happened 24 years later (Worcester manuscript) or 24 and a half years after his accession to the throne (Abingdon manuscript), that is, after he "shared the wealth for twenty four and a half years in succession of winters" ("*XXIIII wintra gerimes weolan brytnode*").[110] The formulaic expression "*wintra gerimes welan brytnian*", "to give away wealth by the count of winters" is reproduced in the poem for the second time (also in a formula), in the context of the reference to the dominion of the Danes: "28 winters wasted wealth" ("*XXVIII wintra gerimes welan brytnodon*").[111] Whereas the Scandinavian invaders "wasted wealth" (*welan brytnodon*[112]), King Edward "distributed wealth" (*weolan brytnode*[113]) to his faithful people:[114] the verb *brytnian*, 'to distribute, to waste', is used both times in formulas which carry opposite connota-

---

[109] *Andreas*, lines 1320-1326.

[110] *Poem on the death of King Edward*, lines 6b-7. Edward came to power after the death of Harthacnut in June 1042, and died in January 1066; therefore, he ruled for 23 and a half years.

[111] *Poem on the death of King Edward*, lines 20b-21. Danish rule began when Sweyn exiled Æthelred to Normandy in November 1013, and ended with the death of Harthacnut in June 1042, i.e. lasted 28 and a half years with interruptions.

[112] *Ibid.*, line 21b.

[113] *Ibid.*, line 7b.

[114] Renée Trilling interprets the phrase "*weolan brytnode*" as "calling up images of the lord dealing out golden rings to his loyal companions in the hall" (TRILLING, *The Aesthetics of Nostalgia*, p. 210).

tions. With the help of the formulaic style, the composer of the poem depicts how the Viking invaders plunder the country, squandering its wealth, and simultaneously recreates the image of Edward as the leader of a Germanic *comitatus* who bestowed treasures on his warriors.

The images of a ruler distributing wealth ("*XXIIII wintra gerimes / weolan brytnode*"[115] – "shared the wealth for twenty four and a half years in succession of winters") or of invaders squandering wealth ("*XXVIII wintra gerimes welan brytnodon*"[116] – "28 winters wasted wealth"), which occurred in the *Chronicle* poem, evoke associations not only with Germanic heroic poetry, but also with Christian epic. The formula *welan bryttian*, 'to distribute wealth', is used in *Genesis* and in *Daniel*: *Ne þearf ic yrfestol / eaforan bytlian //ænegum minra, / ac me æfter sculon // mine woruldmagas / welan bryttian*[117] – "I (Abraham) have no need to establish a throne for any of my heirs, but after me my relatives will have to share my riches"; *þæt he Babilone / abrecan wolde, // alhstede eorla, / þær æðelingas // under wealla hleo / welan brytnedon*[118] – "That he (the ruler of Media) would destroy Babylon, the places of the temples of the princes, where the nobles wasted wealth in the shelter of the walls".

It is difficult to establish the exact connotations of the formula *welan bryttian* in *Genesis A* and in *Daniel*; in dictionaries it is usually interpreted in a positive sense, using the verb 'enjoy', in which case it can be compared with the formula related to King Edward the Confessor. However, the context of both *Genesis A* and *Daniel* implies negative connotations: in the first case, Abraham complains to the Lord that he has not got a son; therefore, his riches will go to his relatives who will squander them. And in the second it is used in connection with Belshazzar, who squanders wealth together with the nobles. If the interpretation of the formula *welan bryttian* in Christian epic as endowed with denigrating connotations is accepted, then its semantic similarity to the formula applied to the Scandinavian invaders in the poem about King Edward could be suggested.

The formula *welan bryttian* is by no means the only one in the poem whose semantics are played on. Another case in point is the formulaic denotation of the ruler, emphasising the genealogy of Edward, who is called the "offspring of Æthelred" (*byre Æðelredes*).[119] The creator of the poem plays on the name of

---

[115] *Poem on the death of King Edward*, lines 6a-7.
[116] *Ibid.*, lines 20b-21.
[117] *Genesis A*, lines 2177-2179.
[118] *Daniel*, lines 688-690.
[119] *Poem on the death of King Edward*, line 10b. Katherine O'Brien O'Keefe points out the importance of the phrase "*byre Æðelredes*" and of the double use of *æðela* within "the historical

Æthelred's father, calling Edward "expert in advice" (*"cræftig ræda"*[120]), because Æthelred's name (*Æðel-ræd*) means 'noble council'. However, Æthelred's nickname ('Unreasonable', *'Un-ræd'*), which also uses the root *ræd*, 'advice', can be interpreted as 'lack of advice', or as 'evil, criminal, treacherous advice' (possibly an allusion to the murder of Æthelred's brother Edward the Martyr, which cleared him the way to the throne). The name of Æthelred is mentioned in the poem once again in connection with the Scandinavian invasion, when Canute prevailed over the "clan of Æthelred" (*"kynn Æðelredes"*[121]), that is, over Edward and his younger brother Alfred, whose death is described in the aforementioned poem of the *Anglo-Saxon Chronicle*.

The use of formulas in the poem on the death of Edward must have evoked in the audience associations with the formulaic style of alliterative verse, which was almost out of use by the time of its composition (in the poem about the death of Alfred Ætheling, Edward's brother, included in the *Chronicle* for 1036, there are only four formulas, and rhyme is used in more than half of the lines). In terms of the number of formulas, the frequency of their use and a special associative function, the poem on the death of Edward significantly surpasses any Old English text;[122] it is therefore possible that an excessive use of formulas is turned by the creator of the poem into a stylistic device. The poet must have had special reasons to choose a style saturated with formulas, conveying hidden meanings through the use of highly traditional poetic means. He focussed on the canonical models of the Old English poems, using the characteristic features of alliterative verse and the traditional formulaic style, endowed with associations with heroic poetry. As was aptly pointed out by Renée Trilling, "the self-conscious archaising of poetic form in the twilight of Anglo-Saxon England is itself enough to provoke a sense of nostalgia, especially in modern readers".[123] Like the Germanic epic, the poem about Edward's death is directed not at the present, but at the idealised past, times of peace, a golden age with which Edward's reign was associated after the Norman Conquest when the eulogy about him could have been composed. The excessive use of the formulaic style and the strictest canonical form of alliterative verse at the end of the Anglo-Saxon tradition can also be considered a poetic expression of longing for the past. In the poetic obituary for the last Wessex king, embodied in traditional

---

framework of Athelstan's victory", which makes Edward an embodiment of his line (O'BRIEN O'KEEFE, "Deaths and Transformations", p. 169).

[120] *Poem on the death of King Edward*, line 5b.
[121] *Poem on the death of King Edward*, line 18b.
[122] O'BRIEN O'KEEFE, "Deaths and transformations", pp. 173-178.
[123] TRILLING, *The Aesthetics of Nostalgia*, p. 209.

Anglo-Saxon alliterative verse, formulas, undoubtedly playing the role of an artistic device, were endowed with an associative function, accompanied by honorific and heroicising connotations.

The semantics and the compositional role of formulas have been discussed in this chapter in order to establish a new function of formulaic style in written poetry (in addition to its utilitarian and aesthetic functions singled out in previous scholarship) which has been provisionally called 'associative'. It has been demonstrated that individual formulas in the *Chronicle* poems establish associations with traditional motifs and imagery of heroic and Christian poetry. Word-play in which a formula carries associations with an entire formulaic system, enables the creators of the *Chronicle* poems to bring into prominence key motifs of their components in order to convey additional, deliberately concealed implications. In the *Chronicle* poems formulaic word-play, performing the role of a consciously cultivated aesthetic device which is used in an associative function, is endowed with new idealising or ironically denigrating connotations.

Freeman's Formulas:
Openings, Transitions, and Closes[*]

JONATHAN ROPER

For historic and economic reasons, the oral narration of long traditional folktales lasted for much longer in Newfoundland than it did in most of the rest of the Anglosphere. Especially fortunately for us as researchers, it survived into the age of portable audio-recording. In the 1960s, folklorists from the local university, Herbert Halpert and John Widdowson, visited the Bennett family of St. Paul's, who had been known for their knowledge of folk song from previous research, and "it soon became clear that this family was as remarkable for its storytelling as its singing".[1] Although the practice of storytelling was semi-moribund at this stage, they made numerous audio-recordings, including multiple recordings of the same tale from the same teller, during their repeat visits to St. Paul's, and they published the data in an exemplary academic edition of almost 200 audio-recorded anglophone tales, presented in unusually detailed textualisations.[2]

---

[*] This work has been supported by the Estonian Research Council (grant project PGR 670).
[1] H. HALPERT and J.D.A. WIDDOWSON, with M.J. LOVELACE and E. COLLINS, *Folktales of Newfoundland: The Resilience of the Oral Tradition*, 2 vols. (New York, 1996), p. XXXII.
[2] HALPERT and WIDDOWSON, *Folktales of Newfoundland*.

New Light on Formulas in Oral Poetry and Prose, ed. Daniel SÄVBORG and Bernt Ø. THORVALDSEN, *Utrecht Studies in Medieval Literacy*, 57 (Turnhout: Brepols, 2023), pp. 327-351.

This material is of interest to me (if I may be allowed a personal note) not just because the Newfoundland tale tradition presents clear analogues to, and indeed direct connections with, the English tale material I have looked at before, but also because my own chief field site has been the village immediately to the north of St. Paul's. Using, like Halpert and Widdowson, the method of repeat visits, I found between 2000 and 2015 that almost every traditional genre of folk poetry, including riddles, songs, charms, anecdotes, jokes, legends, and even party-plays, was either active or still recallable to mind in this area. But the longest genre, the wonder tale, had by now disappeared. In this sense, Halpert and Widdowson worked at exactly the right time, while audio-recording was possible and the wonder tale tradition was only semi-, and not fully, moribund.

Half a dozen years after their academic edition, Widdowson produced a semi-popular book based on the material entitled *Little Jack*.[3] Examining such texts, things seem promising for formula hunters. Here, for instance, is the simplified version one a tale told by Mose Troke in 1964:

> There was a king one time who had a daughter, and whoever could tell him a story without an end was to marry his daughter and have half the kingdom. And whoever tried but could not tell him such a story would have their heads cut off.
>
> There were several fellows who tried it; they thought they would go and get the king's daughter. And one fellow said he would try it, so he started out and he told his story.[4]

When we turn to the the verbatim transcript of this tale, we find something much less smooth:

> A king one time _ I'll tell you [th]is one now. Er ... a king one time _ he got a ... a daughter. An' ... whoever _ 'd tell un a story without a end _ was to marry his daughter _ an' have a half o' the kingdom. An' whoever couldn't tell un _ they had ... they had their head cut off.
>
> Ah there was several fellers tried it _ thought they'd go an' get the king's daughter. An' one feller _ said HE'D try it. /So/ _ he started out an' he made his story. /fo/[5]

---

[3] J.D.A. WIDDOWSON, *Little Jack and Other Newfoundland Folktales* (St John's, Newfoundland, 2002).
[4] HALPERT and WIDDOWSON, *Folktales of Newfoundland*, p. LXV.
[5] HALPERT and WIDDOWSON, *Folktales of Newfoundland*, p. LXVI.

And so it turns out that the exemplary level of detail in the transcriptions (and the system of notation devised to express this detail) presents something of an obstacle for those interested in finding formulas. All the hesitations, false starts, elisions ('is' for 'this'), misencodings ('fo' for 'so'), idiosyncratic emphases, and repetitions, in a nutshell all the things that are usually edited out when speech is transcribed, confound the mind focussed on formulas, and frustrates those word searches based on producing lists of 2-grams, 3-grams, 4-grams. We cannot, à la Nikolayev,[6] use an algorithm and extract the recurrent text-strings of this texts, because the perfectly formed sentences we find in the semi-popular edition are so often interrupted in the finely detailed transcriptions. The semi-popular edition's data is too unrealistic, too good. If there are formulas in it, then they are often formulas broken and paused.

Perhaps this might lead us to lament that the texts in the academic edition have not been 'tidied up', but the cleaning of folklore texts, like the cleaning of archaeological treasures, can remove things it might be better not to remove. Whereas work is often a matter of making the most of bad data, using well-transcribed audio-recordings, such as those of Halpert and Widdowson, is a matter of making the most of good data. Indeed, the material is so rich it allows us to look at different tellings of the same tale by the same teller, something which can help establish the norms followed by talented storytellers. In this chapter, I have chosen to look at the tales told by one of their key informants, Freeman Bennett (1896-1981), from whom they recorded a total of 26 narratives in a variety of genres, including wonder tales. In extracts from his tales, I have marked what would seem to be formulas in bold. The other unusual features of the transcribed tales are part of Halpert and Widdowson's transcription style.

One tale that Freeman told the researchers three times was a version of the type ATU 304.[7] The plot of this story is simple enough. A married couple and their only son leave home due to poverty. Jack soon parts from his parents and comes across a castle with three giants in it, whom he manages to kill by the use of trickery. He is then rewarded by the king, and everyone lives happily ever after. Freeman learnt the tale from Eli Roberts of the neighbouring community of Sally's Cove circa 1920, when Freeman would have been in his mid-

---

[6] D. NIKOLAYEV, "A new algorithm for extracting formulas from poetic texts and the formulaic density of Russian *bylinas*", *Oral Tradition* 30.1 (2015), pp. 111-136.

[7] ATU 304. For ATU, see: H.-J. UTHER, *The Types of International Folktales: A Classification and Bibliography, Based on the System of Antti Aarne and Stith Thompson*, 3 vols. (Helsinki, 2004).

twenties. When he was recorded half a century later (in 1966, 1970, and 1971, to be precise), he called the tale 'Peter and Minnie', after the parents of Jack. Maybe this was because in his rendition it is not just Jack and the king's daughter who have a happy ending, but Jack's parents too, and possibly also because, given his age at the time he told the folklorists the tale, he identified more with the parents than with Jack.

In their commentary, the fieldworkers invoked the "listeners of former days" and spoke of becoming "part of the audience he had once known",[8] statements which allow us to understand both the moribund nature of the practice and how, through their intervention, it was coming to life again. Even though we have remarkably good data, we still cannot be said to be entirely comparing like with like in this case, as Freeman did not often get to narrate this tale in his everyday life, which means that there are some pockets of confusion in both the first and second tellings arising from the tale not having been told recently. Unusually, the tale grew longer with each telling, which is not something typical when retelling the same story to the same person. The fieldworkers specifically remark that Freeman and his brother Everett, another skilled storyteller, would "narrate a shorter, less elaborate though often smoother version of a tale on a second or third occasion".[9] They suggest this may be, naturally enough, due to "their knowledge that the collector has heard it from them before and they may therefore think that more elaboration is unnecessary", or else that it may rather be due to the "streamlining of the tale after the process of calling it to mind after a lapse of many years". This streamlining is not the case with these three versions of this particular tale as recorded from Freeman: the earliest version was about 3400 words long, the second was about 3900 words long, and the third had grown to around 4600 words in length.

One observation that supports the fieldworkers' impression that initial tellings by the Bennetts were faltering recollections and that subsequent tellings were more streamlined, was that first tellings were often at a slower pace than subsequent ones. But, as far as the pace of the tellings under the microscope here, the pace of the first is in fact the quickest, at around 4.2 words per second, while that of the second and third are slower at around 3.6 and 3.7 words per second, respectively. While their observations are likely correct as far as other tales are concerned, they are belied here.

---

[8] HALPERT and WIDDOWSON, *Folktales of Newfoundland*, p. 1065.
[9] HALPERT and WIDDOWSON, *Folktales of Newfoundland*, p. 1007.

Opening Formulas

What can we say about the first of these groups of formulas, opening formulas? In chronological order of recording, these are the three openings which introduce Jack and his parents, and which set the narrative ball rolling by having them decide to leave home and move to the city (and here I quote at length):

1966 version:

> Well once upon a time in olden times you know - there was a ... well there ... perhaps there'd [be] a family livin here an' perhaps in another ... thirty mile there'd be another family see? Well now't would be a long ways 'fore they'd get to the ... to the settlement. Well anyhow there was a family we 'll say he was li[vin] ... they was livin HERE. An' uh ... only just Uh ... their uh ... only just the three of 'em, they had one son. Now their son's name was Jack. It got poor times, well they never had very much an' ... an' uh ... he said to his father well he said uh ... "We got to shift out o' this place" he said "we can't stay here" he said "we'll have to go out" he said "to the ... to the city" he said "that we can ... so we can earn a livin" he said "we got nothing to eat". He said "An' we can't stay here". Ol' man said "Yes" he said "we'll have to go. Well" he said "we'll pack up tomorrow morning" he said "an' we'll go". So by god _ next morning _ they packed up.

1970 version:

> Well once upon a time _ in uh ... i ... in olden times ya know, that's away back in pod auger days that is _ there was a ... well there ... there was a ... family living well ... we'll say up to ... Sally's Cove, that's about ten mile from this. Oh further than that, so far as to this to Bonne Bay. Well they ... they lived there for ... oh good many years an' they uh ... got on alright. An' last goin' off uh ... the times got so bad _ they got down an' out an' uh ... nothing to eat see? Well uh ... th' ol' man said, he said "Well" he said uh ... "we'll have to leave" _ he said "an' go out" he said uh ... "go out" he said "to the (city)". "Go out" he said "to the city". An' well _ th' ol' woman said "Yes" she said "we'll have to do something _ 'cause" she said "we got nothing to eat. " Well uh ... Jack _ they had a little feller there, his name was Jack, they only had one ... one ... boy _ one child. "Well" he said "alright" he said "tomorrow morning" he said "we'll go". Well _ in the morning they got up an' they packed up.

1971 version:

Well once upon a time _ in olden times ya know well might be uh ... perhaps five or six hundred year ago _ well uh ... I can ... I can only just mind that anyhow! I wasn't very ol'. Not ... not five or six hundred year ago! But anyhow I ... I ... I can mind a little bit about it. There was a ... one time see ther ... there used to be a ... a family livin here, well now they'd be a long ways see from the ... from the city, they might be _ two days' walk. Well now this family was livin here he had one son. An' his name was Jack. An' there was only the three of 'em, well _ they lived there for uh ... twenty-five or thirty year. Well the times got so bad _ they uh ... never got much to eat. He said to his uh ... father an' mother, he said "I think" he said "we'll _ go out to the city" he said "an' see" he said "can we get a job out there" he said "an' a place to stay" he said "'cause we can't live here" he said "no longer". He said uh ... "We can't live here". "Well" she said "alright" she said "we'll go".[10]

These three excerpts do the same work in setting up their stories: first, they establish this is a story that happened "once upon a time", i.e. it will be a story where all sorts of things will happen that do not happen in real life. Then the parents and their son Jack are introduced, their poverty (and hunger) is described and presented as the reason for them to leave home. Already we have a sense of the unusual nature of the story in that it is not just Jack who leaves home, but also his parents.

In terms of formula, we can clearly see each rendition begins with the opening formula "well, once upon a time, in olden times you know". "Well once upon a time" is a classic opening formula in anglophone tale-telling, but what follows is more typical of Freeman. "In olden times you know" seems to function as an explanation or underlining of the meaning of "once upon a time". It is almost as though it is a translation of "once upon a time". It is the "you know" that suggests it is a kind of translation of a compulsory but formal phrase into common language. It is reminiscent of a feature of weather forecasts in Britain at one time, when utterances like this might be heard: "Tomorrow it will be twenty-one degrees Centigrade, that's seventy degrees Fahrenheit". The temperature was first given, as it officially should be, in Centigrade, and then it was translated into the more understandable Fahrenheit. Could it be that before regaining currency in Newfoundland via mass media, the phrase 'once upon a time' was not immediately intelligible to Freeman's listeners? Of course, that weather forecasting formula was current only for one period in time, and nowadays the temperatures are given out exclusively in Centigrade. By analogy, we could imagine a modern Freeman beginning tales simply with

---

[10] HALPERT and WIDDOWSON, *Folktales of Newfoundland*, p. 35, 56, 66.

'once upon a time', now that is well-known enough not to need any 'translation'.

"Well once upon a time" is part of a larger structure that continues "there was / were a".[11] The insertion of the "in olden times you know" means there is already a gap between the two halves of the structure, and Freeman inserts further material in all three renditions. In the 1966 telling, the "there was a" seems to follow immediately, but this is a false dawn as Freeman then digresses, as he often does as the start of his wonder tales, to talk about the local settlement pattern, and implicitly how while the date of the story may be distant, its location is close. We might re-lineate the excerpt to show this:

there was a ...
 well there ... perhaps there'd [be] a family livin here an' perhaps in another ... thirty mile there'd be another family see? Well now 't would be a long ways 'fore they'd get to the ... to the settlement. Well anyhow
there was a family we'll say he was li[vin] ... they was livin HERE

and one could imagine an editor of this story simplifying the opening to "Once upon a time there was a family living here". To do so would miss out not only the hesitations and false starts, but also the play Freeman makes with various evidentiality markers such as "perhaps" and "we'll say", which underline the provisionality and the fictionality of his storyworld.

In the 1970 telling, before the family is mentioned there is only the briefest of digressions: "that's away back in pod auger days that is" – a phrase that the editors of the collection cannot analyse (and nor can I), but which they recognise must denote a time long past. This is immediately followed by Freeman placing them in the vicinity of St. Paul's, in this case in Sally's Cove, the village immediately to the south, and perhaps not coincidentally the village of Eli Roberts, the man who told him the story. By contrast, in the third (and most confident) telling, the digression at this point in the story comes with Freeman's comedic presentation of himself as being around when the events took place, "perhaps five or six hundred year ago". He was not very old then, he says, and "can only just mind [i.e. remember] that anyhow!". As well as being amusing, such remarks are also a clue as to the key in which we should take the story, namely that of fiction. This tongue-in-cheek presentation of himself as being a youngster at the date of the long past events is found at the start of some of his

---

[11] J. ROPER, "Opening and closing formulas in tales told in England", in: *Weathered Words: Formulaic Language and Verbal Art*, ed. FROG and W. LAMB (Cambridge, MA, 2022), pp. 411-434, at pp. 412-413.

other tales. In one tale he remarks "that was before Newfoundland was discovered",[12] which, if it is not simply to be taken as a deliberately paradoxical impossibility, suggests that the tale is happening back in Europe, or a Europe-like tale-world.

We find some other repeated phrases in the three orientations that might also be thought of as formulaic. There seems to be a formula "[his] name was Jack" that appears immediately before or after the mention of them having only one son (cited here in chronological order: 1966, 1970, 1971):

> they had one son. Now their son's **name was Jack**.
>
> **his name was Jack**, they only had one ... one ... boy - one child.
>
> Well now this family was livin here he had one son. An' **his name was Jack**.

And there seems to be something of a formula with words like "the times got so bad" underlying these three extracts:

> It got poor times, well they never had very much an' ...
>
> the times got so bad -they got down an' out an' uh ... nothing to eat see?
>
> Well the times got so bad _ they uh ... never got much to eat.

It is hard to make firm claims on the basis on only three tellings. But "the times got so bad" does not occur in any other of Freeman's 23 recorded stories, which suggests at least the possibility that it is, unlike "once upon a time", a formula connected only with a single tale. There are some other strings, "a family living" + LOCATION, "go to the city", "we have to leave", "can't stay/live here", "we'll go", that might be formulas for Freeman, at least as far as this tale is concerned, and should be investigated another time. But the "[his] name was Jack" string is unambiguously a formula – perhaps not surprisingly so, when we consider that most of Freeman's stories have a hero called Jack. The relevant examples run as follows:

> Well now they growed up. An' uh ... they got ... he got good education _ Jack did, **his name was Jack**. But they used to call un ... the teachers used to call un Hard Head _ 'cause he was ... hard to learn see?

---

[12] HALPERT and WIDDOWSON, *Folktales of Newfoundland*, p. 488.

Freeman's Formulas 335

> Well once upon a time in olden times _ there was a feller uh ... **his name was Jack** see.
>
> Well one time _ in olden times _ there was a man an' he had uh ... three or four children see. An' one's **name was ... was Jack**.
>
> now there was a feller HIS **name was Jack**.
>
> And uh ... they had one son. An' **his name was Jack**.
>
> And _ there was a feller an' **his name was Jack**.
>
> this was a family was livin off see an' uh ... they had one son _ an' **his name was Jack**.
>
> Well once upon a time in olden times ya know _ there was a ... a little feller _ well he was 'bout the size o' Kevin there [*points to small boy*] _ when his uh ... father an' mother died see? Now that's th' only one they had an' **his name was Jack**.
>
> Well once upon a time there ... ..as a a man an' his ... wife an' they only had one son see? An' uh ... **his name was Jack**.[13]

The first example is quite interesting in its positioning, as it comes after Freeman had somewhat tangled up the opening where upon the first mention of the boy the formula would usually appear. Freeman is still a flexible enough narrator to bring up the formula near the start and to use it to contrast it with Jack's name with his nickname 'Hard Head'.

There is one more example of this formula in his stories, this time followed by a revealing commentary from Freeman:

> Well now one time _ there was a feller, course his name was Jack, all their names was Jack those fellers in the stories 'cause they (were) ... they was all smart men they'd always come out on top.[14]

It is worth noting that not just do we get the formula in "course his name was Jack" in this explanation, but we also find it echoed in the commentary "all their names was Jack".

---

[13] HALPERT and WIDDOWSON, *Folktales of Newfoundland*, pp. 388, 403, 415, 512, 743, 840, 853, 998, 1011.

[14] HALPERT and WIDDOWSON, *Folktales of Newfoundland*, p. 760.

There are also some exceptions which are also informative. In cases where three brothers featured in the body of the story the "his name was Jack" formula was not used:

> Well he had ... three ... three sons. He had Bill, Tom an' Jack.
>
> An' he had three sons _ Jack _ Tom an' Bill.
>
> one time there was uh· ... three boys see? Jack _ Tom. an' Bill.[15]

In one highly atypical tale, that may ultimately derive from popular print fiction that has been somewhat oralised, the chief hero is Black George. During the course of the tale he meets two men who become his helpers, Bill and Jack. Even though this is Black George's story, and the opening and close of the tale focus on him, the formula appears when his helpers are named:

> one's name was Bill an' the other's name was Jack.[16]

If, as this example suggests, Jack and Bill are the two names that will be chosen from the trio of Jack, Bill, and Tom when only two are required, it is noteworthy that 'Jack' and 'Bill' appear in first and third positions in the lists of three brothers above. This suggests that it is the second position in these lists, where 'Tom' always appears, that is the most unmarked.

There is only one other case of a protagonist not called Jack, and that is a brief droll story featuring a character called Abraham who turns out to be the butt of the humour. Although the story is very different from any told about Jack, perhaps we can see the undergirdings of the formula used to introduce Jack here too?

> [One] (time) there's a ... a little feller ya know, he was only a ... small feller _ an' **his name was** Abraham see?

---

[15] HALPERT and WIDDOWSON, *Folktales of Newfoundland*, pp. 590, 599, 619.
[16] HALPERT and WIDDOWSON, *Folktales of Newfoundland*, p. 971.

Transition Formulas

In the *Weathered Words* article,[17] I suggested that there were three key points in a traditional folktale: in addition to the opening and the closing, there was a point of transition near the start of the story where the narration moves from the 'eternal' imperfective set up (where we are told that 'once' there was a character who lived somewhere and and had a goal or a lack) into action, or in other words, from the general condition to what's happening on a particular day. And it was suggested on the basis of the pre-audiorecording era English material that a typical formula marking this transition was 'one day', or similar forms such as 'one morning' or 'one night', etc. How does this play out in Freeman's material?

Sometimes we find a transition like the ones found in the pre-audiorecorded era data. For example, in a 1971 telling of a tale Freeman called 'Jack and the Goose', we do find the familiar transition:

> Well once upon a time _ in olden times _ there was a ... a little settlement uh ... well he was smaller than this, there ... there might have been only ... seven or eight families into un. [*clears throat*] I can only just mind it, well uh ... 'tis uh ... might be uh ... four or five hundred year ago for all I knows. (Said) uh ... I can just mind un anyhow, I wasn't very old then [*laughs*] And uh ... they [a family] had one son. An' his name was Jack. [*clears throat*] Well uh ... he never had no work to do there, he couldn't earn no money an' he said to his uh ... father **one morning** he said "I think" he said "I'm goin somewhere" he said "to look" he said "see can I get a job".[18]

The text shows that after beginning with "Well once upon a time" and then making fun with the idea that he can only just remember such a time, Freeman mentions the existence of a family with one son, Jack. The statement "he never had no work to do there" represents a durative rather than a punctual state, as does "he couldn't earn no money", so we are still in the realm of the set-up with these statements. Then the transition comes, marked by the words "one morning", showing Jack leaving home and the start proper of his story, here figured in dialogue.

Another example in a story he called 'The Basketmaker':

---

[17] ROPER, "Opening and closing formulas in tales told in England".
[18] HALPERT and WIDDOWSON, *Folktales of Newfoundland* p. 743.

> One time ... in olden times ya know _ in olden times. now if you an' me was livin here _ I was livin here an' you was livin out there _ an' you had a ... girl _ an' I had a son _ well now _ we would marry 'em when they was small children see? So very good. That's what they done. This ... this uh ... feller. They was two farmers see? They was livin close 'longside, well one had a daughter an' the other one had a son. An' when they was born they married 'em see?
>
> Well when they growed up. to be big ... boy an' a big girl well they ... they took up goin together, well now they didn't know nothing about being married. Well they was ... goin together goin to school. Well they ... used to be goin together. So very good uh ... after they growed up _ a man an' woman _ she said uh ... to .. / Jack / **one day** she said ... he said to her. he said uh ... "What about us gettin married?"[19]

Once again, the written transcript is not easy to parse. After beginning "One time", Freeman then addresses the fieldworker, explaining the situation in the past where neighbours engaged their offspring to one another as children. He marks the end of this section with his favoured discourse marker "So very good". Then he presents the two farmers, who had a son and a daughter, who were betrothed at their births. They grew to adulthood ("man an' woman"). This section also ends with the discourse marker "So very good". And now we get the transition from set-up to action. This is a somewhat confused passage, as Freeman twice begins saying that the young woman spoke to the young man (and he also does not say 'Jack' but 'Bill'), rather than the young man speaking to the young woman. If we made our own clearer, corrected version of this, it might read:

> **One day** he said to her: "What about us getting married?"

Another example is found in 'Jack Lives Without Eating', which begins like this:

> Well one time you know _ in olden times _ a long time back that's uh ..when I was a young feller, that's a couple or three hundred year ago uh ... well was only a young feller then. And _ there was a feller an' his name was Jack. An' he started to look for some work. And _ he leaved in the morning and walked all day[20]

The orientation runs from "Well one time" to "an' his name was Jack". Probably with "An' he started to look for some work", and definitely with "And ... he

---

[19] HALPERT and WIDDOWSON, *Folktales of Newfoundland*, pp. 521-522.
[20] HALPERT and WIDDOWSON, *Folktales of Newfoundland*, p. 840.

leaved in the morning" we are in the action of the story proper. Just like "one morning", here "in the morning" is the marker of transition to the realm of events.

But while these examples of transitions are close to what I found in the English texts, there are also less marked transitions in Freeman's material. One reason is because there is often what might be called a 'prologue' between the opening formula and the story proper, even longer than in 'The Basketmaker' example we saw above. In 'Jack and the Slave Islands', after the opening formula there is a long prologue (abbreviated here) before we come to the story proper. This long section rehearses how the rich man forbidding his servant from marrying his daughter, the servant and the daughter making an agreement, the servant travelling to America and making his fortune, and the couple marrying. These events might make for a story in themselves another time, but here they are prologue for the real story – the wager on his wife's chastity that Jack will make with the fellow he meets on the pier. And sure enough we find that the transition from is marked by "one day" (and here I have made the text more legible):

> Well she came and they got married. Well now he had his ships going, three ships, going from one place to another. And **one day** all the ship got in together, and this man went down on the pier, walking around on the pier and talking about one thing and another, and by-and-by he brought up the [topic of] women.

In one view, prologues should be considered as being more part of the orientation than the story proper. One reason for this would be that, although verbal uses are highly non-standard, there seem to be more imperfective uses in the prologue ("his daughter was getting around with un", "he was doing so good", "he had his uh ... ships goin") than in the story proper, something which is typical of orientations. And in sentences such as "An' _ he build his house. An' he start this ... his business", even verbal forms which are meant to represent particular events rather than general states (i.e. which would be 'built' and 'started' in Standard English) have an ambiguous status as these non-standard finite forms are the same as their non-finite forms. In another view, prologues do narrate events and thus should be considered together with the story proper. But it might be best to solve this moot question by recognising that 'prologues', where they appear, form a distinct section of their own.

As well as the additional complexity such extended prologues bring to the stories, Freeman often also favours shifting from the orientation to the action via the dialogue of the characters, rather than moving straight to the action, which again makes it harder to say where exactly the transition comes. All in all, transition formulas as 'one day' and 'one morning' which were apparent in the print material are not to be found so frequently nor so clearly in Freeman's tales. No doubt there are various reasons why 'One day' has not become as world-famous a formula as 'Once upon a time' or 'Happily ever after', and one of them may be that is too typical a construction (unlike the other two unusual and more memorable forms), but another reason might be because it is less used that those two.

Closing Formulas

In the stories recorded from Freeman, fewer closing formulas are evident than opening formulas. Widdowson describes how the shorter stories typically end

> with a brief statement of the hero or heroine's success or, in the case of humorous tales, a punchline. Occasionally, the narrator simply says "that ends the story" or a similar concluding statement, or repeats the title of the tale at the end.[21]

Firstly we might note that "that ends the story" is a traditional means of ending tales, as researchers at least as early as Robert Petsch have recognised. He called it the '*C'est tout*' ending.[22] Secondly, the narrator repeating the title of the tale at the end is not something typically found in tradition, and may be an artefact of the collecting situation where the fieldworkers often asked for the title of the story at the start of the telling. In such a context, it may seem reasonable to reprise these words at the end.

As far as the shorter jocular tales are concerned, it is noteworthy that while they begin in a way similar to wonder tales, they do not end in the same way. Freeman begins one such droll tale like any other tale: "One time there was a man and his wife" (though it does swiftly signal the register it is to be taken in by the following words "and they had a pig to kill"). But it ends with these words:

---

[21] J.D.A. WIDDOWSON, Folktales in Newfoundland oral tradition: Structure, style, and performance", *Folklore* 120.1 (2009), pp. 19-35, at p. 28.

[22] ROPER, "Opening and closing formulas in tales told in England", p. 426.

"What I meaned," he said, "'to put it away an' when all the rest was gone, we'd have that half a pig. Now", he said, "you've give the half a pig away. Now", he said, "all we've got is half".[23]

These words, which underline the foolishness of the wife in the story, are not formulaic and are quite different from those used to end the wonder tales. A similarly jocular story begins with the words "One time there's a ... a little feller, ya know".[24] This would seem to be a plainer equivalent of words he uses another time to begin a longer tale: "Well once upon a time in olden times ya know _ there was a ... a little feller".[25] But whereas the longer tale ends in a traditionally formulaic manner:

> Well _ they got married an' uh ... they lived there an' he went an' he'd brought the doctor an' his wife in an' he has his old grandmother an' they all lived together an' _ when I left they had three children. Huh! (laughs)[26]

the droll tale ends with its punchline:

> "Take the damn fish" he said "if you wants un" he said "I don't want un".[27]

We find such descriptions of marriage, and the number of children the couple had had by the time the narrator leaves them, in many of Freeman's tales, including the three versions of the tale we started looking at, 'Peter and Minnie'. Indeed 'when I came away they / he had two / three children' is Freeman's preferred happy ending rather than something such as 'Happy ever after'. But before he can reach such a resolution there is much to be gone through. In the earliest (1966) version of 'Peter and Minnie', after Jack has killed the giants and rescued the king's daughter, we do not immediately arrive at a happy ending, as he and his parents continue to live in poverty. It is not until the King's daughter identifies Jack, after hearing his relation of what he did in the castle, that things move toward a resolution:

> She jumped up an' she went out an' she locked the door.
> 'Way she goes after the king.

---

[23] HALPERT and WIDDOWSON, *Folktales of Newfoundland*, p. 835.
[24] HALPERT and WIDDOWSON, *Folktales of Newfoundland*, p. 910.
[25] HALPERT and WIDDOWSON, *Folktales of Newfoundland*, p. 998.
[26] HALPERT and WIDDOWSON, *Folktales of Newfoundland*, p. 1006.
[27] HALPERT and WIDDOWSON, *Folktales of Newfoundland*, p. 910.

> "Oh" she said, "father" she said "I got the man!"
> He said "Have ya?"
> "Yes". Said "I got un"
> Over the king comes.
> "Well now" _ the king said _ "I been after that man" he said "this ten year". He said "An' I got un he said "this morning.
> Now" _ he said _ "Jack" he said "you got to marry my daughter" _ he said "an' I 'm goin to give yous this hotel" he said "an' yous can live in un".[28]

While a similar denouement occurs in Freeman's two subsequent tellings of this tale, this section's length and content is highly variable in the three tellings. In the 1970 telling it is much longer, featuring the departure of the king's daughter, and Jack's mother blaming him, whereas in the 1971 telling, the mini-episodes occur in reverse order. In any event, following the tying up of loose ends that means the hero has a bride and a dwelling, the closing formula appears:

> an' when I leaved they had two children.
> That ends the story.[29]

In fact, we have two closes here. The first is the traditional one that involves the revelation that they were not simply married, but were successfully able to establish a family. It also presents the implicit claim that the narrator was an eye-witness of this (which presumably is how he might have gained the knowledge to be able to claim to tell the story), and that he left them to return to the workaday world where such stories can be told, if not lived. The act of leaving Jack is also a sign that we, as listeners, are leaving the tale. Such endings are common throughout European and European-derived popular narratives.

The second closing formula here is 'That ends the story'. As just mentioned, while it may seem like a prosaic utterance from everyday speech, it is a traditional formula, and can serve as a reminder that formulas are not always the 'poeticisms' we expect; they can be more everyday. And in the other two tellings of 'Peter and Minnie', it also appears:

> He said "An' you can have me daughter". (See) an' that end the story.[30]

---

[28] HALPERT and WIDDOWSON, *Folktales of Newfoundland*, p. 41.
[29] HALPERT and WIDDOWSON, *Folktales of Newfoundland*, p. 41.
[30] HALPERT and WIDDOWSON, *Folktales of Newfoundland*, p. 62.

Freeman's Formulas 343

> But Jack had ... lots o' money then, he was alright, well _ that end the story.[31]

We also find the 'that ends the story' formula elsewhere in Freeman's repertoire:

> "Well" he said "so long as he sove my life" he said "I'll save his life". He said an' he ... an' he got clear. That ends the story.[32]

In fact, the formula seems to have been quite widespread in Newfoundland. Mose Troke told a tale, which features a tale within the tale. He seems to play off the formula by having the teller within the story tell the King, when he complains about the long repetitive tale he is being told, that

> when the ... the locustes gets all the corn _ called out ... carried away out o' the barn _ that'll be the end o' the story.[33]

Likewise, when later commenting on the tale, Mose Troke said:

> he didn't lose his head! He wouldn't ... he **never end the story**! He **never end the story**.[34]

We can list here the twelve occurrences of the '(and) **when I left** (they had)' formula in Freeman's documented repertoire:

> "Jack" /he/ said "you got to marry my daughter" _ he said "an' I'm goin to give yous this hotel" he said "an' yous can live in un" an' **when I leaved** they had two children. That ends the story. [laughs]

> An' **when I left** they had three children an' ol' ... an' ol' man. well they was gettin ol' then, they was 'bout seventy or eighty year ol' then. But Jack had ... lots o' money then, he was alright, well _ that end the story. [laughs]

> **when leaved** Jack an' she was livin the best kind an' had three or four children. Huh!

> **when I leaved** they had three s ... three children. (laughs)

[31] HALPERT and WIDDOWSON, *Folktales of Newfoundland*, p. 74.
[32] HALPERT and WIDDOWSON, *Folktales of Newfoundland*, p. 604.
[33] HALPERT and WIDDOWSON, *Folktales of Newfoundland*, p. 944.
[34] HALPERT and WIDDOWSON, *Folktales of Newfoundland*, p. 945, emphasis added.

an' when they ... **when I left** they had three children.

Jack married his daughter an' **when I left** _ they had oh they had a big family, they had uh .. _ five or six youngsters I think when I left. I was in there. I was in there talking to 'em. (laughs) That's all of it.

an' **when I left** he was married an' he had three or four children. [laughter]

when I left he was ... he was married an' had three or four children. [laughs]

an' **when I left** they had a couple or three children.

an' **when I left** they was married an' had two youngsters.

an' _ **when I left** they had three children. Huh! [laughs]

... **when I left** they had _ couple o' children I think, well they was ... livin ... happy together. (That) end the story. [laughs][35]

The noun is always 'children', except in the two cases where it is 'youngsters'. The number of children varies, but three (including "three or four") is the most popular number. The outliers are the two cases where "two youngsters" are mentioned. It may be that 'youngsters' was chosen here because of the different register of the tale, that, as mentioned, would seem to be a recently oralised piece of popular fiction. This does not apply in the second case, but it, again, is an outlier in terms of the number of children: "five or six".

It turns out that 'five or six' is something of a formula, or a formula fragment, for Freeman. Of the seven occurrences of "five or six" in the corpus of almost 200 tales, all were spoken by Freeman. As well as the current occurrence, we also find him telling of five or six "dollars", "years ago", "hundred years ago", "baskets", "eyes", "thousand dollars", and "men".[36] The last example is interesting as he begins like this: "So there's six ..." before seeming to correct himself to the formula "five or six men"[37]. To get an idea of how unusual it is that such a sequential number-pair should only be spoken by one teller, we can consider the neighbouring pairs, "four or five" and "six or seven"

---

[35] HALPERT and WIDDOWSON, *Folktales of Newfoundland*, pp. 41, 74, 128, 396, 411, 755, 767, 844, 858, 976, 1006, 1018.

[36] HALPERT and WIDDOWSON, *Folktales of Newfoundland*, pp. 39, 60, 66, 525, 621, 765, 918.

[37] HALPERT and WIDDOWSON, *Folktales of Newfoundland*, p. 918.

(both of which alliterate, and so might be thought to be more likely to occur). There are 13 occurrences of "four or five" – 3 of which are in Freeman's tales, 4 of which are in John Roberts' tales, and 6 of which are in Mike Kent's tales. The numbers are much more telling that they seem in absolute terms, as John Roberts only told two tales, and Mike Kent four, whereas Freeman told 26. And as Freeman knew John Roberts as a narrator, he would have heard such instances of "four or five" in the context of tales, and thus, it seems, was deliberately avoiding them (or deliberately favouring another pair in their stead). As for "six or seven", there are just three occurrences in the tales, none of which come in Freeman's tales. So "five or six" is a number-pair idiosyncratically favoured by Freeman, though there may be nothing more to read into this than simple stylistic idiosyncracy.

It is worth noting that the '*C'est tout*' ending then follows this formula in a third of the cases. And thanks to Halpert and Widdowson's mode of transcription we can tell that in many cases shortly after the **'when I left'** formula, Freeman laughed. Laughing perhaps at the exaggeration implicit of him being there, as well as because laughter is another marker of the end of the story. Note that it is not in his jests, but in his wonder tales and realistic tales that we find this formula that bring the narrator's laughter in its wake.

Observations on the Nature of Formulas

This look, however brief, at one teller's formulas, has, I hope, been enlightening. My main point of external comparison has been with earlier pre-audiorecording data, which it largely, though not entirely, squares with, and allows us to re-imagine in a more lively way. No doubt a comparison with the usages of other members of his family and with other tellers in western Newfoundland would be informative too. Such investigations might make it possible not simply to make lists of formulas within a single tradition but we might be able to say something about the ambit of those formulas as well. Is a formula found only within the stories of an individual teller, or of a small group of contacts and kin, or of a region, or of the entire anglosphere? Is a formula typical of a single tale-type (e.g. 'What big eyes you have'), or of a sub-genre, of a broad genre, or of a mode (e.g. the wonder tale)? To be able to give full answers to such interesting questions would require a large amount of high-quality data. As regards the amount of data, without a large number of texts, we might mistake absence of evidence for evidence of absence as regards formulaic usage. Among other questions arising from a low quantity of data is the question of whether a formula-like usage with only a single example is a formula in tradition or just a *hapax legomenon*.

And yet such endeavours are fraught with difficulty. Freeman began one wonder tale like this:

> once upon a time ya know that's in _ olden times that's away back uh _ not in our days at all.[38]

Halpert and Widdowson remark "the opening lines also include a hint in the phrase 'not in our days at all' of more elaborate formulas found in other tales in this collection". What they are alluding to are formulas recorded by Halpert elsewhere on the island of Newfoundland:

> once upon a time an' a time very good /time/ it was _ not in your time _ 'deed in my time _ in olden times. (When) quart bottles hold half a gallon an' house paper[ed] with pancakes. an' pigs run about, forks stuck in their ass _ see who wanted to buy pork.[39]

> Well once upon a time an' that very good time it was _ 'twas neither in MY time or YOUR time _ the time that birds used to go round buildin nests in old men's whiskers _ an' pigs goin around with forks stuck in their ... quarters singin out who'd buy pork.[40]

Such formulas were also found far to the south in the Caribbean,[41] and over on the other side of the Atlantic, as for example in the stories of William Colcombe in Herefordshire:

> Once upon a time _ a very good time it was _ when pigs were swine and dogs ate lime and monkeys chewed tobacco, when houses were thatched with pancakes, streets paved with plum puddings, and roasted pigs ran up and down the streets with knives and forks on their backs crying "Come and eat me!" That was a good time for travellers.[42]

---

[38] HALPERT and WIDDOWSON, *Folktales of Newfoundland*, p. 487.
[39] HALPERT and WIDDOWSON, *Folktales of Newfoundland*, p. 316.
[40] HALPERT and WIDDOWSON, *Folktales of Newfoundland*, p. 461.
[41] ROPER, "Opening and closing formulas in tales told in England".
[42] E.M. LEATHER, *The Folk-Lore of Herefordshire: Collected from Oral and Printed Sources* (Hereford, 1912), p. 174.

Freeman's Formulas 347

But did Freeman really know such elaborate opening formulas for which the only Newfoundland evidence is from the other side of island, more than 300 miles away as the crow flies (and much longer in practice)? It would seem more likely that he knew simpler, less elaborated formulas, such as the one reported from a nineteenth-century Londoner:

> Once upon a time, and a very good time it was, though it was neither in your time, nor my time, nor nobody else's time.[43]

But if we do imagine that the formula *was* known to Freeman, then how should we consider the text as we have it? In that case, was the formula complete in itself or was it a defective version of a longer formula? And if it was the latter, where does the formula reside?

Joseph Jacobs long ago remarked upon the repetition of verbs of motion in English folktales. His example was "So he went along and went along and went along".[44] And there are examples of this in, for example, his version of 'Jack and the Beanstalk':

> So Jack climbed and he climbed and he climbed and he climbed and he climbed and he climbed and he climbed till at last he reached the sky. And when he got there he found a long broad road going as straight as a dart. So he walked along and he walked along and he walked along till he came to a great big tall house, and on the doorstep there was a great big tall woman.[45]

(The first example with six occurrences of 'climbed' is best understood as a double example of the typical threefold occurrence made in order to emphasise the tremendous height of the beanstalk.) Jacobs does not comment on the function of such strings, but Halpert and Widdowson say that they indicate "the passage of time or the intensity of an action",[46] which seems right. And sure enough, we find this kind of structure in the Newfoundland material. For example, in Stephen Snook's storytelling, we find the following: "Jack smopped an' smopped an' smopped away"; "So he dropped an' dropped an' dropped"; and "So anyhow Jack ... went on an' went on an' went on".[47] Is this a formula? If

---

[43] H. MAYHEW, *London Labour and the London Poor*, 3 (London, 1861), p. 391.
[44] J. JACOBS, *More English Fairy Tales* (London, 1894), p. 238.
[45] J. JACOBS, *English Fairy Tales* (London, 1890), p. 62.
[46] HALPERT and WIDDOWSON, *Folktales of Newfoundland*, p. 97.
[47] HALPERT and WIDDOWSON, *Folktales of Newfoundland*, p. 97.

so, Snook remembers it as "he dropped and dropped and dropped"? But perhaps not. Perhaps the rule in his mind was more like:

he VERB OF MOTION-$_{past}$ and VERB OF MOTION-$_{past}$ and VERB OF MOTION-$_{past}$

Such a structure might at times produce strings such as 'He went along and went along and went along', and other times 'He walked and walked and walked', and at yet other times 'He travelled and travelled and travelled'. If the latter hypothesis is correct, and it is stored more as a structure (or a rule) than as a set of words, then perhaps we should distinguish between formulas proper and other kinds of repeated structures. Perhaps these structures need another name (and if they are various, then names plural). Conversely, if we still want to consider these structures as formulas, then we need a model of formula which recognises some formulas as fixed and others as variable.

As well as classic formulas such as 'Once upon a time', there were what we might call 'vanilla formulas' in Freeman's material, and in the Newfoundland tale material more broadly.[48] For example, the most common 2-gram in the Newfoundland tale corpus is the dialogue indicator "he said", and the second most common is "she said". Are these to be considered as formulas? It seems to me that the instincts of most scholars would be to answer: No. But on what grounds? They cannot be excluded on the grounds of length if other two-word sequences, such as 'golden hair', can be considered as formulas. Nor are they exclusible on grounds of prosody, as they serve a punctuating function and a rhythmic effect within the telling. After all, Freeman could have supplied the dialogue without any 'he said's, simply differentiating the speakers by tricks of the voice or by accompanying gestures, but he chose not to.

Perhaps one argument in favour of excluding 'he said' from the category of formula is there is nothing genre-specific about it. Unlike 'golden hair', 'he said' can turn up in any number of genres. Even the most common 3-gram 'yes he said' and 4-gram 'oh yes he said' _ which might possibly hold a stronger claim to formulaicity, also seems to lack any folktale feel. 'Oh yes, he said', which might be found in any kind of discourse. We are used to thinking of formulas as being unusual combinations of words, such as 'once upon a time', 'over seven hills', or 'wine-dark sea', but there are vanilla formulas too, strings as simple as 'by and by' or 'very good'. In these Newfoundland tales, 'by and

---

[48] On such 'vanilla formulas', see J. ROPER, "Formulas in folk verse and folk prose: Overlap or independence?", *Narodna Umjetnost: Croatian Journal of Ethnology and Folklore Research* 59.1 (2022), pp. 7-21.

by' seems to be used to mark the beginning of a narrative segment, and 'very good' to make the end of such segments (rather than denoting, as they conventionally do, that something is good). But perhaps we are misled when we focus on register here – perhaps it is not the quality of the recurrent word-strings, but the quantity of their recurrence that make them formulaic in any particular text or genre.

Much attention is given to formulas, but might formulas not be *sui generis* after all? When I was studying alliteration, for a long time I focussed on alliteration, ignoring other forms of sound repetition. But later on, I came to feel that all kinds of sound repetition should be my topic, with alliteration as only one part of this. I feel something similar about formulas in folktales: they are one of the sub-classes of repetition to be found there, and they warrant study, just as the other forms of repetition too – and indeed such a broader focus might tell us more about formulas too. Folktales are both a free and a fixed genre, and a large part of that fixity consists in repetition: in other words, folktales are repetition machines. As well as formulas, we find, at the small scale, repetitions of dialogue indicators, discourse markers, and reduplicated verbs, and at a larger scale, entire episodes retold by characters within the story. We are familiar with tales in which the first character tries and fails, the second then tries and fails, and the third tries and succeeds. There are also tales, often humorous in nature, where a character does something successfully, then a second character attempting replicate this is unsuccessful. Alan Dundes has an article on such tales.[49] Episodes which are in large part the same also occur in the tale we have been focusing on, Freeman's renderings of 'Peter and Minnie'. First Jack kills the three giants, then he tells the king's daughter how he killed the three giants. These parts are narrated largely in the same words, one in the third person, the other in the first person. If folktales are repetition machines, how much of that repetition is due to storytelling grammar and how much might be called formulaic?

One more issue that transcripts of real, untidy narration raise for us, is that the tales are different from the tidied up versions that editors have usually presented us with, whether in books or articles. Examining the high-quality transcripts produced by Halpert and Widdowson leads us to realise that in practice formulas may be much less clean-cut than they have typically been presented as being in edited transcripts of folktales. People do not produce only perfect formulas any more than they produce only perfect sentences. I have noticed

---

[49] A. DUNDES, "The binary structure of 'unsuccessful repetition' in Lithuanian folk tales", *Western Folklore* 21.3 (1962), pp. 165-174.

cases at academic conferences where the speaker, attempting to draw a contrast between x and y, actually says something like 'x is ... , but x is ...', when they should have said 'x is ... , but y is ...'. The speaker got a word wrong, but the listeners still managed to get the right idea by listening to the structure rather than to the one wrong word. There was even one example of this during the presentations at the conference that this book is based on. And, sure enough, it seems that the listeners to folktales are also able to do the same – ignore an occasional wrong word by following the structure. Halpert and Widdowson remark on the case of one Newfoundland tale that:

> It is probable, for example, that in the lengthy sentence just quoted above the teller intended to say "behead him" but appears to say "behead 'em" which adds to the confusion. Such details are usually immaterial to the audience in the storytelling context and are easily overlooked as the listeners concentrate attention on the main thrust of the plot.[50]

If 'overheard' did not already have a well-established meaning, we might rewrite the final sentence "are easily overheard as the listeners concentrate attention on the main thrust of the plot". Such a change would be especially relevant, as this is the kind of error that is ignorable in speech (whether that be of lecturers or of storytellers) more easily than it is in writing. If thoughts may be communicated successfully between two minds even with errors in their linguistic form, how much do mistakes matter at a verbal level? There must be an unsupportable level of error – but perhaps the supportable level of verbal error within a formulaic genre such as folktale is much higher than we ('we' meaning here: 'people used to writing') might suppose.

While bad data is disappointing, it is easier to use than rich data. Such data does show us, however, that the formulas are more apparent in the edited transcriptions than in the words the teller speaks. What do we find in the texts are 'formulas' – or should we call them 'paused formulas', 'broken formulas' or 'quasi-formulas'? Does this mean that, in the primary context these tales had their life, the formulas were primarily in the mind of the teller and in the minds of a familiar audience rather than in the words that went between them? And in this case, might an editor's interventions make up for the exigencies of performance, and be restorative of what the teller meant to have said and of what the listeners thought they heard? The topic of verbal error leads on to another question: where are the formulas? Are they in the spoken words of the teller? Or in

---

[50] HALPERT and WIDDOWSON, *Folktales of Newfoundland*, p. 429.

the edited transcriptions of those words? Or rather in mind of the teller? Or perhaps in the minds of an audience familiar with the tradition?

We might end with this thought. We tend to think of folktales as being full of formulas but perhaps we have been thinking of them wrongly? Print replicas (or simulacra) of oral folktales, such as the Grimms' tales, are as misleading in respect of formulas, as they have been shown to be in other regards. The Grimms' style of folktale is one with many formulas, but the further the Grimms' published tales got from their putative oral prototypes through the seven editions published in their lifetimes, the greater the presence of verbal formulas in them became. While the Grimms' tales are an outstanding example of literary documents with a folk flavour, their lesson seems to be that this flavour is not the flavour of the oral tale, but that of the book folktale. Genuine oral folktales, such as we find in Halpert and Widdowson's collection, may be far less formula-rich than we have come to think that they should be and feature formulas that are far less rich in style than we have come to think they should have been.

The Aesthetics of Russian Folktale Formulas: A View from Translation Studies

TATIANA BOGRDANOVA

Introduction

The present article is intended as another step in dealing with the aesthetics of the Russian folktale formulas viewed through the prism of translations.[1] Its theoretical part is revised and updated in the light of the recent discussions of formula research,[2] while further emphasis is made pertaining to theory in the field of translation history studies, as well as to the examination of translated folklore texts (the empirical part of the paper).

---

[1] See T. BOGRDANOVA, "*Morozko*: Russian folklore formulas in British translations", in: *Weathered Words: Formulaic Language and Verbal Art*, ed. FROG and W. LAMB (Cambridge, MA, 2020), pp. 350-371.

[2] *Weathered Words: Formulaic Language and Verbal Art*, ed. FROG and LAMB. See also S. RANKOVIĆ, "Immanent seas, scribal havens: distributed reading of formulaic networks in the sagas of Icelanders', *European Review* 22 (2014), pp. 45-54; W. LAMB, "Verbal formulas in Gaelic traditional narrative: Some aspects of their form and function", in: *Registers of Communication*, ed. by A. AGHA and FROG (Helsinki, 2015): *Studia Fennica Linguistica* 18), pp. 225-246; and D. SÄVBORG, "The formula in Icelandic saga prose", *Saga-Book*, 42 (2018), pp. 51-86.

New Light on Formulas in Oral Poetry and Prose, ed. Daniel SÄVBORG and Bernt Ø. THORVALDSEN, *Utrecht Studies in Medieval Literacy*, 57 (Turnhout: Brepols, 2023), pp. 353-368.

BREPOLS ❧ PUBLISHERS   DOI <10.1484/M.USML-EB.5.133559>

I will argue that this largely innovative approach sheds useful light on the way Russian folklore formulas were understood and interpreted by British translators for their audiences. Moreover, in my opinion, the relevance of the texts under discussion will only grow, granted that these are initial contributions to the 'amalgam' of rewritings of the Russian folktale. In fact, it is the collective effort of translators that produces the necessary cumulative effect to initiate the interested reader into the poetic world of Russian folklore.

The selections for comparative analysis were made from W.S.R. Ralston's *Russian Folk-Tales* (1873), Andrew Lang's *Red* and *Yellow Fairy Books* (1890, 1894) and Arthur Ransome's *Old Peter's Russian Tales* (1916), based on *Narodnye russkie skazki A.N. Afanas'eva* (Popular Russian Tales by A.N. Afanasyev) (1984-1985).[3] The focus will be on Russian supernatural figures, this time on *Koshchei the Deathless* and *Baba Yaga*.

The Aesthetics of Russian Folktale Formulas

In general, formulas are categories of traditions and are characteristic of every culture, where they serve as a stabilising factor, a mechanism facilitating their unique characters; thus no culture exists without its tradition.[4] Regular recycling of forms, reproducing stereotypical models, is a characteristic feature both of cultures on the whole and of their specific areas, such as languages: "[m]ost people use ready-made clichés in their speech and writings".[5] Everyday conversations may appear to be spontaneous, while in fact they are chiefly based on repetitions of *standartnykh rechevykh blokov* ('standard speech

---

[3] For more detail on the translators and their translation strategies, see T. BOGRDANOVA "Russian folklore for the English reader: William Ralston as an intercultural agent", in: *New Horizons in Translation Research and Education*, 1, ed. N. POKORN and K. KOSKINEN (Joensuu, 2013), pp. 28-44 and <http://urn.fi/URN:ISBN:978-952-61-1288-6>; EAD., "Arthur Ransome's rewriting of the Russian folktale historicised", *Slavonica* 21.1-2 (2016), pp. 79-94; and EAD., *Translators of Folklore in the British-Russian Interaction: Cultural Mediators' Agency At the Turn of the Twentieth Century* (Joensuu, 2019: *Publications of the University of Eastern Finland: Dissertations in Education, Humanities, and Theology* 138).

[4] G.I. MAL′TSEV, *Traditsional′nye formuly russkoi narodnoi neobriadovoi liriki* [Traditional Formulas of Russian Folk Non-Ritual Lyrics] (Leningrad, 1989), p. 6. Translations from Russian are by the present author, unless stated otherwise.

[5] V.V. VINOGRADOV, *Sovremennyi russkii literaturnyi iazyk* [Modern Russian literary language] (Moscow, 1938), p. 121; quoted in MAL′TSEV, *Traditsional′nye formuly russkoi narodnoi neobriadovoi liriki*, p. 6; cf. A. LIBERMAN, "Humans as formulaic beings", in: *Weathered Words*, ed. FROG and LAMB, pp. 108-118.

The Aesthetics of Russian Folktale Formulas 355

blocs') and clichés.⁶ Thus, the relevance of traditional formulas of Russian non-ritual songs, for example, may be recognised both in terms of folkloristics and cultural studies. However, according to the Russian folklorist, of far more importance is the study of these facts in their particular cultural and historical contexts, with a focus on their aesthetic character and poetic features.⁷

Karl Reichl also points out that "[f]ormulaic diction has to be understood in the context in which it occurs, and it has to be interpreted within the framework of an oral poetics"; this is the way to avoid "misunderstandings", which "easily arise if oral and popular poetry is measured against written literature and if the function and the poetics of the formula in oral narrative poetry are ignored".⁸ The idea of an oral poetics, dating back to the time of Herder and Goethe, has received, according to the scholar, a new impetus in the context of Oral Theory,⁹ as well as in that of ethnopoetics and literary criticism. Formulas are singled out in these approaches for their "important role in defining the style of oral poetry"; therefore their appreciation is impossible without an understanding of the "aesthetics of traditional style (Parry)".¹⁰

In his interesting study of traditional formulas of Russian non-ritual songs, Georgii Mal´tsev argues that differentiation should be made between formulas as a distinct morphological type (ranging from a single word to a stereotypical situation)¹¹ and as a category singled out on the basis of their aesthetics. The

---

⁶ N.Iu. SHVEDOVA, *Ocherki po sintaksisu russkoi razgovornoi rechi* [Essays on the syntax of Russian colloquial speech] (Moscow, 1960); O.A. LAPTEVA, "Normativnost´ literaturnoi razgovornoi rechi" [Normativity of non-codified literary speech], in: *Sintaksis i norma* [Syntax and norm], ed. G.A. ZOLOTOVA (Moscow,1974), pp. 5-42; quoted in MAL´TSEV, *Traditsional´nye formuly russkoi narodnoi neobriadovoi liriki*, pp. 6-7. Frog and William Lamb commend the accessibility and wide-ranging utility of the definition of a formula as: "a sequence, continuous or discontinuous, of words or other elements, which is, or appears to be, prefabricated: that is, stored and retrieved whole from memory at the time of use, rather than being subject to generation or analysis by the language grammar" (A. WRAY, *Formulaic Language and the Lexicon* (Cambridge, 2002), p. 9, quoted by FROG and W. LAMB, "A Picasso of perspectives", in: *Weathered Words*, ed. FROG and LAMB, pp. 5-34).

⁷ MAL´TSEV, *Traditsional´nye formuly russkoi narodnoi neobriadovoi liriki*, p. 7.

⁸ K. REICHL, "Formulas in oral epics: The dynamics of metre, memory and meaning", in: *Weathered Words*, ed. FROG and LAMB, p. 52.

⁹ Cf. J.M. FOLEY, *Immanent Art: From Structure to Meaning in Traditional Oral Epic* (Bloomington and Indianapolis, 1991).

¹⁰ REICHL, "Formulas in oral epics", p. 52-53.

¹¹ Honko emphasises the paramount role of repeatable expressions (multiforms) in oral epic art, including descriptions of standard events (receiving guests, having a grand meal, sending a letter, etc.) that contain formulas, elaborated phrases, standard images and minor episodic elements varying in length, degree of embellishment and emphasis (L. HONKO, "Text as process and practice: Textualization of oral epics", in: *Textualization of Oral Epics*, ed. L. HONKO (Berlin

recurrent, stereotypical character of a formula is in fact determined by its aesthetic meaning, which also serves as a clue to understanding the position of a formula within a traditional canon. Importantly, by way of discovering particular aesthetic ideas associated with formulaic forms, one gets insights into the aesthetics of a given oral poetry.[12]

While the aesthetics of formulas are the aesthetics of the general, of the typical, they are also culture-specific and thus should be investigated for particular cases and poetic traditions. This is no easy task, granted the "extreme complexity of codes that fund oral formulae and complexity of meanings generated or transferred by them", for example, in Serbian oral epics.[13] Even if identified, like ritual and ethical models or elements of social stratification, these are only the "tip of the iceberg", whose underwater massif ("hidden knowledge") is the traditional system as a whole.[14]

Interestingly, these studies with their focus on the complexity of interplay between the aesthetics of formulas and their respective traditions find a parallel in John Miles Foley's theory of "immanent art".[15] In one of his publications Foley argues, for example, for a more faithful understanding of verbal art by attending to its "untextuality", i.e. the

> richly contexted array of meanings that can be communicated only through the special, 'dedicated' set of channels that constitute the multivalent experience of performance, or that can be accessed in diminished form through the augmented rhetoric of the dictated text.

This means an appeal to "what lies beyond any collection of linguistic integers by insisting on the value-added signification of these integers as perceived by

and New York, 2000: *Trends in Linguistics: Studies and Monographs* 128), pp. 3-56).

[12] MAL'TSEV, *Traditsional'nye formuly russkoi narodnoi neobriadovoi liriki*, p. 33.

[13] L. DELIĆ, "Poetic grounds of epic formulae", *Balcanica* 46 (2013), pp. 51-78, at p. 73, and <DOI 10.2298/BALC1344051D>.

[14] MAL'TSEV, *Traditsional'nye formuly russkoi narodnoi neobriadovoi liriki*, pp. 44, 68-69; DELIĆ, "Poetic grounds of epic formulae", pp. 73-75, emphasis in the text. Of interest in this respect may be the project of a dictionary of folklore language intended for linguists, which is based on a thesaurus description of folklore texts, i.e. a description of dictionary items, with their semantic associations explained. The semantic fields of items in such a thesaurus result from the analysis of a number of various texts interpreted as a single entity. Based on texts of a particular folklore genre (e.g. *byliny* or wedding songs), this dictionary will present the picture of a fragment of a given folklore worldview (S.E. NIKITINA, *Ustnaia narodnaia kul'tura i iazykovoe soznanie* [Oral Folk Culture and Linguistic Awareness] (Moscow, 1993)).

[15] FOLEY, *Immanent Art*.

an audience suitably equipped to accord them their special valences".[16] Thus, in terms of Foley's "traditional referentiality", "formulae trigger an aesthetically rich play of association by reaching out of their immediate narrative contexts and drawing on the semantic acumen of the entire tradition".[17]

Much has been done in the field of *skazkovedenie* ('folktale studies') in Russia,[18] and due attention has been given to Russian folktale formulas as well.[19] However, in the light of the recent research of the aesthetics of the formula, discussed in some detail above, new perspectives for further research are opening up. I suggest that translation studies and, especially, translation history studies, my own field of specialisation, should be seriously considered for potentially useful insights into formula aesthetics in particular, and folklore in general.[20]

Translation History Studies: An 'Amalgam' of Rewritings[21]

As Maria Tymoczko points out, translators working with, for example, "traditional tales", face significant obstacles: they have to deal with issues related to material and social culture, including law, economics, history, as well as values, world view, etc.; then, there are serious problems with the transfer-

---

[16] J.M. FOLEY, "Word-power, performance, and tradition', *The Journal of American Folklore* 105 (417) (1992), pp. 275-301, at p. 294. Available at <DOI: 10.2307/541757>.

[17] FOLEY, *Immanent Art,* p. 7; RANKOVIĆ, "Immanent seas".

[18] V.Y. PROPP, *Morphology of the Folktale,* rev. and ed., with a preface by L.A. WAGNER (Austin, 1968); ID., *Russkaya skazka* [The Russian Folktale] (Leningrad, 1984); and ID. *Istoricheskie korni volshebnoi skazki* [Historical Roots of the Wonder Tale] (Moscow, 1998). Of relevance is also the work of Ralston, the great lover of Russian folklore and its ardent populariser (W.R.S. RALSTON, *The Songs of the Russian People, As Illustrative of Slavonic Mythology and Russian Social Life* (London, 1872), and ID., *Russian Folk-Tales* (London, 1873); see M.P. ALEKSEEV and Y.D. LEVIN, *Vil'iam Rol'ston – propagandist russkoi literatury i fol'klora: S prilozheniem pisem Rol'stona k russkim korrespondentam* [William Ralston, the Propagandist of Russian Literature and Folklore: With Ralston's Letters to Russian Correspondents] (Moscow, 1994).

[19] N.M. VEDERNIKOVA, *Russkaia narodnaia skazka* [The Russian Folktale] (Moscow, 1975); I.A. RAZUMOVA, *Stilisticheskaia obriadnost' russkoi volshebnoi skazki* [Stylistic Ritualism of the Russian Wonder Folktale] (Petrozavodsk, 1991).

[20] See, e.g. J. ROPER, "Opening and closing formulas in tales told in England", in: *Weathered Words,* ed. FROG and LAMB, pp. 372-390.

[21] In my opinion, of potential interest in this respect are also the concepts of 'multiformity' or 'textual plurality' that influence the scribes' performance (R.F. PERSON JR., "Formula and scribal memory: A case study of text-critical variants as examples of category-triggering', in: *Weathered Words,* ed. FROG and LAMB, pp. 146-168.

ence of literary features (genre, form, etc.), and issues of linguistic interface. For the receiving audience, the stories told by the translator are new: they are the more radically new, the more remote the source culture and literature are.[22] In other words, of central importance is the question of how far translators are ready to go to render that "underwater massif, the traditional system as a whole", when dealing with folktale texts and their formulas, the "tip of the iceberg".[23]

Folklore texts are in fact complex encoded messages that may be 'read' or understood at two levels at least. Firstly, to understand Russian texts, e.g. one has to possess a sufficient command of the language, as well as of the basics of the culture; this will lead to the first, direct reading of the texts. However, to fully grasp their encoded meanings (and hence their formulas) and thus transfer to the second level of reading, one needs to be well versed in the folklore tradition in question.[24] Clearly, translators dealing with folklore texts should aspire to operate on the second level.

However, importantly, texts, according to André Lefevere, do not exist simply in their primary form; rather, texts are surrounded by a great number of "refracted texts", i.e. texts that have been processed for certain audiences, children for instance, or have been adapted to a certain poetics or a certain ideology.[25] He argues that for the general Anglo-American reader, for example, *Crime and Punishment*, "is, and always will be, an amalgam" of translations, histories of Russian literature, articles in popular magazines, and theatre productions.[26] Translation is thus understood as one form of refraction, a form of writing that is a rewriting. Notably, this discourse of retelling and rewriting may be used as "a potent" framework for the discussion of the translation of a non-canonical or marginalised literature, such as early Irish works and traditional tales.[27]

It is in the amalgam of rewritings of Russian tales that one may find clues to a better understanding, and hence better appreciation, of the tale and its mag-

---

[22] M. TYMOCZKO, "The metonymics of translating marginalized texts" *Comparative Literature* 47.1 (1995), pp. 11-24, at pp. 12-14; cf.FOLEY, "Word-power, performance, and tradition".

[23] Translations are seen as a necessary part of folklore textualisations (J.M. FOLEY, 'From oral performance to paper-text to cyber-edition", *Oral Tradition* 20 (2005), pp. 233-263, at p. 237; cf. HONKO, "Text as process and practice", p. 3).

[24] NIKITINA, *Ustnaia narodnaia kul´tura i iazykovoe soznanie.*

[25] A. LEFEVERE, "Literary theory and translated literature", *Dispositio: The Art and Science of Translation* 7.19-20 (1982), pp. 3-22, at p. 13; available at: <https:www.jstor.org/stable/1491223>.

[26] LEVERERE, "Literary theory and translated literature", pp. 13-14.

[27] TYMOCZKO, "The metonymics of translating marginalized texts", pp.12-14.

ical world. To illustrate this, let us examine in some detail the rewritings of particular Russian tales, focussing on renderings of the aesthetics of formulas associated with powers of darkness.

The Aesthetics of Darkness: Koshchei the Deathless

W.S.R. Ralston is rightly considered to have been the one serious Russian scholar in Great Britain in 1860s and 1870s, still known for his translations of Russian folklore.[28] His *Russian Folk-Tales* (1873) was the most extensive collection of Russian tales in English up to the mid-twentieth century.[29]

According to Ralston,

> the stories which are current among the Russian peasantry are for the most part exceedingly well narrated. Their language is simple and pleasantly quaint, their humour is natural and unobtrusive, and their descriptions, whether of persons or of events, are often excellent.[30]

He singles out 'mythological' folktales (*volshebnye skazki*, 'magic or wonder tales') for their individual character and, in particular, for portrayals of 'powers of darkness'.[31] These are divided into two groups: male, with the most prominent figures of the Snake, Koshchei the Deathless, and the Morskoi Tsar (King of the Waters), and the other group of the female principal characters, such as the Baba Yaga, or Hag, her close connection the Witch, and the Female Snake.[32]

Ralston finds it important to explain further that Koshchei is merely one of the many incarnations of the dark spirit known in its many monstrous shapes in the folktales. His name is by some mythologists derived from *kost'* or a bone; the corresponding verb signifies to become ossified, petrified, or frozen, either because he is bony of limb, or because he produces an effect akin to freezing or petrifaction.[33] He is called Koshchei the Immortal or the Deathless for his supe-

---

[28] R. MAY, *The Translator in the Text: On Reading Russian Literature in English* (Evanston, 1994); ALEKSEEV and LEVIN, *Vil'iam Rol'ston*.
[29] W.F. RYAN, "W.R.S. Ralston and the Russian Folktale", (Presidential address given to The Folklore Society, 4 April 2008), *Folklore* 120.2 (2009), pp. 123-132, at pp. 127-128.
[30] RALSTON, *Russian Folk-Tales*, p. 6.
[31] See also, e.g. J.V. HANEY, *An Introduction to the Russian Folktale* (Armonk, NY, 1999).
[32] RALSTON, *Russian Folk-Tales*, p. 65.
[33] *Morozko*, another of evil spirits found in the skazkas, may produce a similar effect (BOGRDANOVA, "*Morozko*: Russian folklore formulas in British translations").

riority to the ordinary laws of existence.[34] In the history of Marya Morevna, selected by the translator as one of the best of the *skazki*, Koshchei the Deathless plays a leading part.[35]

A proponent of literal translation strategy, Ralston sees his task in creating black and white photographs of the originals.[36] The strategy is effectively realised in every one of the fifty one tales he chose to translate, including the one under discussion.

This folktale begins with Prince Ivan marrying his three sisters to the first suitors who come to ask them in marriage, in accordance with his parents' advice, and then starting to travel to see the world. During his travels he comes across the fair Princess Marya Morevna. This princess belongs to a class of heroines of many stories, "who slaughters whole armies before she is married, and then becomes mild and gentle", and thus can be compared to an Amazon.[37] However, their happy marriage is soon in trouble, when in the absence of his wife Prince Ivan disobeys her instructions and opens a secret closet:

Mar'ia Morevna, prekrasnaia korolevna, vziala ego s soboi v svoe gosudarstvo; pozhili oni vmeste skol'ko-to vremeni, i vzdumalos' korolevne na voinu sobirat'sia; pokidaet ona na Ivana-tsarevicha vse khoziaistvo i prikazyvaet: "Vezde khodi, za vsem prismatrivai; tol'ko v etot chulan ne mogi zagliadyvat'!"	The fair Princess, Marya Morevna, carried him off into her own realm. They spent some time together, and then the Princess took it into her head to go a-warring. So she handed over all the housekeeping affairs to Prince Ivan, and gave him these instructions: "Go about everywhere, keep watch over everything; only do not venture to look into that closet there".
On ne vyterpel, kak tol'ko Mar'ia Morevna uekhala, totchas brosilsia v chulan, otvoril dver', glianul – a tam visit Koshei Bessmertnyi, na dvenadtsati tsepiakh prikovan. Prosit Koshei u Ivana-tsarevicha: "Szhal'sia nado mnoi, dai mne napit'sia! Desyat' let ia zdes' muchaius', ne el, ne pil – sovsem v gorle	He couldn't help doing so. The moment Marya Morevna had gone he rushed to the closet, pulled open the door, and looked in - there hung Koshchei the Deathless, fettered by twelve chains. Then Koshchei entreated Prince Ivan, saying, "Have pity upon me and give me

---

[34] RALSTON, *Russian Folk-Tales*, pp. 84-85.

[35] *Narodnye russkie skazki A.N. Afanas'eva* [Popular Russian Tales by A.N. Afanasyev], ed. L.G. BARAG and N.V. NOVIKOV, 1 (Moscow, 1984), pp. 300-305; RALSTON, *Russian Folk-Tales*, pp. 85-96.

[36] BOGRDANOVA, "Russian Folklore for the English Reader"; EAD., "Translators of folklore"; and ead. "*Morozko*: Russian folklore formulas in British translations".

[37] RALSTON, *Russian Folk-Tales*, p. 97.

peresokhlo!" Tsarevich podal emu tsel-oe vedro vody; on vypil i esche zaprosil: "Mne odnim vedrom ne zalit' zhazhdy; dai eshe!" Tsarevich podal drugoe vedro; Koshei vypil i zaprosil tret'e, a kak vypil tret'e vedro – vzial svoyu prezhniuiu silu, triakhnul tsepiami i srazu vse dvenadtsat' porval. "Spasibo, Ivan-tsarevich! – skazal Koshei Bessmertnyi. – Teper' tebe nikogda ne vidat' Mar'i Morevny, kak ushei svoikh!" – i strashnym vikhrem vyletel v okno, nagnal na doroge Mar'iu Morevnu, prekrasnuiu korolevnu, podkhvatil ee i unes k sebe. A Ivan-tsarevich gor'ko-gor'ko zaplakal, snariadilsia i poshel v put'-dorogu: "Chto ni budet, a razyschu Mar'iu Morevnu!" (*Narodnye russkie skazki A. N. Afanas'eva*, p. 301)

to drink! Ten years long have I been here in torment, neither eating nor drinking; my throat is utterly dried up". The Prince gave him a bucketful of water; he drank it up and asked for more, saying: "A single bucket of water will not quench my thirst; give me more!" The Prince gave him a second bucketful. Koshchei drank it up and asked for a third, and when he had swallowed the third bucketful, he regained his former strength, gave his chains a shake, and broke all twelve at once. "Thanks, Prince Ivan!" cried Koshchei the Deathless, "now you will sooner see your own ears than Marya Morevna!" and out of the window he flew in the shape of a terrible whirlwind. And he came up with the fair Princess Marya Morevna as she was going her way, laid hold of her, and carried her off home with him. But Prince Ivan wept full sore, and he arrayed himself and set out a wandering, saying to himself: "Whatever happens, I will go and look for Marya Morevna!" (RALSTON, *Russian Folk-Tales*, pp. 87-8).

What we have here is "the Bluebeard incident of the forbidden closet":[38] by opening the closet, Prince Ivan encounters Koshchei the Deathless himself and sets free the power of evil. To win over Maria Morevna and to regain peace and happiness, our hero has to fight and kill the fiend. The description stresses Koshchei's great strength ("fettered by twelve chains"; "gave his chains a shake, and broke all twelve at once") and supernatural powers ("Koshchei the Deathless"; "ten years long have I been here in torment, neither eating nor drinking"; "out of the window he flew in the shape of a terrible whirlwind"). As one may notice, the formulas are mostly repeated three times: "the Prince gave him a bucketful of water"; "the Prince gave him a second bucketful"; "he drank it up and asked for more"; "Koshchei drank it up and asked for a third"; etc. The

[38] RALSTON, *Russian Folk-Tales*, p. 97.

formulas are repeated to call one's attention to important details, as well as to add to the rhythm of the narration. Formulaic direct speech, used as an expressive and effective stylistic device, sheds an additional light on the forceful character of Koshchei, whom Prince Ivan so meekly obeys in the episode in question.

In the continuation of the text, one can see that the folktale abounds in repetitions. For example, Prince Ivan makes three attempts to rescue Maria Morevna; however, these are equally unsuccessful because each time Koshchei's magic horse comes to his help:

A Koshei na okhote byl; k vecheru on domoi vorochaetsia, pod nim dobryi kon' spotykaetsia. "Chto ty, nesytaia kliacha, spotykaesh'sia? Ali chuesh' kakuyu nevzgodu?" Otvechaet kon': "Ivan-tsarevich prikhodil, Mar'iu Morevnu uvez". – "A mozhno li ih dognat'?" – "Mozhno pshenitsy naseiat', dozhdat'sia, poka ona vyrastet, szhat' ee, smolotit', v muku obratit', piat' pechei khleba nagotovit', tot khleb poest', da togda vdogon' ekhat' – i to pospeem!" Koshei poskakal, dognal Ivan-tsarevicha: "Nu, – govorit, – pervyi raz tebia proschayu za tvoyiu dobrotu, chto vodoi menia napoil; i v drugoi raz proschu, a v tretii beregis' – na kuski izrubliu!" Otnial u nego Mar'iu Morevnu i uvez; a Ivan-tsarevich sel na kamen' i zaplakal (Narodnye russkie skazki A. N. Afanas'eva, p. 302).

Now Koshchei was out hunting. Towards evening he was returning home, when his good steed stumbled beneath him. "Why stumblest thou, sorry jade? scentest thou some ill?" The steed replied: "Prince Ivan has come and carried off Marya Morevna." "Is it possible to catch them?" "It is possible to sow wheat, to wait till it grows up, to reap it and thresh it, to grind it to flour, to make five pies of it, to eat those pies, and then to start in pursuit and even then to be in time." Koshchei galloped off and caught up Prince Ivan. "Now," says he, "this time I will forgive you, in return for your kindness in giving me water to drink. And a second time I will forgive you; but the third time beware! I will cut you to bits" (Ralston, *Russian Folk-Tales* 90).

The episode is repeated three times, with small variations. For example, the second time the horse says: "It is possible to sow barley, to wait till it grows up, to reap it and thresh it, to brew beer, to drink ourselves drunk on it, to sleep our fill, and then to set off in pursuit and yet to be in time".[39] As promised, the first two times Prince Ivan is forgiven by his rival but the third time Koshchei "caught Prince Ivan, chopped him into little pieces, put them in a barrel, smeared it with pitch and bound it with iron hoops, and flung it into the blue

---

[39] RALSTON, *Russian Folk-Tales*, pp. 90-91.

sea".[40] But when the hero is rescued and revived by his brothers-in-law (the Falcon, the Eagle, and the Raven) with the help of the Water of Death and the Water of Life, he again continues on his quest. This time he first goes to the Baba Yaga to serve and win himself a magic steed, more powerful than his rival's. Thanks to his magic horse, Prince Ivan is finally able to succeed and restore his own happiness, as well as the peace and happiness in the whole world.[41]

Notably, this and another tale of Ralston's collection were selected by Andrew Lang for his *Red Fairy Book* (1890), the second in the series of his fairy books.[42] The stories were borrowed verbatim, with the due reference made to the source. However, 'Marya Morevna' appears under a new title, 'The Death of Koshchei the Deathless',[43] along with German, French, Norwegian, and Rumanian stories.[44]

The Aesthetics of Darkness: The Baba Yaga

The story of Marya Morevna deals with another evil character of the Russian folklore tradition, which deserves a separate discussion. The Baba Yaga is a female fiend who often features in Russian folktales as "a tall, gaunt hag, with dishevelled hair".[45] Ralston's description of this formidable character of the Russian *skazka* is as follows:

---

[40] RALSTON, *Russian Folk-Tales*, p. 91.

[41] A.V. ZHUCHKOVA, and K.N. GALAY, "Funktsional'noe znachenie mifologicheskogo obraza Koscheia Bessmertnogo i ego otrazhenie v russkikh volshebnykh skazkakh" [The mythological image of Koshchei the Deathless and his reflection in the Russian magic fairy tales], *Vestnik slavianskikh kul'tur* 3 (2015), pp. 165-174.

[42] Andrew Lang, the folklorist, classicist, romantic poet, and literary scholar is mostly remembered today as the editor of enormously popular *Colour Fairy Books* published between 1889 and 1910 (S.M. HINES, *"The Taste of the World": A Re-evaluation of the Public History and Reception Context of Andrew Lang's Fairy Book Series, 1899-1910* (PhD thesis, University of Edinburgh, 2013)). Both Ralston and Lang belonged to the "great team of British folklorists" (R. DORSON, *The British Folklorists* (Chicago, 1968), p. 199).

[43] *The Red Fairy Book*, ed. A. LANG (London, [1890] 1907), pp. 42-53.

[44] As reviewers pointed out, the appeal of this volume ("a favourite of the season") was that it introduced new stories to the reader (HINES, *"The Taste of the World"*, p. 166).

[45] The database of one of the recent studies devoted to the Baba Yaga includes a selection of some hundred stories from the Russian North (A.V. NIKITINA and M.V. REILI, "Baba-Iaga v skazkakh Russkogo Severa" [Baba Yaga in the folktales of Russian North], in: *Russkii fol'klor* [Russian Folklore], ed. A.Y. KASTROV (St. Petersburg, 2008: *Materialy i issledovaniia* 33), pp. 28-74).

Sometimes she is seen lying stretched out from one corner to the other of a miserable hut, through the ceiling of which passes her long iron nose; the hut is supported by fowl's legs and stands at the edge of a forest towards which its entrance looks. When the proper words are addressed to it, the hut revolves upon its slender supports, so as to turn its back instead of its front to the forest. Sometimes (...) the Baba Yaga appears as the mistress of a mansion, which stands in a courtyard enclosed by a fence made of dead men's bones. When she goes abroad she rides in a mortar, which she urges on with a pestle, while she sweeps away the traces of her flight with a broom.[46]

In this tale the house of the Baba Yaga is surrounded by twelve poles set in a circle, "and on each of eleven of these poles was stuck a human head, the twelfth alone remained unoccupied". The terms of service were simple: Prince Ivan will have his heroic steed if he takes good care of Baba Yaga's mares; otherwise, he "mustn't be annoyed at finding your head stuck on top of the last pole up there". However, "the moment he had driven the mares afield, they cocked up their tails, and away they tore across the meadows in all directions. Before the Prince had time to look round, they were all out of sight".[47] Things would have ended badly for the hero but for the help of thankful animals in return to his previous good services procured to them:

Thereupon he began to weep and to disquiet himself, and then he sat down upon a stone and went to sleep. But when the sun was near its setting, the outlandish bird came flying up to him, and awakened him saying: "Arise, Prince Ivan! the mares are at home now".[48]

Again, one may notice that the episodes and formulas are repeated.

Notably, the Baba Yaga is not just another enchantress who works wonders with the usual magic apparatus; she is much more powerful: "the entire animal world lies at her disposal" and Day and Night are found among her servants.[49] As a "fair specimen" among the *skazki* where she features as a prominent figure, the translator chose another folktale dealing with a poor step-daughter who is sent into the forest to fetch a needle and thread from her step-mother's sister.[50] But her aunt turns out to be "the Baba Yaga, the Bony-Shanks".

---

[46] RALSTON, *Russian Folk-Tales,* p.138.
[47] RALSTON, *Russian Folk-Tales,* p. 93.
[48] RALSTON, *Russian Folk-Tales,* p. 93.
[49] RALSTON, *Russian Folk-Tales,* p. 138.
[50] *The Baba Yaga* (RALSTON, *Russian Folk-Tales,* pp. 139-142); *Baba-iaga* (*Narodnye russkie skazki A.N. Afanas'eva*, pp.124-127).

Straightaway the Baba Yaga gives the command to her servant-maid: "Go and heat the bath, and get my niece washed; and mind you look sharp after her. I want to breakfast off her" ("*Stupai, istopi baniu da vymoi plemiannitsu, da smotri, khoroshen'ko; ia khochu eiu pozavtrakat'*").[51]

The girl, however, manages to escape:

Baba-iaga brosilas' v khatku, uvidela, chto devochka ushla, i davai bit' kota i rugat, zachem ne vytsarapal devochke glaza. "Ia tebe skol'ko sluzhu, – govorit kot, – ty mne kostochki ne dala, a ona mne vetchinki dala". Baba-iaga nakinulas'na sobak, na vorota, na berezku i na rabotnitsu, davai vsekh rugat' i kolotit'. Sobaki govoriat ei: "My tebe skol'ko sluzhim, ty nam goreloi korochki ne brosila, a ona nam khlebtsa dala". Vorota govoriat: "My tebe skol'ko sluzhim, ty nam voditsy pod piatochki ne podlila, a ona nam maslitsa podlila". Berezka govorit: "Ia tebe skol'ko sluzhu, ty menia nitochkoi ne pereviazala, ona menia lentochkoi pereviazala". Rabotnitsa govorit: "Ia tebe skol'ko sluzhu, ty mne triapochki ne podarila, a ona mne platochek podarila" (*Narodnye russkie skazki A.N. Afanas'eva*, pp. 126-127).

The Baba Yaga rushed into the hut, saw that the girl was gone, and took to beating the Cat, and abusing it for not having scratched the girl's eyes out. "Long as I've served you", said the Cat, "you've never given me so much as a bone; but she gave me bacon". Then the Baba Yaga pounced upon the dogs, on the doors, on the birch-tree, and on the servant-maid, and set to work to abuse them all, and to knock them about. Then the dogs said to her, "Long as we've served you, you've never so much as pitched us a burnt crust; but she gave us rolls to eat." And the doors said, "Long as we've served you, you've never poured even a drop of water on our hinges; but she poured oil on us." The birch-tree said, "Long as I've served you, you've never tied a single thread round me; but she fastened a ribbon around me." And the servant-maid said, "Long as I've served you, you've never given me so much as a rag; but she gave me a handkerchief" (Ralston, *Russian Folk-Tales*, p. 141).

As one may notice, here are the formulas, which are repeated even more than three times, while Ralston reproduced them with great accuracy. Importantly, too, he managed to render the expressive rhythm and stylistic nuances of the original.[52] On the one hand, there are a series of verbal forms, such as

---

[51] RALSTON, *Russian Folk-Tales*, p. 139; *Narodnye russkie skazki A.N. Afanas'eva*, p. 126.
[52] Rhymes or rhythmic prose alongside other euphonic devices such as assonance and alliteration enhance the integrity as well as the artistic effect of formulas (VEDERNIKOVA,

'rushed', 'saw', 'took to beating' and 'abusing', 'pounced upon', 'set to work to abuse them all, and to knock them about', which render the Baba Yaga's promptness of action and her terrible fury. On the other hand, there are a series of complaints of her servants, all beginning with "Long as I've served you", which help to create the monotonous musical tone, characteristic of the style of *skazki*. The effectiveness of Ralston's text stands out when compared with a similar passage from the translation of a similar folktale in Lang's *Yellow Fairy Book*:

> When the witch saw that the children had escaped her, she was furious, and, hitting the cat with a porringer, she said: "Why did you let the children leave the hut? Why did you not scratch their eyes out?" But the cat curled up its tail and put its back up, and answered: "I have served you all these years and you never even threw me a bone, but the dear children gave me their own piece of ham". Then the witch was furious with the watch-dog and with the birch-trees, because they had let the children pass. But the dog answered: "I have served you all these years and you never gave me so much as a hard crust, but the dear children gave me their own loaf of bread". And the birch rustled its leaves, and said: "I have served you longer than I can say, and you never tied a bit of twine even round my branches; and the dear children bound them up with their brightest ribbons".[53]

Importantly, much of the original colour of the story is lost, when its Russian formula – the Baba Yaga – is missing in Lang's text.

Finally, let us examine Arthur Ransome's variant of the same episode:[54]

> And presently Baba Yaga came to the window. "Are you weaving, little niece?" she asked. "Are you weaving, my pretty?" "I am weaving, auntie," says the thin black cat, tangling and tangling, while the loom went clickety clack, clickety clack. "That's not the voice of my little dinner," says Baba Yaga, and she jumped into the hut, gnashing her iron teeth; and there was no little girl, but only the thin black cat,

---

Russkaia narodnaia skazka pp. 65-66; RAZUMOVA, *Stilisticheskaia obriadnost' russkoi volshebnoi skazki*, p. 22).

[53] In *The Yellow Fairy Book*, ed. A. LANG (London, [1894] 1906), pp. 219-220. In this book there are several Russian stories. The one of interest for the present discussion is 'The Witch' (pp. 216-221). There are at least three stories which were presumably used as the sources for the English translation; two of them have the title *Baba Iaga* (*Narodnye russkie skazki A.N. Afanas'eva*, pp. 124-127) and still another is *Vasilisa Prekrasnaia* (pp. 127-132), in which the Baba Yaga plays a prominent role as well.

[54] In "Baba Yaga and the Little Girl with the Kind Heart" the two variants of the Russian original *Baba Iaga* are creatively combined (RANSOME, *Old Peter's Russian Tales* (Edinburgh, 1957), pp. 76-91).

sitting at the loom, tangling and tangling the threads. "Grr", says Baba Yaga, and jumps for the cat, and begins banging it about. "Why didn't you tear the little girl's eyes out?" "In all the years I have served you", says the cat, "you have only given me one little bone; but the kind little girl gave me scraps of meat".

Baba Yaga threw the cat into a corner, and went out into the yard. "Why didn't you squeak when she opened you?" she asked the gates. "Why didn't you tear her to pieces?" she asked the dog. "Why didn't you beat her in the face, and not let her go by?" she asked the birch tree. "Why were you so long in getting the bath ready? If you had been quicker, she never would have got away", said Baba Yaga to the servant. And she rushed about the yard, beating them all, and scolding at the top of her voice.

"Ah!" said the gates, "in all the years we have served you, you never even eased us with water; but the kind little girl poured good oil into our hinges".

"Ah!" said the dog, "in all the years I've served you, you never threw me anything but burnt crusts; but the kind little girl gave me a good loaf".

"Ah!" said the little birch tree, "in all the years I've served you, you never tied me up, even with thread; but the kind little girl tied me up with a gay blue ribbon".

"Ah!" said the servant, "in all the years I've served you, you have never given me even a rag; but the kind little girl gave me a pretty handkerchief".

Baba Yaga gnashed at them with her iron teeth. Then she jumped into the mortar and sat down. She drove it along with the pestle, and swept up her tracks with a besom, and flew off in pursuit of the little girl.[55]

Ransome's retelling of the Russian *skazka*, intended for children, follows the plot line closely, but the author also feels free to add detail and colour (e.g. sound effects like "the loom went clickety clack, clickety clack"; "'Grr', says Baba Yaga"; "'Ah!' said the dog"; etc.) so that his story is amplified to acquire additional effects. Notably, repetitions are conspicuous, beginning with separate words ("tangling and tangling") and ending with phrases and sentences ("Why didn't you squeak when she opened you?" she asked the gates; "Why didn't you tear her to pieces?" she asked the dog; etc.). Finally, these add to the rhythm of the narrative, hence rendering the overall artistic effect and aesthetics of the formulaic original. As this example shows, Ransome is at his best while reproducing the rhythmic formulaic prose of the original, but also sensitive in rendering the folklore tradition with its particular folktale formulas (e.g. "Baba Yaga"; "She drove it along with the pestle, and swept up her tracks with a besom").[56]

---

[55] RANSOME, *Old Peter's Russian Tales*, pp. 87-88.
[56] There are all kinds of such formulas, including double, but usually triple ones, repetitions of episodes that may extend from separate words to substantial sections of texts, contributing to

Concluding Remarks

Folklore texts are not easy to understand and to interpret. Translators have to be versed in the "the inexplicit but always implicit tradition" to be able to explore their encoded meanings, including the aesthetics of culture-specific formulas, and to render them to their audiences.

A close reading of translated texts compared with originals, as well as between the translations themselves has shed useful light on the different ways Russian folklore formulas were understood and interpreted by British translators for their respective audiences. Notably, the collective effort of the translators produced an 'amalgam' of rewritings of the Russian folktale, their cumulative effect allowing the reader to access the magic world of the Russian folktale and to appreciate its poetics.

---

their fluent, sing-song character (RAZUMOVA, *Stilisticheskaia obriadnost' russkoi volshebnoi skazki*, pp. 36-53, 98).